31651

D0269766

POPULAR ALGAM

Psychoanalytic Literary Criticism

LONGMAN CRITICAL READERS

General Editor:

STAN SMITH, Professor of English, University of Dundee

Published titles:

K. M. NEWTON, *George Eliot*

MARY EAGLETON, *Feminist Literary Criticism*

GARY WALLER, *Shakespeare's Comedies*

JOHN DRAKAKIS, *Shakespearean Tragedy*

RICHARD WILSON AND RICHARD DUTTON, *New Historicism and Renaissance Drama*

PETER BROOKER, *Modernism/Postmodernism*

PETER WIDDOWSON, *D. H. Lawrence*

RACHEL BOWLBY, *Virginia Woolf*

FRANCIS MULHERN, *Contemporary Marxist Literary Criticism*

ANNABEL PATTERSON, *John Milton*

CYNTHIA CHASE, *Romanticism*

MICHAEL O'NEILL, *Shelley*

STEPHANIE TRIGG, *Medieval English Poetry*

ANTONY EASTHOPE, *Contemporary Film Theory*

TERRY EAGLETON, *Ideology*

MAUD ELLMANN, *Psychoanalytic Literary Criticism*

Psychoanalytic Literary Criticism

Edited and Introduced by

Maud Ellmann

Longman
London and New York

Longman Group UK Limited,
Longman House, Burnt Mill,
Harlow, Essex CM20 2JE, England
and Associated Companies throughout the world.

*Published in the United States of America
by Longman Publishing, New York*

First published 1994

ISBN 0–582–08348–6 CSD
ISBN 0–582–08347–8 PPR

British Library Cataloguing-in-Publication Data

A catalogue record for this book is
available from the British Library

Library of Congress Cataloging-in-Publication Data

Psychoanalytic literary criticism/edited and introduced by Maud Ellmann.
    p.   cm.–(Longman critical readers)
  Includes bibliographical references and index.
  ISBN 0–582–08348–6 (CSD).—ISBN 0–582–08347–8 (PPR)
  1. Psychoanalysis and literature. 2. Criticism. I. Ellmann, Maud, 1954– .
II. Series.
PN56.P92P725   1994
801'.92—dc20   94–1983
                                                                                   CIP

Set by 5 in 9 on 11½ Palatino
Produced by Longman Singapore Publishers (Pte) Ltd.
Printed in Singapore

276125

Contents

General Editors' Preface

The outlines of contemporary critical theory are now often taught as
a standard feature of a degree in literary studies. The development
of particular theories has seen a thorough transformation of literary
criticism. For example, Marxist and Foucauldian theories have
revolutionised Shakespeare studies, and 'deconstruction' has led to a
complete reassessment of Romantic poetry. Feminist criticism has left
scarcely any period of literature unaffected by its searching critiques.
Teachers of literary studies can no longer fall back on a standardised,
received, methodology.

Lecturers and teachers are now urgently looking for guidance
in a rapidly changing critical environment. They need help in
understanding the latest revisions in literary theory, and especially
in grasping the practical effects of the new theories in the form of
theoretically sensitised new readings. A number of volumes in the
series anthologise important essays on particular theories. However,
in order to grasp the full implications and possible uses of particular
theories it is essential to see them put to work. This series provides
substantial volumes of new readings, presented in an accessible form
and with a significant amount of editorial guidance.

Each volume includes a substantial introduction which explores
the theoretical issues and conflicts embodied in the essays selected
and locates areas of disagreement between positions. The pluralism
of theories has to be put on the agenda of literary studies. We can no
longer pretend that we all tacitly accept the same practices in literary
studies. Neither is a *laissez-faire* attitude any longer tenable. Literature
departments need to go beyond the mere toleration of theoretical
differences: it is not enough merely to agree to differ; they need
actually to 'stage' the differences openly. The volumes in this series
all attempt to dramatise the differences, not necessarily with a view
to resolving them but in order to foreground the choices presented
by different theories or to argue for a particular route through the
impasses the differences present.

The theory 'revolution' has had real effects. It has loosened the grip
of traditional empiricist and romantic assumptions about language and
literature. It is not always clear what is being proposed as the new
agenda for literary studies, and indeed the very notion of 'literature'
is questioned by the post-structuralist strain in theory. However, the
uncertainties and obscurities of contemporary theories appear much
less worrying when we see what the best critics have been able to do

with them in practice. This series aims to disseminate the best of recent criticism and to show that it is possible to re-read the canonical texts of literature in new and challenging ways.

RAMAN SELDEN AND STAN SMITH

The Publishers and fellow Series Editor regret to record that Raman Selden died after a short illness in May 1991 at the age of fifty-three. Ray Selden was a fine scholar and a lovely man. All those he has worked with will remember him with much affection and respect.

Acknowledgements

I should like to thank my husband, Chris Baldick, for his generous help throughout this project.

We are grateful to the following for permission to reproduce copyright material;

Cambridge University Press for extracts from the article 'The Psycho-analytic Reading of Tragedy' prologue to *The Tragic Effect: The Oedipus Complex in Tragedy* by André Green, translated by Alan Sheridan (1979); Columbia University Press for the chapter 'Gerard de Nerval, the Disinherited Poet' from *Black Sun: Depression and Melancholia* by Julia Kristeva, translated by Leon S. Roudiez (1989), © Columbia University Press; Faber and Faber Ltd and HarperCollins Publishers, Inc. for the poem 'Daddy' from *Ariel* by Sylvia Plath, © 1963 by Ted Hughes; Johns Hopkins University Press for extracts from the article 'Oedipal Textuality: Reading Freud's Reading of *Oedipus*' from *Decomposing Figures: Rhetorical Readings in the Romantic Tradition* by Cynthia Chase (1986) and extracts from 'Beyond Oedipus: The Specimen Story of Psychoanalysis' by Shoshana Felman from *Lacan and Narration: The Psychoanalytic Difference in Narrative Theory* edited by Robert Con Davis (1983); The MIT Press for the chapter 'Two Ways to Avoid the Real of Desire: The Sherlock Holmes Way' from *Looking Awry: An Introduction to Jacques Lacan Through Popular Culture* by Slavoj Žižek (1991); Oxford University Press, Inc. for the article 'Freud and the Sublime: A Catastrophe Theory of Creativity' from *Agon: Towards Revisionism* by Harold Bloom (1982), © 1982 by Oxford University Press, Inc.; Routledge, a division of Routledge Chapman and Hall Ltd, and the author, Daniel Ferrer for the chapter 'To the Lighthouse' from *Virginia Woolf and the Madness of Language* by Daniel Ferrer translated by Rachel Bowlby (1990); the author, Anita Sokolsky for her essay 'The Manic Side of the Depression: Jane Austen and Screwball Comedy'; Virago Press and Harvard University Press for the chapter 'Daddy' from *The Haunting of Sylvia Plath* by Jacqueline Rose (1991), © 1991 by Jacqueline Rose.

Introduction

> As for psychoanalysis, it's neither
> more nor less than blackmail.
>
> James Joyce

The textual unconscious

Gertrude Stein once complained that a work of art could be
acknowledged as a masterpiece only when it ceased to irritate the
public. 'If every one were not so indolent,' she argued, 'they would
realize that beauty is beauty even when it is irritating and stimulating
not only when it is accepted and classic.'[1] Yet Freud's masterpieces
– for better or worse – have never lost their power to irritate, even
when their beauty is accepted and their strangeness tamed. And
Freudian literary criticism causes a peculiar form of irritation, differing
from other symptoms of the condition Paul de Man described as
the 'resistance to theory'.[2] There is nothing like Freudian theory to
elicit sniggers of embarrassment or snorts of disbelief, and even the
abstrusities of Lacan can reduce a classroom to cascades of giggles.
Reactions against psychoanalysis tend to be visceral, the body rejecting
with convulsions what the intellect refuses to assimiliate.

Yet Freud came to realise that a gut resistance to psychoanalysis
often signified a deeper recognition of its dangers than a prompt
assimilation of its principles. A little indigestion was a healthy sign.
He was outraged by the way the medical profession in America
appropriated his ideas while stifling their controversial implications.
Philip Rieff points out that liberal culture in America tends to absorb
and even canonise its own detractors, reducing such masters of acerbity
as Freud to hired critics or 'entertainers in the negative'.[3] Furthermore,
the immigrants who imported psychoanalysis to the United States had
compelling reasons to insist on adaptation to the social order as they
found it.[4] Consequently, they tended to ignore Freud's searing criticism
of society and, turning their attention to the individual, perceived

1

their task as one of bolstering the ego to alleviate the sufferings of maladjustment. Known as 'ego-psychology', this school of thought has been subjected to a fierce assault by Jacques Lacan, who sees the ego as the source of our delusions, rather than the key to our deliverance. While the ego-psychologists urged the conquest of the unconscious, enlisting Freud's famous slogan, 'Where id was there ego shall be' (*Wo Es war soll Ich werden*); Lacan takes these words to mean that the 'I' [*Ich*] is subject to the 'it' [*Es*]; and that the goal of psychoanalysis is to acknowledge the fiasco of the humanist tradition based on the Socratic dictum – *know thyself*.[5]

Freud tended to regard all criticism of his theories as a symptom of resistance to unwelcome truths; so it is worth remembering that psychoanalysis frequently deserves the scorn with which it is repudiated. In literary studies, for example, psychoanalytic criticism often disregards the textuality of texts, their verbal surface, in favour of the Freudian motifs supposedly encrypted in their depths. Typically the work of art is treated as a window to the artist's sex-tormented soul. Frederick Crews, in a notorious analysis of Joseph Conrad's *Heart of Darkness*, interprets Marlow's pilgrimage to central Africa as a 'journey into the maternal body'.[6] He cites as evidence the rank and matted vegetation of the wilderness '"that seemed to draw [Kurtz] to its pitiless breast by the awakening of forgotten and brutal instincts, by the memory of gratified and monstrous passions".' Kurtz, the sinner at the heart of darkness, represents the father, while Marlow is the son who interrupts the primal scene, the 'unspeakable rites' of parental intercourse.[7] Marie Bonaparte comes to similar conclusions in her study of Edgar Allan Poe: in 'The Pit and the Pendulum', for instance, she argues that the dungeon represents the mother's womb, invaded by the murderous pendulum, which represents the father's penis lunging in the act of intercourse.[8] Imaginative as it is, this interpretation overlooks the literary resonances of the text and also suggests a strange anatomical naivety.

Of course, it is unfair to cite such howlers out of context, since both these critics have a subtler grasp of literature than they sometimes permit themselves to show. While Bonaparte sidesteps aesthetic questions, she produces readings that rival Poe's own chillers in their paranoiac intricacy and extravagance. Crews, however, seems to have talked himself out of psychoanalysis precisely by applying it too heavyhandedly, for he recently repudiated psychoanalytic criticism as a whole.[9] What both these critics have in common, though, is that they focus on the content of the text at the expense of literary form. One consequence of this procedure is that both ignore the temporal dimension of the narrative, reducing Poe's and Conrad's well-paced plots to motionless tableaux; it is as if the critics, rather than the authors, were compelled to reproduce a 'primal scene'. In this sense the stories psychoanalyse their own interpreters: the scenes of sexual possession discovered in the texts tell us less about the authors than about the critics, and less about eroticism than about the will to power over literary ambiguity. Only by attending to the rhetoric of texts, to the echoes and recesses of the words themselves, can we recognise the otherness of literature, its recalcitrance as well as its susceptibility to theorisation. Without this vigilance to language, psychoanalysis is doomed to rediscover its own myths grotesquely multiplied throughout the course of literature.

Peter Brooks observes that classic psychoanalytic criticism 'displaces the object of analysis from the text to some person', be it the author, the reader, or the characters, all of whom are viewed as independent personalities rather than as functions of the text itself.[10] This person-centred form of criticism mirrors American ego-psychology insofar as both exalt the individual, failing to perceive how the transubjective force of the unconscious undermines the perilous cohesion of the self. The most famous psychoanalytic study of a literary character is Ernest Jones's *Hamlet and Oedipus* (1949), which takes up Freud's suggestion in *The Interpretation of Dreams* (1900) that Hamlet is unable to avenge his father's death because he secretly identifies himself with the assassin. 'Hamlet is able to do anything,' Freud writes, 'except take vengeance on the man who did away with his father and took that father's place with his mother, the man who shows him the repressed wishes of his own childhood realised.'[11] Jones endorses this interpretation, but suggests that Hamlet's hesitation is a symptom of his wish to kill his *mother*, which stymies his attempts to kill his *uncle*. 'When a man who has been betrayed is emotionally moved to murder, whom should he kill, the rival lover or the lady? It is a nice question', Jones writes.[12] Gertrude herself confirms his suspicion that *Hamlet* is a matricidal tragedy, closer to the *Oresteia* than to *Oedipus*: for she is terrified that Hamlet means to murder her when he invades her closet, speaking daggers; and the ghost is forced to intervene to protect her from the prince's misdirected vengeance.

Jones's reading, though inspired, makes the fundamental error of treating Hamlet as a real person, vexed by unconscious impulses unfathomable even to the text itself. Jones defends this error by protesting that the anguished prince has more vitality than the moribund majority of living people. True – but Hamlet has the disadvantage that he cannot contradict his psychoanalyst. Unlike a real analysand, he cannot lie down on the couch and free associate about his dreams or recapitulate the traumas of his infancy. Amusing as it is to speculate about his early history, Hamlet *never had a childhood*. Jones ignores the difference between a human being made of flesh and a character composed of words, and thereby overlooks the verbal specificities of Shakespeare's text to focus on its universal archetypes.

Where literature is concerned, Ernest Jones makes greater claims than Freud himself for the efficacy of the psychoanalytic method of interpretation. Freud, although he saw himself as the conquistador of the unconscious, admitted that the mysteries of art defeated his explanatory powers. 'Before the problem of the creative artist analysis must, alas, lay down its arms' (SE XXI 177). Psychoanalysis, he said, can only speculate about the author's raw materials – the psychic upheavals of early childhood – and has no explanation for the alchemy that turns those tribulations into art. Yet in spite of such disclaimers, Freud could not resist what he described as a 'particular fascination' with the workings of the artist's mind (SE XXII 254). In addition to his insights about Sophocles and Shakespeare, Freud wrote psychobiographical accounts of Leonardo and Dostoevsky and a study of the Moses of Michelangelo. His most sustained analyses of literature may be found in his essay on Jensen's *Gradiva* (1907: SE IX 1–97) – a tale in which an archaeologist, investigating buried relics of Pompeii, rediscovers buried yearnings of his childhood – and also in his essay 'The "Uncanny"' (1919: SE XVII 217–56), which examines Hoffmann's macabre fantasy, 'The Sandman'. The hero of this story, Nathaniel, suffers from a terror that the Sandman, a bogeyman of childhood, is pursuing him in different incarnations with the purpose of tearing out his eyes: a symptom Freud predictably interprets as castration-phobia. In spite of this reductiveness, however, Freud's essay has fascinated psychoanalytic critics, especially his definition of the uncanny as the return of the familiar in an unfamiliar form. In a thrilling etymology, Freud demonstrates how the German word *heimlich* (meaning homely or familiar) 'develops in the direction of ambivalence, until it finally coincides with its opposite, *unheimlich*' (SE XVII 226); thus suggesting that the very word has grown uncanny to itself. Freud's essay has inspired at least nine new readings of 'The Sandman' in the last few years, each arguing in different ways that Freud employs the theory of castration to evade the more disturbing themes in Hoffmann's work, such as the death drive and the compulsion to repeat.[13] These articles reflect a shift of emphasis away from sexuality to death in recent psychoanalytic criticism, which has become increasingly concerned with mourning, haunting, and repetition rather than the misadventures of the penis.[14] This new emphasis is rather a relief; yet it may also represent the latest way of disavowing Freud's most troubling discovery – the centrality of sexuality to psychic life. Freud, by contrast, would agree with Yeats that intellect is inextricable from sexuality, and that even the most beautiful and lofty things arise out of the foul rag-and-bone shop of the heart.

Freud's sporadic forays into literary criticism scarcely indicate the depth of his indebtedness to literature. Lionel Trilling argued in 1947 that 'the Freudian psychology makes poetry indigenous to the very constitution of the mind'. Long before Lacan announced that the unconscious was structured like a language, Trilling had discovered that psychoanalysis was 'a science of tropes, of metaphor and its variants, synecdoche and metonymy'.[15] Lacan, more recently, has reaffirmed that dreams and symptoms owe their form to the principles of figurative speech: the unconscious processes of condensation and displacement correspond respectively to metaphor and to metonymy, which the linguist Roman Jakobson identifies as the twin axes of language.[16] If the unconscious operates according to the strategems of rhetoric, this means that psychoanalysis and literary criticism are united by a common object of investigation: the boundless creativity of tropes. Moreover, Freud's most famous theory was inspired by a work of literature, *Oedipus the King*; and indeed, it could be argued that the whole tradition of psychoanalytic theory that extends from Freud to Jacques Lacan consists of variations on the theme of Oedipus.

For this reason, the remainder of this introduction explores the ways that psychoanalysis and *Oedipus* reflect on one another. First we shall see how Freud makes use of the dramatic form as well as the incestuous and parricidal themes of *Oedipus*; next, how Freud identifies himself with Oedipus as the detective inculpated in the crime. The third section examines Freud's account of the Oedipus complex, and reveals how critics have adapted this account to investigate erotic triangles in literature. In the fourth section we turn to Lacan's reinterpretation of the Oedipus complex as a fable of the child's entry into language and desire. According to Fredric Jameson, Lacan's life work should be understood 'not as the transformation of Freud into linguistics, but as the disengagement of a linguistic theory that was implicit in Freud's practice but for which he did not yet have the appropriate conceptual instruments. . . .'[17] Lacan's emphasis on language has captivated many literary critics; his apotheosis of the penis, on the other hand, has generated much controversy. This introduction therefore ends with a discussion of the sexual politics of psychoanalysis, showing how feminists have either rehabilitated or rejected what Malcolm Bowie has described as Lacan's 'guileful priapic cult'.[18]

The essays in this volume have been selected for their clarity and ingenuity, in the hope that readers with little prior knowledge may discover the enticements, as well as the vexations, of current psychoanalytic criticism. Even so, most of the critics represented here assume some acquaintance with Freud's and Lacan's theories. For this reason, it is useful to return to basics, especially in a discipline so prone to jargon, and to rediscover the dynamic force of theories often frozen into formulae. Only by abandoning the clichés can we hope to understand how psychoanalysis continues to intrigue and irritate its enemies and advocates alike.

The psychic theatre

'King Oedipus, who slew his father Laius and married his mother Jocasta, merely shows us the fulfilment of our own childhood wishes . . . and we shrink back from him with the whole force of the repression by which those wishes have since that time been held down within us' (SE IV 262–3). In this passage from *The Interpretation of Dreams* Freud inaugurates the theory of the Oedipus complex. But he makes it clear that the 'riveting power' of *Oedipus* does not derive from the events alone but from the process of dramatic revelation, the sheer *theatricality* with which the hero's crime is 'brought out into the open and realised as it would be in a dream' (SE IV 264). Often overlooked, the literary form of *Oedipus*, rather than the myth *per se*, pervades Freud's whole conception of the psyche. Many of his key terms correspond to those of the theatre or the cinema, such as 'acting out', 'projection', and 'screen memories'.[19] The interpretation of dreams lies at the heart of psychoanalysis, and Freud identifies 'dramatisation' as the primary technique of dreaming.[20] The dream, he says, is the hallucinatory fulfilment of a wish, in which desires are replaced by their embodiments: thoughts become deeds, fears become monsters. In Freud's terms, 'thing-presentations' take the place of 'word-presentations', and in this way the dream creates a world of 'picture-thoughts' (to borrow Hegel's term for the embodied discourse of the stage).[21] If dreams resemble drama, drama also owes its form to dreams; rather than mirroring the outer world, the theatre gives external form to the internal dramaturgy of the mind, where anything may be invoked and brought to life.

One of my dreams illustrates the process of dramatisation rather neatly, so I shall follow the well-established Freudian tradition of enlisting one's own dreams into the argument. I once dreamt that I was stranded on a desert island where my only companions were puffins, penguins, and pelicans. When I described this dream to a friend, she exclaimed, 'They're all *books!*' And sure enough, I had conjured up a comic image of the life of letters – stuck on a desert island with nothing but books: Puffins and Penguins and Pelicans. Notice that the dream's dramatic form disguised its meaning, which only re-emerged when the visual puns were translated into words.

Those words, moreover, had to be repeated back to me before I could perceive their true significance. As Freud explains, 'everyone possesses in his unconscious mental activity an apparatus which enables him to interpret other people's reactions, that is, to undo the distortions which other people have imposed on the expression of their feelings' (SE XIII 159). If this anecdote exposes my obtuseness it also shows why Freud distinguishes between the dream as dreamt, and the words the patient uses to describe the dream. The technique of dramatisation seems to be designed specifically to *hide us from ourselves*; and the task of the interpreter is to discern the words encoded in the pictographic script of dreams.

In *The Interpretation of Dreams*, Freud insists upon the principle that the dream is a fulfilment of a wish, and leaves no loophole for dissension: even when a patient presents him with a dream that seems to contradict this axiom, he argues slyly that the dream fulfils her wish to invalidate his theory that the dream is the fulfilment of a wish (SE IV 151). Freud maintained this doctrine stubbornly until the First World War, when the dreams of shell-shock victims finally forced him to rethink the pleasure principle. These dreams, he found, compulsively returned to the traumatic moments of the victims' lives; and it was clear that no pleasure, in any ordinary meaning of the word, could be derived from these horrendous nightmares. In *Beyond the Pleasure Principle* (1919), Freud compares the 'compulsion to repeat', as manifested in these dreams, to a game in which his grandson would fling a cotton-reel out of his cot, emitting a sadistic 'oooo', and then retrieve it with an 'aaaa' of satisfaction. Freud interprets these two syllables as rudiments of the German words *fort* [gone] and *da* [here], and argues that the child is attempting to master the anxiety of separation from his mother by 'staging' her absences and presences. According to Freud, this game resembles tragic drama, which inflicts upon the audience the painful experience of loss, while wresting pleasure out of the aesthetic mastery of that experience. Freud observes, however, that his grandson stages the painful 'first act, that of departure', much more often than the pleasurable drama of return (SE XVIII 14–17); thus revealing a 'demonic' element in the compulsion to repeat that overrides the pleasure principle. On this basis Freud posits the presence of another 'power in mental life which we call the instinct of aggression or of destruction according to its aims, and which we trace back to the original death instinct of living matter' (SE XXIII 243). The extraordinary speculative chapters of *Beyond the Pleasure Principle* pit the death drive against the life drive, arguing that *the aim of all life is death*', and that the instincts are the urges '*inherent in organic life to restore an earlier state of things*', the earliest of which is death itself (SE XVIII 38, 36). Thus the pleasure principle, which aims for 'constancy' or equilibrium within the organism, is hijacked by the instincts of destruction, which crave the final constancy of death, the chill repose of inorganic matter.[22]

In the *fort/da* game, it is specifically the element of drama that alerts Freud to the presence of the death drive. But the compulsion to repeat, as revealed in the child's addicted gambling with loss, also underlies the drama of analysis. Freud argues that whatever is repressed is destined to repeat itself, whether in the form of symptoms, dreams, or 'acting-out': 'a thing which has not been understood inevitably reappears; like an unlaid ghost, it cannot rest until the mystery has been solved and the spell broken' (SE X 122). Possessed by such unconscious mysteries, the patient 'is obliged to *repeat* the repressed material as a contemporary experience instead of, as the physician would prefer to see, *remembering* it as something belonging to the past' (SE XVIII 18). In its early days the psychoanalytic cure was based on the Aristotelian catharsis, whereby the revelation of the patient's past would release buried feelings, just as tragedy gave vent to pity and fear. When Freud abandoned the use of hypnosis in the 1890s, he gradually dispensed with the cathartic model but replaced it with the equally Thespian concept of the 'transference'. In the transferential model, the psychoanalytic session provides a theatre in which patients re-enact the conflicts of their early history, 'transferring' their forgotten feelings towards their parents or their siblings onto the neutral figure of the analyst. Thus the analyst is forced to play a part, and play it badly, so that the patient may be freed from the compulsion to repeat the script of childhood. Freud writes, 'the patient does not *remember* anything of what he has forgotten or repressed, but *acts* it out. . . . He *repeats* it, without . . . knowing that he is repeating it' (SE XII 150). The success of the analysis depends upon converting re-enactment into memory: through the 'talking cure', the language of remembrance takes the place of the compulsive rehearsals of the past.[23]

In view of the primacy of language in psychoanalytic theory and technique, it is crucial that *Oedipus the King*, its founding text, should be a tragedy of words rather than a tragedy of deeds. None of the events that shaped the hero's destiny actually occurs on stage: we only glimpse them through the medium of language. Freud points out that the play consists of 'nothing other than the process of revealing, with cunning delays and ever-mounting excitement', the parricide and incest that we all supposedly commit in fantasy. This 'process of revealing', Freud contends, 'can be likened to the work of a psychoanalysis', in which the secrets of the patient's infancy are slowly and painfully unveiled (SE IV 261–2). So incest and parricide provide the punchlines of the play but they do not constitute its only fascination. The power of *Oedipus* depends upon the *process* of discovery rather than the crimes revealed; like a psychoanalysis, its terror lies in the interpretive activity itself, the sheer audacity of looking back into the past and rediscovering the violence of childhood. Thus it is curious that many myths revolve around the prohibition of the backward glance: Lot's wife turns into a pillar of salt when she looks back at her homeland left behind; Orpheus is permitted to conduct Eurydice out of the underworld only under the condition that he does not look back at her. When he does so anyway, Eurydice is lost forever. It seems that Orpheus's yearning for the past exceeds his desire to lead it back into the light; he is the artist whose desire to look back, to challenge the darkness, exceeds his desire to communicate his knowledge to the living world.[24] Similarly, Oedipus's backward glance costs him his eyes.

The reason Oedipus looks back into the past is to decipher the mysteries of the present; and in this sense he could be seen as the founder of the psychoanalytic method. He addresses the Chorus with the question, 'Where would a trace / of this old crime be found?'[25] This is a question of interpretation; and throughout the play he strives to reconstruct a meaning out of the remains of lost and uncorroborated deeds. Now, it is in the role of the *interpreter* that Freud identifies himself with Oedipus, even more than as a father-slayer and a mother-lover, although these transgressions are profoundly intervolved. Just as Oedipus solved the riddle of the sphinx, so Freud was to solve the riddle of dreams; in 1931 he declared that *The Interpretation of Dreams* contained the most valuable of his discoveries: 'Insight such as this falls to one's lot but once in a lifetime.'[26] This statement hints that Freud was blinded by his own insight: it is as if he saw so much that he could never see again, punished like Oedipus for gazing back into the phantasmagoria of infancy. Another strange coincidence is that Freud wrote *The Interpretation of Dreams* in the year after his father died, and described the book as 'a portion of my own self-analysis, my reaction to my father's death' (SE IV xxvi). Does the dream book represent an atonement with the father? Or is it an attempt to overcome him, in a re-enactment of the parricidal fantasies whose price is blindness? Perhaps Freud would have accepted both alternatives, since he believed the work of mourning to consist of the struggle to preserve, but also to destroy, the things we love.

Freud discovers his own fantasies in Sophocles's tragedy in the same way that Oedipus discovers his own guilt enciphered in the blight of Thebes. For Oedipus is the interpreter who finds that he himself is the solution to the mystery; he is the meaning of the strange events; he is the criminal indicted by his own detection. Both Freud and Oedipus realise to their dismay that they are implicated in the crimes they crack, the riddles they decipher. This is why both interpreters produce reductive readings, as if they were imprisoned, like Narcissus, by their own self-images: Oedipus leaps to his conclusion as soon as he suspects his culpability, neglecting all the inconsistencies within the evidence that links him to the Phocal crime; while Freud neglects the formal and historical particularities of *Oedipus* to focus on its revelation of his own desires, universalised into the fantasies of humankind.

Yet Oedipus and Freud both show that interpretation necessarily invokes the dreams of the interpreter, implicating the reader in the secrets of the text. For Lacan, this complicity between the subject reading and the object read represents the crux of Freud's discoveries. Freud's 'first interest was in hysteria', he writes:

> He spent a lot of time listening, and, while he was listening, there resulted something paradoxical . . . that is, a *reading*. It was while listening to hysterics that he *read* that there was an unconscious. That is, something which he could only construct, and in which he himself was implicated; he was implicated in it in the sense that, to his great astonishment, he noticed that he could not avoid participating in what the hysteric was telling him, and that he felt affected by it. Naturally everything in the resulting rules through which he established the practice of psychoanalysis is designed to counteract this consequence, to conduct things in such as way as to avoid being affected.[27]

In other words, it is impossible to understand analysands or literary texts without participating in their dreams or their delusions. The critic necessarily conspires in the text's imaginings: the act of reading is a process of mutual seduction, whereby the reader and the read arouse each other's fantasies, expose each other's dreams.[28] It is when we think we penetrate the text's disguises that we are usually most deluded and most ignorant, for what we see is nothing but our unknown selves. Traditional psychoanalytic critics, such as Bonaparte and Crews, fall into this trap precisely by asserting their authority over the literary text, and by claiming they can see through *it* better than it sees through *them*. In this form of criticism, as Shoshana Felman argues, 'literature is considered as a body of *language* – to *be interpreted*', whereas 'psychoanalysis is considered as a body of *knowledge* . . . called upon *to interpret*. Psychoanalysis, in other words, occupies the place of a *subject*, literature that of an *object*; the relation of interpretation is structured as a relation of master to slave. . . .'[29]

To some degree or other all interpretation must curtail the meanings of the text in order to render them intelligible. Perhaps this is why so many of our words for understanding also carry connotations of possession, violation, and constraint: we 'grasp' or 'seize' or 'apprehend' the things we know, much as we might apprehend a fugitive from justice. What psychoanalysis can teach us is to substitute the art of listening for the seizure of meaning. The literary text, like the analytic patient, provides the terms of its interpretation, and the reader has to learn to wrestle with this idiom rather than replace it with prepacked theories. After all, it was patients, rather than theorists, who inspired many of Freud's major principles – little Hans, for instance, invented the castration complex, while the hysteric Anna O. identified the 'talking cure' – and what Freud failed to get from his analysands he usually picked up from literature (SE X 5–149; SE II 30). What literature confirms is not so much Freud's doctrines as his insights into the unconscious, which persistently eludes his efforts to reduce it to an orthodoxy. The unconscious is the movement of escape itself. It manifests itself in accidental actions, verbal slips, and dreams, proving that the ego is not even master of its mansion, but haunted by another force that interferes with its intentions, distorting the meanings of its words and deeds. Thus if Lacan sees Oedipus as the archetypal psychoanalytic subject, this is not because of his offences but because *he does not know he has committed them*. The next sections of this introduction show how the divergence between Freud and Lacan hinges on the lessons they derive from *Oedipus*.

Freud's Oedipus

Almost every school of psychoanalysis after Freud has defined itself in terms of its interpretation of the Oedipus complex. Freud described the Oedipus as the *Kernkomplex*, the kernel complex at the troubled core of personality[30]; yet although he alluded to Oedipus throughout his writings, he never tried to encapsulate his theory in a single work. This omission cannot be passed off as carelessness: it stems from the divarications of the complex itself and its resistance to final resolutions. It is Jocasta, Oedipus's mother, who describes the syndrome most succinctly:

> As to your mother's marriage bed, – don't fear it.
> Before this, in dreams too, as well as oracles,
> many a man has lain with his own mother.
> But he to whom such things are nothing bears
> his life most easily
>
> (*Oedipus the King*, lines 980–984).

The trouble with Jocasta's version is that she equates desire for the mother with the urge for coitus. In psychoanalysis, as Freud observes,

11

the concept of sex 'goes lower and also higher than its popular sense'.[31] Lower, in the sense that infantile sexuality is 'polymorphously perverse', capricious in its aim and object and ill-distinguished from the excremental functions; higher, in the sense that sexual desire is the force that fuels the loftiest productions of the mind. As Yeats writes, speaking of Freud, 'The passions, when . . . they do not find fulfilment, become vision': the visions of the poet, like the visions of the dream, represent the 'sublimation' – the sublime transfiguration – of the shackled cravings of the flesh.[32] When Freud speaks of the infant's incestuous desire for the mother he is referring to a welter of libidinous imaginings, unrestricted to the genitals and including the sadistic drives to devour or eviscerate the mother's body, which Melanie Klein elaborates so luridly.[33] In any case, the infant yearns to possess its mother unconditionally by destroying father and siblings, the rival claimants of her love.

Freud originally believed that boys desire their mothers, girls their fathers, as the consequence of an innate predisposition. It was only later that he realised that the first erotic object for both sexes is the mother; while the way that boys and girls resolve their mother-love determines their respective sexual identities. The little boy relinquishes the mother because he fears castration at the father's hands, having attributed the absence of the penis in the girl to such a punishment. The little girl, by contrast, blames her 'castration' on her mother's stinginess or incapacity, appealing to her father for a baby as a penis-substitute. While the little boy resolves the Oedipus complex by abandoning the mother and identifying with the father, in the expectation of inheriting paternal power, the little girl's trajectory is less straightforward, for she must find a way of identifying with the mother she has loved and spurned in order to resign herself to femininity, with all the disempowerment entailed. Freud confesses that the theory of castration works better in the case of boys, for in the case of girls, 'our material – for some imcomprehensible reason – becomes far more obscure and full of gaps [*dunkler und lückenhafter*]'. In this unwitting pun, Freud betrays the fact that the 'gap' imputed to the little girl really represents the gaps in his analysis, the shortcomings of the theory which presumes to 'know' her. As Freud admits, 'it is hardly possible to give a description which has general validity' (SE XXI 233). Yet this resistance to generalisation on the part of girls is constantly forgotten by psychoanalytic theory, in its search for an invariable recipe for femininity.

Freud's account of gender has incited furious debate in psychoanalytic circles, and I examine this controversy a little later. In the meantime, it is worth observing that Freud is paying heed to poets rather than biologists in insisting that human sexuality is fundamentally

misguided, excessive, and ambivalent, and above all radically at
odds with the injunction to increase and multiply. Both sexes, Freud
contends, direct their earliest erotic feelings towards their mothers,
their earliest destructive urges towards their fathers, and it is only
through a drastic realignment, if at all, that they assume the sexual
identities allotted to them in society. In addition to the 'positive' form
of the Oedipus complex, Freud postulates a 'negative' or homosexual
variety, in which the boy desires his father and envies his mother as
a rival:

> a boy has not merely an ambivalent attitude towards his father and
> an affectionate object-choice towards his mother, but at the same
> time he also behaves like a girl and displays an affectionate feminine
> attitude to his father and a corresponding jealousy and hostility
> towards his mother.[34]

This scheme implies that the homosexual position is just as primal as
the heterosexual, and that neither is more natural, more normal, nor
more righteous than the other.

Perhaps the most disturbing implication of the Oedipus complex
is that love is never merely a relationship between two people, but
always a contest between three, even if the third is present only as a
psychic obstacle. Because of this triangular enmeshment, sexual identity
is torn between the impulses to identify, desire, or compete with both
maternal and paternal prototypes. This model of triangular desire has
inspired several thought-provoking works of psychoanalytic criticism.
René Girard, for instance, has redeployed it to examine the erotic
triangles that dominate the European novel.[35] Almost all these triangles
involve two men competing for the favours of a woman; but Girard
insists that the bond between the rivals is often more intense than
the bond that draws them both to the beloved.[36] Thus the woman,
ostensibly the object of desire, is reduced to the go-between in an erotic
tug-of-war between the men. What is more, the beloved is often chosen
by the lover, not because of her intrinsic charms, but because she is
the object of another man's infatuation. A good example may be found
in Shakespeare's *Sonnets*, where the speaker, the young man, and the
Dark Lady compete for one another's love:

> That thou has her, it is not all my grief,
> And yet it may be said I loved her dearly;
> That she hath thee is of my wailing chief,
> A loss in love that touches me more nearly.
> Loving offenders, thus I will excuse ye:
> Thou dost love her because thou know'st I love her. . . .[37]

Here the speaker admits that he is more distressed by the young man's betrayal than by the woman's. Although he 'loved her dearly', his envy for her overwhelms his love: 'That she hath thee is of my wailing chief.' In the end, however, he excuses both offenders by reflecting that their passion for each other is merely the mimesis of his love for them: 'Thou dost love her because thou know'st I love her.'

Mikkel Borch-Jacobsen agrees with Girard that rivalry and love are near of kin: what triggers desire is not an object, nor even the absence of an object, but the impulse to *identify with the desire of another*. For this reason there is no 'essential bond between desire and its object':

> the desire for an object is a desire-effect; it is *induced*, or at least secondary, with respect to the imitation – the mimesis – of the desire of others. In other words, desire is mimetic before it is anything else.[38]

This desire to identify with a desirer involves oneupmanship as well as emulation, belligerence as well as love:

> Mimesis is . . . the matrix of desire and, by the same token, the matrix of rivalry, hatred, and (in the social order) violence: 'I want what my brother, my model, my idol wants – and I want it in his place.' And, consequently, 'I want to kill him, to eliminate him'.[39]

Freud himself points out that identification is 'ambivalent from the very first'; he attributes this ambivalence to early fantasies of cannibalism, in which the infant dreams of eating the beloved object in order to identify with it, but also to destroy it at the moment of incorporation. As Freud observes, 'the object that we long for and prize is assimilated by eating and is in that way annihilated as such' (SE XVIII 105).

One difficulty with Girard's analysis is that he overlooks the role of gender in triangulation, and in particular the way that women's subjugation skews the symmetry of the relationships. Freud rectifies this omission, albeit unknowingly, in a brief but resonant analysis of dirty jokes, which exposes violent inequities between the sexes.[40] 'Smut', he argues, 'is originally directed towards women and may be equated with attempts at seduction.' If the woman yields, speech gives way to action; if she resists, however, the act of sexual aggression is diverted into the linguistic detour of a joke. Left to her own devices, the woman inevitably falls; so her resistance must be reinforced by the presence of 'another man', 'a third person', who now becomes the joker's addressee. Among the lower orders, Freud contends, the presence of the woman encourages obscenity; but in the higher levels of society, her presence brings the joking to an end, for men of rank 'save up' their smut for times when they can be 'alone together'. In this fable of the genesis of wit, the impulse to assault the woman's body is transfigured into the desire to amuse another man with words. The third person takes over the role vacated by the woman: 'When the first person finds his libidinal impulse inhibited by the woman, he develops a hostile trend against that second person and calls on the originally interfering third person as his ally.' Meanwhile the woman, first the object, then the butt, and finally the sacrificial victim of the joke, disappears to leave the joker and his interlocutor to their delight. Freud's analysis of smut offers a chilling model of male discourse as a kind of verbal gang rape, founded on the degradation and exclusion of the woman, who is reduced to nothing but a violated apparition: 'A person who laughs at smut that he hears is laughing as though he were the spectator of an act of sexual aggression' (SE VII 97–102).

This effacement of woman from the triangle is taken up by Eve Kosofsky Sedgwick in her groundbreaking study *Between Men* (1985). In this work, Sedgwick criticises Girard for his indifference not only to women's oppression but also to homophobia, which she perceives as crucial to the maintenance of patriarchy. Whereas Girard treats male bonding as if it were continuous with male eroticism, Sedgwick points out that the homo*social* bonds of patriarchy depend precisely on the disavowal of their homo*sexual* constituent, resulting in the vicious persecution of gay men. Heterosexism is therefore doubly fraudulent: the ostensible desire for women serves as pretext for affirming bonds with other men and for denying the sexual component of those bonds.[41] Claude Lévi-Strauss provides the scaffolding for this theory in his argument that 'the total relationship of exchange which constitutes marriage is not established between a man and a woman, but between two groups of men, and the woman figures only as one of the objects in the exchange, not as one of the partners.'[42] The next section of this introduction shows how Lacan develops the anthropology of Lévi-Strauss to reformulate Freud's concept of the Oedipus complex.

Lacan's Oedipus

Lévi-Strauss argues that the taboo against incest is the fundamental law of human culture. All societies prohibit sexual relationships between the near of kin, although that nearness is construed in diverse ways. This taboo marks the conquest of nature by culture: as Lacan puts it, this 'primordial Law . . . in regulating marriage ties superimposes the kingdom of culture on that of a nature abandoned to the law of [copulation]'. Kinship laws, which govern the system of combinations in mating, correspond to linguistic laws governing the combinations of words in a sentence or letters in a word. For this reason Lacan sees the taboo against incest as 'identical with an order of language. For without kinship nominations, no power is capable of instituting the order of preferences and taboos which bind and weave the yarn of lineage through succeeding generations.'[43] For Lacan, as for Lévi-Strauss, incest is bad grammar.[44]

Lacan's theory, like so many other psychoanalytic principles, finds its origin in Sophocles's *Oedipus*, where the complicity between the laws of kinship and the laws of language brings about the hero's fall. The reason Oedipus is so much more tormented by the crime of incest than the crime of parricide is that the former overthrows the nomenclature of the family. Being brother to his children, child to his wife, lover to his mother, father to his siblings, Oedipus has *sinned against the name*. As Girard puts it, 'incestuous propagation leads to formless duplications, sinister repetitions, a dark mixture of unnameable things: "a monstrous commingling of fathers, brothers, sons; of brides, wives, and mothers!"'[45] The miasma enveloping the city is interpretive as well as atmospheric: for Oedipus's crimes against his family have deranged the grammar of kinship, transforming Thebes into a barren unintelligible place. The monstrous commingling of the members of the family is reflected in a monstrous commingling of meanings.

Lacan argues that every human infant enters its existence in this undifferentiated and miasmic state, which Freud described as 'oceanic feeling'.[46] To achieve subjectivity, the infant has to be conscripted into the lexicon of kinship, in which its identity as child, son or daughter, is determined by its difference from other subjects, such as mothers, fathers, brothers, sisters, uncles, aunts. The new-born infant has no self because it is oblivious to difference, adrift among sensations, appetites, phantasmagoria. Lacan describes the infant as an 'hommelette', meaning a little man, a manlet or homunculus; an omelette, or an eggy mess of possibilities; and finally a Hamlet, or a scrambled Oedipus.[47] Why Hamlet? Freud argues that *Hamlet* reveals the 'secular advance of repression in the emotional life of mankind', because the hero's wishes have gone underground, and we discern them only in the deeds he cannot do, rather than the deeds he does (SE IV 264). By contrast, Oedipus actually commits the murder and the incest that his descendents merely agonise or dream about. In this sense, Oedipus is the only man in history *without* an Oedipus complex, as Cynthia Chase has wittily observed (see below, p. 62).

For Lacan, however, the difference between the tragedies lies elsewhere. In the first place, the crime attributed to Oedipus occurs within his own generation, whereas the crime that Hamlet is commissioned to avenge belongs to the unfinished business of the older generation. Hence Hamlet's cry, 'O cursèd spite / That ever I was born to set it right!' Secondly, Oedipus assumed the onus of the Theban regicide, and atoned for his alleged incest with his eyes. 'Oedipus paid,' writes Lacan; 'he represents the man whose heroic lot is to carry the burden of requited debt'. Hamlet's father, on the contrary, was 'cut off even in the blossoms of [his] sin,' burdening his son with his 'inexpiable debt'.[48] So Hamlet is an omelette because he has no selfhood of his own; he is haunted to the core by the undiscoverable secrets of the father. Even his name implies the interpsychic nature of his guilt, since it confuses the distinction between Hamlet son and Hamlet phantom.

How is the hommelette to be cooked into a human subject? Lacan argues that the infant, originally merged in a 'primal dyad' with the mother, has to break this symbiosis in order to establish the limits of its body and desires. The crucial moment of this separation occurs in the 'mirror stage', a period between the ages of six and eighteen months in which the infant falls for the enchantment of its own reflection in the mirror, or recognises its behaviour in the imitative gestures of another person.[49] At this phase of development, the infant experiences its body as a random concatenation of its parts: a 'heterogeneous mannequin, a baroque doll, a trophy of limbs', in Lacan's words.[50] In contrast to this experience of fragmentation, the mirror offers a mirage of bodily coordination and control that the infant greets with jubilation. Its joy, however, is ill-founded, for the image of coherence is a decoy and a trap. Just as Ovid's Narcissus pines away because he can neither capture his reflection nor escape from it, so the infant yearns for a statuesque completeness that never coincides with its tumultuous experience. As Lacan writes, 'the human individual fixes upon himself an image that alienates him from himself', literally losing himself in his own reflection.[51] In this double-bind, it is impossible to make the ego whole because the fantasy of wholeness is the wellspring of its self-estrangement.

'Je est un autre', wrote Rimbaud.[52] Lacan would agree that the I is always someone else, an alibi, since it is founded on identification with a spectral form external to itself, whether its own reflection or the equally quixotic image of an other. Thus the ego is a ghost, or rather a consortium of ghosts, consisting of the replicas of lost or

absent objects of desire.[53] Identification belongs to the modality that
Lacan has defined as the 'imaginary': a specular domain of images,
reflections, simulacra. The imaginary arises in the mirror stage, but
this is not a 'stage' in the developmental sense, which the ego might
outgrow and leave behind, but a stage in the spatial sense, a *stade*
or stadium, in which the ego constantly identifies itself with new
personae in the effort to evade division, distance, difference, deferral,
death. Malcolm Bowie, in his superb introduction to Lacan, argues that
'the imaginary is the scene of a desperate delusional attempt to be and
to remain "what one is" by gathering to oneself ever more instances
of sameness, resemblance, and self-replication; it is the birthplace of
the narcissistic "ideal ego".'[54] Through identification, the ego strives
to overcome the strangeness of the object by making it a double, an
accomplice, a *semblable*. The result is a wilderness of mirrors in which
self and object oscillate perpetually, each eclipsed under the shadow of
the other.

The reason that the infant first resorts to identification is to deny its
separation from the mother by incorporating her persona in its ego.[55]
For this reason Lacan regards the Imaginary as a maternal realm,
and he argues that this dual universe of mother and child has to be
disrupted by a third term if the principle of difference is to prevail over
the whirlpool of similitudes. It is the father who intervenes between
the mother and the child, breaking up their spectral reciprocities. His
function is to introduce the law against incest into the Oedipal drama
of the home. By forbidding 'incest' – or merger – with the mother, the
father instates the symbolic order, which distinguishes parent from
child, mother from father, sister from brother. If this theory seems to
assume that every child has a loving mother and a jealous father, Lacan
insists that these are both symbolic roles transcending the individuals
performing them. The real father cannot be conflated with the symbolic
father, the paternal function or the '*Nom-du-Père*': here the pun on
non-du-père implies that the Name-of-the-Father is *not*-of-the-father, not
intrinsic to the man as such but donned upon him like a giant's robe
upon a dwarfish thief.[56] (I quote *Macbeth* because this play, like *Hamlet*,
exposes the absurdity of the attempt to *be* the father, and insinuates
that those who take his role are always dwarfish thieves or player
kings.)

By promoting the name over the person of the father, Lacan is
taking up a hint of Freud's that paternal power is linguistic rather
than corporeal. In a crucial passage of *Moses and Monotheism* (1939),
Freud suggests that patriarchy represents the triumph of doubt over
truth, of word over flesh: 'since maternity is proved by the evidence
of the senses while paternity is a hypothesis, based on an inference
and a premiss' (SE XXIII 114). Similarly, Stephen Dedalus in Joyce's

Ulysses describes the father as the 'legal fiction' invented to efface the
fact of motherhood. The 'mystery' of paternity, he says, is founded on
the void, 'upon incertitude, upon unlikelihood'; the father is a 'ghost
by absence' from the act of birth, and potentially 'a ghost by death'
as well.[57] Lacan agrees that under the dominion of the *Nom-du-Père*,
'nothing exists except on an assumed foundation of absence'.[58] What is
more, the father's name outlives its bearer, anticipating the extinction
of the very monster that it brings to life. Thus the name, from the
beginning, is an epitaph, a ghost, destined to outlive the dissolution of
the flesh; and Lacan insists that death inheres in language as a whole,
where every vocable enfolds a void, entombs a silence.

For language originates in absence: the infant resorts to words
only when the things it wants are unavailable. As Lacan writes, 'the
symbol manifests itself first of all as the murder of the thing, and this
death constitutes in the subject the eternalization of his desire' (*Ecrits*,
p. 104). Fear of castration brings about the cruelest loss of all, since it
forces the infant to renounce the mother. Henceforth, all pleasures will
be substitutive, for sexuality consists of the pursuit of metaphorical
alternatives to lost felicities: indeed, desire in Lacan is nothing other
than the drive to linguistic substitution.

Lacan borrows most of his assumptions about language from
Ferdinand de Saussure, who stated in his *Course in General Linguistics*:
'in a language there are only differences, *and no positive terms.*'[59]
According to Saussure, meaning is determined not by the intrinsic
properties of signs, but rather by their negative relationships to other
signs, their counter-magnetism. This theory implies that words and
meanings are forever shifting under the semantic contagion of their
neighbours: the signified (the concept) cannot be anchored to the
signifier (the written or acoustic substance of the word). For Lacan,
however, it is the phallus that provides the needed anchorage in
language. As signifier of the difference between the sexes, the phallus
comes to stand for all the differences that structure the symbolic order:
in Lacan's less than lucid formula, the phallus is 'the signifier destined
to designate as a whole the effects of the signified, in that the signifier
conditions them by its presence as a signifier' (*Ecrits*, p. 124). In other
words, the phallus is the kingpin in the bowling alley of signification:
knock it over, and all the other signs come tumbling down. It takes the
place of God as the absolute guarantee of meaning, the only difference
being that the phallus is the absence that precedes all lacks, rather
than the presence that precedes all beings. If this theory seems a bit
far-fetched, phallo-sceptics should beware; for Lacan warns us that
the price of the denial or 'foreclosure' of the phallus is psychosis.
Language is a sacrificial order which exacts its pound of flesh: and it is
better to believe oneself castrated, or to live in terror of the knife, than

19

to forfeit all the differences enshrined within the phallus that render
the universe intelligible.

Before the phallus

Lacan has been accused of phallicism, phallocentrism, and even
phallogocentrism: his critics often seem to be competing for the
length of their neologisms in the absence of the controversial member.
Whatever the effects of the phallus on the psyche, there can be no
doubt of its divisive impact on the psychoanalytic movement; indeed,
the phallus could be described as arch-signifier of the raging differences
between the schools. These ruptures began as early as the 1920s when
Karen Horney challenged the theory of penis-envy, arguing that it
was men who envied women the capacity to reproduce; while the
overvaluation of the penis was contrived to compensate the male sex
for its womblessness.[60] For this heresy, Horney was expelled in 1941
from the New York Psychoanalytic Institute; hardly an uncommon fate
in a movement which has grown, like the psyche it describes, through
splitting, excommunication, and repression, rather than accumulated
wisdom. Lacan, too, dissociated himself from the *Société psychanalytique
de Paris* in 1953; but after forming the *École freudienne*, he found
himself so besieged by renegades that he dissolved his own school
in 1980, with the words, 'je persevère': in other words, I persevere
as *père sévère*, the severe and unrelenting father, in order to defend
the father and the phallus from the efforts of other theorists, such as
Melanie Klein, to instate the mother in the central role.[61]

In *The Second Sex* (1949), Simone de Beauvoir argued that Freud had
constructed a masculine model of development and then imposed it,
with minimal adjustments, onto women, while ignoring the political
constraints on women's lives. If girls desire a penis, de Beauvoir
insisted, it is 'only as a symbol of the privileges enjoyed by boys'.[62] In
other words, women have good reason to envy an organ that promises
authority and freedom; in fact, it would be much more slavish *not* to
envy such an organ than to feel oneself deprived and 'cut off short'.
This argument, compelling as it is, assumes the psychic and the social
to be interchangeable, a view that Lacan vigorously challenges.[63] He
insists that the penis, the real organ, be distinguished from the phallus,
its unconscious counterpart, because the role the phallus plays as
signifier is incommensurable with the functions of the penis in reality.

If many feminists repudiate the theory of castration, others prove
its staunchest advocates. Juliet Mitchell, in *Psychoanalysis and Feminism*
(1974), defends the theory of castration because it means that gender

is determined by fantasy rather than by fact.[64] Since one sex mourns the penis, while the other sex is terrified of losing it, yet neither is castrated in reality, it is clear that the organ with which they are obsessed is symbolic or chimerical, not real. This means that 'gender', unlike 'sex', is an artifact of culture, subject like all artifacts to transformation, whereas the genitals persist unchangeably throughout the centuries, indifferent to all campaigns in favour of the convex or the concave. The infantile fiction of castration actually disavows the real distinction between the sexes by asserting they were once the same, before the females were emasculated. According to Freud, children concoct this fantasy out of the slightest hints in order to evade the anatomical realities of sexuality; and since this gruesome tale of mutilation institutes the world of gender, the whole adventure of sexual difference begins in blunder.

Juliet Mitchell's study liberated feminist theory from a narrow-minded hostility to psychoanalysis. Yet her argument in favour of Lacan stands or falls upon a dubious opposition, much cherished by opponents of essentialism, whereby 'nature' is regarded as immutable, and 'culture' as amenable to transformation. Lately Eve Kosofsky Sedgwick has cast a salutary scepticism on this opposition: if 'nature' is constant (and genetic engineering challenges this axiom), there is little evidence that 'culture' welcomes change, particularly any change that benefits the subjugated.[65] In the daily struggles of women's lives, moreover, it is just about as useful to reflect that sexism is 'cultural', not 'natural', as to dream of liberation in the afterlife (or after the revolution, in the Marxist eschatology).[66] In practice, it is very difficult to disentangle 'nature' from 'culture', particularly as regards the phallus which, 'cultural' as it is meant to be, bears an unmistakable resemblance to its 'natural' equivalent; the only difference being that the phallus is invested with the power to perform the tricks that the penis often fails abysmally to execute. For instance, the phallus defies gravity, being perpetually tumescent (Freud believed that aeroplanes in dreams were flying phalloi [SE V 394]); the penis, by contrast, spends the greater part of its existence drooping earthward, in deference, perhaps, to the chthonic goddesses. Any woman who has witnessed the humiliations that the penis can inflict upon its bearer is more likely to be piteous than envious, and to be grateful for the dignified discretion of the clitoris. On a more serious note, so many inequities in our society depend on having or not having a *penis* that it seems irrelevant to fret about the phallus, its otherworldly emanation. A reputable English department recently appointed the only man out of a shortlist of six candidates with the explanation that 'he had something that none of the others had'. In a world where the possession of a penis opens up so many opportunities and privileges, and legitimates so much injustice and brutality, it is not surprising that the male organ has been credited with magic powers.

Elizabeth Grosz insists that the prestige accorded to the phallus in psychoanalysis derives from the privileges of the penis in reality. She writes:

> In spite of Lacan's claims, the phallus is not a 'neutral' term functioning equally for both sexes, positioning them both in the symbolic order. As the word suggests, it is a term privileging masculinity, or rather, the penis. The valorization of the penis and the relegation of the female sexual organs to the castrated category are effects of a socio-political system that also enables the phallus to function as the 'signifier of signifiers', giving the child access to a (sexual) identity and speaking position within culture. Its position as a threshold signifier is symptomatic of the assumed patriarchal context in Freud's and Lacan's work.[67]

Stricter Lacanians would argue that the phallus is an arbitrary signifier, so neutral and devoid of content that it carries no ideological sting.[68] Its only function is to signify the law of difference that weans the infant out of the imaginary and substitutes the negativity of language for the plenitude of incest. John Fletcher has remarked that the phallus, in this account of things, is reduced into a kind of civil servant: what is lost is the violence that Freud evokes in his descriptions of the infant's fantasies of mutilation. What is also lost is the polyvalency that Freud attributes to the *penis*, because the *phallus*, in Lacan, stands for anchorage of meaning rather than semantic metamorphosis. In Freud, on the contrary, the *penis* belongs to a chain of fantasmatic objects, including babies, faeces, gifts, and money, which are treated as 'symbolic equations' by the unconscious, since they belong to the subject but may also be detached and yielded into the possession of the other.[69] It is through these circulating objects, which Lacan has described as 'exchange-values', that the infant explores the boundary that divides its body and bodily products from the interpsychic merchandise of others. The *objet petit a* is Lacan's term for these nomadic objects; yet he fails to recognise that their mobility subverts the transcendental status of the phallus.[70] There is no reason, in his *own* terms, to award priority to any organ, nor even to assign the phallus, as *objet petit a*, to either sex; yet whenever its mystique is challenged, Lacan leaps to its defence, as if his theories were themselves in danger of dismemberment.

At his best, Lacan overcomes his own idolatry and restores the phallus to the 'signifying chain', in which the human subject is entrapped from birth. Lacan declares, 'symbols in fact envelop the life of man in a network so total that they join together, before he comes into the world, those who are going to engender him . . . so total that they bring to his birth . . . the shape of his destiny . . . so total that they follow him . . . even beyond his death' (*Ecrits*, p. 68). Desire, founded in loss, never closes on a final signified but presses on from sign to sign in pursuit of an impossible satiety: and thus the signifying chain consists of 'rings of a necklace that is a ring in another necklace made of rings' (*Ecrits*, p. 153). Within 'the rigorously non-elitist world of the signifying chain', the phallus functions as an 'exchange-value' rather than a gold standard.[71] To illustrate the process of exchange, Lacan uses Poe's story, 'The Purloined Letter', in which the letter of the title circulates between the Queen, the Minister, and finally the detective, who restores it, not to its owner (for a letter belongs to no one, neither its sender nor its addressee) but to its original position in the triangle.[72] Though Lacan never explicitly identifies the letter with the phallus, he invites the reader to make this inference: for the letter, like the phallus, functions as an empty signifier, whose meaning depends on its position rather than its contents, which are never disclosed. The fact that the letter/phallus ends up in the possession of the Queen suggests that the mother, rather than the father, is its rightful guardian. Similarly, Melanie Klein argues that children attribute the penis to the mother, not the father, equating it with all the other treasures, such as food and babies, hidden in her enviable womb. Lacan dismisses Klein's account as 'fantastic phallophagia' [phallus-eating]; yet this reaction indicates a fear that the women who have played such an important role in psychoanalysis may devour its paternal gurus, phalluses and all.[73] Frankly, Lacan's conception of the phallus is so difficult to understand that theorists who explain it often find themselves believing in it, in the sheer exhilaration of defeating its opacity.

In France, Luce Irigaray has attempted to evade the problems of the phallus by focusing on the pre-Oedipal dimension of the female psyche, which Freud once compared to the 'Minoan–Mycenean civilisation' buried underneath the ruins of patriarchal Greece (SE XXI 226). In 1985, when Irigaray published her first manifesto, *Speculum of the Other Woman*, Lacan abruptly dismissed her from her teaching post in his department at Vincennes, thus making her another victim of the psychoanalytic ritual of disinheritance. As opposed to Freud, who saw the murder of the father as the founding act of civilisation, Irigaray asserts that 'the whole of our culture in the west depends upon the murder of the mother'.[74] In Greek mythology, for instance, Orestes's murder of the mother leads to the triumph of the patriarchal order of Apollo over the chthonic goddesses; in Christianity, the mother-goddess is not exactly murdered but demoted to a mortal woman who merely incubates the father's fecundating breath, so that

God, together with the Holy Ghost, may take full credit for the act of procreation.[75] According to Irigaray, such myths reveal that Western thought is governed by one of the 'sexual theories of children' that Freud investigates, whereby there is only one sex, which is male, the female being nothing but a mutilated and corrupted copy of that sex.[76] Likewise, the psychoanalytic theory of castration, rather than accounting for the *difference* of femininity, reduces women to the other of the Same, pale shadows of a monosexual identity.

For this reason Irigaray insists upon the need to devise new forms of representation to express the specificity of womanhood. She proposes that the female sex no longer be regarded as a lack, a wound, or a black hole, but rather as 'two lips' forever joined in one embrace. 'Always at least two', these lips cannot be appropriated into masculine conceptions of the one, the proper, or the self-identical; 'continually interchanging', they are 'neither identifiable nor separable from one another . . . it is the *touch* which for the female sex seems to me primordial; these *two lips* are always joined in an embrace'.[77] In Irigaray's utopia, where women would enunciate their own sex, rather than deferring to the phallus, their language would defy grammatical divisions, making words as warm and slippery as lips:

> what a feminine syntax might be is not simple nor easy to state, because in that 'syntax' there would no longer be either subject or object, 'oneness' would no longer be privileged, there would no longer be proper meanings, proper names, 'proper' attributes. . . . Instead, that syntax would invoke nearness, proximity, but in such an extreme form that it would preclude any distinction of identities, any establishment of ownership, thus any form of appropriation.[78]

This theory has angered many feminists, since it seems to be advising women to 'get in touch with their bodies' (as if they were ever permitted to forget about those bodies), and to speak through their vulvas rather than their mouths. Irigaray seems to be relegating women to the formless and irrational, where they have been relegated since the pre-Socratics, who ascribed to men the qualities of reason, form, and spirit, while unloading on to women the rejected qualities of instinct, physicality, and indeterminacy.[79] Other feminists, however, defend Irigaray against the charge of biological essentialism: Jan Montefiore, for example, argues that the metaphor of 'two lips' cannot be taken literally, for it is '*not* a definition of women's identity in biological terms', but 'a counter-proposal to the psychoanalytic association of the right to speech with possession of the phallus'; an attempt to create 'a possible vocabulary for the female imagination other than the Freudian

opposition "phallic/castrated"'.[80] Montefiore makes a convincing case;
but it is troubling that Irigaray, judging by her style, can conceive of
female discourse only in the form of gush, as if incontinence were the
equivalent of liberation. To speak as women, it seems we are obliged
to echo the unpunctuated rhapsody of Molly Bloom, in which the flow
of words is ill-distinguished from the flow of bodily secretions; yet the
notion that liquidity in discourse is superior to dryness is based on
a bizarre confusion of the orifices. Whatever the future of women in
language, it would be sad if Irigaray's ethics of 'mucosity' displaced the
keener energies of women's wit, for 'brevity', as Dorothy Parker has
observed, 'is the soul of lingerie'.

Julia Kristeva also turns her attention to the pre-Oedipal in
order to explore what Freud as described as the 'dark continent'
of femininity; yet her work, in my opinion, is much richer and
more complex than Irigaray's. In her doctoral thesis, translated as
'*Revolution in Poetic Language*', Kristeva distinguishes two orders within
language: the *symbolic*, dominated by the father, the phallus, and
the law; and the *semiotic*, haunted by the vengeful traces of a lost
pre-Oedipal maternal world. These terms owe much to Nietzsche's
opposition in *The Birth of Tragedy* between the Apollonian and
Dionysian principles: the *semiotic*, like the Dionysian, is associated
with sonority and rhythm, with the *stuff* of speech, in which language
coalesces with the body and the orchestration of the drives; whereas
the *symbolic*, like the Apollonian, articulates these primal forces into
rational, intelligible forms. Logically and chronologically prior to the
institution of the symbolic, the semiotic first makes itself heard in the
echolalias of infants; and it survives as a pulsional pressure within
language, resurfacing wherever the acoustic matter of the signifier
threatens to disrupt the sense.[81] As Terry Eagleton comments, 'the
semiotic is the "other" of language which is nonetheless intimately
entwined with it'; it is the nonsense woven indistinguishably into
sense.[82] Though there are traces of Romantic irrationalism in this
theory, as indeed in all of psychoanalytic thought, Kristeva insists
that the forces of the semiotic must be harnessed by those of the
symbolic lest they should erupt into a fanaticism of the instincts,
such as fascism. Avant-garde art, she argues, circumvents fascism
by channelling the semiotic into an exploration of the limits of
language, where the fixities that grammar imposes on the world
succumb to flux. Virginia Woolf, for instance, urges writers to 'let
your rhythmical sense open and shut, open and shut, boldly and
freely, until one thing melts in another'; she is suggesting that the
rhythms associated with the body, with the opening and closing
of its orifices, have the power to dissolve the boorish solidity of
things.[83]

In her more recent work Kristeva uses the term 'abjection' to describe this deliquescence of identities. Abjection literally means 'casting out'; for according to Kristeva, it is through this process of expulsion that the infant establishes the limits of its body, rejecting whatever is perceived as alien, unclean, or improper to the self. What is expelled, however, can never be obliterated, but hovers at the borders of identity, troubling the subject with reminders of its own estranged corporeality. Emissions such as sweat, tears, vomit, urine, faeces, mucus, semen, blood and mother's milk are 'abject' because they overflow the limits of the body, confusing the inside with the outside; and 'abjection is above all ambiguity', Kristeva writes: it is that which 'disturbs identity, system, order'.[84] In her writings on horror, melancholia, and love, Kristeva shows how art and literature grapple with abjection: her essay on Gérard de Nerval's sonnet 'El Desdichado' ['The Disinherited'], reprinted in this volume, is a difficult but powerful example of her methods.[85]

According to Lacan, Freud constantly attempted to evade his own most radical discovery: the polyvalency of the unconscious. As we have seen, the same critique applies to Lacan's ambivalent conception of the phallus. In his work, the phallus sometimes represents a floating currency; sometimes, a funerary monument to lack. Against these pessimistic intuitions, though, Lacan's priapism reasserts itself, and he brandishes the phallus as a magic wand to guide us through the hurlyburly of signification, a point of fixity amidst a wilderness of ambiguity. Thus he defends himself against his own perception of the instability of language, the 'incessant sliding of the signified under the signifier' (*Ecrits*, p. 154). But it is precisely the instability of signs that opens them to history, so that shibboleths like the phallus may change their meaning according to the values and prejudices of the age. In effect, the mystification of the phallus blinds Lacan to his own insight into the rhetorical exuberance of the unconscious, which is his crucial contribution to the art of literary criticism.

Towards the psychoanalysis of literature

The essays in the present volume demonstrate the rich diversity of current psychoanalytic criticism. Yet they are united in the principle that there are more things in literary texts than are dreamt of in Freudian philosophy; and that the reader cannot claim the role of master any more than the text can be restricted to the role of slave. Rather, text and reader each reveal the inadvertent intuitions of the other: and it is out of this exchange that psychoanalytic theory is evolving still, in spite of its practitioners' attempts to petrify its dogma.

The first part of this collection is devoted to drama, and contains three essays on Sophocles's Oedipus plays, which never cease to provoke new insights and new heresies. In the first essay, André Green explores affinities between the stage of drama and the stage of dreams. Cynthia Chase, in 'Oedipal Textuality', shows how Freud's discovery of the unconscious uncannily repeats the tragedy of *Oedipus*; for Freud confessed that he was 'gripped' by Oedipus because he recognised his own desires in the hero's crimes. Lacan, however, is suspicious of the whole idea of recognition, as Shoshana Felman points out in her essay, 'Beyond Oedipus'. Freud saw the goal of psychoanalysis as the capacity to take possession of one's past, and Oedipus accomplishes this task in *Oedipus the King*. For Lacan, on the contrary, the hero must be dispossessed of home and kingdom and every other prop to his identity before he can confront his exile not only from the state but from himself. He must recognise that recognition is itself a narcissistic mirage.

The second part of this collection turns to narrative, opening with Slavoj Žižek's Lacanian investigation of detective fiction. In the next two essays, Anita Sokolsky and Daniel Ferrer both make use of Freud's analysis of mourning and melancholia to explore the significance of loss in narrative: Sokolsky examines the rich anger of Jane Austen's *Persuasion*, while Ferrer analyses *To the Lighthouse*, the novel in which Virginia Woolf claimed to have exorcised her parents' ghosts.[86]

The final essays in this volume concentrate on poetry, the literary form that Freud had least to say about. The critics represented here make up for this omission, showing how psychoanalytic theory may enhance the close analysis of poetry, rather than forsaking rhetoric for generalities. In the first essay, Harold Bloom celebrates Freud as both the theorist and the great prose-poet of the sublime. The poetry of the sublime, Bloom argues, represents a manic triumph over loss: 'a terror uneasily allied with pleasurable sensations of augmented power, and even of narcissistic freedom, freedom in the shape of that wildness that Freud dubbed "the omnipotence of thought", the greatest of all narcissistic illusions'.[87] Kristeva, on the other hand, examines the depressive side of the sublime, the abject experience of loss. She argues that the melancholic does not mourn an object of desire but 'the Thing', which she describes as 'the real that does not lend itself to signification'. The Thing is a loss without limits, prior to the object, and prior to the advent of signification, whereby objects are identified and salvaged from the waste of the unnameable. In his sonnet 'El Desdichado', Gérard de Nerval uses the metaphor of the 'black sun' in order to invoke this unimaginable Thing: 'an insistence without presence, a light without representation.'[88] Kristeva's reading of this sonnet demonstrates how rhythm and semantic polyvalency provide a kind of orchestration for a loss too oceanic to be named.

Jacqueline Rose also explores the ways that poetry contends with the unnameable which, in the case of Sylvia Plath, assumes the deadly image of the Holocaust. In Kristeva's terms, the Holocaust could be described as the Thing in modern history, the loss that defeats signification, rendering language irrelevant at best, or barbarous at worst. Plath has been accused of trivialising the Holocaust by making it a metaphor for her own despair; but it is metaphor, Rose argues, that keeps the past alive, and prevents the Holocaust from disappearing into fictionality. When the metaphoric function is impaired, even the survivors of the Holocaust are unable to believe in their experience, and thus the past remains unburied, unappeased. 'Take metaphor out of language and there is no memory, no history, left', Rose claims (below, p. 229). This is not to say that the past is nothing but a metaphor, but rather that metaphor provides a doorway to the lost events that shape our world and organise our psychic life. If psychoanalysis has often been accused of a disdain for history, historians have also tended to neglect the role of the unconscious in the living and remembering of world events. What history needs is a science of tropes – that is, a psychoanalysis – to understand the ways in which the conflicts of the world are reconfigured in the conflicts of the mind.

Notes

1. GERTRUDE STEIN,'Composition as Explanation' (1926) in *Look At Me Now And Here I Am: Writings and Lectures 1909–45*, ed. Patricia Meyerowitz (Harmondsworth: Penguin, 1967), p. 23.

2. PAUL DE MAN, *The Resistance to Theory*, introd. Wlad Godzich (Minneapolis: Minnesota University Press, 1986).

3. PHILIP RIEFF, *Freud: The Mind of the Moralist* (1959; Chicago: University of Chicago Press, 1979), p. 303.

4. See JULIET FLOWER MCCANNELL, *Figuring Lacan: Criticism and the Cultural Unconscious* (London: Croom Helm, 1986), p. 1.

5. SIGMUND FREUD,'The Dissolution of the Psychical Personality', *New Introductory Lectures* XXXI, in the Standard Edition of *The Complete Psychological Works of Sigmund Freud*, trans. James Strachey (London: Hogarth, 1953–74), vol. XXII, p. 80. Henceforth cited as SE. For Lacan's interpretation of Freud's famous dictum, see JACQUES LACAN, *Ecrits*, trans. Alan Sheridan (London: Tavistock, 1977), p. 129.

6. FREDERICK CREWS, 'Conrad's Uneasiness – and Ours', in *Out of My System: Psychoanalysis, Ideology, and Critical Method* (New York: Oxford University Press, 1975), p. 56.

7. JOSEPH CONRAD, *Heart of Darkness*, ed. Robert Kimbrough (New York: W.W. Norton, 1963), pp. 67, 51; quoted in CREWS, 'Conrad's Uneasiness', p. 56.

8. MARIE BONAPARTE, *The Life and Works of Edgar Allan Poe: A Psycho-Analytic Interpretation*, trans. John Rodker (1933; London: Imago, 1949), p. 590.

9. See CREWS, *Skeptical Engagements* (New York: Oxford University Press, 1986), Intr., pp. xi–ixx.

10. PETER BROOKS, 'The Idea of a Psychoanalytic Literary Criticism', in *Discourse in Psychoanalysis and Literature*, ed. Shlomith Rimmon-Kenan (London: Methuen, 1987), p. 2.

11. FREUD, *The Interpretation of Dreams* (1900), SE IV 265. See also Freud's letter to Wilhelm Fliess of 15 October, 1897, where he points out Hamlet himself 'had contemplated the same deed against his father out of passion for his mother. . . . And does he not in the end, in the same way as my hysterical patients, bring down punishment on himself by suffering the same fate as his father of being poisoned by the same rival?' (*The Complete Letters of Sigmund Freud to Wilhelm Fliess, 1887–1904*, trans. Jeffrey Moussaieff Masson (Cambridge, Mass: Harvard University Press, 1985), p. 273.

12. ERNEST JONES, *Hamlet and Oedipus* (1949; New York: W.W. Norton, 1976), p. 92.

13. See, *inter alia*, SAMUEL WEBER, 'The Sideshow or: Remarks on a Canny Moment', *Modern Language Notes*, **88** (1973): 1102–33; HÉLÈNE CIXOUS, 'Fiction and its Phantoms: A Reading of Freud's *Das Unheimliche*', *New Literary History*, **7** (1976): 525–48; NEIL HERTZ, 'Freud and the Sandman', in J. Harrari (ed.), *Textual Strategies: Perspectives in Post-Structuralist Criticism* (London: Methuen, 1979), pp. 296–321; rpt in NEIL HERTZ, *The End of the Line: Essays on Psychoanalysis and the Sublime* (New York: Columbia University Press, 1985), pp. 97–121; BERNARD RUBIN, 'Freud and Hoffmann: "The Sandman",' in *Introducing Psychoanalytic Theory*, ed. Sander L. Gilman (New York: Brunner/Mazel, 1982), pp. 205–17; FRANÇOISE MELTZER, 'The Uncanny Rendered Canny: Freud's Blind Spot in Reading Hoffmann's "Sandman", in Gilman (ed.), *Introducing Psychoanalytic Theory*, pp. 218–39. For a useful summary of these positions, see ELIZABETH WRIGHT, *Psychoanalytic Criticism: Theory in Practice* (London: Methuen, 1984), pp. 142–50.

14. Much of this work has been inspired by JACQUES DERRIDA, 'To Speculate – on "Freud"', in *The Post Card: From Socrates to Freud and Beyond*, trans. Alan Bass (1980; Chicago: University of Chicago Press, 1987), pp. 257–409. The other founders of this school are NICOLAS ABRAHAM and MARIE TOROK; their works include *The Wolf Man's Magic Word: A Cryptonomy*, trans. Nicholas Rand, with a preface 'Fors' by Jacques Derrida (Minneapolis: University of Minnesota Press, 1986); 'The Shell and the Kernel', *Diacritics*, **9**: 1 (1979): 16–31; 'Psychoanalytic Esthetics: Time, Rhythm, and the Unconscious', *Diacritics*, **16**: 3 (1986): 3–14. For the theory of intergenerational haunting, see also NICOLAS ABRAHAM, 'Notes

on the Phantom: A Complement to Freud's Metapsychology' (1975), in *The Trial(s) of Psychoanalysis*, ed. Françoise Meltzer (Chicago: University of Chicago Press, 1988), pp. 75–80. For a general account of the significance of Abraham and Torok's work for literary criticism, see ESTHER RASHKIN, 'Tools for a New Psychoanalytic Literary Criticism: The Works of Abraham and Torok', *Diacritics*, **18**: 4 (1988): pp. 31–52. For a brilliant application of these theories to *Hamlet*, see NICHOLAS ROYLE, 'The Distraction of "Freud"', in *Oxford Literary Review*, **12**: 1–2 (1990): 101–38.

15. LIONEL TRILLING, 'Freud and Literature' (1947), in *The Liberal Imagination* (London: Heinemann, 1964); rpt in Perry Meisel (ed.), *Freud: A Collection of Critical Essays* (Englewood Cliffs, NJ: Prentice-Hall, 1981), pp. 107, 108.

16. See LACAN, *Ecrits*, pp. 146–78; and ROMAN JAKOBSON, 'Two Aspects of Language and Two Types of Aphasic Disturbances', in *Studies on Child Language and Aphasia* (The Hague: Mouton, 1971), pp. 49–73. For a discussion of the influence of Jakobson on Lacan, see ANIKA LEMAIRE, *Jacques Lacan*, trans. David Macey (London: Routledge, 1977), p. 43.

17. FREDRIC JAMESON, 'Imaginary and Symbolic in Lacan: Marxism, Psychoanalytic Criticism, and the Problem of the Subject', in *Literature and Psychoanalysis: The Question of Reading: Otherwise*, ed. Shoshana Felman (Baltimore: Johns Hopkins University Press, 1982), pp. 386–7.

18. See MALCOLM BOWIE, *Lacan* (London: Fontana, 1991), p. 130. See also LACAN, 'The Signification of the Phallus', *Ecrits*, pp. 281–91; and FREUD, letter to Fliess, 14 April, 1898: 'Priapus stood for permanent erection, a wish fulfilment representing the opposite of psychological impotence' (Masson (ed.), *The Complete Letters of Sigmund Freud to Wilhelm Fliess*, p. 308).

19. See FREUD, 'Screen Memories' (1903), SE III 301–22; 'Remembering, Repeating, and Working-Through' (1914), SE XII 147–56; 'Splitting of the Ego in the Process of Defence' (1940), SE XXIII 273–8.

20. 'Condensation, together with the transformation of thoughts into situations ("dramatization"), is the most important and peculiar characteristic of the dream-work' ('On Dreams' [1901], SE V 653).

21 FREUD, *The Interpretation of Dreams* (1900), SE IV 295–6; HEGEL, *The Phenomenology of Spirit*, trans. A.V. Miller (New York: Oxford University Press, 1977), p. 443.

22. Freud's first statement of the 'principle of constancy' appears in *Studies on Hysteria* (1893–5), SE II 197. See JEAN LAPLANCHE, *Life and Death in Psychoanalysis*, trans. Jeffrey Mehlman (Baltimore: Johns Hopkins University Press, 1976); JACQUES DERRIDA, 'To Speculate – on Freud'; and PETER BROOKS, 'Freud's Masterplot', in *Reading for the Plot; Design and Intention in Narrative* (New York: Vintage, 1985), pp. 90–112, for ingenious readings of *Beyond the Pleasure Principle*.

23. The term 'talking cure' was devised by Josef Breuer's patient Anna O.; she also referred to psychoanalysis as 'chimney-sweeping': see FREUD and BREUER, *Studies on Hysteria* (1893–5), SE II 30.

24. For Eurydice's side of the story, see HD, 'Eurydice', *Collected Poems 1912–1944*, ed. Louis L. Martz (New York: New Directions, 1983), pp. 51–5.

25. SOPHOCLES, *Oedipus the King*, trans. David Grene, in *Sophocles, I: The Complete Greek Tragedies*, intr. David Grene (Chicago: University of Chicago Press, 1954), p. 15, lines 108–9.

26. SE IV xxxii. See also CYNTHIA CHASE, 'Oedipal Textuality', below, p. 57; and Freud's letter to Fliess of 4 July, 1901, where he speaks of a book by L. LAISTNER called *The Riddle of the Sphinx* (1889), which 'maintains that myths go back to dreams' (Masson (ed.), *The Complete Letters of Sigmund Freud to Wilhelm Fliess*, pp. 444–5).

27. Cited in SHOSHANA FELMAN, 'Turning the Screw of Interpretation', in Felman (ed.), *Literature and Psychoanalysis*, p. 118. Felman's essay on HENRY JAMES's novella 'The Turn of the Screw' is one of the finest examples of psychoanalytic criticism to date.

28. See JOHN FORRESTER, *The Seductions of Psychoanalysis: Freud, Lacan and Derrida* (Cambridge: Cambridge University Press, 1990), esp. pp. 264–5.

29. SHOSHANA FELMAN, 'To Open the Question', in Felman (ed.), *Literature and Psychoanalysis*. p. 5.

30. *Kernkomplex* is translated in SE as 'nuclear complex': see FREUD, 'On the Sexual Theories of Children' (1908), SE IX 214. See also JEAN LAPLANCHE and JEAN-BAPTISTE PONTALIS, *The Language of Psycho-Analysis* (1967), trans. Donald Nicholson-Smith (London: Hogarth, 1973), p. 286n.

31. FREUD, '"Wild" Psycho-Analysis' (1910), SE XI 222; this essay is discussed by FELMAN in 'Turning the Screw of Interpretation', pp. 108–10.

32. W.B. YEATS, *Per Amica Silentia Lunae* (1917), in *Mythologies* (New York: Collier, 1969), p. 341.

33. See, for instance, MELANIE KLEIN, 'The Importance of Symbol Formation in the Development of the Ego' (1930) (usually known as the case study of 'little Dick'), in *Love, Guilt, and Reparation and other Works, 1921–1945* (London: Hogarth, 1977), pp. 219–32.

34. FREUD, 'The Ego and the Id' (1923), SE XIX 33. See also RICHARD KLEIN, rev. of *Homosexualities in French Literature*, *MLN*, **95** (1980): 1070–80.

35. RENÉ GIRARD, *Deceit, Desire and the Novel: Self and Other in Literary Structure*, trans. Yvonne Freccero (1961; Baltimore: Johns Hopkins Univeristy Press, 1965). A particularly original use of the theory of Oedipal triangulation may be found in LEO BERSANI, *A Future for Astyanax: Character and Desire in Literature* (Boston: Little, Brown and Co., 1976).

36. For a discussion of the absence of women in Girard's analysis, see TORIL MOI, 'The Missing Mother; The Oedipal Rivalries of René Girard', *Diacritics*, **12**: 2 (1982): 21–31.

37. SHAKESPEARE, Sonnet 42, in *The Sonnets and A Lover's Complaint*, ed. John Kerrigan (Harmondsworth: Penguin, 1986), p. 97. See EVE SEDGWICK's compelling reading of this sonnet in *Between Men: English Literature and Male Homosocial Desire* (New York: Columbia University Press, 1985), pp. 28–30.

38. MIKKEL BORCH-JACOBSEN, *The Freudian Subject* (1982), trans. Catherine Porter (Stanford: Stanford University Press, 1988), p. 26.

39. BORCH-JACOBSEN, *The Freudian Subject*, p. 27.

40. FREUD, *Jokes and their Relation to the Unconscious*, SE VII 97–102.

41. See SEDGWICK, *Between Men*, pp. 16–17, 21–5, and *passim*.

42. CLAUDE LÉVI-STRAUSS, *The Elementary Structures of Kinship* (Boston: Beacon, 1969), p. 115; cited in GAYLE RUBIN, 'The Traffic in Women: Notes Toward a Political Economy of Sex', in *Toward an Anthropology of Women*, ed. Rayna Reiter (New York: Monthly Review Press, 1975), p. 174.

43. JACQUES LACAN, 'The Function and Field of Speech and Language in Psychoanalysis', in *Ecrits: A Selection*, trans. Alan Sheridan (London: Tavistock, 1977), p. 66.

44. CLAUDE LÉVI-STRAUSS, *Structural Anthropology*, trans. Clair Jacobson and Brooke Grundfest Schoepf (Harmondsworth: Penguin, 1972), chs 2 and 3. See also ELIZABETH COWIE, 'Woman as Sign', *m/f*, 1 (1978): 49–63.

45. See RENÉ GIRARD, *Violence and the Sacred* (Baltimore: Johns Hopkins University Press, 1979), p. 75.

46. FREUD, *Civilisation and its Discontents* (1930), SE XXI 68.

47. JACQUES LACAN, *The Four Fundamental Concepts of Psycho-Analysis*, ed. Jacques-Alain Miller, trans. Alan Sheridan (London: Hogarth Press, 1977), p. 197.

48. JACQUES LACAN, 'Desire and the Interpretation of Desire in *Hamlet*', in *Literature and Psychoanalysis*, ed. Felman, pp. 43–4; *Hamlet*, ed. Cyrus Hoy (New York: W.W. Norton, 1963), I v 187–188; I v 76.

49. LACAN, 'The Mirror Stage as Formative of the Function of the I as Revealed in Psychoanalytic Experience' (1949), in *Ecrits: A Selection*, trans. Alan Sheridan (London: Tavistock, 1977), pp. 1–7.

50. Cited in MALCOLM BOWIE, *Lacan*, p. 27.

51. LACAN, 'Aggressivity in Psychoanalysis' (1948), in *Ecrits*, p. 19.

52. ARTHUR RIMBAUD, letter to Georges Izambard (1871), in *Oeuvres-Vie*, ed. Alain Borer with Andrée Montègre (Arléa, 1991), p. 184.

53. See LEO BERSANI's compelling description of 'the moribund nature of the ego . . . its status as a kind of cemetery of decathected object-choices', in *The Freudian Body: Psychoanalysis and Art* (New York: Columbia University Press, 1986), pp. 93–100.

54. BOWIE, *Lacan*, p. 92.

55. ELIZABETH GROSZ makes this point very clearly in *Jacques Lacan: A Feminist Introduction* (London: Routledge, 1990), pp. 50–1.

56. See LACAN, 'On a Question Preliminary to any Possible Treatment of Psychosis' (1955–6), in *Ecrits*, p. 217. See also *Ecrits*, p. 67: 'It is in the *name of the father* that we must recognize the support of the symbolic function which, from the dawn of history, has identified this person with the figure of the law. This conception enables us to distinguish clearly . . . the unconscious effects of this function . . . from the real relations that

the subject sustains with the image and the action of the person who embodies it. . . .'

57. JAMES JOYCE, *Ulysses* (Harmondsworth: Penguin Student Edition, 1984), pp. 170, 155.

58. Cited in BOWIE, *Lacan*, p. 92.

59. FERDINAND DE SAUSSURE, *Course in General Linguistics*, ed. Charles Bally and Albert Sechehaye with Albert Riedlinger, trans. Roy Harris (London: Duckworth, 1983), p. 118.

60. See KAREN HORNEY, *Feminine Psychology* (London: Routledge and Kegan Paul, 1967). A very useful summary of the femininity debate in psychoanalysis may be found in HAZEL ROWLEY and ELIZABETH GROSZ, 'Psychoanalysis and Feminism,' in *Feminist Knowledge: Critique and Construct*, ed. Sneja Gunew (London: Routledge, 1990), pp. 175–204. PARVEEN ADAMS's 'Representation and Sexuality', *m/f*, 1 (1978): 65–82, contains an important defence of Lacan's theory of castration against Ernest Jones's deceptively egalitarian alternative.

61. Cited in JACQUELINE ROSE, 'Introduction – II', in *Jacques Lacan and the École Freudienne*, ed. Juliet Mitchell and Jacqueline Rose (London: Macmillan, 1982), p. 53n.

62. SIMONE DE BEAUVOIR, *The Second Sex*, trans. H.M. Parshley (1949; Penguin: Harmondsworth, 1972), p. 74.

63. As TERESA BRENNAN has pointed out, 'social relations can reinforce (as well as oppose) trans-historical psychical factors'. See TERESA BRENNAN, 'An Impasse in Psychoanalysis and Feminism', in Sneja Gunew (ed.), *A Reader in Feminist Knowledge* (London: Routledge, 1991), p. 134.

64. JULIET MITCHELL, *Psychoanalysis and Feminism* (Harmondsworth: Penguin, 1974), Part I. See also the two introductions by JULIET MITCHELL and JACQUELINE ROSE to their edition of *Feminine Sexuality: Jacques Lacan and the École Freudienne* (London: Macmillan, 1982), pp. 1–57.

65. See EVE KOSOFSKY SEDGWICK, *Epistemology of the Closet* (Berkeley: University of California Press, 1990), p. 42: 'Advice on how to 'make sure your kids turn out gay, not to mention your students, your parishioners, your therapy clients, or your military subordinates, is less ubiquitous than you might think. By contrast, the scope of institutions whose programmatic undertaking is to prevent the development of gay people is unimaginably large.' Sedgwick points out that the theory of a biological, unalterable homosexuality might provide a measure of resistance to these institutions, by disputing the idea that gay identity is culturally determined and therefore culturally manipulable.

66. See EVE KOSOFSKY SEDGWICK, *Epistemology of the Closet* (Berkeley: University of California Press, 1990), p. 41.

67. ELIZABETH GROSZ, *Lacan: A Feminist Introduction*, p. 122.

68. See, for instance, ELLIE RAGLAND-SULLIVAN, who writes: 'the phallic signifier is intrinsically neutral, meaningless in its own right, and only takes its power from association catalyzed in the Oedipal drama' ('Jacques Lacan: Feminism and the Problem of Gender Identity', *SubStance* [1982], **36**: 10).

69. FREUD, 'On Transformations of Instinct as Exemplified in Anal Erotism' (1917), SE XVII 130, 128. Castration phantasies reveal that the penis is also regarded as detachable and therefore as analogous to all the other currencies in this unconscious interchange. See also SE XIX 178–9.

70. See LACAN, 'Of the Gaze as *Objet Petit a*', in *The Four Fundamental Concepts of Psycho-Analysis*, pp. 67–119.

71. See MALCOLM BOWIE, *Lacan*, p. 125.

72. JACQUES LACAN, Seminar on 'The Purloined Letter', *Yale French Studies*, **48** (1972): 39–72. This seminar, along with famous responses by Jacques Derrida and Barbara Johnson, has been republished in *The Purloined Poe: Lacan, Derrida, and Psychoanalytic Reading*, ed. John P. Muller and William J. Richardson (Baltimore: Johns Hopkins University Press, 1988).

73. Quoted by BOWIE, *Lacan*, p. 147.

74. LUCE IRIGARAY, 'Women – Mothers, the Silent Substratum of the Social Order', in *The Irigaray Reader*, ed. Margaret Whitford (Oxford: Blackwell, 1991), p. 47. Irigaray's best-known works translated into English are *This Sex Which is Not One*, trans. Catherine Porter with Carolyn Burke (Ithaca: Cornell University Press, 1985); and *Speculum of the Other Woman*, trans. Gillian C. Gill (Ithaca: Cornell University Press, 1985). MARGARET WHITFORD provides a cogent defence of Irigaray in *Luce Irigaray: Philosophy in the Feminine* (London: Routledge, 1991); see also Whitford's shorter introduction, 'Rereading Irigaray', in Teresa Brennan (ed.), *Between Feminism and Psychoanalysis* (London: Routledge, 1989), pp. 106–26.

75. ERNEST JONES anticipates Irigaray's theory of the primal matricide in 'A Psycho-Analytic Study of the Holy Ghost Concept', in *Essays in Applied Psycho-Analysis*, vol. II (London: Hogarth, 1951), pp. 358–73.

76. See FREUD, SE IX 205–6; and LUCE IRIGARAY, *This Sex Which Is Not One*, p. 78, and *Speculum of the Other Woman*, pp. 48–9. See also JANE GALLOP, *The Daughter's Seduction* (London: Macmillan, 1982), pp. 68–9.

77. See IRIGARAY, Interview in *Ideology and Consciousness*, **1** (1977): 64–5. See also IRIGARAY, 'Sexual Difference', in *The Irigaray Reader*, p. 175.

78. IRIGARAY, *This Sex Which Is Not One*, p. 134.

79. See GENEVIEVE LLOYD, *The Man of Reason: 'Male' and 'Female' in Western Philosophy* (London: Methuen, 1984), pp. 1–9.

80. JAN MONTEFIORE, *Feminism and Poetry* (London: Pandora, 1987), p. 149.

81. See JULIA KRISTEVA, 'From One Identity to Another', in *Desire in Language: A Semiotic Approach to Literature and Art*, ed. Leon S. Roudiez, trans. Thomas Gorz, Alice Jardine and Leon S. Roudiez (Oxford: Blackwell, 1980), pp. 124–47; and KRISTEVA, 'Revolution in Poetic Language', in *The Kristeva Reader*, ed. Toril Moi (Oxford: Blackwell, 1986), pp. 89–136. JOHN LECHTE provides a useful overview of Kristeva's work in *Julia Kristeva* (London: Routledge, 1990). See also JUDITH BUTLER's trenchant critique of Kristeva in *Gender Trouble: Feminism and the Subversion of Identity* (London: Routledge, 1990), where she argues that 'the prediscursive maternal body is itself a production of a given historical discourse, an *effect* of culture rather than its secret cause' (pp. 80–1).

82. TERRY EAGLETON, *Literary Theory: An Introduction* (Oxford: Blackwell, 1983), p. 188.

83. VIRGINIA WOOLF, *Collected Essays*, ed. Leonard Woolf (New York: Harcourt, Brace and World, 1967), vol. 2, p. 191. For an excellent reading of Woolf in the light of Kristeva, see MAKIKO MINOW-PINKNEY, 'Virginia Woolf "Seen from a Foreign Land"', in *Abjection, Melancholia, and Love: The Work of Julia Kristeva*, ed. John Fletcher and Andrew Benjamin (London: Routledge, 1990), pp. 157–77.

84. JULIA KRISTEVA, *Powers of Horror: An Essay on Abjection*, trans. Leon. S. Roudiez (New York: Columbia University Press, 1982), p. 4.

85. The works in question are *Powers of Horror* (first published 1980), *Tales of Love* (1983), trans. Leon S. Roudiez (New York: Columbia University Press, 1987); and *Black Sun: Depression and Melancholia* (1987), trans. Leon S. Roudiez (New York: Columbia University Press, 1989).

86. Another excellent psychoanalytic reading of *To the Lighthouse* may be found in MARY JACOBUS, '"The Third Stroke": Reading Woolf with Freud', in *Grafts: Feminist Cultural Criticism*, ed. Susan Sheridan (London: Verso, 1988), pp. 93–110.

87. HAROLD BLOOM, *Agon: Towards a Theory of Revisionism* (New York: Oxford University Press, 1982), p. 101; and below, p. 182.

88. KRISTEVA, *Black Sun*, p. 13.

Part One

Drama

1 Prologue: The Psycho-Analytic Reading of Tragedy*

ANDRÉ GREEN

In *The Tragic Effect*, André Green offers psychoanalytic readings of several European tragedies in which the Oedipus complex assumes its 'negative' form of male hostility against the female: Aeschylus's *Oresteia*, in which the son murders the mother; Shakespeare's *Othello*, in which the husband kills the wife; and Racine's *Iphigénie à Aulis*, in which the father slays the daughter. While using psychoanalysis to interpret drama, Green also uses drama to interpret psychoanalysis, and insists that each is implicated in the other. He argues that Freudian theory owes more to drama than to any other form of art because of the affinity between the theatre and the dream. The theatre, by imposing darkness and silence on the audience, simulates the state of sleep, in which the disregarded wishes of the day burst forth in the hallucinations of the dreaming mind.

Hegel argues that tragedy depends upon the contradiction between the 'power that knows and reveals itself to consciousness, and the power that conceals itself and lies in ambush'; and Green agrees that this tension between 'knowing and not-knowing' constitutes the crux of tragic form.† 'The art of the theatre is the art of the *malentendu*, the misheard and the misunderstood', Green writes (below, p. 41). The theatre places the spectator in the position of the infant who, excluded from any knowledge of its origins, must seek this knowledge by interpreting its parents' dialogue; just as the audience, excluded from the drama, must fathom its enigma by interpreting the actors' speech. According to Green, the boundary of the stage performs the same function as the boundary established by repression in the psyche, because

---

*ANDRÉ GREEN, 'The Psycho-Analytic Reading of Tragedy', Prologue to *The Tragic Effect: The Oedipus Complex in Tragedy*, trans. Alan Sheridan (Cambridge: Cambridge University Press, 1979), pp. 1–5; 7–9; 18–23; 25–7. © 1979, English translation Alan Sheridan.
†HEGEL, *The Phenomenology of Spirit*, trans. A.V. Miller (New York: Oxford University Press, 1977), p. 446.

the images that pass before the audience correspond to those which surface in our dreams: the fleeting figures of a knowledge both debarred and inescapable.

Play is in fact neither a matter of inner psychic reality nor a matter of external reality . . . The place where cultural experience is located is in the *potential space* between the individual and the environment (originally the object).

. . .

I am assuming that cultural experiences are in direct continuity with play, the play of those who have not yet heard of games.

D.W. Winnicott, 1971, 96 and 100

I. A text in representation: ways from ignorance to knowledge[1]

There is a mysterious bond between psycho-analysis and the theatre. When Freud cites *King Oedipus, Hamlet* and *The Brothers Karamazov* as the most awe-inspiring works of literature, he notes that all three are about parricide; less importance has been attached to the fact that two of the three are plays. One naturally wonders whether, for all the interest he showed in the other arts, the theatre did not have a special significance for Freud – a significance that outweighed his interest in the plastic arts (despite Michelangelo's 'Moses' or Leonardo's 'St Anne'), in poetry (despite Goethe, Schiller or Heine), in the tale (despite Hoffman), in the novel (despite Dostoievsky and Jensen). Sophocles and Shakespeare are in a class of their own, especially Shakespeare; Freud recognized in him a master whose texts he analyses as if they were the discoveries of some illustrious precursor. But he seems to have had a special affection for the theatre in general.

Scene and other scene[2]

Why is this? Is it not that the theatre is the best embodiment of that 'other scene', the unconscious? It is that other scene; it is also a stage whose 'edge' materially presents the break, the line of separation, the frontier at which conjunction and disjunction can carry out their tasks between auditorium and stage in the service of representation – in the same way as the cessation of motility is a precondition for the deployment of the dream. The texture of dramatic representation is not the same as that of the dream, but it is very tempting to compare it with phantasy. Phantasy owes a great deal to the reworking

by the secondary process of elements that belong rather to the
primary processes, these primary processes being then subjected to
an elaboration comparable to that of ceremonial, in the ordering of
dramatic actions and movements, in the coherence of theatrical plot.[3]
But there are many differences between the structure of phantasy and
the structure of the theatre. Phantasy is closer to a form of theatre
in which a narrator describes an action occurring in a certain place,
but in which, though he is not unconcerned, he does not himself
take part. Phantasy is much more reminiscent of the tale, or even the
novel. Its links with the 'family romance'[4] reinforce this comparison.
In the dream, on the other hand, we find the same equality, *de jure*, if
not *de facto*, that reigns between the various protagonists sharing the
space of the stage. So much so that, in the dream, when the dreamer's
representation becomes overloaded, the dreamer splits it into two and
sets up another character to represent, separately, one or more of his
characteristics or affects. Broadly speaking, it would be more correct to
say that the theatre may be situated *between* dream and phantasy.

Perhaps we should turn to the simplest, most obvious fact. Does
not the theatre owe its peculiar power to the fact that it is an exchange
of language, a succession of bare statements without benefit of
commentary? Between the exchanges, between the monologues,
nothing is vouchsafed about the character's state of mind (unless he
says it himself); nothing is added to these statements that refers to the
physical setting, the historical situation, the social context, or the inner
thoughts of the characters. There is nothing but the unglossed text of
the statements.

In much the same way, the child is the witness of the daily domestic
drama. For the *infans* that he remains long after his acquisition of
language, there is nothing but the gestures, actions and statements
of his parents. If there is anything else, it is up to him to find it and
interpret it. The father and mother say this or that, and act in this or
that way. What they really think, what the truth really is, he must
discover on his own. Every theatrical work, like every work of art, is
an enigma, but an enigma expressed in speech: articulated, spoken
and heard, without any alien medium filling in its gaps. That is why
the art of the theatre is the art of the *malentendu*, the misheard and the
misunderstood.

The space of the stage: the spectator in the spectacle

But this structure creates a space, is conceivable only in a space, that
of the stage. The theatre defines its own space, and acting in the
theatre is possible only in so far as one may occupy positions in that

space. The spectacle presents not so much a single, overall view to be understood, more a series of positions that it invites the spectator to take up in order that he may fully participate in what is offered him on the stage. We have to consider, as Jacques Derrida does, the question of the 'enclosure' of representation. Just as the dream depends on the enclosure of the dreamer, the enclosure of sleep – beyond which there is no dream, but either waking or somnambulism – the limits of the theatre are those of the stage.

The theatrical space is bounded by the enclosure formed as a result of the double reversal created by the exchanges that unfold between the spectator and the spectacle, on either side of the edge of the stage. We may try to eliminate this edge; it is only reconstituted elsewhere. This is the invisible frontier where the spectator's gaze meets a barrier that stops it and sends it back – the first reversal – to the onlooker, that is, to himself as source of the gaze. But, since the spectacle is not meant to enclose its participants in a solipsistic solitude, nor to restrict its own effects by keeping its elements separate from each other, we must account for this in a different way. This return to the source has established a relation between source and object: the spectacle encountered by the gaze as it passes beyond the stage barrier. Nonetheless, the edge of the stage preserves its function of separating source and object. The spectator will naturally compare this with his experience of a similar encounter, where the same relation of conjunction and disjunction is set up, linking the object of the spectacle with the objects of the gaze that a different barrier, namely repression, places beyond his reach. It is as if those objects ought not to have been in full view, yet, by some incomprehensible paradox, will not allow the perceiver ever to escape them. They force him to be for ever subjected to their return, experienced in a form at once inescapable, unpredictable and fleeting. The permanence of the object seen in the spectacle is like the lure that tempts us to think that the solicitation might this time lead to the capture always denied hitherto. By arousing a hope that the secret behind the moment of disappearance of the repressed objects will be revealed, it allows the spectacle to unfold so as the better to surprise that secret.

This reversal on to oneself is always accompanied by a second reversal – the reversal into its opposite – whose meaning is more difficult to grasp. The first reversal enables us to measure, as it were, the fundamental otherness of the spectacle for the spectator. If the spectator allowed this otherness, he would either leave or go to sleep, and that would be the end of a spectacle that had never begun. But this otherness solicits him. Though unable to reject this otherness as totally alien, the gaze detaches itself to some extent from its object, otherwise the total participation of the spectator with the forces of the spectacle would merge them beneath the eye of a God bringing about from on high the coalescence of auditorium and stage. The gaze explores the stage from the point at which the spectator is himself observed by his object. The boundary between auditorium and stage is duplicated by the boundary between the stage as visible space and the invisible space off-stage. Together, these two spaces are opposed in turn to the space of the world, whose steady pressure maintains the space of the theatre between its walls.

The contradiction felt by the spectator is such that whereas the project of going to the spectacle initially created a break between the theatre and the world, the fact of being at the spectacle replaces the confrontation between the space of the theatre and that of the world (which has become invisible and so excluded from the spectator's consciousness) by the confrontation between the visible theatrical space and the invisible theatrical space. The world is the limit of the theatre and, to some extent, its *raison d'être*. But the relation of otherness between the subject and the world is replaced by the otherness of the spectator in respect of the objects of the gaze – an otherness no longer based simply on a boundary (the walls of the theatre, or the barrier formed by the edge of the stage), but on another space, one hidden from the gaze. As a result, there occurs a projection of the relationship between theatrical space and the space of the world on to the theatrical space, itself split into a visible theatrical space (the space of the stage) and an invisible theatrical space (the space off-stage). This latter space calls for exploration, for it is not only the space by which illusion is created; it is also that in which the false is fabricated. The space of the stage is the space of the plot, the enigma, the secret; the space off-stage is that of manipulation, suspicion, plotting. However, this space is circumscribable, since it is confined within the walls of the great chamber that is the theatre. (Its unlimited character in the cinema – here the chamber is the camera, but the entire world may be swallowed up in it – makes it impossible to explore these means as a lure for the cinema-spectator.) Thus the limit formed by the edge of the stage is extended to the limits of the space of the stage, this space offering itself as one to be transgressed, passed beyond, through its link with the invisible space off-stage.

This transgression is invited, therefore, by that which constitutes its second limit, a radically uncrossable limit, which denies the gaze of the spectator access to the invisible space off-stage. Since we have to renounce this second transgression as impossible, all that remains possible is the broadest incorporation of the stage space connoted by the term 'illusory', according to which what is incorporated is the opposite of the truth. That is the sense of the second reversal. By a shift of perspective, one might say, from veracity to veridicity, this reversal will affect the unsaid, the unspoken element, of the stage space: its unconscious, invisible problematic which, *qua* non-veridical, will be caught in the movement of return into its opposite, joining itself to the first reversal, which consists of a turning round upon oneself.[5]

So, whereas the spectacle takes place outside oneself, is alien to oneself, there is constituted the 'negative hallucination' of the unsaid of the stage on which all the said is inscribed. The hallucinatory value of representation, which the edge of the stage has materialized by the relation of otherness, both conjoint and disjoint, is inscribed on the opacity of the space off-stage in which the false is fabricated. Here the spectator finds himself in a place as metaphorical as that suggested by the appearance of those objects whose repression allows no more than fleeting residues to filter through. They too can be assembled into a constructed scenario. But this construction blocks, so to speak, the view of their original source, where the subject would have to recognize his own silhouette. This is like the negative hallucination in which the subject looks at himself in the mirror and sees all the elements of the setting around him, but not his own image. The impression that one sees without seeing, hears without hearing, speaks without making oneself understood, is also to be found, in a more fragmentary way, in dream space. This is not the result of some deficiency that weakens the living tissue of the dream, making it like a bloodless body – as is shown by the contrast to be found in some dreams between the effect of hyper-reality and the unintelligibility of their messages. The space off-stage frames this 'blank' of the stage on which the action is inscribed.

The conjunction of this double reversal makes possible that which is sent back to the spectator as his gaze, refused entry to the space beyond the stage. Out of this refusal is constituted the theatrical space in which outside and inside are no longer meaningful within the enclosure of the two reversals. Yet their two-sidedness – as in the figure constituted by the joining of the double reversal – which was once the expression of the opposition between the theatre and the world, has become the opposition in which the spectator is the theatre, and also the opposition between the said and the unsaid.

Aristotle

Reflection on the theatre extends from Aristotle to Antonin Artaud. Aristotle laid down canons that were accepted until fairly recently. The signifier/signified problematic is already to be found in the six elements that Aristotle distinguishes in tragedy. In this respect, the *Poetics* constitutes a composite whole that moves from thematic analysis, an analysis of the fable, to a linguistic analysis whose links with the preceding analysis are never made quite clear.

In his analysis of the fable, Aristotle notes the part played by phantasy and gives it precedence over reality: 'It is not the poet's business to tell what has happened or the kind of things that would happen – what is possible according to probability or necessity' (Aristotle, 29). The aim is simply to arouse fear and pity; and Aristotle declares, without further explanation, that this result is never better attained than when illustrated by relations of kinship: 'When sufferings are engendered among the affections – for example, if murder is done or planned, or some similar outrage is committed, by brother on brother, or son on father, or mother on son, or son on mother – that is the thing to aim at' (Aristotle, 35).

The family, then, is the tragic space *par excellence*, no doubt because in the family the knots of love – and therefore of hate – are not only the earliest, but also the most important ones. But the fable must culminate in a recognition – a passage from ignorance to knowledge. Recognition by representation. The tragic space is the space of the unveiling, the revelation, of some original kinship relation, which never works more effectively than through a sudden reversal of fortune, a peripeteia.

It might be objected that this is taking things too literally. The theatre is the art of mimesis. What follows from this? If the theatre is the art of imitation – the art of the false, say its detractors – it is because Aristotle sees in imitation a specifically human characteristic: 'The impulse to imitate is inherent in man from his childhood; he is distinguished among the animals by being the most imitative of them, and he takes the first steps of his education by imitating. Everyone's enjoyment of imitation is also inborn' (Aristotle, 20). The psycho-analyst is delighted: Aristotle presents him with two of his favourite parameters, childhood and pleasure.

This remark will have a wider implication if one compares it with Aristotle's recommendation to take the bonds formed by kinship as material for the fable. For the climax towards which the fable is tending is recognition, which has its fullest effect only when it is wholly bound up with the sudden reversal of the action in the peripeteia. If we acquire our earliest knowledge through imitation, and if the passage from ignorance to knowledge (recognition) is effected by a sudden reversal, may we not think, from a more modern standpoint, that it is a question not so much of imitation as of identification? This sudden reversal would appear to centre on the relation of identification and desire, on the one hand, and, on the other, on the bipartite function of identification, since it is an identification that contradicts the two terms of the parental couple. (And this more especially because catharsis presupposes identification, since its true meaning is not a purification of the passions, which is a Christian interpretation of tragedy, but the treatment of emotion by emotion, with the aim of discharging it. However, this discharge must not be conceived as some kind of antiphlogistic effect, since its action is more in the nature of an 'assuagement accompanied by pleasure', which implies a participation in which the Other[6] is involved.)

The series of examples given by Aristotle of kinship relations depicted in tragedy says nothing about any action between the parents, or about the effect of the father on his children (only the reverse case is cited). This is a strange omission in a text that refers so often to Orestes and Iphigenia, yet ignores the nature of the relations between their parents.

At the level of the signified, the kinship-relations model seems most effective in the matter of mimesis. At the level of the signifier, Aristotle observes that by far the most important thing is to excel in metaphors (Aristotle, 50). My remarks below are freely based on Lacan's notion of the paternal metaphor. It is a happy chance that links the kinship relation to metaphor. It is as if the kinship relation were metaphorical of all the others – and, within it, in the shadow in which Aristotle keeps it, the relation that unites the parents or the relation that expresses the effect of the father on his children to an even greater degree than the others; as if metaphor, at the level of the signifier in poetic creation, rediscovered at the level of language the creation about which the parental metaphor implicitly speaks.

A fable centred around kinship relations indicates not what has been but what might have been, as if it had occurred as the myths recount it. Dramatic art embodies these myths in speech. All theatre is embodied speech. The tragedy of Oedipus is impossible; how can the life of a single man pile up such a set of coincidences? It is not for the psycho-analyst to answer; but rather for the countless spectators of *King Oedipus*, who might say, with Aristotle, 'a convincing improbability is preferable to what is unconvincing even though it is possible' (Aristotle, 58).

II. Towards a psycho-analytic reading of tragedy

What right has the psycho-analyst to meddle in the business of tragedy? Freud proceeded with extreme caution in his search among the common stock of culture for examples of the expression of the unconscious. Today, when psycho-analysis is less concerned to seek validations outside its own field of practice, is it still proper to seek material for interpretation in works of art? Many people, including some psycho-analysts, believe that the period must now end in which psycho-analytic investigation turned to cultural productions, myths or works of art, to provide evidence for a possible mapping of the unconscious outside the domain of neurosis. Psycho-analysis has provided enough proof of its scientific character, and ought to confine its efforts to the strict framework, defined by its own rigorous parameters, of psycho-analytic treatment. The view is well founded; the field of psycho-analysis will always remain the locus in which the exchanges between analyst and analysand unfold. When the analyst ventures outside the analytic situation, in which he is in direct contact with the unconscious, as it were, he must proceed with caution. The work of art is handed over to the analyst; it can say nothing more than is incorporated in it and cannot, like the analysand, offer an insight into the work of the unconscious *in statu nascendi*. It cannot reveal the state of its functioning through the operation that consists in analysing by free association – that is to say, by providing material that reveals its nature in the very act by which it makes itself known. It does not possess any of the resources that make analysis bearable: that of going back on what one has said, rejecting the intolerable connection at the moment when it presents itself, putting off the moment of an emerging awareness, even denying, by one of the many ways available to the analysand, the correctness of an interpretation or the obviousness of some truth brought by repetition to the front of the stage and needing to be deciphered. The work remains obstinately mute, closed in upon itself, without defences against the treatment that the analyst may be tempted to subject it to.

It would be illusory to believe that one can use a work to provide proof of psycho-analytic theories. Psycho-analysts know that this enterprise is vain, since no degree of consciousness can overcome unconscious resistance. In certain cases, it happens that a fragment of psychical reality manages to overcome repression and seems to emerge with exceptional ease. One then has regretfully to admit, powerless to do anything about it, that the effect is usually followed by a reactivation of the psychical conflict of which this fragment is an integral part. Persuasion, whatever those unacquainted with psycho-analytic experience may think, has never been one of the analyst's instruments; however much he is tempted to use it to get himself out of some impasse in a difficult case, its use will always prove disappointing. The same can be said when the analyst presents the results of his analytic work on some cultural object. If he does not stay close enough to the lines of force that govern the architecture of his object, the truth that even a partly correct analysis contains runs a strong risk of not being recognized, for all its rightness, because the factors opposed to crossing the barriers of the censor find solid support in objections which, though superficial, are reinforced by rationalization. It is therefore particularly necessary to be vigilant in the account of any such investigation. In psycho-analytic treatment, the repetition compulsion again and again offers to disclose the meaning of a conflictual organization, which one can then approach in a fragmentary way. In the analysis of a work of art, everything is said in a single utterance by whoever assumes the task of interpretation, and no inkling is given of the long process of elaboration that has made it possible to arrive at the conclusions now advanced in connected form.

These few remarks are not intended to reassure those who fear the intrusion of psycho-analysis into a domain in which it could have a restricting effect. No interpretation can avoid constraining the work, in the sense that it necessarily forces it into the frame provided by a certain conceptual approach. The work may then be seen from a different perspective, with a new meaning that enlarges it by inserting it in a wider frame of reference. To speak is above all to choose this restricted economy within the enclosure of discourse, in order to give oneself ways towards a development that is impossible if one says nothing.

These warnings are primarily intended to remind myself of the conditions that govern this venture of literary interpretation, that should guide my initial grasp of the work and the subsequent development of my analysis. In any case, the psycho-analyst has less need to defend himself against the charge of violating the work by imposing his version on it, in that a whole recent current of criticism makes it clear that no one is entirely free of this charge when he comes into contact with a work, that every work is itself a kind of reading, calling for a new reading that is the reader's only access to it. Any reading is by definition interpretative; an attribution of meanings is always going on even in the person who thinks himself the most humble of exegetes. Where is a tyrannical relation between reader and text most likely to become established: in the reader who admits his reading is a conjectural enquiry forcing the decipherer to find his way even as he attempts to draw the implicit map of the work, or in the reader who rules out any movement from his own position and merely repeats old schemata that he supposes to be eternal, though historical analysis would show that they are merely the fossilization of acquired knowledge? Who abuses cultural products most: he who seeks in them for a new vision that he supposes them to be still capable of producing, despite the accumulation of readings already in existence, or he who dispenses with radical questioning and brings to the works a mere paraphrastic commentary saturated with the presuppositions of common knowledge? It is just because psycho-analysis provides this radical questioning, this conjectural interrogation, this appeal to what is not given from the outset as cause of an effect, that it has a role in the renewal of criticism.

But even as part of this movement, its role will be a difficult one. Psycho-analysis will always be suspect. It will be criticized, for example, for setting up a relation between the author and the work, as if it were doing so in the spirit of the old biographical criticism, which saw the work as an extension of the experiences of the author's life. Yet psycho-analysis sees it in a relation of discontinuity with them. Biographical criticism saw the work as an echo or a reverberation of some event whose influence was measured in a relation of immediate understanding, according to an implicit scale of common feelings. The link established between author and work by psycho-analysis does not postulate a direct influence between the events of a life and the content of the work, but situates these historical elements in a conflict. These elements are set in the perspective of another problematic, which has been essentially misunderstood because it belongs to repressed childhood, the modes of combination of present and past no longer being accessible to the individual who experiences them, even though they may have a considerable conscious charge. So the work becomes the other network, by which rehandled modes of combination echo what has been reawakened of the unknown past by the present. This repeated past provides the material for a new relation, which keeps a significatory link with its roots that will help to illuminate it retrospectively. A hypothesis about the meaning of this relation for the author helps us to grasp the coherence of the work, which gains in comprehensibility without losing any of its mystery. The reawakening of some significatory constellation underlies this mobilization, which has transformatory power by virtue of its identity with the things from which it is separated by repression. This content is doubly articulated: by the original complexual organization and by the repetition manifested in the present 'event'. None of this puts the author at the mercy of his conflicts – at least, no more than anyone else, since each of us is the system of relations of the various agencies at work in the conflict.

Would it be possible, anyway, to show that there is no relation between a man and his creation? (This is not a thread I mean to follow here, but I must draw attention to the suspiciously passionate way in which any link between author and work is usually 'refuted'.) From what power could creation be nourished if not from those at work in the creator? The psycho-analytic point of view cannot accept that we have disposed of the problem of the genesis of works of art when we have invoked some absolute mystery of creation where the desire to create is not rooted in its unconscious ramifications. Nor can we be content with the idea that the work has the existential significance of a 'supersession' – a view, admittedly, expressed less often by the creator than by commentators on his production. The creator himself always remains aware of its character as a temporary halt on a journey whose aim is above all to ensure the stock of means that will enable him to continue the search.

In the last resort, what people fear most of all about the psycho-analyst is the threat that he will apply some pathological label to the creator or his creations. The keywords in the psycho-analytic vocabulary – though they have value only when placed in the structural ensemble from which they derive their coherence – continue to intimidate; no one feels secure from the unpleasant feeling he would have if, unexpectedly, this vocabulary were applied to him. In our time, this fear has taken on a curiously paradoxical form. We all talk about the pervert and proclaim our potential brotherhood with him; but the mere mention of the word 'normality' is ruthlessly pounced on and denounced. Yet the psycho-analytic texts never postulate a norm – analysts have been attacked enough by physicians and psychiatrists for doing just that – except as a relative term that must be posited somewhere if we are to understand differences of degree or gradations between one structure and another. Resistance to psycho-analytic terminology makes itself felt as soon as it emerges from an unthreatening world of generalization, a world in which its resort to metaphorical terms allows us to harbour the secret hope that we are dealing with the language of some new mythology. It is easy to forget that psycho-analysis has been persecuted precisely for abolishing the frontiers between health and illness and showing the presence in the so-called normal man of all the potentialities whose pathological forms reflect back a magnified, caricatural image. It was Roland Barthes who wrote this condemnation of traditional criticism: 'It wishes to preserve in the work an absolute value, untouched by any of those unworthy "other elements" represented by history and the lower depths of the *psyche*: what it wants is not a constituted work, but a *pure* work, in which any compromise with the world, any misalliance with desire, is avoided' (Barthes, 37). These remarks can be applied to a good deal of the new criticism, or to those upholders of a theory of writing who defend a sort of literary absolutism.

When a psycho-analyst enters the universe of tragedy, it is not to 'pathologize' this world; it is because he recognizes in all the products of mankind the traces of the conflicts of the unconscious. And although it is true that he must not, as Freud rightly remarked, expect to find there a perfect correspondence with what his experience has led him to observe, he is right in thinking that works of art may help him to grasp the articulation of actual but hidden relations, in the cases that he studies, through the increased distortions that accompany the return of the repressed. Freud never thought that he had anything to teach gifted creators of authentic genius, and he never hid his envy of the exceptional gifts that allowed them, if not direct access, at least considerably easier access to the relations that govern the unconscious.

The exploitation of these gifts is directed towards obtaining the 'bonus of pleasure' that is made possible through the displacements of sublimation; this would tend to establish a relation of disjunction between the product of artistic creation and the symptom. For the first has the effect of negating the action of repression; but the second, because it is the expression of the return of the repressed, erupts into the consciousness only after paying the entrance fee of displeasure at the prohibition of satisfaction. Satisfaction, then, is indissolubly linked to the need for punishment associated with the guilt engendered by desire, whose symptom thus becomes its herald. The satisfaction of desire cannot be separated from submission to the sanction of the prohibition that weighs upon it.

This difference between symptom and creation now makes it possible to indicate their resemblance, if not their similarity. In both symptom and creation, the processes of symbolic activity are at work, as they are also in the dream or the phantasy. So artistic creation, 'pathological' creation and dream creation are linked by symbolic activity, their difference being situated in the accommodation that each offers to the tension between the satisfaction bound up with the realization of desire and the satisfaction bound up with the observance of its prohibition. Neurosis, Freud would say, is the individual, asocial solution of the problems posed to the human condition. At the social level, morality and religion propose other solutions. Between the two, at the meeting-point of the individual and society, between the personal resonance of the work's content and its social function, art occupies a transitional position, which qualifies the domain of illusion, which permits an inhibited and displaced *jouissance*[7] obtained by means of objects that both are and are not what they represent.

Breaking the action of repression does not mean exposing the unconscious in all its starkness, but revealing the effective relation between the inevitable disguising and the indirect unveiling that the work allows to take place. The unconscious sets up a communication between a sentient, corporeal space and the textual space of the work. Between the two stand prohibition and its censor; the symbolic activity is the disguise and the exclusion of the unacceptable, and the substitution of the excluded term by another less unacceptable one, more capable of slipping incognito into the area that is closed to it. Indeed, if every text is a text only because it does not yield itself up in its entirety at a first reading, how can we account for this essential dissimulation other than by some prohibition that hangs over it? We can infer the presence of this prohibition by what it allows to filter through of a conflict of which it is the outcome, marked by the lure it offers, calling on us to traverse it from end to end. We shall often feel a renewed disappointment, faced by its refusal to take us anywhere except to the point of origin from which it took its own departure.

The trans-narcissistic object

Our aim, therefore, is to rediscover, in a work whose specific nature is the labour of representation unfolding according to its own procedures, an analogue of what Freud described in his first intuitions about the functioning of the psychical apparatus. This process is the play of a pluri-functional system, which never progresses continuously and in a single direction; it goes back over inscriptions that have already been traced and slides away from obstacles; it reproduces its message with a distortion that forces us back to it; receives some new impulsion that overcomes a resistance; or breaks into fragments. It recomposes these dissociated fragments into a new message incorporating other elements from another fragmented totality, preserving at the essential level that nucleus of intelligibility without which no new crossing of the boundary can be made. It preserves itself from annihilation and consequent oblivion by a protective distortion which prevents it being recognized. The work of representation, which unceasingly maintains an effect of tension in the spectator, is the reconstitution of the process of formation of the phantasy, just as the analysis of the dream, through the resistance to the work of association and to the regroupings that this work operates, replicates the construction of the dream process.

This brings us, then, to our object: the psycho-analytic reading of a tragedy, a reading situated in the potential space between text and representation. Here a question inevitably arises: how are we to understand the *jouissance* felt by the spectator of a tragedy, when the spectacle arouses pity and terror? This question brings us back to Aristotle's problem, for which Freud tried to provide a new answer. The work of art, says Freud, offers an 'incentive bonus' to whoever experiences it. 'We give the name of an *incentive bonus*, or a *fore-pleasure*, to a yield of pleasure such as this, which is offered to us so as to make possible the release of still greater pleasure arising from deeper psychical sources' (*S.E.*, IX, 153). There is a discharge, then, but it is a partial discharge, desexualized by aim-inhibition and displacement of sexual pleasure. But we still have to account for the effect of tragedy.

How may we extend or replace the hypothesis of catharsis as a purging of the passions? Tragedy certainly gives pleasure, but pleasure tinged with pain: a mixture of terror and pity. But there is no tragedy without a tragic hero, that is, without an idealized projection of an ego that finds here the satisfaction of its megalomaniac designs. The hero is the locus of an encounter between the power of the bard, who brings the phantasy to life, and the desire of the spectator, who sees his phantasy embodied and represented. The spectator is the ordinary person to whom nothing of importance happens. The hero is the man who lives through exceptional adventures in which he performs his exploits, and who, in the last resort, must pay the gods dearly for the power he acquires in this way. Becoming a demi-god, he enters into competition with the gods, and so must be crushed by them, thus assuring the triumph of the father.

The spectator's pleasure will be compounded of his movement of identification with the hero (pity, compassion) and his masochistic movement (terror). Every hero, and therefore every spectator, is in the position of the son in the Oedipal situation: the son must become (move towards being) like the father. He must be brave and strong, but he must not do everything the father does. He must show proper respect for the father's prerogatives (his *having*), namely those of paternal power, sexual possession of the mother, and physical power, the right of life and death over his children. In this respect, the father, even when dead, indeed especially when dead, sees this power still further increased in the beyond: totem and taboo.

Tragedy, then, is the representation of the phantasy myth of the Oedipus complex, which Freud identified as the constitutive complex of the subject. Thus the frontiers between the 'normal' individual, the neurotic and the hero became blurred in the subjective structure that is the subject's relation to his progenitors. The encounter between myth and tragedy is obviously not fortuitous. First, because every history, whether it is individual or collective, is based on a myth. In the case of the individual, this myth is known as phantasy. Second, because Freud himself includes myth in the psycho-analytic field: 'It seems quite possible to apply the psycho-analytic views derived from dreams to products of ethnic imagination such as myths and fairy-tales' (*S.E.*, XIII, 185). (In his study of the structure of myths, Lévi-Strauss refers to the myth, without further explanation, as an 'absolute object'.) Freud rejects the traditional interpretation of myths as mere attempts to explain natural phenomena, or as cult practices that have become unintelligible. It is highly likely that he would have much to say about the structuralist interpretation. For the essential function of these collective productions was, in Freud's view, the assuaging of unsatisfied or unsatisfiable desires. This is my interpretation too;

53

it finds support in the foundations of the Oedipus complex, which forbids parricide and incest and so condemns the subject to seek other solutions if he is to satisfy these desires. Tragedy is, at a collective level, one of these substitute solutions. The psycho-analytic reading of tragedy, therefore, will have as its aim the mapping of the traces of the Oedipal structure concealed in its formal organization, through an analysis of the symbolic activity, which is masked from the spectator's perception and acts on him unknown to himself.

Notes

1. [In French, *'représentation'* covers much the same ground as the English 'representation'. Both words are used to translate the German *'Vorstellung'*, a word with a long history in German philosophy and one which Freud took up and developed in his own way. (See entry under 'Idea' in LAPLANCHE and PONTALIS, 200–1.) However, the French word also translates 'performance', in the theatrical sense. It is natural, therefore, for Green to play on both senses of the word – the psychological and the theatrical. For this reason I have avoided the word 'performance' in this translation.]

2. [The French *'scène'* translates both 'stage' and 'scene'. Here, however, I felt obliged to use the English 'stage' where this was unequivocally meant. The 'other scene' is the reference to Freud's notion of the dream as 'another scene' (*'ein anderer Schauplatz'*).]

3. [For an account of the primary and secondary processes, the reader is referred to LAPLANCHE and PONTALIS, 339–41. Broadly speaking, they correspond to unconscious mental activity, governed by the pleasure principle, and conscious mental activity, governed by the reality principle.]

4. [The term *'Familienroman'*, or 'family romance', was coined by Freud as a name for phantasies in which the subject imagines that his relationship to his parents is other than it really is (as when he imagines, for example, that he is really a foundling). Such phantasies are grounded in the Oedipus complex. (See LAPLANCHE and PONTALIS, 160.)]

5. [In psycho-analysis, the 'turning round upon the subject's own self' is a process whereby the drive replaces an independent object by the subject's own self. It is a form of 'reversal into the opposite'. (See LAPLANCHE and PONTALIS, 399.)]

6. [Like many of Lacan's terms, *'Autre'* or *'grand Autre'* is extremely difficult to define. Lacan himself resists such definitions, regarding them as a dead hand on the vital potentiality of language. The best way to understand Lacan's concepts is operationally; that is, seeing them at work in a number of contexts. One of Lacan's best-known formulas is: 'The unconscious is the discourse of the Other.' The Other, says Lacan, is 'the locus of the deployment of speech (the other scene, *ein anderer Schauplatz*, of which Freud speaks in "The Interpretation of Dreams")' (LACAN, 264), 'The Other as previous site of the pure subject of the signifier holds the master

position, even before coming into existence, to use Hegel's term against him, as Absolute Master' (305).]

7. [There is no adequate translation in English for the French *'jouissance'*. 'Enjoyment' conveys the sense, contained in *'jouissance'*, of 'enjoyment' of rights, of property, etc. Unfortunately, the word has lost much of its Shakespearean power in modern English. In French, *'jouissance'* also has the sexual connotation of 'ejaculation'. (*'Jouir'* is the slang equivalent of 'to come'.) Green is using the term here in the Lacanian sense, in contra-distinction with 'pleasure'. For Lacan, pleasure obeys the law of homoeostasis that Freud evokes in 'Beyond the Pleasure Principle', whereby, through discharge, the psyche seeks the lowest possible level of tension. *Jouissance* transgresses this law and, in that respect, it is beyond the pleasure principle.]

References

ARISTOTLE *Poetics*. Trans. L.J. Potts as *Aristotle on the Art of Fiction*. Cambridge: Cambridge University Press, 1953.

BARTHES, ROLAND *Sur Racine*. Paris: Seuil, 1963.

FREUD, SIGMUND *S.E.*: Standard Edition of *The Complete Psychological Works*. Trans. James Strachey. London: Hogarth Press, 1953–1974.

LACAN, JACQUES *Ecrits: A Selection*. Trans. Alan Sheridan. London: Tavistock, 1977.

LAPLANCHE, J. and PONTALIS, J.-B *The Language of Psycho-Analysis*. Trans. Donald Nicholson-Smith. London: Hogarth Press, 1973.

2 Oedipal Textuality: Reading Freud's Reading of *Oedipus**

CYNTHIA CHASE

In 'Oedipal Textuality', Cynthia Chase turns Freud's techniques on Freud himself, using his own tactics of suspicion to re-examine his analysis of *Oedipus*. Her essay belongs to that 'return to Freud' heralded by Lacan, who demanded close rereading of Freud's texts to rescue their dark truths from the sugarcoated versions of the ego-psychologists. Chase's style of interpretation also shows the influence of Jacques Derrida and Paul de Man, both of whom insist that theory is a form of writing, as inexhaustible as literature itself, in which the writer's rhetoric not only enshrines but frequently exceeds his thought, leading into unforeseen associative networks.

In 'Oedipal Textuality', Chase draws an analogy between sexuality, which is repressed in psychic life, and textuality, which is repressed by psychoanalytic criticism in its dogmatic efforts to reduce all texts to sex. In *Oedipus Rex*, she argues, the hero's *sexual* transgression re-emerges long after the event, through the process of *textual* interpretation. She compares this structure to the temporality of trauma, described by Freud as 'deferred action' [*Nachträglichkeit*], whereby the shattering events of early life are never experienced as such but only through belated repetition. Freud's patient 'Emma', who suffered from a phobia of going into shops, exemplifies the workings of *Nachträglichkeit* (SE I 353–6): as a child, Emma was sexually assaulted in a shop, but because she was too young to understand the adult's gesture, the incident remained a foreign body in her psyche, unassimilable to the narrative of memory. At a later date, however, a banal encounter in a shop revived the traces of this lost event, inducing Emma's phobia, in which the idea of the shop, now standing for both scenes, was recharged with unconscious violence. Thus the moment of trauma can be located neither in the first event, nor in its later repetition,

---

*CYNTHIA CHASE, 'Oedipal Textuality: Reading Freud's Reading of *Oedipus*', in *Decomposing Figures: Rhetorical Readings in the Romantic Tradition* (Baltimore: Johns Hopkins University Press, 1986), pp. 175–83; 183–91; 193–5. © 1986, Johns Hopkins University Press.

but between these acts and in their very non-coincidence. The same structure may be found in *Oedipus,* Chase argues, in which the hero's secrets only surface *après coup,* through the process of their verbal repetition.

Where is my voice scattered abroad on wings?

Oedipus

You *should* have meant! What do you suppose is the use of a child without any meaning? Even a joke should have some meaning – and a child's more important than a joke, I hope.

The Red Queen

Of all the fictions that Freud calls upon to render an account of the psyche – from 'The Emperor's New Clothes' in *The Interpretation of Dreams* to the legend of Moses in *Moses and Monotheism* – the drama of Oedipus is his most recurrent and insistent reference. Sophocles' protagonist provides the name for what Freud frequently presented as his major discovery. The Oedipus complex still challenges definition from contemporary analysts and theorists, and writers' interpretive stances can be situated according to their characteristic uses of this one concept. With the matter of Oedipus so chronically urgent and undecided, one recent perspective in particular seems promising, one which aligns psychoanalysis with the theory of drama and theorizes a dramatic structure informing the psychic order.[1] For if a drama could signify for Freud such crucial propositions of psychoanalytic thought, then the signifying mode of drama warrants inquiry. Freud *reads* *Oedipus*: the Oedipus complex draws its specificity from the Sophoclean tragedy, rather than just from the ostensible semantic content of the Oedipus legend. To rethink Freud's concept, we ought not only to reread its first formulation, his claim in *The Interpretation of Dreams* that *Oedipus*'s unfolding 'can be likened to the work of a psychoanalysis,'[2] but also to reconsider its primary source, Sophocles' version of the myth.

Freud uses the drama of Oedipus to tell a story about psychic development and to describe the status of sex in human existence. Perhaps we can use the drama of Oedipus to tell a story about the development of Freudian thought and to describe the status of the *text* in psychoanalytic thinking. We could take our cue from the initial, exemplary project of psychoanalytic investigation, *The Interpretation of Dreams,* and take as clue Freud's dream of solving the riddle of the Sphinx – an actual dream mentioned in a letter to Wilhelm Fliess on May 31, 1897. Freud was also dreaming of solving the riddle of dreams,[3] and the solution written out in the *Traumdeutung* in certain ways resembles the answer to the dreamlike enigma of the Sphinx. By constructing the analogy between them, we may be led to grasp some distinctive traits of Freudian interpretation as well as the crucial features of the Oedipus story that rendered it significant for Freud.

The writing of *The Interpretation of Dreams* takes form both unconsciously and consciously as what will come to be described as an 'Oedipal' endeavor. Like the inquiry of Sophocles' protagonist, it is an investigation in relation to and for the sake of the father, the end result of which is the disclosure of a parricidal effect: the discovery of the Oedipus complex. In his preface to the second edition, Freud identifies the writing of the book as 'a portion of my own self-analysis, my reaction to my father's death' – 'a significance I only grasped after I had completed it' [*ID*, p. xxvi]. Freud's own most manifest 'Oedipus complex' is the drive to interpretation and 'self-analysis' dramatized by Sophocles' hero, which is initially at least, in the tragedy as in *The Interpretation*, a more prominent 'complex' (an excessively insistent and self-exceeding intention) than any parricidal or incestuous tendency. The complex Freud shares with Oedipus is, first, the drive to discover an Oedipus complex. We may take this as an initial pretext for seeking the relationships between *The Interpretation of Dreams*, interpretation, and writing, on the one hand, and on the other hand the Oedipus complex conceived as a theory of the child's relationships to his father and mother. Reading Sophocles with Freud could help to illustrate the complicity of Oedipal sexuality with a certain textuality.

Turning points in the legendary career of Oedipus, and the legible career of Freud, take place with the formulation of an enigma or riddle. First there is the question of Oedipus's parentage, which the Pythia answers with an unassimilable structural definition: your mother is she whose lover and your father he whose murderer you shall be. Then comes the riddle posed by the female-male being, creature of Apollo, the Sphinx: what is the thing that changes shape, with two feet and four feet, with a single voice, that has three feet as well? Finally, there is the enigma of the Phocal crime: 'How can we ever find the track of ancient guilt now hard to read?' Freud riddles: Do dreams have meaning? What meaning? Why is it distorted? And in the course of interrogating the significance of dreams he comes to interrogate the significance of audience response to dramatic presentations, and the particular enigma of the universal effectiveness of *Oedipus Tyrannus* for generation after generation of audiences.

This is the riddle of the riddle: the enigma of why the riddle of the Phocal crime should be so absorbing. It is solved along with the riddle of dreaming, which Freud answers by positing a censoring agent active in mental life – by discovering repression, and by

positing the unconscious. The riddle of another riddle initiated the
metapsychological inquiries that preoccupied Freud from 1895 on,
even as he completed his *Traumdeutung*. As he wrote in the *Project
for a Scientific Psychology*: 'It is quite impossible to suppose that
distressing sexual affects so greatly exceed all other unpleasurable
affects in intensity. It must be another characteristic of sexual ideas
that can explain how they are alone subjected to repression.'[4] How can
one interpret the fact that sexuality alone (of all 'drives') is uniquely
enigmatic? How can one interpret the enigmatic fact that *Oedipus* (of
all 'tragedies of destiny') is uniquely enthralling? Freud's explanation
for the repression of sexuality first takes shape in his theory of
seduction, or of the *proton pseudos* or 'primal deceit,' formulated in
the *Project* of 1895.[5] It focuses on the decisive effect of a distinctive
temporal structure in sexual development, a proleptic or metaleptic
structure marked by prematuration and deferral, or, in Freud's term,
Nachträglichkeit. The same conception of a peculiar time scheme, Freud's
solution to the riddle of the sexual riddle, becomes the principle of his
reading of the Oedipal riddle, the peculiar power of *Oedipus Tyrannus*.

Freud indicates a solution in the 'peculiar nature of the material,'
a 'voice within us,' a 'factor' or 'moment' of a certain kind. Modern
dramatists, on the theory that *Oedipus* owes its success to its
construction as a 'tragedy of destiny,' to the conflict of 'divine will'
with 'human responsibility,' have tried to achieve the same effect
by constructing plots on the same theme; but, remarks Freud, the
plays based on such *'selbsterfundenen Fabeln'* (plots invented by the
playwrights themselves) have failed to move their audiences. Hence:

> Wenn der König Ödipus den modernen Menschen nicht minder
> zu erschüttern weiss als den zeitgenössischen Griechen, so kann
> die Lösung nur darin liegen, dass die Wirkung . . . nicht auf dem
> Gegensatz zwischen Schicksal und Menschenwillen ruht, sondern
> in der Besonderheit des Stoffes zu suchen ist, an welchem dieser
> Gegensatz erwiesen wird. *Es muss eine Stimme in unserem Innern
> geben, welche* die zwingende Gewalt des Schicksals im Ödipus
> *anzuerkennen bereit ist*, während wir Verfügungen wie in der 'Ahnfrau'
> oder in andern Schicksalstragödien als willkürliche zurückzuweisen
> vermögen. *Und ein solches Moment ist in der Tat in der Geschichte des
> Königs Ödipus enthalten.*[6]

> [If *Oedipus Rex* moves a modern audience no less than it did the
> contemporary Greek one, the explanation can only be that its effect
> does not lie in the contrast between destiny and the human will, but
> is to be looked for in the particular nature of the material on which
> that contrast is exemplified. *There must be* something which makes *a
> voice within us ready to recognize* the compelling force of destiny in the

Oedipus, while we can dismiss as merely arbitrary such dispositions as are laid down in (Grillparzer's) *Die Ahnfrau* or other modern tragedies of destiny. *And a factor of this kind is in fact involved in the story of King Oedipus*.]

(*ID* pp. 295–6. My italics.)

The original German text refers to an inner 'voice which is ready,' not to 'something which makes' it ready, to perform the act of recognition. In the German, then, 'such a *Moment*' refers back to the 'voice which is ready': Freud is pointing to a 'moment' or 'factor' in Sophocles' drama involving recognition carried out by a 'voice' poised for such an act. The relation between that voice and *einem solchen Moment* is a problematic one, the German text suggests; whereas the English translation of *Moment* as 'factor' neatly elides the difficulty, excluding the temporal character of the 'factor' and identifying it with a 'something' in the play's thematic content. Hence the passage is most often read in a way that reduces it to the statement that follows it, to the effect that 'it is the fate of all of us . . . to direct our first sexual impulse towards our mother and our first hatred and our first murderous wish against our father.' But we should make the attempt to read it in conjunction with Freud's remark in the preceding paragraph that the 'process of revealing' that constitutes 'the action of the play . . . can be likened to the work of a psychoanalysis.' Freud is not simply evoking the psychoanalytic practice of disclosing a patient's Oedipus complex. In the context of his practice and writing in this period, Freud's comparison means that *Oedipus Tyrannus* successfully dramatizes the activity of repression and unrepression – the 'abnormal defense' that characterizes 'psychoneurosis' and the peculiar 'process of revealing' that constitutes interpretation of dreams, or psychoanalysis. Freud theorized the relationship between sexuality and repression in the light of the temporal structure he reconstrued in the case histories of his hysterical subjects in the 1890s. In identifying the uniquely revelatory character of *Oedipus*, Freud is remarking the same crucial structure, the same exemplary plot. The parallel between the riddle of *Oedipus*'s power and the riddle of sexual repression can be situated in a certain moment or factor (*ein solches Moment*) in the sequence of sexual development – something for which Freud used the term *trauma*.

Trauma is a key concept in the interpretation of sexual repression first outlined by Freud in the *Project* of 1895, where he reconstructs a kind of plot for the neurosis of a patient fictitiously named 'Emma.' This plot focuses on two moments or scenes, which between them constitute the trauma and install repression. One scene takes place before, the other after, puberty. There is a fateful time lag between the child's passive participation in an adult world imbued with sexuality, and the child's own accession to biological maturity and sexual awareness; the difference or deferral between 'moments' is the decisive factor in causing the extraordinary 'abnormal defense' of 'hysterical' repression, in which the mind blinds itself to the 'first scene' of a sexual encounter. As Jean Laplanche summarizes: there are two scenes 'separated from each other by a temporal barrier which inscribes them in two different spheres of meaning.'[7]

The first scene in Emma's drama, as Freud narrates it, is a putative seduction, an adult's sexual gesture toward her, the sexual nature of which, however, the child cannot sense. After sexual maturity there occurs a second scene that is banal, nonsexual, and distinguished only by the fact that through some detail of resemblance it recalls the first scene. In provoking a sudden recollection of that scene, together with its sexual significance now understood for the first time, the second scene produces within Emma a sexual excitation which takes the ego by surprise, for the danger comes from a memory, from within, not, as the ego's defenses expect, from an outside stimulus. The result is that the second scene institutes not only the normal defensive mechanism of 'attenuating' the threatening tension by associating the sexual idea with others, allowing its assimilation into consciousness, but the more 'primary process' of 'total evacuation of affect': the first scene is completely forgotten, and the second, in its insignificant detail, takes on all the affective significance of the first alien sexual gesture. Freud writes, 'Here we have an instance of a memory exciting an affect which it had not excited as an experience, because in the meantime changes produced by puberty had made possible a different understanding of what was remembered . . . . The memory is repressed which has only become a trauma *by deferred action.*'[8] The peculiar status of the traumatic moment, the sexual factor, stems from the impossibility of locating it in either scene: it is neither in the first, which has a sexual content merely 'as it were, *in itself* and not *for the subject,*' and which 'has no immediate sexual effect, produces no excitation, and provokes no defense', nor in the second, which includes no sexual gesture at all. Like self-blinded Oedipus, Emma feels herself a prey to 'double griefs and double evils' (l. 1320), the things done involuntarily, years before, and the things done just now, by and to the self. It is precisely a neither-nor that empowers the both-and of repression, as the subject blinds herself to the past, to the entry into a world structured by sexual meanings inaccessible to the subject's initial understanding. As Sophocles' Chorus declares, 'Time, all-seeing, surprised you living an unwilled life' (l. 1213).

Like Emma's typical 'psychoneurosis,' Oedipal sexuality concerns a certain lag or limp of the subject in relation to structures of meaning. The 'Oedipus complex' takes its explanatory power not simply from the generality of incestuous desire, but from the rigorous representation, in the Oedipal drama, of the temporal logic of repression. Reading *Oedipus Tyrannus* as structured according to a 'first scene' and a 'second scene' like the history of the repressed subject, we may come to distinguish, in Sophocles' more complex plotting, an enrichment of the conception of repression that will be taken up and implied by Freud in all his subsequent references to our Oedipal sexuality.

An initial recollection of Sophocles' play gives us a 'first scene' in the murder of Laius, the Phocal crime, and a 'second scene' precisely in the drama itself, the moment of the legendary story chosen by Sophocles for representation on the stage, the quest for and recognition of the deed's agent and meaning. The accession to sexual awareness that converts an indifferent episode into a seduction in Emma's case is paralleled in Oedipus's case by an accession to genealogical awareness that converts an accidental manslaughter into patricide. In this perspective, Sophocles' play portrays Oedipus as the one person in history *without* an Oedipus complex in the conventional sense: he has murdered his father and married his mother in an appreciation of expediency rather than in satisfaction of a desire. The one person who actually enacts patricide and incest completely misses the experience – until after the fact, when the parrincest is inscribed as a palimpsest and becomes readable for the first time. The Phocal event, the real, as Lacan writes, exists as what is missed, according to the traumatic logic of psychoanalytic thinking:

> That which is repeated, in fact, is always something produced – the very expression reveals its relation to *tuché* – as if by chance . . . . The function of *tuché*, of the real as encounter [*rencontre*] – an encounter insofar as it can be missed, and as it is essentially an encounter which *is* missed [*rencontre manquée*] – first appeared in the history of psychoanalysis in a form which is itself enough to awaken our attention – as trauma.[9]

In the very drama of the 'one in whom these primaeval wishes of our childhood have been fulfilled' [*ID*, p. 296], there lies inscribed the metaleptic plot structure that makes such fulfilment an impossibility. The sex of the cause is produced only through the *text* of the effect. The 'cause' – the parrincestual experience that has supreme guilt as its 'effect' – is, practically, the effect of its effect. 'Hysterical,' Emma draws the connection: so that was sex! 'Horror-stricken,' Oedipus draws the connection: so that was . . . text! Emma represses the first scene, forgets it absolutely, yet is unable to return to the scene of the crime (shops, where both the first and second moments of the trauma took place; her symptom is a phobic evasion of shopping), and at last commits herself to 'the work of a psychoanalysis.' Oedipus engages in 'a process of revealing, with cunning delays and mounting excitement – a process that can be likened to the work of a psychoanalysis – that Oedipus himself is the murderer of Laius . . . [and] son of the murdered man and of Jocasta'; and at last he 'represses' the scene of the crime by blinding himself. We remark initially, then, the analogy between Emma's hysterical forgetting and Oedipus's self-blinding, and between Emma's engagement in psychoanalysis and Oedipus's analysis of the Phocal crime. There also emerges the possibility – suggested by a certain literal reading of Freud's ambiguous comparison between the plot and an analysis – of leaving the two plot sequences strictly parallel: if Oedipus's self-blinding is his final act in the play, are we to understand that a similar action concludes a psychoanalysis – blinding oneself to the impossibility of cure for a temporally determined predicament? In matching the Sophoclean to the psychoanalytic plot, Freud suggests a critique of psychoanalysis as radical as the most strenuously antiFreudian or antipsychoanalytic critic could compose.[10]

With a facetious equation of Emma's and Oedipus's rhyming revelations we exploit an opportune coincidence – in order to raise the question of the text. Or rather, we begin to read the question of Freud's text, the riddle Freud ravels in citing another text (Sophocles') that exposes questionable relations between text and sex. While an extraordinary sex act is one major component of Oedipus's drama, text acts are just as major and extraordinary a component of the story; if there is a scandal to match (in the modern mind from Jocasta to Girard) that of incest, it is that of oracles. A recent Girardian reading of Sophocles' *Oedipus*, Sandor Goodhart's 'Oedipus and Laius's Many Murderers' refreshes our apprehension of the scandalously textual nature of Oedipus's central act, his affirmation of his guilt as the murderer of Laius.[11] In Sophocles' version of the legendary story, the facts of Laius's murder are never empirically established. Empirical proof of Oedipus's guilt hinges on the testimony of the one eyewitness to the murder, the Herdsman, who is *said* to have said that not one but many assaulters felled the king and his party (ll. 842–7). Oedipus initially focuses on the question of one or many murderers as the fact that will absolve or condemn him. By the time the Herdsman has arrived to testify, however, the arrival of the Corinthian Messenger has shifted all attention to the question of Oedipus's parentage. What finally convinces Oedipus of his guilt is the Herdsman's implication that he, Oedipus ('Swellfoot'), is the child exposed with pierced ankles by Jocasta and Laius in response to the oracle's prediction that he would kill the latter and marry the former.

Goodhart's reading helps us to perceive more readily the parallel between Oedipus's appropriation of guilt and Emma's repression of her 'seduction': both can be seen as phobic gestures responsive to juxtaposed structures, rather than reactions to accumulated empirical evidence. Oedipus reads his guilt in a palimpsest compounding the oracle told to Jocasta and Laius with the oracular definition of his parentage that first drove him from Corinth. What convinces him is a constricting network of texts: the Herdsman's word that he helped 'save for a dreadful fate' the exposed child entrusted to him by the queen, the Messenger's news that he was Polybus's and Merope's adopted heir, his wife's confession to exposing her child, and, above all, the words of the oracles, the Pythia's dreadful structural account of ancestry, and Apollo's fearful designation of a particular infant aggressor.[12] Sophocles arranges for the eyewitness to appear and to testify, but never to be asked the empirical question, Who killed Laius? 'From a semiotic point of view,' says Jonathan Culler, 'what is important here is the play's implicit commentary on the relation between meaning and event, between signs and the "realities" often thought to be independent of them . . . . We are not given a deed from which we infer a meaning but a meaning from which we infer a deed.'[13] In Sophocles' tragedy, then, as Sandor Goodhart writes, 'it is the status of the explanation that identifies those crimes that comes to be questioned . . . . Sophocles has shifted his interest from the myth to its appropriation, and it is this appropriation, in its origin and danger, that is examined.'[14] Precisely this dimension of Sophocles' drama enables it to be a uniquely rich reference for Freud.

Let us return to a Freudian reading of the case of Sophocles' *Oedipus*. The Oedipal drama presents itself for analysis as a 'first scene' made up of all that precedes the point at which the stage representation picks up the story, and a 'second scene' made up of all that is represented on the stage. The first scene itself includes several crucial scenes or moments that can be analyzed in the light of Freud's account of the primary instance of such a 'sexual-presexual' condition, infantile sexuality. The conception of an infantile sexuality ultimately impinges on the theory of seduction, as Freud comes to insist on the literal universality of seduction in at least one form, the earliest gestures of a mother toward her child, which are necessarily imbued with sexual meaning owing to her engagement in the sexualized adult world. The 'first scene,' then, is not just an accidental episode in the case history of a hysteric, but the first entry upon the human scene of every subject. Maternal care (in the first instance, nursing) sensitizes particular parts of the infant's body (in the first instance, the mouth and lips) and establishes an erogenous zone, a specially sensitive and significant region of the body. Initiating the oral phase, this zoning institutes the course of sexual development that, for Freud, spells the individual's destiny. Lacan, following Freud, stresses that this is an entry into not only a preexistent sexual but a preexistent textual order, that of language.[15] The child's accession to speech, like its accession to sexual maturity, comes long after its insertion into a sexual-social structure, through maternal and familial care and subscription in a discursive order, in the first instance by being given a name. Zoning and naming thus constitute the individual's inscription in a sexual-textual or 'Symbolic order.' One of the extraordinary features of the legend of Oedipus, of 'Swellfoot,' is its representation of these modes of facticity as radically identical. Thus the piercing of Oedipus's ankles, the maiming of his feet, is the terrible gesture of parental 'care' that marks the infant's position as the potential murderer of his father and lover of his mother, in the sexual-social order that is precisely a textual, discursive order, the language of the oracle. The parental gesture at once marks a special spot in the infant's body and generates his name, Oidi-pous. The mark and the name in fact determine Oedipus's relation to the Symbolic order and regulate his destiny. The most spectacular instance of this is his competition with the Sphinx: sensitive to *feet* as part of a name for man, Oedipus can provide the identification that destroys the Sphinx and lays the city of Thebes at his feet – where Sophocles sets the Chorus at the beginning of his drama.

Sophocles' text plays repeatedly on the syllable *pous* and expressions involving *feet*. Tiresias speaks of 'a mother's and a father's double-lashing terrible-footed curse'; Creon explains the failure to track down the regicide by saying that the Sphinx compelled the Thebans 'to turn from the obscure to what lay at our feet' (ll. 417–18, 130–1). At another moment, attacking Tiresias's mantic power and celebrating his own power of reasoning, *gnōmē*, Oedipus reminds his listeners how he read the Sphinx's riddle:

> Why, when the dog who chanted verse was here,
> did you not speak and liberate this city?
> Her riddle wasn't for a man chancing by
> to interpret; prophetic art was needed,
> but you had none, it seems – learned from birds
> or from a god. I came along, yes I,
> Oedipus the ignorant, and stopped her –
> by using thought, not augury from birds.
>
> [ll. 391–8]

In a footnote to his translation of this passage, Thomas Gould comments:

> Oedipus uses sarcasm that rebounds bitterly on himself. In Greek, the phrase *Oedipus the ignorant* has an assonance and an apparent

65

etymological connection that make it seem right in a sinister way: *ho mēden eidōs Oidipous. Eidōs* means 'knowing': *oida* means 'I know.' Oedipus seems to be speaking of himself as 'I whose name sounds like *oida* but really signifies the reverse.' (*Oida* and *eidōs* are also related to the verb 'to see'.) *Pous*, the other half of Oedipus' name, means 'foot.' 'As "Knowfoot" (*eidōs tous podas*) he solves the riddle about feet.'

(M.L. Earle, *The Oedipus Tyrannus*)[16]

In the very act of claiming reasoned control over language, Oedipus utters syllables that speak the opposite; the controlling utterance here is not his, but that of a fragmentary language speaking itself. 'Lack – knowing – I know – foot': in the very act of deploying a limited local irony, with his sarcastic references to himself as 'the ignorant,' Oedipus produces an irony of that irony, which fragments meaning into material signifiers. Expressions of double meaning, not usually of the fragmentary punlike kind here, abound in tragic drama, and *Oedipus Tyrannus* has more than twice as many ambiguous forms as Sophocles' other plays.[17] Missed by Oedipus (even and especially in his own speech), these double meanings speak to the spectators (who always already know the story). There is an irony to his 'tragic irony,' however, which ultimately overwhelms the audience just as much as the irony of his local irony overwhelms sarcastic Oedipus. As Gould writes,

> the double meaning is the most tactful possible way to keep the audience focused on the patricide and incest. Each person in the theater, as he is caught up in the fantasy, must imagine himself discovering the same guilt in his past, but he must be kept quite unaware of his involvement in the story or he will recoil with revulsion or defend himself with laughter. Sophocles, by pushing the vision of the crimes almost solely in double meanings, offers the audience a way to escape too conscious an identification with Oedipus in his troubles.

(p. 175)

Sophocles' strategy to prevent our prompt disassociation from the parrincest engages us in interpreting a meaning gradually ramified until it refers to our own condition and confronts us with our complicity with Oedipus. The double meanings thus mark our distance only to draw us in. They impel us to read into them a complex of significations so distant and different from the secret we know in advance that finally we find ourselves written into a representation that traverses and exceeds us.

We may undergo a similar effect in reading the text of Freud. Freud's Oedipus complex exceeds itself in a particular way that the legend of the name of Oedipus represents precisely. It seems that sexual repression, generating the unconscious, implicates the subject in an order not only of the living but also of the dead. Recent psychoanalytic theorists have followed the ghost of a suggestion in Freud's writing that the subject is obscurely constrained not only by his own lively unconscious but by the unconscious of his parents and their parents.[18] This notion would take support from the observation that, as Laplanche explains, 'the slightest parental gesture bear[s] the parents' fantasies . . . the parents themselves had their own parents; they have their "complexes," wishes marked by historicity, so that . . . at two vertices of the triangle [of the child's Oedipus complex] each adult protagonist is himself the bearer of a small triangle and even of a whole series of interlocking triangles.'[19] The 'zoning' and naming of Oedipus reflect Laius's fantasmatic relation to his father, Labdacus, 'the limping one,' with his maimed walk. As the son of his father, Laius makes a father of his son: he ascribes to him the threat of castration (as parrincest) that a son might have ascribed to his kingly father. In giving the child the 'Name-of-the-Father,'[20] in effect, the father empowers him, in fact, to take his (father's) place, for as 'Swellfoot' he solves the riddle of excess feet, and takes the king's place in Thebes.

Freud takes his place as a master, 'the father of psychoanalysis,' when he solves the riddle of dreams and in 1900 publishes the *Traumdeutung*. Rather as Oedipus is enabled to answer the Sphinx by an intimate sense of the significance of feet, Freud is empowered to interpret dreaming by an intimate conviction that it does have meaning, that (to quote the opening sentence of *The Interpretation of Dreams*) 'there is a psychological technique which makes it possible to interpret dreams, and that, if that procedure is employed, every dream reveals itself as a psychical structure which has a meaning and which can be inserted at an assignable point in the mental activities of waking life.' Like Oedipus's simple solution to the Sphinx's bizarre questions, Freud's *Traumdeutung* restores to the light of 'waking life' the weird productions of nighttime fantasy. Each rediscovers the uncanny and *unheimlich* as *heimlich*, canny, homely, 'what lay at our feet.' Each reconstructs a narrative scheme capable of explaining the inconceivable kind of being expressed by the dream or the riddle. Oedipus must identify 'a thing with two feet and four feet, with a single voice, that has three feet as well. It changes shape, alone among the things that move on land or in the air or down through the sea. Yet during the periods when it walks supported by the largest number of feet, then is the speed in its limbs the feeblest of all.'[21] The riddle concerns a coincidence of excess and lack, a collusion of sameness and difference, and a question of 'speed' and a question of 'support.' These are the factors of Freud's riddle as well, if not most patently in *The Interpretation of Dreams*, more clearly at least in his solutions to the general puzzle of repression that dreams manifest. It is unriddled, as we have seen, in terms of the shifting zones and phases of the sexual being. The inadequacy of the 'speed' of sexual development is most evident when the creature has the most 'support': the human infant supported by sexual care (and with the greatest number of relevant 'limbs,' if we recall the theory of the infant's 'polymorphous perversity') is least capable of sexual action. We can even draw a connection between the riddle's emphasis on 'walking *supported*' and Freud's conception of the sexual drive *propped* upon a biological function – in his scheme, as in Oedipus's answer to the Sphinx, at the infantile stage, when the infant's satisfaction in ingesting its mother's milk is supplemented by a pleasure in sucking the mother's breast. These principles of *Anlehnung* and *Nebenwirkung* compose Freud's recurrent report of the genesis of sexuality.[22]

Like Freud, Oedipus solves the riddle of human being by identifying its distinctively temporal structure: his answer is man, who moves on four limbs as an infant, on two feet in his prime, and with the aid of a staff in old age – and whose dilemma is compounded, we might add, by his provision with a 'single voice,' which cannot adequately express the overlapping discontinuous phases of his metamorphosis. Oedipus answers 'man'; he does not answer 'man, I myself'; yet Oedipus himself is the prime example of the bizarre being described by the Sphinx, precisely in the senseless numbering and collapsed syntax of the riddle's opening sentence. Through the very act of reading the riddle, Oedipus will become the one man who exemplifies the Sphinx's challenge not merely in the form of its answer but in its form as riddle. For Oedipus's parrincest (half finished even as he makes his reply to the Sphinx) makes him at once a husband ('with two feet') of his mother, a child among his children ('and four feet'), and the father of his father ('that has three feet as well'). Sophocles dramatizes the riddle by representing Oedipus as king, as exposed child, and as blind old man all in the single scene of the tragedy. Parrincest is a catastrophic convergence and crossing of life-lines – the unspeakable event 'at the place where three roads meet,' and an unreadable palimpsest, the text that cannot be read out with a 'single voice.'

The restriction of 'voice' affects Oedipus's answer to the Sphinx, and we can trace a similar effect in Freud's answer to the riddle of dreams. Freud recurrently neglects to implicate his own theory in his account of the reductive or recuperative rationalization that he finds to be characteristic both of the reporting of dreams and of the elaboration of systematic thought. In *The Interpretation of Dreams* Freud calls this rationalization 'secondary revision,' the activity by which the dream's patent absurdities are viewed from the standpoint of the ego and made to seem to conform to some kind of rational expectation. In *Totem and Taboo* Freud defines systematic thought in general as a type of 'secondary revision.' Yet he continues to claim for psychoanalytic theory the power to distinguish between the primary and the secondary, or the riddles and the answer, without being subject to the recuperative revision it ascribes to all theorizing. This tendency to ignore the implications of the critique of theory for his own emerging theories can be noticed throughout Freud's works, from the *Project for a Scientific Psychology* (1895) to *Negation* (1925).

At other moments, however, and particularly where he addresses the question of literature, as in his generalizing reading of *Oedipus*, Freud insists that no position exists – including that of psychoanalysis – immune to the distortions of secondary revision involved in all writing, no position from which writing or revision could be judged with disinterested final accuracy.[23] The theory of transference, too, as reread by Lacan,[24] situates both the power and the danger of psychoanalysis in the determinate resemblance between analyst and analysand, interpretation and symptom. It initially takes form as a mirror-image relation like that of Oedipus to Oedipus in the Sophoclean plot Freud compares to 'the work of a psychoanalysis.'

There is also another dimension of Freud's texts that converges with the critique of clear thinking, passages that insist on a kind of theoretical obscurity, and that formulate peculiarly elusive riddles. Thus, in the final chapter of the *Traumdeutung* (in the section entitled 'The Forgetting of Dreams'):

> Even in the best interpreted dreams, there is often a place [*eine Stelle*] that must be left in the dark, because in the process of interpreting, one notices a tangle of dream-thoughts arising [*anhebt*], which resists unravelling but has also made no further contributions [*keine weitern Beiträge*] to the dream-content. This is then the dream's navel, the place where it straddles the unknown [*dem Unerkannten aufsitzt*]. The dream-thoughts, to which interpretation leads one, are necessarily interminable [*ohne Abschluss*] and branch out on all sides into the netlike entanglement [*in die netzartige Verstrickung*] of our world of thought. Out of one of the denser places of this meshwork, the dream-wish rises [*erhebt sich*] like a mushroom out of its mycelium.[25]

Samuel Weber, reading this passage in the course of remarks on Freud's *Witz*, calls attention to the riddle it evokes. Freud's text describes the 'dream-navel' as like a 'mycelium,' which the dictionary defines as 'part of the thallus of fungi' – leading the reader on to the definition of *thallus*: 'Thallus . . . Bot. A vegetable structure without vascular tissue, in which there is no differentiation into stem and leaves, and from which true roots are absent.'[26] The riddle of Freud's riddle is that there exists a thing that is without tissue, without differentiation, and without roots. We might be tempted simply to unriddle this as the concept of the unconscious, which also, by definition, is definable only as what it is not. What should be remarked here, however, is not any supposed *ramifications* of the concept, but the resurgence of the thing itself in Freud's text. In its very unreadability, in passages like the one above, Freud's writing generates itself as the thing evoked in the riddle of the dream – or in the riddle of the Sphinx. For if the Oedipus of legend is the one who *is* the very riddle, not just its answer, whose parrincest crisscrosses the numbered phases of existence, so the text of Freud is also the very dream-text that is his riddle, and not just its interpretation. Freud's dream-book is a dream-text and palimpsest, in which the unreadable 'primary' text of 'primary process' is written under and over the systematic 'secondary revision.' This writing is the discourse of the Sphinx, as well as the human response.

The effect of the text, whether as Sphinx or as hero, can only be constituted by a third dimension, by the presence of witnesses – of readers. In Freud's case, the fact of his writing is precisely that third dimension. The psychoanalytic project came into being with the writing that Freud carried on in supplement to his ongoing clinical practice, writings that supplemented the relationship between analyst and analysand by an invocation of readers. We too readily take Freud's writing for granted and forget that it had to be carried on in addition to a practice that generally occupied nine hours a day; that it *was* carried on makes psychoanalysis, from the start, a triangular complex relating an analyst, a subject, and a text with its readers. *The Interpretation of Dreams*, for example, viewed as a self-analysis, is composed as a triangle made up by the analysing subject ('Freud'), the analysed subject ('Freud'), and the text within which the analysis takes place, the text of Freud. Freud's text constitutes the meaning of the analysis by letting it be read – and misread, as readers repeat the Oedipal gesture of appropriating the textual network for an overdetermined signification. Its definitive and continuous dependency on writing makes psychoanalysis what a certain popular view and a certain scientific perspective have long held it to be, a joke. It is a joke, that is, as rigorously defined in Freud's *Jokes and Their Relation to the Unconscious*, which describes how sexual jokes or 'dirty jokes,' in particular, are constituted as jokes – as funny – by the laughter of a third person, not the teller, nor the one on whom the joke is told, but the one to whom it is told, whose laughter alone makes the joke telling. That laughter cannot be controlled or explained, neither by the one who does the laughing, the third person, nor by the first, who does the telling.[27] Like the *fantômes* of parental fantasies that fix the nuclear oedipal triangle in a network of endless interlocking triangles, the laughter of the listener or reader sets the scene of psychoanalysis in the context of an endlessly-to-be-repeated joke.

We could also put it another way: as writing, and reading, psychoanalysis is an endlessly recited tragedy. For it is generated, as joke or tragedy, by the aspiration to a cure, whether conceived as resembling laughter or a catharsis of pity and fear. The structure of *Oedipus Tyrannus* is instructive here, in suggesting how writing is written into the psychoanalytic encounter itself, as 'analysis terminable and interminable' – how it constitutes the scenario of cure, or of interminable interpretation. Thus the tragedy of *Oedipus* consisted in a dramatization, for an audience of Athenians, of a dramatization on the stage, for a Chorus of fictive Thebans, of the drama of Oedipus's discovery of his role in the drama of the Phocal crime. An audience, an effect of witnesses, is built into the drama in the form of the tragic Chorus, which with Sophocles' addition of secondary characters (the High Priest, then Tiresias, then Creon, then Jocasta) takes the position of a third person ('we know that it was Sophocles who introduced the third character,' notes André Green).[28] This third person is an audience up on the stage, radically implicated in Oedipus's interpretations, and unable to predict or withhold its responses of fear, pity, laughter, or revulsion. It is like the third position constituted between and within the analyst and the analysand, a writing that is not just the record of their exchange, but a primary text generated as the unconscious significance of the discourse they together produce. The text that requires a reader, and the reader collapsed in laughter or dread is written into Freud's practice of psychoanalysis, as well as written out in the tomes of texts where analysis accumulated a history.

The time lag that dooms sexual ideas to repression also affects the ideas we have of texts. Reading, like sexual development, is a discontinuous temporal process in which the subject's awareness lags behind her or his ever-shifting enmeshment with a preexistent order of meaning, and not only because of the multiple significations of individual elements of discourse (such as the divergence between literal and figurative senses, and more complex kinds of rhetorical difference). The process must begin as misreading and go on to rereading, and to a rewriting in which the reader becomes legible. Like the Freudian subject's reading of sex, the analytic reader's writing on texts enforces and appropriates coincidences, collapsing the difference between disparate textual scenes. In this reading of Freud's reading of *Oedipus*, for example, not only have we compressed the different stories within each text, but we have stressed the relation of consistency and complicity between Freud's text and Sophocles' rather than a radically illegible discontinuity between them (which could be seen to be equally insistent). That illegible difference might be written (though not here) as the distinctively textual phenomenon, a trauma of unreadability, sited in a neither-nor between two almost incomparable texts. In differentiating such an option from our own writing strategy here, we assume (in every sense) the limp or lag that psychoanalysis, like Sophocles, ascribes to the exemplary subject.

Reading must culminate in a rewriting that cannot fail to be symptomatic. Oedipus is engaged in this dilemma when he encounters the unreadable structure of meanings produced by the Pythia, who tells him, in effect, that his knowledge will catch up with him [l. 788 ff. 'I went to Pytho']. It does – not (*in der Tat*) in the event, but only when Oedipus rereads her pronouncement in conjunction with another oracle and other histories of his case. Pythian prophecy may be saliently characterized as a type of writing, for the tradition describes the Pythia as a frenzied priestess who would cite Apollo and be quoted, by a priest, to the waiting supplicant. Like writing, then, Pythian prophecy is mediated – and female and probably mad, also like writing (when opposed to speech) in the scheme that dominates culture. Psychoanalysis differed with this scheme from the start, when Freud's theory of seduction as a *proton pseudos*, or primary deceit inscribed in the facts, positioned his writing 'beyond the banalities of official "clinical" practice, which regularly invoked bad faith and simulation to account for what it called "pithiatism,"' the lying of hysterics.[29] Freud's temporal scheme of sexual repression enabled him to unriddle these lies as the productions neither of bad faith nor of error, but as the expressions of victims of a fundamental duplicity grounded in the historicity of desire. Here too the Freudian perspective involves a Sophoclean insight, for as the finest scholarly reader of Oedipus remarks, the one issue that is not brought up in the tragedy is the question, Where does the blame lie? 'The battle is not in this case between truth and error. For when one speaks of "error" one does not mean an inevitable failure such as we have here, a flaw not of mind but of the whole human condition, both internal and external.'[30] Oedipus at Colonus dismisses his guilt for his blindness and his limp [ll. 213–88].

Freud ends *Beyond the Pleasure Principle* in the same way. The argument of that work, he is aware, more than usually succumbs to the deferrals and differences that mark his text. In a gesture like that which terminates *Totem and Taboo*, Freud ends by reciting a quotation: 'We may take comfort, too, for the slow advances of our scientific knowledge in the words of the poet:

Was man nicht erfliegen kann, muss man erhinken.

. . .

Die Schrift sagt, es ist keine Sünde zu hinken.'

What one cannot reach flying one must reach limping.

. . .

The Scripture says it is no sin to limp.[31]

Notes

1. See ANDRÉ GREEN, *Un Oeil en trop: Le complexe d'Oedipe dans la tragédie* (Paris: Minuit, 1969), and PHILIPPE LACOUE-LABARTHE, 'Theatrum Analyticum', in *Glyph 2: Johns Hopkins Textual Studies* (Baltimore: Johns Hopkins University Press, 1977).

2. SIGMUND FREUD, *The Interpretation of Dreams* (New York: Avon Books, 1965), p. 295. Quotations from *The Interpretation of Dreams*, henceforth cited as *ID*, are from this edition unless otherwise indicated.

3. FREUD, *The Origins of Psychoanalysis: Letters to Wilhelm Fliess*, trans. E. Mosbacher and J. Strachey (New York: Basic Books, 1954), p. 322: 'Do you suppose that some day a marble tablet will be placed on the house, inscribed with these words: "In this house on July 24, 1895, the Secret of Dreams was revealed to Dr. Sigmund Freud"?'

4. FREUD, *Project for a Scientific Psychology, Complete Psychological Works*, ed. J. Strachey (London: Hogarth Press, 1966), **1**: 352.

5. See JEAN LAPLANCHE, *Life and Death in Psychoanalysis*, trans. Jeffrey Mehlman (Baltimore: Johns Hopkins University Press, 1976), ch. 2, especially p. 30ff. This book, together with THOMAS GOULD, *Oedipus the King, A Translation with Commentary* (Englewood Cliffs, NJ: Prentice-Hall, 1970), generates the ideas of the present essay. Quotations from *Oedipus the King* are taken from Gould's translation.

6. FREUD, *Gesammelte Werke* (London: Imago Press, 1941), **2/3**: 269.

7. LAPLANCHE, *Life and Death*, p. 40, and p. 43, where he quotes Freud: 'The retardation of puberty makes possible the occurrence of posthumous primary process.'

8. FREUD, *Project*, **1**: 410.

9. JACQUES LACAN, *Le Séminaire XI: Les quatre concepts fondamentaux de la psychanalyse* (Paris: Seuil, 1973), p. 54.

10. Cf. SHOSHANA FELMAN's Lacanian-Freudian critique of 'psychoanalysis' – of a psychoanalytic interpretation setting itself in opposition to literature – in 'Turning the Screw of Interpretation', *Yale French Studies*, **55/56** (1977). See pp. 197–8 on the symptom as interpretation.

11. SANDOR GOODHART, 'Oedipus and Laius's Many Murderers', *Diacritics*, **8** (Spring 1978).

12. It would seem that one could distinguish between the two oracles in terms of the difference between anxiety and fear, or in terms of Freud's conception of the threat of anxiety as an endemic hazard like free-floating libido, or alternatively, as a specific hazard like castration. Cf. JEFFREY MEHLMAN, *Revolution and Repetition* (Berkeley and Los Angeles: University of California Press, 1977), pp. 96–7.

13. JONATHAN CULLER, 'Semiotic Consequences', paper presented at the Semiotics Forum, Modern Language Association of America Convention, Chicago, December 1977.

14. SANDOR GOODHART, *Who Killed Laius?*, PhD Diss., State University of New York at Buffalo, 1977, pp. 186, 183.

15. See JOHN BRENKMAN, 'The Other and the One: Psychoanalysis, Reading, *The Symposium.*' *Yale French Studies*, **55/56** (1977), especially pp. 438–43, for a lucid explanation of Lacan's concept of the signifier and of castration.

16. GOULD, *Oedipus the King*, p. 63. Gould also points out that the messenger who recounts Oedipus's blinding speaks of his piercing of his ball-joints, arthra, in 'an unparalleled use of this word'. With this catachresis naming eyes as feet, Sophocles calls attention to Oedipus's completion of his first maiming (and naming). We are also brought to 'see' the two acts as putative and deliberate castrations.

17. JEAN-PIERRE VERNANT, 'Ambiguity and Reversal: On the Enigmatic Structure of Oedipus Rex', *New Literary History*, **9** (1978): 474.

18. See JACQUES DERRIDA, 'Fors', *The Georgia Review*, **21**: 2 (1977).

19. LAPLANCHE, *Life and Death*, p. 45.

20. 'Nom-du-Père'; the concept is Lacan's. See *Ecrits* (Paris: Gallimard, 1966), p. 583.

21. GOULD, *Oedipus the King*, p. 19.

22. In *Three Essays on the Theory of Sexuality*, in re-editions in 1910, 1915, 1920, and 1924–5, *Complete Psychological Works*, **7**: 125–243. See LAPLANCHE, *Life and Death*, ch. 1, especially pp. 18–22.

23. Cf. SHOSHANA FELMAN, 'Turning the Screw', p. 200: 'The fact that literature has no outside, that there is no safe spot assuredly outside of madness, from which one might demystify and judge it, locate it in the Other without oneself participating in it, was indeed ceaselessly affirmed by Freud in the most revealing moments of his text (and in spite of the constant opposite temptation – the mastery temptation – to which he at other times inevitably succumbed).'

24. JACQUES LACAN, *Le Séminaire I: Les Ecrits techniques de Freud* (Paris: Seuil, 1975).

25. FREUD, *Complete Psychological Works*, **5**: 530. Retranslated by Samuel Weber, *The Legend of Freud* (Minneapolis: University of Minnesota Press, 1982), p. 75.

26. WEBER, *The Legend of Freud*, p. 81.

27. FREUD, *Complete Psychological Works*, **8**: 99–101, 144–5. Weber goes on to evoke a special case described by Freud, the bad joke in which the only joke is that there is no joke, and the expectation of the listener is thwarted. This is another instance of that marginal logic whereby the exception comes to appear more exemplary than the norm, for Freud's theory of jokes depends on his being able to refer to this joke of the joke. Weber is suggesting that Freud's text operates as a bad joke or no-joke of this kind. *The Legend of Freud*, pp. 108–15.

28. GREEN, *Un Oeil en trop*, p. 167n.

29. LAPLANCHE, *Life and Death*, p. 34.

30. KARL RHEINHARDT, *Sophokles* (Frankfurt am Main: Klosterman, 1949), p. 127.

31. Freud is quoting the last lines of 'Die beiden Gulden', Strachey's note tells us, which is 'a version by Rückert of one of the Maqâmât of al-Hairiri', quoting 'Die Schrift'. *Beyond the Pleasure Principle, Complete Psychological Works*, **18**: 64. Cf. FRIEDRICH RÜCKERT, *Die Verwandlungen des Abu Said von Serug oder die Makamen des Hariri*, in *Gesammelte Poetische Werke* (Frankfurt am Main: J.D. Sauerländer, 1869) **11**: 239.

3 Beyond Oedipus: The Specimen Story of Psychoanalysis*

SHOSHANA FELMAN

Freud argued in a famous formulation that *'hysterics suffer mainly from reminiscences'* (SE II 7). These reminiscences, banished from consciousness and inexpressible in words, take refuge in the form of the somatic symptoms of hysteria. According to this definition, Oedipus would qualify as an hysteric, too, because his reminiscences have been encrypted in his name, which represents a kind of verbal symptom: Oedipus means 'swellfoot', and it refers to the injuries inflicted on the hero's feet when he was exposed as an infant on the mountainside, in his parents' doomed attempt to circumvent the oracle. If the purpose of analysis is to restore to consciousness the reminiscences displaced onto the flesh, it could be said that Oedipus accomplishes this task in the first instalment of the trilogy. But Shoshana Felman argues that Lacan is not content with this conclusion: on the contrary, he believes that Oedipus's psychoanalysis 'ends only at Colonus', at the moment when the hero flings this terrifying question to the gods: 'Is it now that I am nothing, that I am made to be a man?' (below, p. 83).

While Lacan's remarks on Oedipus are often as obscure as those of the Delphic oracle itself, Felman reconstructs these fragmentary utterances into a theory of subjectivity that moves beyond *Oedipus Rex* into the eschatological mysteries of *Oedipus at Colonus*. For Freud, Oedipus achieves his destiny when he assumes the onus of his crimes; for Lacan, however, Oedipus confronts the lack that constitutes his being only when deprived of everything he owns, even his sins. If the hero recognises who he *is* in *Oedipus the King*, it is at Colonus that he realises through death his 'radical expropriation' from himself (below, p. 88).

*SHOSHANA FELMAN, 'Beyond Oedipus: The Specimen Story of Psychoanalysis',
in *Lacan and Narration: The Psychoanalytic Difference in Narrative Theory*,
ed. Robert Con Davis (Baltimore: Johns Hopkins University Press, 1983),
pp. 1021–35; 1040–5; 1049–53. © 1983, Shoshana Felman.

I

What is a key-narrative?

'We are forever telling stories about ourselves,' writes Roy Schafer, in an essay[1] that most suggestively defines the crux of the relation – and of the differentiation – between psychoanalysis and narration: between the daily practice (need) of telling stories and the narrative experience that is at stake in a practical psychoanalysis:

> We are forever telling stories about ourselves. In telling these stories *to others*, we may . . . be said to perform straightforward narrative actions. In saying that we also tell them *to ourselves*, however, we are enclosing one story within another . . . . On this view, the self is a telling . . . .
>
> Additionally, we are forever telling stories about others . . . we narrate others just as we narrate ourselves . . . . Consequently, telling 'others' about 'ourselves' is doubly narrative.
>
> Often the stories we tell about ourselves are life historical or autobiographical; we locate them in the past. For example, we might say, 'Until I was fifteen, I was proud of my father' or 'I had a totally miserable childhood.' These histories are present telling. The same may be said of the histories we attribute to others. We change many aspects of these histories of self and others as we change, for better or worse, the implied or stated questions to which they are the answers. Personal development may be characterized as change in the questions it is urgent or essential to answer. As a project in personal development, personal analysis changes the leading questions that one addresses to the tale of one's life and the lives of important others.[2]

Freud changed, indeed, our understanding of the leading questions underlying his patients' stories. The constitution of psychoanalysis, however, was motivated not just in the patients' need to tell their stories, nor even merely in Freud's way of changing the essential questions that those narrative complaints addressed, but in Freud's unprecedented *transformation of narration into theory*. In transforming, thus, not just the *questions* of the story but the very *status* of the narrative, in investing the idiosyncrasies of narrative with the generalizing power of a theoretical validity, Freud had a way of telling stories – of telling stories about others and of telling others stories about himself – which made history.

My dear Wilhelm,
   My self-analysis is the most important thing I have in hand, and

promises to be of the greatest value to me, when it is finished . . . . If
the analysis goes on as I expect, I shall write it all out systematically
and lay the results before you. So far I have found nothing completely
new, but all the complication to which I am used . . . . Only
one idea of general value has occurred to me. I have found
love of the mother and jealousy of the father in my own case
too, and now believe it to be a general phenomenon of early
childhood . . . . If that is the case, the gripping power of *Oedipus
Rex* . . . becomes intelligible. The Greek myth seizes on a compulsion
which everyone recognizes because he has felt traces of it in
himself. Every member of the audience was once a budding
Oedipus in phantasy, and this dream-fulfilment played out in
reality causes everyone to recoil in horror, with the full measure
of repression which separates his infantile from his present
state.[3]

'Only one idea of general value has occurred to me. I have found
love of the mother and jealousy of the father in my own case too.'
From the *Letters to Fliess* to *The Interpretation of Dreams*, what Freud
is instituting is a radically new way of writing one's autobiography,
by transforming personal narration into a path-breaking theoretical
discovery. In the constitution of the theory, however, the discovery
that emerges out of the narration is itself referred back to a story
which confirms it: the literary drama of the destiny of Oedipus,
which, in becoming thus a *reference narrative* – the specimen story
of psychoanalysis –, situates the validating moment at which the
psychoanalytic story-telling turns and returns back upon itself, in the
unprecedented, Freudian narrative-discursive space in which narration
becomes theory.

This discovery is confirmed by a legend which has come down to
us from classical antiquity: a legend whose profound and universal
power to move can only be understood if the hypothesis I have
put forward in regard to the psychology of children has an equally
universal validity. What I have in mind is the legend of King
Oedipus and Sophocles' drama which bears his name . . . .
    The action of the play consists in nothing other than the process
of revealing, with cunning delays and ever-mounting excitement – a
process that can be likened to the work of a psycho-analysis – that
Oedipus himself is the murderer of Laius, but further that he is the
son of the murdered man and of Jocasta . . . .
    If *Oedipus Rex* moves a modern audience no less than it did the
contemporary Greek one . . . there must be something which makes

a voice within us ready to recognize the compelling force of destiny in the Oedipus . . . . His destiny moves us because it might have been ours – because the oracle laid the same curse upon us before our birth as upon him. It is the fate of all of us, perhaps, to direct our first sexual impulse towards our mother and our first hatred and our first murderous wish against our father. Our dreams convince us that this is so. King Oedipus, who slew his father Laius and married his mother Jocasta, merely shows us the fulfilment of our childhood wishes . . . . While the poet . . . brings to light the guilt of Oedipus, he is at the same time compelling us to recognize our own inner minds, in which those same impulses, though suppressed, are still to be found.[4]

Freud's reference to the Oedipus as a key-narrative – the specimen story of psychoanalysis – is structured by three questions which support his analytical interrogation:

(1) *The question of the effectiveness of the story* (Why is the story so compelling, moving? How to account for the story's *practical effect* on the audience – its power to elicit affect, its symbolic efficacy?)

(2) *The question of the recognition* (The story has power over us because it 'is compelling us to *recognize*' something in ourselves. What is it that the story is compelling us to recognize? What is at stake in the recognition?)

(3) *The question of the validity of the hypothesis, of the theory* ('a legend whose profound and universal power to move can only be understood if the *hypothesis* I have put forward in regard to the psychology of children has an *equally universal validity*').

Any further inquiry into, or rethinking of, the significance of the Oedipus in psychoanalytic theory and practice, would have to take into account the implications of those three questions: the question of the narrative's *practical efficacy* (and hence, its potential for a clinical efficacy: its practical *effect* on us, having to do not necessarily with what the story *means*, but with what it *does* to us); the question of the meaning of the *theoretical recognition* (what do we recognize when we recognize the Oedipus?); and the question not just of the mere validity of Freud's hypothesis, but of the very *status of the theoretical validation through a narrative*, that is, the question of the relationship between truth and fiction in psychoanalysis.

I would suggest, now, that Lacan's reading of Freud renews, indeed, each of these questions in some crucial ways; and that an exploration of this renewal – an exploration of the way in which the Oedipus mythic reference holds the key to a Lacanian psychoanalytic understanding – may hold the key, in turn, to the crux of Lacan's innovative and enriching insight into what it is that Freud discovered, and consequently, into what it is that psychoanalysis is all about.

The psychoanalytic story: Oedipus the King

Nowhere is there in Lacan's writings any systematic exposition of Lacan's specific understanding of the significance of the Oedipus. As is often the case, Lacan's insight has to be derived, through a reading labor, from an elliptical and fragmentary text, from sporadic comments, from episodic highlights of (often critical and corrective) interpretations, and from the omnipresent literary usage of the reference to the Oedipus in Lacan's own rhetoric and style. My attempt at a creative systematization of what may be called Lacan's revision of the Oedipus would organize itself, in a structure of its own, as a relation between (the refraction of an insight through) three dimensions: (1) *the purely theoretical dimension*: how does Lacan understand (or modify the traditional understanding of) the basic psychoanalytic concept of 'the Oedipus complex'? (2) *The practical and clinical dimension*: what is, in Lacan's eyes, the practical relevance of the Oedipus *to the clinical event*, to the practical dealings with a patient? (3) *The literary dimension*: How does Lacan understand the way in which the text of Sophocles *informs* psychoanalytic knowledge?[5]

While Freud reads Sophocles's text in view of the consolidation – the confirmation – of his theory, Lacan re-reads the Greek text, after Freud, with an eye to its specific pertinence not to theory but to psychoanalytic *practice*. Freud, already, had compared the drama of the Oedipus to the process of a practical psychoanalysis ('The action of the play consists in nothing other than the process of revealing . . . *a process that can be likened to the work of a psychoanalysis'*.) But while this comparison between the literary work and the work of the analysand leads Freud to the confirmation of his *theory*, a theory of wish, of wish-fulfilment and of primordial Oedipal desires (incestuous and patricidal), Lacan's different analytic emphasis on the relevance of Oedipus to the clinician's *practice*, is not so much on wish as on the *role of speech* – of language – in the play.

What Freud discovered in, or through, the Oedipus – the *unconscious nature of desire* – implies, in Lacan's view, a *structural relation between language and desire*: a desire that articulates itself, substitutively, in a symbolic metomymic language which, thereby, is no longer recognizable by the subject.

It is always at the juncture of speech, at the level of its apparition, its emergence, . . . that the manifestation of desire is produced. Desire emerges at the moment of its incarnation into speech – it is coincident with the emergence of symbolism.

(S-II, 273)

No wonder then, that *Oedipus Rex*, dramatizing as it does *the primal scene* of *desire*, in effect takes place on *the other scene* of *language*. 'The unconscious', says Lacan, 'is the discourse of the other.' *Oedipus Rex* could be viewed as nothing other than a spectacular dramatization, a calculated pedagogical demonstration, of this formula. For Oedipus' unconscious is quite literally embodied by the discourse of the Other – of the oracle.

Oedipus' unconscious is nothing other than this fundamental discourse whereby, long since, for all time, Oedipus' history is out there – written, and we know it, but Oedipus is ignorant of it, even as he is played out by it since the beginning. This goes way back – remember how the Oracle frightens his parents, and how he is consequently exposed, rejected. Everything takes place in function of the Oracle and of the fact that Oedipus is truly other than what he realizes as his history – he is the son of Laius and Jocasta, and he starts out his life ignorant of this fact. The whole pulsation of the drama of his destiny, from the beginning to the end, hinges on the veiling of this discourse, which is his reality without his knowing it.

(S-II, 245)[6]

The unconscious is this subject unknown to the self, misapprehended, misrecognized, by the ego.

(S-II, 59)

The Oedipal question is thus at the center of each practical psychoanalysis, not necessarily as a question addressing the analysand's desire for his parents, but as a question addressing the analysand's misapprehension, misrecognition [*méconnaissance*] of his own history.

The subject's question in no way refers to the results of any specific weaning, abandonment, or vital lack of love or affection; it concerns the subject's history inasmuch as the subject misapprehends, *misrecognizes* it; this is what the subject's actual conduct is expressing in spite of himself, insofar as he obscurely seeks to *recognize* this history. His life is guided by a problematics which is not that of his life-experience, but that of his destiny, that is – what is the meaning, the significance of his history? What does his life-story mean?

An utterance is the matrix of the misrecognized part of the subject, and this is the specific level of the analytic symptom – a level which is de-centered with respect to the individual experience, since it is, precisely, what the historical text must integrate.

(S-II, 58)

Analysis is, indeed, nothing other than this process of historical integration of the spoken – but misrecognized – part of the subject. To do this, the subject must – like Oedipus – *recognize* what he *misrecognizes*, namely, his desire, and his history, inasmuch as they are, both, unconscious (that is, insofar as his *life-history* differs from what he can know, or own, as his *life-story*).

What we teach the subject to *recognize* as his unconscious is his history – that is to say, we help him to complete the present historization of the facts that have already determined a certain number of historical 'turning-points' in his existence. But if they have played this role, they did so already as facts of history, that is to say, in so far as they have been *recognized* in a certain sense or censored in a certain order.

(E 261, N 52, TM)

As in Freud's case, the reference of the clinical practice of psychoanalysis to the literary drama of the Oedipus hinges on the central question of the *recognition* (as opposed to what the subject had, beforehand, censored or misrecognized, misapprehended, or repressed). Recognition is, indeed, for Freud as for Lacan, the crucial *psychoanalytic stake* both of the clinical and of the literary work.

The nature of the recognition is, however, somewhat differently conceived, in Freud's discussion of the Oedipus as validating psychoanalytic *theory*, and in Lacan's discussion of the Oedipus as illuminating psychoanalytic *practice*. In Freud's analysis, Oedipus recognizes his desire (incest, patricide) as (unwittingly) fulfilled, whereas Sophocles's reader recognizes in himself the same desire, as repressed. The recognition is thus constative, or *cognitive*. In Lacan's different emphasis, however, the psychoanalytic recognition is radically tied up with language, with the subject's analytic speech-act, and as such, its value is less cognitive than *performative*[7]: it is, itself, essentially a speech-act, whose symbolic action *modifies* the subject's history, rather than cerebrally observing or recording it, at last correctly.

To bring the subject to *recognize* and to *name* his desire, this is the nature of the efficacious action of analysis. But it is not a question of recognizing something that would have already been there – a given

– ready to be captured. In naming it, the subject creates, gives rise to something new, makes something new present in the world.

(S-II, 267)

Analysis can have for its goal only *the advent* of an authentic speech and the realization by the subject of his history, *in relation to a future*.

(E 302, N 88, TM)

The analytical speech-act by which the subject recognizes, and performatively names, his desire and his history (insofar as the misapprehension of the one has in effect structured the other), has to be completed, consummated, by an ultimate analytic act of speech which Lacan calls 'the *assumption* of one's history', that is, the ultimate acceptance – and endorsement – of one's destiny, the acknowledgement of responsibility for the discourse of the Other in oneself, but also the forgiving of this discourse.

It is certainly this *assumption* of his history by the subject, in so far as it is constituted by the speech addressed to the other, that constitutes the ground for the new method that Freud called Psycho-analysis.

(E 257, N 48)

Oedipus the King, however, in Lacan's eyes, while recognizing, naming his desire and his history, does not truly *assume* them; at the end of *Oedipus Rex*, Oedipus accepts his destiny, but does not accept (forgive) himself. This is why Lacan would like to take us, as he puts it (in a formula that once again is resonant with many meanings), *beyond Oedipus*: that is, first of all beyond *Oedipus the King* and into Sophocles' tragic sequel, *Oedipus at Colonus*.

If the tragedy of *Oedipus Rex* is an exemplary literary work, psychoanalysis should also know this *beyond* which is realized by the tragedy of *Oedipus at Colonus*.

(S-II, 245)

II

Beyond Oedipus: Oedipus at Colonus

It is only in the tragic sequel that the true *assumption* of his destiny by Oedipus takes place:

In *Oedipus at Colonus*, Oedipus says the following sentence: '*Is it now that I am nothing, that I am made to be a man?*' This is the end

of Oedipus' psychoanalysis – Oedipus' psychoanalysis ends only at
Colonus . . . . This is the essential moment which gives its whole
meaning to his history.

(S-II, 250)

What Lacan refers to is the following scene, which I will now quote
twice, in two different translations:

Oedipus
And did you think the gods would yet deliver me?

Ismene
The present oracles give me that hope.

Oedipus
What oracles are they? What prophecy?

Ismene
The people of Thebes shall desire you, for their safety,
After your death, and even while you live.

Oedipus
What good can such as I bring any man?

Ismene
They say it is in you that they must grow to greatness.

Oedipus
Am I made man in the hour when I cease to be?

(Watling's translation[8])

. . .

Oedipus
You have some hope than that they [the gods] are concerned
With my deliverance?

Ismene
        I have, father.
The latest sentences of the oracle . . .

Oedipus
How are they worded? What do they prophesy?

Ismene
The oracles declare their strength's in you –

Oedipus
When I am finished, I suppose I am strong!

(Grene's translation[9])

84

'Is it now that I am nothing that I am made to be a man?' What is it, then, which makes for Oedipus' humanity and strength at the very moment at which he is 'finished', at the moment when, reduced to nothing, he embodies his forthcoming death? What is it that Oedipus, beyond the *recognition* of his destiny, here *assumes*, and which exemplifies 'the end of his analysis'? He *assumes the Other* – in himself, he assumes his own *relation* to the discourse of the Other, 'this subject beyond the subject' (S-II, 245); he assumes, in other words, his radical de-centerment from his own ego, from his own self-image (Oedipus the King) and his own (self-) consciousness. And it is this radical acceptance, and assumption, of his own *self-expropriation* that embodies, for Lacan, the ultimate meaning of Oedipus' analysis, as well as the profound Oedipal significance of analysis as such.

This significance is historically consummated by Oedipus at the moment when he awaits – and indeed *assumes* – his death. But this is not just a coincidence: the assumption of one's death is inherent to the analytical assumption:

> You will have to read *Oedipus at Colonus*. You will see that the last word of man's relation to this discourse which he does not know is – death.
>
> (S-II, 245)

Why death? Here Lacan is at his most hermetic, at his most elliptical. I believe, however, that this ellipsis embodies one of his most complex, profound and important psychoanalytic insights, and I will try – at my own risk – to shed some light on it by continuing, now, the analysis of *Oedipus at Colonus* 'beyond' what Lacan explicitly articulates, by using some Lacanian highlights borrowed from other texts (other contexts). Let me first make an explanatory detour.

The Oedipus complex, in its traditional conception, encompasses two fantasized ('imaginary') visions of death: the father's death (imaginary murder), and the subject's own death in return (imaginary castration). The Oedipus complex is resolved through the child's identification with his father, constituting his superego; in Lacan's terms, the resolution takes place through the introjection of the Father's Name[10] (embodying the Law of incest prohibition), which becomes constitutive of the child's unconscious. As the first, archetypal linguistic symbol ('name') which represses, and replaces, or displaces, the desire for the mother, the father's name (and consequently, in the chain of linguistic or symbolic substitution, any word or symbol used metaphorically or metonymically, that is, all symbols and all words), in effect incorporates the child's assumption of his own death as a condition – and a metaphor – for his *renunciation*. Since symbolization

85

is coincident with the constitution of the unconscious (the displacement of desire), 'the last word of man's relation to this discourse which he does not know' – his unconscious – 'is [thus] death': to symbolize is to incorporate death in language, *in order to survive*.

> So when we wish to attain in the subject what was before the serial articulations of speech, and what is primordial to the birth of symbols, we find it in death, from which his existence takes on all the meaning it has.
>
> (E 320, N 105)

> Thus the symbol manifests itself first of all as the murder of the thing, and this death constitutes in the subject the eternization of his desire.
>
> The first symbol in which we recognize humanity in its vestigial traces is the grave, and the intermediary of death can be recognized in every relation through which man is born into the life of his history.
>
> (E 319, N 104, TM)

What, now, happens in *Oedipus at Colonus* which is new with respect to the story (to the *recognition story*) of *Oedipus the King* (besides the subject's final death)?

Precisely the fact that Oedipus *is born*, through the assumption of his death (of his radical self-expropriation), *into the life of his history*. *Oedipus at Colonus* is about the transformation of Oedipus' story into history: it does not tell the drama, it is *about the telling* (and retelling) of the drama. It is, in other words, about the *historization* of Oedipus' destiny, through the *symbolization* – the transmutation into speech – of the Oedipal desire.

Oedipus
My star was unspeakable.

Chorus
          Speak!

Oedipus
My child, what can I say to them?

Chorus
Answer us, stranger; what is your race,
Who was your father?

Oedipus
God help me, what will become of me, child?

Antigone
Tell them; there is no other way.

(Scene 1, 89)

. . .

Oedipus
           Or do you dread
My strength? My actions? I think not, for I
Suffered those deeds more than I acted them,
As I might show if it were fitting here
To tell my father's and my mother's story . . .
For which you fear me, as I know too well.

(Scene 2, 91)

. . .

Chorus
What evil things have slept since long ago
It is not sweet to awaken;
And yet I long to be told –

Oedipus
           What?

Chorus
Of that heartbreak for which there was no help,
The pain you have had to suffer.

Oedipus
For kindness' sake, do not open
My old wound, and my shame.

Chorus
It is told everywhere, and never dies;
I only want to hear it truly told.

(Scene 2, 102)

. . .

Oedipus
There is, then, nothing left for me to tell
But my desire; and then the tale is ended.

(Scene 3, 105)

. . .

Messenger
Citizens, the briefest way to tell you
Would be to say that Oedipus is no more;

87

But what has happened cannot be told so simply –
It was no simple thing.

(Scene 8, 147)

Embodying the linguistic drama – the analytical speech-act – of
Oedipus' assumption of his radical expropriation, *Oedipus at Colonus*
tells, thus, not simply the story of the telling of the story of the
Oedipus, the drama of symbolization and historization of the Oedipal
desire, but *beyond that* ('beyond Oedipus'), as the final verses indicate,
the story of *the transmutation of Oedipus' death* (in all senses of the word,
literal and metaphoric) *into the symbolic language of the myth.*

> The fact that Oedipus is the Patronymic hero of the Oedipus complex
> is not a coincidence. It would have been possible to choose another
> hero, since all the heroes of Greek mythology have some relation
> to this myth, which they embody in different forms . . . . It is not
> without reason that Freud was guided towards this particular myth.
>   Oedipus, in his very life, is entirely this myth. He himself is
> nothing other than the passage of this myth into existence.
>
> (S-II, 267–8)

> It is natural that everything would fall on Oedipus, since Oedipus
> embodies the central knot of speech.
>
> (S-II, 269)

Freud at Colonus

At the same time that *Oedipus at Colonus* dramatizes the 'eternization'
of the Oedipal desire through its narrative symbolization, that is,
Oedipus' birth into his symbolic *life*, into his historical, mythic
survival, the later play also embodies something of the order of an
Oedipal *death-instinct*, since Oedipus, himself the victim of a curse
and of a consequent parental rejection, pronounces, in his turn,
a mortal curse against his sons. Oedipus' destiny is thus marked
by a repetition-compulsion, illustrating and rejoining, in Lacan's
eyes, Freud's tragic intuition in *Beyond the Pleasure Principle*. Like
the later Freud, the later Sophocles narrates, as his ultimate human
(psychoanalytic) insight, *the conjunction between life and death.*

> Oedipus at Colonus, whose entire being resides in the speech ·
> formulated by his destiny, concretizes the conjunction between
> death and life. He lives a life which is made of death, that sort
> of death which is exactly there, beneath life's surface. This is also

where we are guided by this text in which Freud is telling us, 'Don't believe that life . . . is made of any force . . . of progress, life . . . is characterized by nothing other than . . . its capacity for death' . . . .

Freud's theory may appear . . . to account for everything, including what relates to death, in the framework of a closed libidinal economy, regulated by the pleasure principle and by the return to equilibrium . . . .

The meaning of *Beyond the Pleasure Principle* is that this explanation is insufficient . . . . What Freud teaches us through the notion of primordial masochism is that the last word of life, when life has been dispossessed of speech, can only be this ultimate curse which finds expression at the end of *Oedipus at Colonus*. Life does not want to heal . . . . What is, moreover, the significance of the healing, of the cure, if not the realization, by the subject, of a speech which comes from elsewhere, and by which he is traversed?

(S-II, 271–2)

What Lacan endeavors here is obviously not a simple reading of the literary Oedipus in terms of Freud's theory, but rather, a rereading of Freud's theory in terms of the literary Oedipus. Lacan's emphasis, as usual, is *corrective* with respect to a certain psychoanalytical tradition that tends to disregard Freud's speculations in *Beyond the Pleasure Principle* as 'overpessimistic' and 'unscientific', not truly belonging in his theory. For Lacan, however, *Beyond the Pleasure Principle* is absolutely crucial to any understanding of psychoanalysis, since it embodies *the ultimate riddle* which Freud's insight has confronted – and attempted to convey:

. . . Freud has bequeathed us his testament on the negative therapeutic reaction.

The key to *this mystery*, it is said, is in the agency of a primordial masochism, that is, in a pure manifestation of that death instinct whose *enigma* Freud propounded for us at the climax of his experience.

We cannot turn up our noses at this problem, any more than I can postpone an examination of it here.

For I note this same *refusal to accept this culminating point of Freud's doctrine* by those who conduct their analysis on the basis of a conception of the *Ego* [ego psychology], and by those who, like Reich, go so far in the principle of seeking the ineffable organic expression beyond speech that . . . [they expect from analysis something like an] orgasmic induction.

(E 316, N 101, TM)

In reading Freud across *Oedipus at Colonus*, Lacan is doing much more than to suggest an affinity of subjects between Freud's and Sophocles's later works (the constitutive, structural relation between life and death: primordial masochism, death-instinct, repetition compulsion). Lacan is *using the relation* between *Oedipus at Colonus* and *Oedipus the King* (the undeniable relation, that is, of the later literary work to the specimen narrative of psychoanalysis) in order to illuminate and to make a claim for the importance of *Beyond the Pleasure Principle*. *Oedipus at Colonus*, says Lacan, is taking us *beyond Oedipus*, in much the same way as Freud is taking us *Beyond the pleasure principle*. By this multi-levelled, densely resonant comparison, Lacan is elliptically, strategically suggesting two things:

(1) that *Beyond the Pleasure Principle* stands to *The Interpretation of Dreams* (the work in which Freud narrates, for the first time, his discovery of the significance of *Oedipus the King*) in precisely the same relation in which *Oedipus at Colonus* stands to *Oedipus the King*;

(2) that the significance of the *rejection* of Freud's later text by a certain psychoanalytical establishment (embodying the *consciousness* of the psychoanalytic movement, that is, its own perception of itself, its own self-image), is itself part of an Oedipal story: the story, once again, of the *misrecognition* – misapprehension and misreading – of a history and of a discourse.

> The unconscious is that part of the concrete discourse . . . which is not at the disposal of the subject in re-establishing the continuity of his conscious discourse.
>
> (E 258, N 490)

> The unconscious is that chapter of my history which is marked by a blank . . .: it is the censored chapter.
>
> (E 259, N 50)

The Oedipal significance of *psychoanalysis' misrecognition of its own discourse*, of its own history, can only be seen from Colonus. In confining itself, however, to *Oedipus the King* and to Freud's concomitant discovery of the wish-fulfilment (as theorized in the *Interpretation of Dreams*), the psychoanalytic movement, far from going – as did Freud – *beyond Oedipus*, is still living only the last scene of *Oedipus the King*, in repeating consciousness' last gesture of denial: the *self-blinding*.

Lacan, on the other hand, strives to make the psychoanalytic movement *recognize* what it misrecognizes, and thus reintegrate the repressed – the censored Freudian text – into psychoanalytic history – and theory.

Why is Freud's *Beyond the Pleasure Principle* so important? Why is it not possible to *dispense with* this final phase of Freud's thought, in much the same way as it is impossible to dispense with *Oedipus at Colonus*? Because, let us not forget, 'Oedipus' analysis *ends* only at Colonus . . . . This is the essential moment which gives its whole meaning to his history' (S-II, 250). In what sense can *Beyond the Pleasure Principle* be said to give its whole *meaning* to psychoanalytic *history*? In the sense that what is *beyond* the wish for pleasure – the *compulsion to repeat* – radically displaces the conception both of history and of meaning, both of what and how history means and of how meaning comes to be, and is historicized. This radical displacement of the understanding both of meaning and of temporality (or history), far from being episodic, marginal, dispensable, is essential both to psychoanalytic theory (what has happened in the subject's past) and to psychoanalytic practice (what is happening in the subject's present: the concrete unfolding of unconscious history in the repetition of the transference [E 318, N 102]). Since the compulsion to repeat is, in Lacan's view, the compulsion to repeat a *signifier*, *Beyond the Pleasure Principle* holds the key not just to history or to transference but, specifically, to the *textual functioning* of signification, that is, to the insistence of the signifier in a signifying chain (that of a text, or of a life).

What is, then, psychoanalysis if not, precisely, a *life-usage of the death-instinct* – a practical, productive usage of the compulsion to repeat, through a *replaying* of the symbolic meaning of the *death* the subject has repeatedly experienced, and through a recognition and *assumption* of the meaning of this death (separation, loss) by the subject, as a symbolic means of his coming to terms not with death but, precisely, with his *life*?

> The game is already played, the dice are already thrown, with this one exception, that we can take them once more in our hand, and throw them once again.
>
> (S-II, 256)

This is what a practical psychoanalysis is all about; and this is what Freud tells us in his later speculative narrative, which seeks its way beyond the pleasure principle, beyond his earlier discovery of wish-fulfilment, beyond his earlier wish-fulfilling way of dreaming Sophocles.

'The Oedipus complex', says Lacan in one of those suggestive, richly understated statements (pronounced in an unpublished Seminar), 'the

Oedipus complex is – a dream of Freud.' This apparently transparent sentence is, in effect, a complex re-statement of the way psychoanalysis is *staked* in the discovery that *The Interpretation of Dreams* narrates: a complex re-statement both of Freud's *discovery of the theory* of wish-fulfilment as the meaning – and the motivating force – of dreams, and of Freud's *discovery of the narrative* of Oedipus as validating the discovery of the theory. It was, in effect, through his self-analyis, out of his own dream about his father that revealed to Freud his own Oedipal complexity, that Freud retrieved the founding, psychoanalytic meaning of the literary Oedipus. 'The Oedipus complex is a dream of Freud.'

But if Colonus resonates so forcefully in Lacan's heart, strikes such a forceful chord in Lacan's insight, it is because Lacan, perhaps unconsciously, identifies with Oedipus at Colonus. While Freud identifies quite naturally with Oedipus the King or the conquistador, *the riddle-solver* (who is, incidentally, a father-killer and a mother-lover: *King to his own mother*), even as he knows that this stupendous riddle-solving in effect will bring about 'the Plague',[11] Lacan identifies quite naturally with Oedipus *the exile* (a survivor of the Plague), since Lacan has been, precisely *as a training analyst*, expropriated, *excommunicated* from the International Psychoanalytical Association.

> I am here, in the posture which is mine, in order to address always the same question – *what does psychoanalysis mean?* . . .
>
> The place from which I am re-addressing this problem is in effect a place which has changed, which is no longer altogether inside, and of which one does not know whether it is outside.
>
> This reminder is not anecdotic: . . . I hand you this, which is a fact – that my teaching, designated as such, has been the object of a quite extraordinary *censorship* declared by an organism which is called the *Executive Committee* of an international organization which is called *The International Psychoanalytical Association*. What is at stake is nothing less than the prohibition of my teaching, which must be considered as *null and void* insofar as it concerns the habilitation of psychoanalysis; and this proscription has been made the condition for the affiliation of the psychoanalytic society of which I am a member with the International Psychoanalytic Association . . . .
>
> What is at stake is, therefore, something of the order of what is called . . . a *major excommunication* . . .
>
> I believe . . . that, not only by the echoes it evokes, but by the very structure it implies, this fact introduces something which is at the very principle of our interrogation concerning psychoanalytic practice.
>
> (S-XI, 9)

Colonus thus embodies, among other things, not just Lacan's own exile, Lacan's own story of ex-propriation from the International Psychoanalytical Association, but Lacan's dramatic, tragic understanding that psychoanalysis is radically *about expropriation*, and his *assumption* of his story, his assumption, that is, all at once of his own *death* and of his own *myth* – of the *legacy* of this expropriation – as his truly destined psychoanalytic legacy and as his truly training psychoanalytic question: 'Is it now that I am nothing, that I am made to be a man?'

'It was ordained: I recognize it now', says Oedipus at Colonus (Scene 1, 81). It may be but my own dream, but I can hear, indeed, Lacan's voice in the very words of Oedipus the exile:

Oedipus
That stranger is I. As they say of the blind,
Sounds are the things I see.

(Scene 1, 85)

. . .

Ismene
The oracles declare their strength's in you –

Oedipus
When I am finished, I suppose I am strong!

(Scene 2, 96)

. . .

Oedipus
I come to give you something, and the gift
Is my own beaten self: no feast for the eyes;
Yet in me is a more lasting grace than beauty.

Theseus
What grace is this you say you bring to us?

Oedipus
In time you'll learn, but not immediately.

Theseus
How long, then, must we wait to be enlightened?

Oedipus
Until I am dead, and you have buried me.

(Scene 3, 106)

Psychoanalysis at Colonus

At the same time, then, that Lacan is talking about *Oedipus at Colonus*, he is telling and retelling, not just Freud's, and his own, psychoanalytic story, but the very story of psychoanalysis, *seen from Colonus*: the story of Freud's going beyond Freud, of Oedipus' going beyond Oedipus, the story of psychoanalysis' inherent, radical, and destined self-expropriation. Lacan thus recapitulates at once the meaning of the story in which Freud is taking us beyond his own solution to the riddle, and the narrative voice – or the narrative movement – by which Freud *expropriates*, in fact, not just his own solution, but *his own narrative*.

In subscribing to Freud's psychoanalytic *self-recognition* in the Oedipus, as the moment of psychoanalysis' self-appropriation, its coming into the possession of its ('scientific') knowledge, and in censoring *Beyond the Pleasure Principle* as 'non-scientific', the psychoanalytical establishment has, precisely, tried to censor, to repress this final Freudian self-expropriation, and this ominous narrative annunciation, by the 'father of the psychoanalytic movement', of an inherent *exile of psychoanalysis*: an exile from the presence-to-itself of psychoanalytic truth; an exile from a *non-mythical access* to truth; an exile, that is, from any final rest in a knowledge guaranteed by the self-possessed kingdom of a theory, and the constrained departure from this kingdom into an uncertain psychoanalytic *destiny of erring*.

Counter this rejection of Freud's text, counter this repression, not just of Freud's insight, but of the very revolution involved in Freud's narration (in the unprecedented, self-trespassing, self-expropriating status of his narrative), Lacan has raised his training, psychoanalytic voice; but this protestation is, then, censored in its turn. Whatever the polemical pretexts, or the political reasons, given by the Censors, it is clear that the profound (and perhaps unconscious) thrust of the repressive gesture is the same: to eradicate from psychoanalysis the threat of its own self-expropriation (to repeat the Oedipal gesture of self-blinding); to censor, thus, in Freud as well as in Lacan, the radically self-critical, and *self-transgressive*, movement of the psychoanalytic discourse; to pretend, or truly to believe, that this self-transgression and this self-expropriation, far from being *the* essential, revolutionary feature of the psychoanalytic discourse, is (nothing other than) a historic accident, one particular historic chapter, to be (easily) erased, eliminated.

However, the repeated psychoanalytic censorships illustrate only the effectiveness (the working truth) of Freud's *Beyond the Pleasure Principle* (or of Sophocles'/Lacan's *Oedipus at Colonus*): in dramatizing the compulsion to repeat in the very midst of the psychoanalytic

institution, they bear witness to the very Freudian story, illustrate
the very Freudian myth of (something like) a *death-instinct* of
psychoanalysis itself: the (Oedipal) repetition of a curse in a discourse
that is destined to bestow speech as a blessing.

Through his call for 'a return to Freud' – a *return to Colonus* – Lacan
himself embodies, in the history of the psychoanalytic movement,
a return of the repressed. This is why, like Oedipus at Colonus,
he too announces (and his entire style is but a symptom of this
announcement) the return of a riddle.

Theseus
What grace is this you say you bring to us?

Oedipus
In time you'll learn, but not immediately.

Theseus
How long, then, must we wait to be enlightened?

Oedipus
Until I am dead, and you have buried me.

Lacan's narrative is, however, at the same time a dramatic repetition, a
reminder, of the radical *impossibility of ever burying* the (speech of the)
unconscious. The riddle, thus, persists. And so does Lacan's story,
whose subject, in all senses of the word, is, precisely, *the insistence of
the riddle*.

What, however, is a riddle, if not a narrative delay ('In time you'll
learn'), the narrative analytical *negotiation* of some truth or insight,
and their metaphorical approximation *through a myth*? The rejection
of *Beyond the Pleasure Principle* under the pretext that, as myth, it
is 'unscientific' ('just a myth'), involves, in Lacan's view, a radical
misunderstanding both of what a myth is all about and of the status of
the myth, as such, in Freud's narration and in psychoanalytic theory.
(But then again, the *misrecognition of a myth* is what psychoanalysis –
and Oedipus – are all about.)

In the final analysis . . . we can talk adequately about the libido only
in a *mythic* manner . . . . This is what is at stake in Freud's text.

(S-II, 265)

In trying to decipher the significance of Freud's work, Lacan
insists not just on the significance of Freud's myths, but, even more
importantly, on the (too often overlooked) significance of Freud's
acknowledgement of his own myths:

> At this point I must note that in order to handle any Freudian concept, reading Freud cannot be considered superfluous, even for those concepts that are homonyms of current notions. This has been well demonstrated, I am opportunely reminded, by the misadventure that befell Freud's theory of the instincts, in a revision of Freud's position by an author less than alert to Freud's explicit statement of the mythical status of this theory.
>
> (E 246, N 39, TM)

Freud's own terms of acknowledgement of his own myth are, indeed, enlightening:

> The theory of the instincts is so to say our mythology. Instincts are mythical entities, magnificent in their indefiniteness. *In our work, we cannot* for a moment *disregard them, yet we are never sure* that we are seeing them clearly.
>
> (Standard, XXII, 95)

Myth, in Freud, is not a supplement to, or an accident of, theory: it is not *external* to the theory: it is the very vehicle of theory, a vehicle of *mediation between practice and theorization*. This complex acknowledgement by Freud of the mythic status of his discourse is reflected, echoed, mediated in Lacan's response:

> I would like to give you a more precise idea of the manner in which I plan to conduct this seminar.
>
> You have seen, in my last lectures, the beginning of *a reading of what one might call the psychoanalytic myth*. This reading goes in the direction, not so much of criticizing this myth, as of *measuring the scope of the reality* with which it comes to grips, and to which it gives its *mythical reply*.
>
> (S-I, 24)

The analytical experience, says Lacan, has been involved, since its very origins, not simply with fiction, but with the 'truthful' structural necessity of fiction, that is, with its symbolical non-arbitrariness (E 12, 17). Like the analytical experience, the psychoanalytic myth is constituted by '*that very truthful fictitious structure*' (E 449). Insofar as it is mediated by a myth, the Freudian theory is not a literal translation or reflection of reality, but its *symptom*, its *metaphorical* account. The myth is not pure fantasy, however, but a narrative symbolic *logic* that accounts for a very real *mode of functioning*, a very real *structure of relations*. The myth is not reality; but neither is it what it is commonly (mis-)understood to be – a simple opposite of reality. Between reality and the psychoanalytic myth, the relation is not one of opposition, but one of (analytic) *dialogue*: the myth comes to grips with something in reality that it does not fully apprehend, comprehend, or master, but to which it gives an answer, a *symbolical reply*. The function of the myth in psychoanalytic theory is thus evocative of the function of interpretation in the psychoanalytic dialogue: the Freudian mythical account can be thought of as Freud's theoretical *gift of speech*.

What does that mean? In much the same way as the gift of speech of analytical interpretation, within the situation of the dialogue, acts not by virtue of its accuracy but by virtue of its *resonance* (whose impact is received in terms of the listener's structure), works, that is, by virtue of its openness to a linguistic passage through the Other, so does the psychoanalytic myth, *in resonating in the Other*, produce a *truthful structure*. The psychoanalytic myth, in other words, derives its *theoretical effectiveness* not from its truth-value, but from its truth-encounter with the other, from its capacity for *passing through the Other*; from its openness, that is, to an *expropriating passage* of one insight through another, of one story through another: the passage, for example, of *Oedipus the King* through *Oedipus at Colonus*; or the passage of the myth of 'Instinct' through this later and more troubling myth of 'Death':

> As a moment's reflection shows, the notion of the *death instinct* involves a *basic irony*, since its meaning has to be sought in the conjunction of two contrary terms: instinct in its most comprehensive acceptation being the law that governs in its succession a cycle of behaviour whose goal is the accomplishment of a vital function; and death appearing first of all as the destruction of life . . . .
>
> This notion must be approached through its *resonances* in what I shall call *the poetics of the Freudian corpus, the first way of access to the penetration of its meaning,* and the essential dimension, from the origins of the work to the apogee marked in it by this notion, for an understanding of its dialectical repercussions.
>
> (E 316–17, N 101–2)

> The psychoanalytic experience has discovered in man the imperative of the Word as the law that has formed him in its image. It manipulates the poetic function of language to give to his desire its symbolic mediation. May that experience enable you to understand at last that *it is in the gift of speech that all the reality of its effects resides*; for it is by way of this gift that all reality has come to man and it is by his continued act that he maintains it.
>
> If the domain defined by this gift of speech [says Lacan to an audience of psychoanalysts] is to be sufficient for your action as also for your knowledge, it will also be sufficient for your devotion.
>
> (E 322, N 106)

Contrary to received opinion, Lacan's preoccupation is not with theory *per se* (with games of 'intellectualization'), but always, with his *practice* as a psychoanalytical clinician. He is, first and foremost, a practitioner; a practitioner who happens to be thinking – and rethinking – about what he is doing in his practice. His *theory* is nothing other than his training practice – his practice as an educator, as a training analyst – who introduces others to the pragmatic issues (questions) of the practice.

Now, this *commitment to the practice of psychoanalysis as science*, concomitant with the *acknowledgement that psychoanalytic theory is fundamentally and radically composed of myth* – that the knowledge, that is, which is theorized out of the practice cannot transgress its status as a *narrative expropriating its secured possession as a knowledge* – has repercussions both in theory and in practice. It means that, to be truly scientific, the practice has to be conceived as antecedent to the knowledge: it has to be forgetful of the knowledge.

> Science, if you look into it, has no memory. It forgets the peripeties out of which it has been born; it has, in other words, a dimension of truth which psychoanalysis puts into practice.
>
> (E 869)

> [To be a good psychoanalyst is to find oneself] in the heart of a concrete history where a dialogue is engaged, in a register where no sort of truth can be found in the form of a knowledge which is generalizable and always true. To give the right reply to an event insofar as it is significant is . . . to give a good interpretation. And to give a good interpretation at the right timing is to be a good analyst.
>
> (S-II, 31)

> Any operation in the field of analytic action is anterior to the constitution of knowledge, which does not preclude the fact that in operating in this field, we have constituted knowledge . . . .
>
> For this reason, the more we know, the greater the risks we run. Everything that you are taught in a form more or less pre-digested in the so-called institutes of psychoanalysis (sadistic, anal stages, etc.) – is of course very useful, especially for non-analysts. It would be stupid for a psychoanalyst systematically to neglect it, but he should know that this is not the dimension in which he operates.
>
> (S-II, 30)

The peculiar scientific status of psychoanalytic practice is then such that psychoanalysis (as an individual advent and process) is always living and re-living the very moment of the *birth of knowledge*: the moment, that is, of *the birth of science*. Like Oedipus at the beginning of his mythical itinerary, psychoanalysis has *no use for the Oedipus myth* insofar as it has entered, through the oracles, the domain of public discourse. Like Oedipus, psychoanalysis has no use for a preconceived knowledge of the mythic story, no use for the story insofar as the story is, precisely, in advance, well known. *In practice,* there is no such thing as a specimen story. The very notion of a specimen story as applied to the reading or interpretation of another story is thus always a misreading, a mistake.

> This mistake exists in every form of knowledge, insofar as knowledge is nothing other than the crystallization of symbolical activity which it forgets, once constituted. In every knowledge already constituted there is thus a dimension of error, which consists in the forgetting of the creative function of truth in its nascent form.
>
> (S-II, 29)

Paradoxically enough, it is precisely insofar as it embodies *its own forgetting* that the Oedipus myth is constitutive of the *science* of psychoanalysis. And this science only takes itself complacently (non-problematically) to be a science when it in effect *forgets* the fictive, generative moment of its birth, when it forgets, in other words, that it owes its creativity – the *production* of its knowledge – to a myth. In this respect, psychoanalysis, which treats the Real by means of the symbolic, is not so different, moreover, from any other science (physics, for example). There is a fictive moment at the genesis of every science, a generative fiction (a hypothesis) at the foundation of every theory.

To borrow a metaphor from physics, one could say that the generative, fictive psychoanalytic myth is to the *science* of psychoanalysis what the Heisenberg principle is to contemporary physics: the element of mythic narrative is something like an *uncertainty principle* of psychoanalytic theory. It does not conflict with science – it *generates it* – as long as it is not believed to be, erroneously, a *certainty principle.*

The question of science in psychoanalysis is, thus, for Lacan, not a question of cognition but a question of commitment. And the concomitant acknowledgement of the psychoanalytic myth is, on the other hand, not a question of complacency in myth, but a question of exigency in and beyond the myth.

Science is the drive to *go beyond.* The scientist's commitment is at once to acknowledge myth and to attempt to *go beyond the myth.* Only when this (mythical, narrative) movement of 'going beyond' stops, does science stop. Only when the myth is not acknowledged, is *believed to be a science*, does the myth prevail at the expense of science. It is precisely when we believe we are *beyond* the myth that we are (indulge in) fiction. There is no 'beyond' to myth – science is always, in one way or another, a new (generative) myth.

There is no *beyond* to the narrative movement of the myth. But the narrative movement of the myth is precisely that which always takes us – if we dare go with it – *beyond itself.*

'Many complain', writes Kafka[12], 'that the words of the wise are always merely parables and of no use in daily life, which is the only life we have':

> When the sage says, *'go beyond,'* he does not mean that we should cross to some actual place, which we could do anyhow if the labor were worth it; he means some fabulous yonder, something unknown to us, something too that he cannot designate more precisely, and therefore, cannot help us here in the very least. All these parables really set out to say merely that the incomprehensible is incomprehensible, and we know that already. But the cares we have to struggle with every day: that is a different matter.
>
> Concerning this a man once said: Why such reluctance? If you only followed the parables you yourselves would become parables and with that rid of all your daily cares.
>
> Another said: I bet that is also a parable.
>
> The first said: You have won.
>
> The second said: But unfortunately only in parable.
>
> The first said: No, in reality: in parable you have lost.[13]

Notes

1. ROY SCHAFER, 'Narration in the Psychoanalytic Dialogue', in *On Narrative*, ed. W.J.T. Mitchell (Chicago and London: The University of Chicago Press, 1981).

2. Ibid., p. 31.

3. FREUD, Letter to Wilhelm Fliess of 15 Oct. 1897, in *The Origins of Psychoanalysis*, trans. E. Mosbacher and J. Strachey (New York: Basic Books, 1954), pp. 221–4.

4. FREUD, *The Interpretation of Dreams*, in *The Standard Edition of the Complete Psychological Works of Sigmund Freud*, trans. from the German under the General Editorship of James Strachey (London: The Hogarth Press and the Institute of Psychoanalysis, 1964), vol. IV, pp. 261–3. Unless otherwise indicated, quotations from Freud's works will refer to this edition: following quotations, in parenthesis, roman numerals will signal volume number, and arabic numerals page number, of the Standard Edition.

5. For lack of space, I had to skip here a detailed analysis of the first and second dimensions. This essay will therefore concentrate on the third dimension, trying to implicate the first two through the third.

6. The following abbreviations are here used to refer to Lacan's works:
   S-I (followed by page number), for: J. LACAN, *Le Séminaire, livre I: Les Ecrits techniques de Freud* (Paris: Seuil, 1975);
   S-II (followed by page number), for: J. LACAN, *Le Séminaire, livre II: Le Moi dans la théorie de Freud et dans la technique psychanalytique* (Paris: Seuil, 1978);
   S-XX (followed by page number), for: J. LACAN, *Le Séminaire, livre XX: Encore* (Paris: Seuil, 1975).
   All quoted passages from these Seminars are here in my translation.
   S-XI (followed by page number), for: *Le Séminaire, livre XI: Les Quatre concepts fondamentaux de la psychanalyse* (Paris: Seuil, 1973). The following abbreviation 'N' (followed by page number) will refer to the corresponding English edition: *The Four Fundamental Concepts of Psychoanalysis*, trans. Alan Sheridan (New York: Norton, 1978).
   E (followed by page number), for: *Ecrits* (Paris: Seuil, 1966); the following abbreviation 'N' (followed by page number) will designate the page reference in the corresponding Norton edition, *Ecrits: A Selection*, trans. Alan Sheridan (New York: Norton, 1977). When the reference to the French edition of the *Ecrits* ('*E*') is not followed by a reference to the Norton English edition ('N'), the passage quoted is in my translation and has not been included in the 'Selection' of the Norton edition.
   The abbreviation 'TM' – 'translation modified' – will signal my alterations of the official English translation of the work in question.
   As a rule, in the quoted passages, italics are mine, unless otherwise indicated.

7. I am using here the term 'performative' in the sense established by J.L. AUSTIN. Cf. 'Performative Utterances', in *Philosophical Papers* (London and New York: Oxford University Press, 1970) and *How to Do Things with Words* (Cambridge, Mass.: Harvard University Press, 1975). For a different perspective on the relation between speech-acts and psychoanalysis (as well as on the theoretical relation between Austin and Lacan), see my book, *The Literary Speech-Act: Don Juan with J.L. Austin, or Seduction in Two Languages* (Ithaca: Cornell University Press, 1983). [Original edition in French: *Le Scandale du corps parlant: Don Juan avec Austin, ou La Séduction en deux langues* (Paris: Seuil, 1980).]

8. SOPHOCLES, *Oedipus at Colonus*, in SOPHOCLES, *The Theban Plays*, trans. E.F. Watling (Baltimore: Penguin Classics, 1947; reprinted 1965), Scene 2, p. 83.

9. SOPHOCLES, *Oedipus at Colonus*, trans. David Grene, in SOPHOCLES I, *The Complete Greek Tragedies*, ed. D. Grene and R. Lattimore (Chicago and London: The University of Chicago Press, 1954), Scene 2, p. 96. All subsequent quotations from *Oedipus at Colonus* will refer to this edition, by scene number followed by page number.

10. Cf. E 277–8, N 66–7: 'Even when in fact it is represented by a single person, the paternal function concentrates in itself both imaginary and real relations, always more or less inadequate to the symbolic relation which constitutes it.

> It is in the *name of the father* that we must recognize the support of the symbolic function which, from the dawn of history, has identified his person with the figure of the law.'

11. Aboard the ship which transported him to the US to give the Clark lectures, Freud, apparently, said to Jung (who reported it to Lacan): 'They don't know that we bring with us the Plague . . . .'

12. FRANZ KAFKA, 'On Parables', in *Parables and Paradoxes* (New York: Schocken Books, 1970), p. 11.

13. The present essay is (part of) a chapter from my book, *Jacques Lacan and the Adventure of Insight: Psychoanalysis in Contemporary Culture* (Cambridge, Mass.: Harvard University Press, 1987).

Part Two

Narrative

4 Two Ways to Avoid the Real of Desire*

SLAVOJ ŽIŽEK

It is a condition of all classic detective fiction, Peter Brooks has observed, 'that the detective repeat, go over again, the ground that has been covered by his predecessor, the criminal' (*Reading for the Plot* [New York: Vintage, 1985], p. 24). In this sense the investigator must identify with the assassin, just as the analyst must identify with the analysand, or the reader with the literary text. Freud, an avid reader of Arthur Conan Doyle, was well aware of the affinities between his own investigative work and that of the detective; and Lacan, too, based one of his most famous seminars on Poe's detective story, 'The Purloined Letter'.†

In the following essay, Slavoj Žižek uses detective fiction to elucidate Lacan's conception of the real, which is distinguished both from the imaginary and from the symbolic order. Yet the real is not, as one might think, the realm in which the illusions of the other orders are dispelled: the real is the irruption of the unrepresentable. In the case of Emma's trauma, discussed by Chase, the real intrudes in the form of an assault to which the child cannot give a meaning or a name; after sexual maturity, a second scene, bearing a contiguous resemblance to the first, induces a belated understanding of the earlier encounter. At this point, it is not the seductive gesture from without, but the sexual excitation from within, that convulses Emma's psyche; as Chase puts it, 'the danger comes from a memory, from within, not, as the ego's defences expect, from an outside stimulus' (above, p. 61). Lacan describes trauma as a 'missed encounter' with the real, since it belongs to neither the first scene nor the second, neither the outer nor the inner world: the real is both 'inward and outward' (Malcolm Bowie,

---

*SLAVOJ ŽIŽEK, 'Two Ways to Avoid the Real of Desire', in *Looking Awry: An Introduction to Jacques Lacan through Popular Culture* (Cambridge, Mass.: MIT Press, 1991), pp. 48–66; 175–6. © 1991, Massachusetts Institute of Technology.
†The Wolf-Man (SERGE PANKEJEV) remembers Freud's enthusiasm for detective novels in *The Wolf-Man by the Wolf-Man*, ed. MURIEL GARDINER (New York: Basic Books, 1971), p. 146. LACAN's seminar on 'The Purloined Letter' is discussed in the Introduction above, p. 23.

Lacan, p. 110); it is the point at which the unknown without (the desire of the other) solicits the unknown within (the demonic power of the drives). In detective fiction, Žižek argues, the real is represented by the murder: 'an event that cannot be integrated into symbolic reality because it appears to interrupt the "normal" causal chain' (below, p. 117).

Žižek divides detective fiction into two genres, both of which conspire to avoid the real. In the first, or 'classical', variety, the detective, such as Sherlock Holmes, has to reintegrate the real into the symbolic order shattered by the murder. To do so, he must exculpate the suspects by localising all the guilt within a scapegoat, whose role is to conceal the truth that any of the others could have been the murderer. According to Žižek, the classical detective remains aloof and undefiled by the crime, getting *paid* so as not to get *involved*; whereas the 'hard-boiled' detective, such as Philip Marlowe, implicates himself in the free-floating guilt precisely by disclaiming any payment that would let him off the hook. In this hard-boiled genre, it is the *femme fatale* who stands for the resurgence of the real. The detective must reject the *femme fatale*, not only because her 'boundless enjoyment' threatens his identity as subject, but because she ultimately moves beyond the pleasure principle and assumes the death drive as her fate, death being the final triumph of the real.

THE SHERLOCK HOLMES WAY

The detective and the analyst

The easiest way to detect changes in the so-called *Zeitgeist* is to pay careful attention to the moment when a certain artistic (literary, etc.) form becomes 'impossible,' as the traditional psychological-realist novel did in the 1920s. The '20s mark the final victory of the 'modern' over the traditional 'realist' novel. Afterward, it was, of course, actually still possible to write 'realist' novels, but the norm was set by the modern novel, the traditional form was – to use the Hegelian term – already 'mediated' by it. After this break, the common 'literary taste' perceived newly written realist novels as ironic pastiches, as nostalgic attempts to recapture a lost unity, as outward inauthentic 'regression,' or simply as no longer pertaining to the domain of art. What is of interest here, however, is a fact that usually goes unnoticed: the breakdown of the traditional 'realist' novel in the '20s coincides with the shift of accent from the detective *story* (Conan Doyle, Chesterton, etc.) to the detective *novel* (Christie, Sayers, etc.) in the domain of popular culture. The novel form is not yet possible with Conan Doyle, as is clear from his novels themselves: they are really just extended short stories with a long flashback written in the form of an adventure story (*The Valley of Fear*) or they incorporate elements of another genre, the Gothic novel (*The Hound of the Baskervilles*). In the '20s, however, the detective story quickly disappears as a genre and is replaced by the classic form of the 'logic and deduction' detective novel. Is this coincidence between the final breakdown of the 'realist' novel and the rise of the detective novel purely contingent, or is there significance in it? Do the modern novel and the detective novel have something in common, in spite of the gulf separating them?

The answer usually escapes us because of its very obviousness: both the modern novel and the detective novel are centered around the same formal problem – the *impossibility of telling a story in a linear, consistent way*, of rendering the 'realistic' continuity of events. It is of course a commonplace to affirm that the modern novel replaces realistic narration with a diversity of new literary techniques (stream of consciousness, pseudodocumentary style, etc.) bearing witness to the impossibility of locating the individual's fate in a meaningful, 'organic' historical totality; but on another level, the problem of the detective story is the same: the traumatic act (murder) cannot be located in the meaningful totality of a life story. There is a certain self-reflexive strain in the detective novel: it is a story of the detective's effort to tell the story, i.e., to reconstitute what 'really happened' around and before the murder, and the novel is finished not when we get the answer to 'Whodunit?' but when the detective is finally able to tell 'the real story' in the form of a linear narrative.

An obvious reaction to this would be: yes, but the fact remains that the modern novel is a form of art, while the detective novel is sheer entertainment governed by firm conventions, principal among them the fact that we can be absolutely sure that at the end, the detective will succeed in explaining the entire mystery and in reconstructing 'what really happened.' It is, however, precisely this 'infallibility' and 'omniscience' of the detective that constitutes the stumbling block of the standard deprecatory theories of the detective novel: their aggressive dismissal of the detective's power betrays a perplexity, a fundamental incapacity to explain how it works and why it appears so 'convincing' to the reader in spite of its indisputable 'improbability.' Attempts to explain it usually follow two opposing directions. On the one hand, the figure of the detective is interpreted as 'bourgeois' scientific rationalism personified; on the other, he is conceived as successor to the romantic clairvoyant, the man possessing an irrational, quasisupernatural power to penetrate the mystery of another person's mind. The inadequacy of both these approaches is evident to any admirer of a good logic and deduction story. We are immensely disappointed if the denouement is brought about by a pure scientific procedure (if, for example, the assassin is identified simply by means of a chemical analysis of the stains on the corpse). We feel that 'there is something missing here,' that 'this is not deduction proper.' But it is even more disappointing if, at the end, after naming the assassin, the detective claims that 'he was guided from the very beginning by some unmistakable instinct' – here we are clearly deceived, the detective must arrive at the solution on the basis of *reasoning* not by mere 'intuition.'[1]

Instead of striving for an immediate solution to this riddle, let us turn our attention to another subjective position that arouses the same perplexity, that of the analyst in the psychoanalytic process. Attempts to locate this position parallel those made in relation to the detective: on the one hand, the analyst is conceived as somebody who tries to reduce to their rational foundation phenomena that, at first sight, belong to the most obscure and irrational strata of the human psyche; on the other hand, he again appears as successor to the romantic clairvoyant, as a reader of dark signs, producing 'hidden meanings' not susceptible to scientific verification. There is a whole series of circumstantial evidence pointing to the fact that this parallel is not without foundation: psychoanalysis and the logic and deduction story made their appearance in the same epoch (Europe at the turn of the century). The 'Wolf Man,' Freud's most famous patient, reports in his memoirs that Freud was a regular and careful reader of the Sherlock Holmes stories, not for distraction but precisely on account of the parallel between the respective procedures of the detective and the analyst. One of the Sherlock Holmes pastiches, Nicholas Meyer's *Seven Per-Cent Solution*, has as its theme an encounter between Freud and Sherlock Holmes, and it should be remembered that Lacan's *Ecrits* begins with a detailed analysis of Edgar Allan Poe's 'The Purloined Letter,' one of the archetypes of the detective story, in which Lacan's accent is on the parallel between the subjective position of Auguste Dupin – Poe's amateur detective – and that of the analyst.

The clue

The analogy between the detective and the analyst has been drawn often enough. There are a wide range of studies that set out to reveal the psychoanalytic undertones of the detective story: the primordial crime to be explained is parricide, the prototype of the detective is Oedipus, striving to attain the terrifying truth about himself. What we would prefer to do here, however, is to tackle the task on a different, 'formal' level. Following Freud's casual remarks to the 'Wolf Man,' we will focus on the respective *formal procedures* of the detective and the psychoanalyst. What distinguishes, then, the psychoanalytic interpretation of the formations of the unconscious – of dreams, for example? The following passage from Freud's *Interpretation of Dreams* provides a preliminary answer:

> The dream-thoughts are immediately comprehensible, as soon as we have learnt them. The dream-content, on the other hand, is expressed as it were in a pictographic script, the characters of which have to be transposed individually into the language of the dream-thoughts. If we attempted to read these characters according to their pictorial value instead of according to their symbolic relation, we should clearly be led into error. Suppose I have a picture-puzzle, a rebus, in front of me. It depicts a house with a boat on its roof, a single letter of the alphabet, the figure of a running man whose head had been conjured away, and so on. Now I might be misled into raising objections and declaring that the picture as a whole and its component parts are nonsensical. A boat has no business to be on the roof of a house, and a headless man cannot run. Moreover, the man is bigger than the house, and if the whole picture is intended to represent a landscape, letters of the alphabet are out of place in it since such objects do not occur in nature. But obviously we can only form a proper judgement of the rebus if we put aside criticisms such as these of the whole composition and its parts and if, instead, we try to replace each separate element by a syllable or word that can be presented by that element in some way or other. The words which are put together in this way are no longer nonsensical but may form a poetical phrase of the greatest beauty and significance. A dream is a picture-puzzle of this sort and our predecessors in the field of dream-interpretation have made the mistake of treating the rebus as a pictorial composition: and as such it has seemed to them nonsensical and worthless.[2]

Freud is quite clear when faced with a dream, we must absolutely avoid the search for the so-called 'symbolic meaning' of its totality or of its constituent parts; we must *not* ask the question 'what does the house mean? what is the meaning of the boat on the house? what could the figure of a running man symbolize?' What we must do is translate the objects back into words, replace things by words designating them. In a rebus, things literally *stand for their names*, for their signifiers. We can see, now, why it is absolutely misleading to characterize the passage from word presentations (*Wort-Vorstellungen*) to thing presentations (*Sach-Vorstellungen*) – so-called 'considerations of representability' at work in a dream – as a kind of 'regression' from language to prelanguage representations. In a dream, 'things' themselves are already 'structured like a language,' their disposition is regulated by the signifying chain for which they stand. The signified of this signifying chain, obtained by means of a retranslation of 'things' into 'words,' is the 'dream-thought.' On the level of meaning, this 'dream-thought' is in no way connected in its content with objects depicted in the dream (as in the case of a rebus, whose solution is in no way connected with the meaning of the objects depicted in it). If we look for the 'deeper, hidden meaning' of the figures appearing in a dream, we *blind* ourselves to the latent 'dream-thought' articulated in it. The link between immediate 'dream-contents' and the latent 'dream-thought' exists only on the level of wordplay, i.e., of nonsensical signifying material. Remember Aristander's famous interpretation of the dream of Alexander of Macedon, reported by Artemidorus? Alexander 'had surrounded Tyre and was besieging it but was feeling uneasy and disturbed because of the length of time the siege was taking. Alexander dreamt he saw a satyr dancing on his shield. Aristander happened to be in the neighborhood of Tyre . . . . By dividing the word for satyr into *sa* and *tyros* he encouraged the king to press home the siege so that he became master of the city.' As we can see, Aristander was quite uninterested in the possible 'symbolic meaning' of the figure of a dancing satyr (ardent desire? joviality?): instead, he focused on the *word* and divided it, thus obtaining the message of the dream: *sa Tyros* = Tyre is thine.

There is, however, a certain difference between a rebus and a dream, which makes a rebus much easier to interpret. In a way, a rebus is like a dream that has not undergone 'secondary revision,' whose purpose is to satisfy the 'necessity for unification.' For that reason, a rebus is immediately perceived as something 'nonsensical,' a bric-a-brac of unconnected, heterogeneous elements, while a dream conceals its absurdity through 'secondary revision,' which lends the dream at least a superficial unity and consistency. The image of a dancing satyr is thus perceived as an organic whole, there is nothing in it that would indicate that the sole reason for its existence is to lend an imaginary figuration to the signifying chain *sa Tyros*. Herein lies the role of the imaginary 'totality of meaning,' the final result of the 'dream-work': to blind us – by means of the appearance of organic unity – to the effective reason for its existence.

The basic presupposition of psychoanalytic interpretation, its methodologic a priori, is, however, that every final product of the dream work, every manifest dream content, contains *at least one* ingredient that functions as a stopgap, as a filler holding the place of what is necessarily *lacking* in it. This is an element that at first sight fits perfectly into the organic whole of the manifest imaginary scene, but which effectively holds within it the place of what this imaginary scene must 'repress,' exclude, force out, in order to constitute itself. It is a kind of umbilical cord tying the imaginary structure to the 'repressed' process of its structuration. In short, secondary revision never fully succeeds, not for empirical reasons, but on account of an a priori structural necessity. In the final analysis, an element always 'sticks out,' marking the dream's constitutive lack, i.e., representing within it its exterior. This element is caught in a paradoxical dialectic of simultaneous lack and surplus: but for it, the final result (the manifest dream text) would not hold together, something would be missing. Its presence is absolutely indispensable to create the sense that the dream is an organic whole; once this element is in place, however, it is in a way 'in excess,' it functions as an embarrassing plethora:

> We are of the opinion that in every structure there is a lure, a
> place-holder of the lack, comprised by what is perceived, but at
> the same time the weakest link in a given series, the point which
> vacillates and only seems to belong to the actual level: in it is
> *compressed* the whole virtual level [of the structuring space]. This
> element is *irrational* in reality, and by being included in it, it indicates
> the place of lack in it.[3]

And it is almost superfluous to add that the interpretation of dreams must begin precisely by isolating this paradoxical element, the 'place-holder of the lack,' the point of the signifier's non-sense. Starting from this point, dream interpretation must proceed to 'denature,' to dissipate the false appearance of the manifest dream-content's totality of meaning, i.e., to penetrate through to the 'dream-work,' to render visible the montage of heterogeneous ingredients effaced by its own final result. With this we have arrived at the similarity between the procedure of the analyst and that of the detective: the scene of the crime with which the detective is confronted is also, as a rule, a false image put together by the murderer in order to efface the traces of his act. The scene's organic, natural quality is a lure, and the detective's task is to denature it by first discovering the inconspicuous details that stick out, that do not fit into the frame of the surface image. The vocabulary of detective narration contains a precise *terminus technicus* for such a detail: *clue*, indicated by a whole series of adjectives: '"odd" – "queer" – "wrong" – "strange" – "fishy" – "rummy" – "doesn't make sense," not to mention stronger expressions like "eerie", "unreal", "unbelievable," up to the categorical "impossible".'[4] What we have here is a detail that *in itself* is usually quite insignificant (the broken handle of a cup, the changed position of a chair, some transitory remark of a witness, or even a nonevent, i.e., the fact that something *did not* happen), but which nonetheless *with regard to its structural position* denatures the scene of the crime and produces a quasi-Brechtian effect of estrangement – like the alteration of a small detail in a well-known picture that all of a sudden renders the whole picture strange and uncanny. Such clues can of course be detected only if we put in parentheses the scene's totality of meaning and focus our attention on details. Holmes's advise to Watson not to mind the basic impressions but to take into consideration details echoes Freud's assertion that psychoanalysis employs interpretation *en détail* and not *en masse*: 'It regards dreams from the very first as being of a composite character, as being conglomerates of psychical formations.'5

Starting from clues, the detective thus unmasks the imaginary unity of the scene of the crime as it was staged by the assassin. The detective grasps the scene as a *bricolage* of heterogeneous elements, in which the connection between the murderer's mise-en-scène and the 'real events' corresponds exactly to that between the manifest dream contents and the latent dream thought, or between the immediate figuration of the rebus and its solution. It consists solely in the 'doubly inscribed' signifying material, like the 'satyr' that means first the dancing figure of the satyr and then 'Tyre is thine.' The relevance of this 'double inscription' for the detective story was already noticed by Victor Shklovsky: 'The writer looks for cases in which two things which do not correspond, coincide nonetheless in some specific feature.'6 Shklovsky also pointed out that the privileged case of such a coincidence is a word-play: he refers to Conan Doyle's 'The Adventure of the Speckled Band' where the key to the solution is hidden in the statement of the dying woman: 'It was the speckled band . . . .' The wrong solution is based on the reading of *band* as *gang*, and is suggested by the fact that a band of gypsies was camped near the site of the murder, thus evoking the 'convincing' image of the exotic gypsy murderer, while the real solution is arrived at only when Sherlock Holmes reads *band* as *ribbon*. In the majority of cases, this 'doubly inscribed' element consists of course of nonlinguistic material, but even here it is already structured like a language (Shklovsky himself mentions one of Chesterton's stories that concerns the similarity between a gentleman's evening wear and a valet's dress).

Why is the 'false solution' necessary?

The crucial thing about the distance separating the false scene staged by the murderer and the true course of events is *the structural necessity*

of the false solution toward which we are enticed because of the
'convincing' character of the staged scene, which is – at least in the
classic logic and deduction story – usually sustained by representatives
of 'official' knowledge (the police). The status of the false solution
is epistemologically internal to the detective's final, true solution.
The key to the detective's procedure is that the relation to the first,
false solutions is not simply an external one; the detective does not
apprehend them as simple obstacles to be cast away in order to obtain
the truth, rather it is only *through* them that he can arrive at the truth,
for there is no path leading immediately to the truth.[7]

In Conan Doyle's 'The Red-Headed League,' a redheaded client calls
on Sherlock Holmes, telling him his strange adventure. He read an
advertisement in a newspaper, offering redheaded men a well-paid
temporary job. After presenting himself at the appointed place, he
was chosen from among a great number of men, although the hair of
many of the others was much redder. The job was indeed well paid,
but utterly senseless: every day, from nine to five, he copies parts of
the Bible. Holmes quickly solves the enigma: next to the house in
which the client lives (and where he usually stayed during the day
when he was unemployed), there is a large bank. The criminals put
the advertisement in the newspaper so that he would respond to it.
Their purpose was to ensure his absence from his home during the
day so that they could dig a tunnel from his cellar into the bank. The
only significance of their specification of hair color was to lure him.
In Agatha Christie's *The ABC Murders*, a series of murders take place
in which the names of the victims follow a complicated alphabetical
pattern: this inevitably produces the impression that there is a
pathological motivation. But the solution reveals quite a different
motivation: the assassin really intended to kill just one person, not for
'pathological' reasons but for very 'intelligible' material gain. In order
to lead the police astray, however, he murdered a few extra people,
chosen so that their names form an alphabetical pattern and thus
guaranteeing that the murders will be perceived as the work of some
lunatic. What do these two stories have in common? In both cases,
the deceitful first impression offers an image of pathological excess,
a 'loony' formula covering a multitude of people (red hair, alphabet),
while the operation, in fact, is aimed at a single person. The solution
is not arrived at by scrutinizing the possible hidden meaning of the
surface impression (what could the pathological fixation on red hair
mean? what is the meaning of the alphabetical pattern?): it is precisely
by indulging in this kind of deliberation that we fall into a trap. The
only proper procedure is to put in parentheses the field of meaning
imposed upon us by the deceitful first impression and to devote all our
attention to the details *abstracted from their inclusion in the imposed field of*

meaning. Why was this person hired for a senseless job *regardless of the fact that he is a redhead*? Who derives profit from the death of a certain person *regardless of the first letter of this person's name*? In other words, we must continually bear in mind that the fields of meaning imposing the 'loony' frame of interpretation on us *'exist only in order to conceal the reason of their existence'*:[8] their meaning consists solely in the fact that 'others' (*doxa*, common opinion) will think they have meaning. The sole 'meaning' of red hair is that the person chosen for the job should believe his red hair played a role in the choice; the sole 'meaning' of the ABC pattern is to lure the police into thinking this pattern has meaning.

   This intersubjective dimension of the meaning that pertains to the false image is most clearly articulated in 'The Adventure of the Highgate Miracle,' a Sherlock Holmes pastiche written by John Dickson Carr and Adrian Conan Doyle, son of Arthur. Mister Cabpleasure, a merchant married to a wealthy heiress, suddenly develops a 'pathological' attachment to his walking stick: he never parts from it, carrying it day and night. What does this sudden 'fetishistic' attachment mean? Does the stick serve as a hiding place for the diamonds that recently vanished from Mrs. Cabpleasure's drawer? A detailed examination of the stick excludes this possibility: it is just an ordinary stick. Finally, Sherlock Holmes discovers that the whole attachment to the stick was staged in order to confer credibility on the scene of Cabpleasure's 'magic' disappearance. During the night prior to his planned escape, he slips out of his home unobserved, goes to the milkman, and bribes him into lending him his outfit and letting him take his place. Dressed as a milkman, he appears next morning in front of his house with the milkman's handcart, takes out a bottle, and enters the house as usual to leave the bottle in the kitchen. Once inside the house, he quickly puts on his own overcoat and hat and steps out *without his stick*; halfway through the garden, he grimaces, as if suddenly remembering that he forgot his beloved stick, turns around, and runs quickly into the house. Behind the entrance door, he again changes into the milkman's outfit, walks calmly to the handcart and moves off. Cabpleasure, it turns out, stole his wife's diamonds; he knew that his wife suspected him and that she had hired detectives to watch the house during the day. He counted on his 'loony' attachment to the stick being observed so that when, on his way through the garden, after noticing the lack of his stick, he shrinks and runs back, his actions appear natural to the detectives observing the house. In short, the sole 'meaning' of his attachment to the stick was to make others think it has meaning.

   It should be clear, now, why it is totally misleading to conceive of the detective's procedure as a version of the procedure proper to 'precise' natural sciences: it is true that the 'objective' scientist also 'penetrates through false appearance into the hidden reality,' but this false appearance with which he has to deal *lacks the dimension of deception*. Unless we accept the hypothesis of an evil, deceitful God, we can in no way maintain that the scientist is 'deceived' by his object, i.e., that the false appearance confronting him 'exists only to conceal the reason of its existence.' In contrast to the 'objective' scientist, however, the detective does not attain the truth by simply canceling the false appearance: he takes it into consideration. When confronted with the mystery of Cabpleasure's stick, Holmes does not say to himself 'Let us leave out its meaning, it is just a lure,' he asks himself a quite different question: 'The stick has no meaning, the special meaning supposedly attached to it is of course just a lure; but what precisely did the criminal achieve by luring us into believing that the stick has special meaning for him?' The truth lies not 'beyond' the domain of deception, it lies in the 'intention,' in the intersubjective function of the very deception. The detective does not simply disregard the meaning of the false scene: he pushes it to the point of self-reference, i.e., to the point at which it becomes obvious that its sole meaning consists in the fact that (others think) it possesses some meaning. At the point at which the murderer's position of enunciation is that of a certain *I am deceiving you*, the detective is finally capable of sending back to him the true significance of his message:

> The *I am deceiving you* arises from the point at which the detective awaits the murderer and sends back to him, according to the formula, his own message in its true significance, that is to say, in an inverted form. He says to him – *in this* I am deceiving you, *what you are sending as message is what I express to you, and in doing so you are telling the truth*.[9]

The detective as the 'subject supposed to know'

Now we are finally in a position to locate properly the detective's ill-famed 'omniscience' and 'infallibility.' The certainty on the part of the reader that, at the end, the detective will solve the case does not include the supposition that he will arrive at the truth notwithstanding all deceitful appearances. The point is rather that he will literally *catch the murderer in his deception*, i.e., that he will trap him by taking into account his cunning. The very deceit the murderer invents to save himself is the cause of his downfall. Such a paradoxical conjunction in which it is the very attempt at deception that betrays us is of course possible only in the domain of 'meaning,' of a signifying structure; it is on this account that the detective's 'omniscience' is strictly homologous to that of the psychoanalyst, who is taken by the patient as the 'subject supposed to know' (*le sujet supposé savoir*) – supposed to know what? The true meaning of our act, the meaning visible in the very falseness of the appearance. The detective's domain, as well as that of the psychoanalyst, is thus thoroughly the domain of *meaning*, not of 'facts': as we have already noted, the scene of the crime analyzed by the detective is by definition 'structured like a language.' The basic feature of the signifier is its differential character: since the identity of a signifier consists in the bundle of differences from other signifiers, the absence of a trait itself can have a positive value. Which is why the detective's artifice lies not simply in his capacity to grasp the possible meaning of 'insignificant details,' but perhaps even more in his capacity to apprehend absence itself (the nonoccurrence of some detail) as meaningful – it is perhaps not by chance that the most famous of all Sherlock Holmes's dialogues is the following from 'Silver Blaze':

'Is there any point to which you wish to draw my attention?'
'To the curious incident of the dog in the night.'
'The dog did nothing in the night.'
'That was the curious incident,' remarked Holmes.

This is how the detective traps the murderer: not simply by perceiving the traces of the deed the murderer failed to efface, but by perceiving the very absence of a trace as itself a trace.[10] We could then specify the function of the detective *qua* 'subject supposed to know' in the following way: the scene of the crime contains a diversity of clues, of meaningless, scattered details with no obvious pattern (like 'free associations' of the analysand in the psychoanalytic process), and *the detective, solely by means of his presence, guarantees that all these details will retroactively acquire meaning*. In other words, his 'omniscience' is an effect of *transference* (the person in a relation of transference toward the detective is above all his Watsonian companion, who provides him with information the meaning of which escapes the companion completely).[11] And it is precisely on the basis of this specific position of the detective as 'guarantor of meaning' that we can elucidate the circular structure of the detective story. What we have at the beginning is a void, a blank of the unexplained, more properly, of the *unnarrated* ('How did it happen? What happened on the night of the murder?'). The story encircles this blank, it is set in motion by the detective's attempt to reconstruct the missing narrative by interpreting the clues. In this way, we reach the proper beginning only at the very end, when the detective is finally able to narrate the whole story in its 'normal,' linear form, to reconstruct 'what really happened,' by filling in all the blanks. At the beginning, there is thus the murder – a traumatic shock, an event that cannot be integrated into symbolic reality because it appears to interrupt the 'normal' causal chain. From the moment of this eruption, even the most ordinary events of life seem loaded with threatening possibilities; everyday reality becomes a nightmarish dream as the 'normal' link between cause and effect is suspended. This radical opening, this dissolution of symbolic reality, entails the transformation of the lawlike succession of events into a kind of 'lawless sequence' and therefore bears witness to an encounter with the 'impossible' real, resisting symbolization. Suddenly, 'everything is possible,' including the impossible. The detective's role is precisely to demonstrate how 'the impossible is possible' (Ellery Queen), that is, to resymbolize the traumatic shock, to integrate it into symbolic reality. The very presence of the detective guarantees in advance the transformation of the lawless sequence into a lawful sequence; in other words, the reestablishment of 'normality.'

What is of crucial importance here is the *intersubjective* dimension of the murder, more properly, of the *corpse*. The corpse as object works to bind a group of individuals together: the corpse constitutes them as a group (a group of suspects), it brings and keeps them together through their shared feeling of guilt – any one of them *could have been* the murderer, each had motive and opportunity. The role of the detective is, again, precisely to dissolve the impasse of this universalized, free-floating guilt by localizing it in a single subject and thus exculpating all others.[12] Here, however, the homology between the procedure of the analyst and that of the detective reveals its limits. That is to say, it is not enough to draw a parallel and affirm that the psychoanalyst analyzes 'inner,' psychic reality, while the detective is confined to 'external,' material reality. The thing to do is to define the space where the two of them overlap, by asking the crucial question: how does this transportation of the analytic procedure onto 'external' reality bear on the very domain of the 'inner' libidinal economy? We have already indicated the answer: the detective's act consists in annihilating the libidinal possibility, the 'inner' truth that each one in the group might have been the murderer (i.e., that we *are* murderers in the unconscious of our desire, insofar as the actual murderer realizes the desire of the group constituted by the corpse) on the level of 'reality' (where the culprit singled out *is* the murderer and thus the guarantee of *our* innocence). Herein lies the fundamental untruth, the existential falsity of the detective's 'solution': the detective plays upon the difference between the factual truth (the accuracy of facts) and the 'inner' truth concerning our desire. On behalf of the accuracy of facts, he compromises the 'inner,' libidinal truth and discharges us of all guilt for the realization of our desire, insofar as this realization is imputed to the culprit alone. In regard to the libidinal economy, the detective's 'solution' is therefore nothing but a kind of realized hallucination. The detective 'proves by facts' what would otherwise remain a hallucinatory projection of guilt onto a scapegoat, i.e., he proves that the scapegoat is effectively guilty. The immense pleasure brought about by the detective's solution results from this libidinal gain, from a kind of surplus profit obtained from it: our desire is realized and we do not even have to pay the price for it. The contrast between the psychoanalyst and the detective is thus clear: psychoanalysis confronts us precisely with the price we have to pay for the access to our desire, with an irredeemable loss (the 'symbolic castration'). The way in which the detective functions as a 'subject supposed to know' also changes accordingly: what does he guarantee by his mere presence? He guarantees precisely that we will be discharged of any guilt, that the guilt for the realization of our desire will be 'externalized' in the scapegoat and that, consequently, we will be able to desire without paying the price for it.

THE PHILIP MARLOWE WAY

The classical versus the hard-boiled detective

Perhaps the greatest charm of the classical detective narrative lies in the fascinating, uncanny, dreamlike quality of the story the client tells the detective at the very beginning. A young maid tells Sherlock Holmes how, every morning on her way from the train station to work, a shy man with a masked face follows her at a distance on a bicycle and draws back as soon as she tries to approach him. Another woman tells Holmes of strange things her employer demands of her: she is handsomely paid to sit by the window for a couple of hours every evening, dressed in an old-fashioned gown, and braid. These scenes exert such a powerful libidinal force that one is almost tempted to hypothesize that the main function of the detective's 'rational explanation' is to break the spell they have upon us, i.e., to spare us the encounter with the real of our desire that these scenes stage. The hard-boiled detective novel presents in this regard a totally different situation. In it, the detective loses the distance that would enable him to analyze the false scene and to dispel its charm; he becomes an active hero confronted with a chaotic, corrupt world: the more he intervenes in it, the more involved in its wicked ways he becomes.

It is therefore totally misleading to locate the difference between the classical and the hard-boiled detective as one of 'intellectual'

versus 'physical' activity, to say that the classical detective of logic
and deduction is engaged in reasoning while the hard-boiled detective
is mainly engaged in chase and fight. The real break consists in the
fact that, existentially, the classical detective is not 'engaged' at all: he
maintains an eccentric position throughout; he is excluded from the
exchanges that take place among the group of suspects constituted
by the corpse. It is precisely on the basis of this exteriority of his
position (which is of course not to be confused with the position of
the 'objective' scientist: the latter's distance toward the object of his
research is of quite another nature) that the homology between the
detective and the analyst is founded. One of the clues indicating
the difference between the two types of detective is their respective
attitudes toward financial reward. After solving the case, the classical
detective accepts with accentuated pleasure payment for the services
he has rendered, whereas the hard-boiled detective as a rule disdains
money and solves his cases with the personal commitment of
somebody fulfilling an ethical mission, although this commitment is
often hidden under a mask of cynicism. What is at stake here is not
the classical detective's simple greed or his callousness toward human
suffering and injustice – the point is much finer: the payment enables
him to avoid getting mixed up in the libidinal circuit of (symbolic)
debt and its restitution. The symbolic value of payment is the same
in psychoanalysis: the fees of the analyst allow him to stay out of
the 'sacred' domain of exchange and sacrifice, i.e., to avoid getting
involved in the analysand's libidinal circuit. Lacan articulates this
dimension of payment precisely apropos of Dupin who, at the end of
'The Purloined Letter,' makes the prefect of police understand that
he already has the letter, but is prepared to deliver it only for an
appropriate fee:

> Does this mean that this Dupin, who up until then was an
> admirable, almost excessively lucid character, has all of a sudden
> become a small time wheeler and dealer? I don't hesitate to see in
> this action the re-purchasing of what one could call the bad *mana*
> attached to the letter. And indeed, from the moment he receives
> his fee, he has pulled out of the game. It isn't only because he has
> handed the letter over to another, but because his motives are clear
> to everyone – he got his money, it's no longer of any concern to
> him. The sacred value of remuneration, of the fee, is clearly indicated
> by the context . . . . We, who spend our time being the bearers
> of all the purloined letters of the patient, also get paid somewhat
> dearly. Think about this with some care – were we not to be paid,
> we would get involved in the drama of Atreus and Thyestes, the
> drama in which all the subjects who come to confide their truth in

119

us are involved . . . . Everyone knows that money doesn't just buy things, but that the prices which, in our culture, are calculated at rock-bottom, have the function of neutralizing something infinitely more dangerous than paying in money, namely owing somebody something.[13]

In short, by demanding a fee, Dupin forestalls the 'curse' – the place in the symbolic network – that befalls those who come into possession of the letter. The hard-boiled detective is, on the contrary, 'involved' from the very beginning, caught up in the circuit: this involvement defines his very subjective position. What causes him to solve the mystery is first of all the fact that he has a certain debt to honor. We can locate this 'settlement of (symbolic) accounts' on a wide scale ranging from Mike Hammer's primitive vendetta ethos in Mickey Spillane's novels to the refined sense of wounded subjectivity that characterizes Chandler's Philip Marlowe. Let us take, as an exemplary case of the latter, 'Red Wind,' one of Chandler's early short stories. Lola Barsley once had a lover who died unexpectedly. As a memento of her great love, she keeps an expensive pearl necklace, a gift from him, but in order to avoid her husband's suspicion she invents the story that the necklace is an imitation. Her ex-chauffeur steals the necklace and blackmails her, guessing that the necklace is real and what it means to her. He wants money for the necklace and for not telling her husband that it is not a fake. After the blackmailer is murdered, Lola asks John Dalmas (a precursor of Marlowe) to find the missing necklace, but when he obtains it and shows it to a professional jeweller, the necklace turns out to be a fake. Lola's great love was also an impostor, it seems, and her memory an illusion. Dalmas, however, does not want to hurt her, so he hires a cheap forger to manufacture a deliberately raw imitation of the imitation. Lola, of course, immediately sees that the necklace Dalmas gives her is not her own and Dalmas explains that the blackmailer probably intended to return her this imitation and to keep the original for himself so that he might resell it later on. The memory of Lola's great love, which gives meaning to her life, is thus left unspoiled. Such an act of goodness is, of course, not without a kind of moral beauty, but it nonetheless runs contrary to the psychoanalytic ethic: it intends to spare the other the confrontation with a truth that would hurt him/her by demolishing his/her ego-ideal.

Such an involvement entails the loss of the 'excentric' position by means of which the classical detective plays a role homologous to the 'subject supposed to know.' That is to say, the detective is never, as a rule, the narrator of the classical detective novel, which has either an 'omniscient' narrator or one who is a sympathetic member of the social milieu, preferably the detective's Watsonian companion – in short, the person *for whom* the detective is a 'subject supposed to know.' The 'subject supposed to know' is an effect of transference and is as such *structurally impossible in the first person*: he is by definition 'supposed to know' by another subject. For that reason, it is strictly prohibited to divulge the detective's 'inner thoughts.' His reasoning must be concealed till the final triumphal denouement, except for occasional mysterious questions and remarks whose function is to emphasize even further the inaccessible character of what goes on in the detective's head. Agatha Christie is a great master of such remarks, although she seems sometimes to push them to a mannerist extreme: in the midst of an intricate investigation, Poirot usually asks a question such as 'Do you know by any chance what was the color of the stockings worn by the lady's maid?'; after obtaining the answer, he mumbles into his moustache: 'Then the case is completely clear!'

The hard-boiled novels are in contrast generally narrated in the first person, with the detective himself as narrator (a notable exception, which would require exhaustive interpretation, is the majority of Dashiell Hammett's novels). This change in narrative perspective has of course profound consequences for the dialectic of truth and deception. By means of his initial decision to accept a case, the hard-boiled detective gets mixed up in a course of events that he is unable to dominate; all of a sudden it becomes evident that he has been 'played for a sucker.' What looked at first like an easy job turns into an intricate game of criss-cross, and all his effort is directed toward clarifying the contours of the trap into which he has fallen. The 'truth' at which he attempts to arrive is not just a challenge to his reason but concerns him ethically and often painfully. The deceitful game of which he has become a part poses a threat to his very identity as a subject. In short, the dialectic of deception in the hard-boiled novel is the dialectic of an active hero caught in a nightmarish game whose real stakes escape him. His acts acquire an unforeseen dimension, he can hurt somebody unknowingly – the guilt he thus contracts involuntarily propels him to 'honor his debt.'[14]

In this case, then, it is the detective himself – not the terrified members of the 'group of suspects' – who undergoes a kind of 'loss of reality,' who finds himself in a dreamlike world where it is never quite clear who is playing what game. And the person who embodies this deceitful character of the universe, its fundamental corruption, the person who lures the detective and 'plays him for a sucker,' is as a rule the femme fatale, which is why the final 'settlement of accounts' usually consists in the detective's confrontation with her. This confrontation results in a range of reactions, from desperate resignation or escape into cynicism in Hammett and Chandler to loose slaughter in Mickey Spillane (in the final page of *I, the Jury*, Mike Hammer answers

'It was easy' when his dying, treacherous lover asks him how he could kill her in the middle of making love). Why is this ambiguity, this deceitfulness and corruption of the universe embodied in a woman whose promise of surplus enjoyment conceals mortal danger? What is the precise dimension of this danger? Our answer is that, contrary to appearance, the femme fatale embodies a radical *ethical* attitude, that of 'not ceding one's desire,' of persisting in it to the very end when its true nature as the death drive is revealed. It is the hero who, by rejecting the femme fatale, breaks with his ethical stance.

The woman who 'does not cede her desire'

What precisely is meant here by 'ethics' can be elucidated by reference to the famous Peter Brooks version of Bizet's *Carmen*. That is to say, our thesis is that, by means of the changes he introduced into the original plot, Brooks made Carmen not only a tragic figure but, more radically, an *ethical* figure of the lineage of Antigone. Again, at first it seems that there could be no greater contrast than that between Antigone's dignified sacrifice and the debauchery that leads to Carmen's destruction. Yet the two are connected by the same ethical attitude that we could describe (according to the Lacanian reading of *Antigone*) as an unreserved acceptance of the death drive, as a striving for radical self-annihilation, for what Lacan calls the 'second death' going beyond mere physical destruction, i.e., entailing the effacement of the very symbolic texture of generation and corruption. Brooks was quite justified in making the aria about the 'merciless card' the central musical motif of the entire work: the aria about the card that 'always shows death' (in the third act) designates the precise moment at which Carmen assumes an ethical status, accepting without reserve the imminence of her own death. The cards that, in their chance fall, always predict death, are the 'little piece of the real' to which Carmen's death drive clings. And it is precisely at the moment when Carmen not only becomes aware that she – as a woman marking the fate of the men she encounters – is herself the victim of fate, a plaything in the hands of forces she cannot dominate, but also fully accepts her fate by not ceding her desire that she becomes a 'subject' in the strict Lacanian meaning of this term. For Lacan, a subject is in the last resort the name for this 'empty gesture' by means of which we freely assume what is imposed on us, the real of the death drive. In other words, up until the aria about the 'merciless card,' Carmen was an object for men, her power of fascination depended on the role she played in their fantasy space, she was nothing but their symptom, although she lived under the illusion that she was effectively 'pulling the strings.' When she finally becomes an object *for herself also*, i.e., when she realizes that she is just a passive element in the interplay of libidinal forces, she 'subjectifies' herself, she becomes a 'subject.' From the Lacanian perspective, 'subjectification' is thus strictly correlative to experiencing oneself as an object, a 'helpless victim': it is the name for the gaze by means of which we confront the utter nullity of our narcissistic pretentions.

To prove that Brooks was fully aware of this, it suffices to mention his most ingenious intervention: the radical change of the denouement of the opera. Bizet's original version is well known. In front of the arena in which the toreador Escamillo pursues his victorious fight, Carmen is approached by the desperate Jose who begs her to live with him again. His demand is met with rebuff, and while the song in the background announces another triumph for Escamillo, Jose stabs Carmen to death – the usual drama of a rejected lover who cannot bear his loss. With Brooks, however, things turn out quite differently. Jose resignedly *accepts* Carmen's final rebuff, but as Carmen is walking away from him, the servants bring her the dead Escamillo – he lost the fight, the bull has killed him. It is Carmen who is now broken. She leads Jose to a lonely place near the arena, kneels down and offers herself to him to be stabbed. Is there a denouement more desperate than this? Of course there is: Carmen might have left with Jose, this weakling, and continued to live her miserable everyday life. The 'happy ending,' in other words, would be the most desperate of all.

And it is the same with the figure of the femme fatale in hard-boiled novels and in *film noir*: she who ruins the lives of men and is at the same time victim of her own lust for enjoyment, obsessed by a desire for power, who endlessly manipulates her partners and is at the same time slave to some third, ambiguous person, sometimes even an impotent or sexually ambivalent man. What bestows on her an aura of mystery is precisely the way she cannot be clearly located in the opposition between master and slave. At the moment she seems permeated with intense pleasure, it suddenly becomes apparent that she suffers immensely; when she seems to be the victim of some horrible and unspeakable violence, it suddenly becomes clear that she enjoys it. We can never be quite sure if she enjoys or suffers, if she manipulates or is herself the victim of manipulation. It is this that produces the deeply ambiguous character of those moments in the *film noir* (or in the hard-boiled detective novel) when the femme fatale breaks down, loses her powers of manipulation, and becomes the victim of her own game. Let us just mention the first model of such a breakdown, the final confrontation between Sam Spade and Brigid O'Shaughnessy in *The Maltese Falcon*. As she begins to lose

her grasp of the situation, Brigid suffers a hysterical breakdown; she
passes immediately from one strategy to another. She first threatens,
then she cries and maintains that she did not know what was really
happening to her, then suddenly she assumes again an attitude of cold
distance and disdain, and so on. In short, she unfolds a whole fan of
inconsistent hysterical masks. This moment of the final breakdown of
the femme fatale – who now appears as an entity without substance,
a series of inconsistent masks without a coherent ethical attitude –
this moment when her power of fascination evaporates and leaves
us with feelings of nausea and disgust, this moment when we see
'nought but shadows of what is not' where previously we saw clear
and distinct form exerting tremendous powers of seduction, this
moment of reversal is at the same time the moment of triumph for the
hard-boiled detective. Now, when the fascinating figure of the femme
fatale disintegrates into an inconsistent bric-a-brac of hysterical masks,
he is finally capable of gaining a kind of distance toward her and of
rejecting her.

The destiny of the femme fatale in *film noir*, her final hysterical
breakdown, exemplifies perfectly the Lacanian proposition that 'Woman
does not exist': she is nothing but 'the symptom of man,' her power
of fascination masks the void of her nonexistence, so that when she
is finally rejected, her whole ontological consistency is dissolved.
But precisely as nonexisting, i.e., at the moment at which, through
hysterical breakdown, she *assumes* her nonexistence, she constitutes
herself as 'subject': what is waiting for her *beyond* hysterization is the
death drive in its purest. In feminist writings on *film noir* we often
encounter the thesis that the femme fatale presents a mortal threat to
man (the hard-boiled detective), i.e., that her boundless enjoyment
menaces his very identity as subject: by rejecting her at the end, he
regains his sense of personal integrity and identity. This thesis is
true, but in a sense that is the exact opposite of the way it is usually
understood. What is so menacing about the femme fatale is not
the boundless enjoyment that overwhelms the man and makes him
woman's plaything or slave. It is not Woman as object of fascination
that causes us to lose our sense of judgment and moral attitude but, on
the contrary, that which remains hidden beneath this fascinating mask
and which appears once the masks fall off: the dimension of the pure
subject fully assuming the death drive. To use Kantian terminology,
woman is not a threat to man insofar as she embodies pathological
enjoyment, insofar as she enters the frame of a particular fantasy. The
real dimension of the threat is revealed when we 'traverse' the fantasy,
when the coordinates of the fantasy space are lost via hysterical
breakdown. In other words, what is really menacing about the femme
fatale is not that she is fatal for *men* but that she presents a case of

a 'pure,' nonpathological subject fully assuming *her own* fate. When
the woman reaches this point, there are only two attitudes left to the
man: either he 'cedes his desire,' rejects her and regains his imaginary,
narcissistic identity (Sam Spade at the end of *The Maltese Falcon*), or he
identifies with the woman as symptom and meets his fate in a suicidal
gesture (the act of Robert Mitchum in what is perhaps the crucial *film
noir*, Jacques Tourneur's *Out of the Past*).[15]

Notes

1. It is needless to add that attempts at a pseudo-'dialectical' synthesis
    conceiving the figure of the detective as the contradictory fusion of
    bourgeois rationality and its reverse, irrational intuition, fare no better: both
    sides together fail to procure what each of them lacks.

2. FREUD, *The Interpretation of Dreams*, SE IV 277–8.

3. JACQUES-ALAIN MILLER, 'Action de la structure', in *Cahiers pour l'Analyse*, **9**
    (Paris: Graphe, 1968), pp. 96–7.

4. RICHARD ALEWYN, 'Anatomie des Detektivromans', in Jochen Vogt (ed), *Der
    Kriminalroman* (Munich: UTB-Verlag, 1971), vol. 2, p. 35.

5. FREUD, *The Interpretation of Dreams*, SE IV 104.

6. VICTOR SHKLOVSKY, 'Die Kriminalerzaehlung bei Conan Doyle', in Vogt (ed),
    Der Kriminalroman vol. 1, p. 84.

7. It is on the basis of this structural necessity of the false solution that
    we can explain the role of one of the standard figures of the classical
    detective story: the detective's naive, everyday companion who is usually
    also the narrator (Holmes's Watson, Poirot's Hastings, etc.). In one of
    AGATHA CHRISTIE's novels, Hastings asks Poirot of what use he is to him
    in his work of detection, insofar as he is just an ordinary, average person,
    full of everyday prejudices. Poirot answers that he needs Hastings *precisely
    on that account*, i.e., precisely because he is an ordinary man who embodies
    what we could call the field of *doxa*, spontaneous common opinion. That
    is to say, after accomplishing his crime, the murderer must efface its traces
    by composing an image that conceals its true motive and points toward a
    false culprit (a classical topos: the murder is accomplished by a victim's
    close relative who arranges things to give the impression that the act was
    performed by a burglar surprised by the unexpected arrival of the victim).
    Whom, precisely, does the murderer want to deceive by means of this false
    scene? What is the 'reasoning' of the murderer when he stages the false
    scene? It is of course the very field of *doxa*, of 'common opinion' embodied
    in the detective's faithful companion. Consequently, the detective does not
    need his Watson in order to point out the contrast between his dazzling
    perspicacity and the companion's ordinary humanity; instead Watson, with
    his commonsense reactions, is necessary in order to exhibit in the clearest

possible way the effect that the murderer intended to produce by his staging of a false scene.

8. MILLER, 'Action de la structure', p. 96.

9. LACAN, *The Four Fundamental Concepts of Psycho-Analysis*, pp. 139–40 (the quotation is, of course, slightly changed to suit our purposes).

10. Which is why the 'retired colourman' in one of the late Sherlock Holmes stories, although ingenious enough, does not really take advantage of all the ruses of deception proper to the order of the signifier. This old official, whose wife was missing and presumed to have escaped with a young lover, suddenly started to repaint his house – why? In order that the strong smell of fresh paint would prevent the visitors from detecting another smell, that of the decaying bodies of his wife and her lover whom he killed and hid in the house. An even more ingenious deception would have been to paint the walls in order to provoke the impression that the smell of paint is meant to cover up another smell, i.e., to provoke the impression that we are hiding something, while in reality there is nothing to hide.

11. Apropos of the 'subject supposed to know', it is absolutely crucial to grasp this link between knowledge and the stupid, senseless *presence* of the subject embodying it. The 'subject supposed to know' is someone who, *by his mere presence*, guarantees that the chaos will acquire meaning, i.e., that 'there is a method in this madness.' Which is why the title of HAL ASHBY's film about the effects of transference, *Being There*, is thoroughly adequate: it is enough for the poor gardener Chance, played by Peter Sellers, to find himself – by means of a purely contingent misapprehension – at a certain place, to occupy the place of transference for the others, and already he operates as the wise 'Chauncey Gardener.' His stupid phrases, scraps of his gardening experience and of what he remembers from watching TV incessantly, are all of a sudden supposed to contain another, metaphorical, 'deeper' meaning. His childish utterances about how to take care of a garden in winter and spring, for example, are read as profound allusions to the thawing of relations between the superpowers. Those critics who saw in the film a eulogy of the simple man's commonsense, its triumph over the artificiality of experts, were totally wrong. In this respect, the film is definitely not spoiled by any compromise, Chance is depicted as completely and painfully idiotic, the whole effect of his 'wisdom' results from his 'being there' at the place of transference. Even though the American psychoanalytical establishment has been unable to swallow Lacan, Hollywood, happily, has been more accommodating.

12. AGATHA CHRISTIE's *Murder on the Orient Express* confirms this by way of an ingenious exception: here, the murder is accomplished by the entire group of suspects, and it is precisely for this reason that they cannot be guilty, so the paradoxical although necessary outcome is that *the culprit coincides with the victim*, i.e., the murder proves to be a well-deserved punishment.

13. JACQUES LACAN, *The Ego in Freud's Theory and in the Technique of Psychoanalysis* (New York: Norton, 1988), p. 204.

14. We have of course left out of consideration the extremely interesting rise of the postwar 'crime novel', which shifts the attention from the detective (either as the 'subject supposed to know' or as the first-person narrator) to the victim (Boileau-Narcejac) or the culprit (Patricia Highsmith,

Ruth Rendell). The necessary consequence of this shift is that the entire temporal structure of the narrative is changed. The story is presented in the 'usual' linear way, with the accent placed on what goes on *before* the crime, i.e., we are no longer concerned with the *aftermath* of crime and with attempts to reconstruct the course of events leading up to it. In BOILEAU-NARCEJAC's novels (*Les Diaboliques*, for example), the story is usually told from the perspective of the future victim, a woman to whom strange things seem to happen, foreboding a horrible crime, though we are not sure until the final denouement if all this is true or just her hallucination. On the other hand, PATRICIA HIGHSMITH depicts the whole diversity of contingencies and psychological impasses that could induce an apparently 'normal' person to commit a murder. Even in her first novel, *Strangers on a Train*, she established her elementary matrix: that of a transferential relationship between a psychotic murderer capable of performing the act and a hysteric who organizes his desire by means of a reference to the psychotic, i.e., who literally *desires by proxy* (no wonder Hitchcock recognized immediately the affinity between this matrix and his motif of the 'transference of guilt'). Incidentally, an interesting case in respect to this opposition between the 'victim' novel and the 'culprit' novel is MARGARET MILLAR's masterpiece *Beast in View*, in which the two coincide: the culprit turns out to be the victim of the crime itself, a pathologically split personality.

15. The fact that this is a matter of a postfantasy 'purification' of desire is attested by an ingenious detail: in the final scene, the wardrobe of Jane Greer unmistakably resembles that of a nun.

5 The Melancholy Persuasion*

ANITA SOKOLSKY

Anita Sokolsky's reading of Jane Austen's *Persuasion* draws on Freud's study of melancholia and on Klein's concept of the 'depressive position', so a brief introduction to these theories may be helpful. In 'Mourning and Melancholia' (1917), Freud argues that the ego identifies itself with its beloved objects in order to preserve them from extinction. This process of identification originates in infantile fantasies of cannibalism, in which the subject strives to take possession of the object by devouring it. In normal circumstances, the ego gradually 'decathects' or disentangles its investments from the object; but in states of melancholia, the incorporated object overwhelms the ego from within. As Freud puts it, 'the shadow of the object [falls] over the ego', and the ego moves towards death, annihilated by the very object it was striving to preserve (SE XIV 249). Thus the endless self-recriminations of the melancholic really represent attacks against the object instated at the core of subjectivity (SE XIV 243–58). Julia Kristeva examines these inversions:

'I love that object,' is what the person seems to say about the lost object, 'but even more so I hate it; because I love it, and in order not to lose it, I imbed it in myself; but because I hate it, that other within myself is a bad self, I am bad, I am non-existent, I shall kill myself.' The complaint against oneself would therefore be a complaint against another, and putting oneself to death but a tragic disguise for massacring an other.

(*Black Sun*, p. 11)

Melanie Klein takes Freud's theory of cannibalism further, arguing that the ego engorges all the objects of its outer world in order to install them in the 'inner world' of fantasy.† The infant's

---

*Anita Sokolsky's essay 'The Melancholy Persuasion', is published for the first time in this volume. © 1994, Anita Sokolsky.

first object is not the mother but the breast, which is itself divided into two opposing fantasies: the good breast, idealised as all-giving; and the bad breast, its withholding counterpart. This primordial relationship to objects is described by Klein as the 'paranoid–schizoid position', since it is characterised by splitting, which is schizoid, and also by the paranoid delusion that the persecuting object will invade the ego, annihilating both the ideal object and the self. The paranoid–schizoid position is superseded by the 'depressive position', in which the infant comes to recognise the mother as a whole person, rather than a bric-à-brac of breast, hands, voice, mouth, gaze. At this point paranoia gives way to melancholia: for the infant is obliged to sacrifice the ideal object, along with its avenging counterpart, having learnt that good and evil are inextricable from one another and embedded in his own divided heart. Thus melancholy in Klein is 'not a luxurious debility, but a hypothetically constitutive moment in the development of identity' (below, p. 130). With Freud's and Klein's accounts of melancholy in the background, Sokolsky shows how Austen's *Persuasion* revels in melancholy at the same time that it consoles the reader with the spectacle of the dejected heroine's recovery. The heroine Anne Elliot, Sokolsky hints, is more in love with loss itself than with the lover she rebuffed before the book begins; and thus she has to be 'persuaded' to abandon the loss that she has nurtured so as to accept a substitute instead, in the resurrected form of Captain Wentworth.

I

Melancholy seems to harbor a revulsion against narrative: there is nothing more to say, or no point in trying to say it. The great loss or grief the melancholic has suffered cannot be eased by rehearsing it. All efforts to persuade one that anything but an irredeemably lost past matters are regarded with wonder or disdain. The only audience who counts – the one whose loss has precipitated the melancholy – cannot or will not hear the protest that without it is not worth mounting. That audience may be a loved one, a class, an historical moment, or a fantasied and amorphous identity. But the renunciation

---

†See KLEIN, 'Mourning and its Relation to Manic-Depressive States' (1940), in *Love, Guilt, and Reparation and Other Works 1921–1945*, intr. R.E. Money-Kyrle (New York: Delta, 1977), pp. 345–6. For a lucid exposition of Klein's theories, see HANNA SEGAL, *Introduction to the Work of Melanie Klein* (New York: Basic Books, 1974).

its disappearance entails will take a similar form: a dispirited and intransigent clamping of the lips in the conviction that to recount one's loss would be to vitiate or disperse it.

The melancholic thus claims the prestige of an affliction which cannot be meliorated, which prides itself on the superiority of its causes to its treatment. But it is not just that the affliction cannot be meliorated, but that on some level the melancholic cannot be persuaded that he or she *is* afflicted. The disconsolate and preoccupied mood that amounts at times to a kind of indolent stupor conceals an exultant sense that the seemingly vanished object persists. One is mute because preoccupied: occupied in advance, as it were, by the very figure whose loss one seems to mourn. Freudian theory sees melancholy as an attempt to deny an acute sense of privation by introjecting the lost object and deflecting attention to a series of inner dramas that covertly play out its loss.[1] Such theory conceives of melancholy less as an inconsolable mood or affect than as a strategy. Or rather, the inconsolable mood *is* a strategy, a self-protective one: the melancholic refuses to accept a devastating loss even while seeming to grieve for it, sustaining the lost object in inchoate and mobile internal dramas that belie his or her mute and static posture. These are the hidden reserves of melancholy. Because these subterranean narratives are scarcely registered, the melancholic seems indolent, whereas in fact he or she is living on a hectic if inaccessible level. And because melancholy ennui or stupor is variably penetrable by the bewildering and seemingly arbitrary impulses to punish or coddle the lost object, impulses which for the most part seem to have been levelled from elsewhere – as indeed in a sense they have, for the lost object cannot well be distinguished from the melancholic's psyche, in fact subsists in what Freud terms a libidinal cathexis on one's ego – he or she either faithfully claims those virtues and flaws, or remains silent so as to stem the underlying loquacity. Melancholy discourse may be understood as a fantasia on its muteness.

Freud wishes to treat the melancholic by meticulously prying that libidinal cathexis away from the ego and attaching it to the analyst-as-lost-object. One replays and discards painful and ambivalent memories so that the introjected loss is finally acknowledged and mourned. But to reach a point of mourning is arduous; the more so if, as Melanie Klein suggests, melancholy is not a luxurious debility, but a hypothetically constitutive moment in the development of identity.[2] Elaborating a dense, precise and animated set of narrative scenarios within melancholy, Klein argues that from the infant's first awareness of separation, the melancholy dynamic is touched off. Drawing on Klein's account, Julia Kristeva posits a primordial sense of loss that precedes individuation and the notion of a lost object.[3] That primordial

loss of the 'thing' spurs a radical suspicion of signifying, for to enter
into the symbolic order one must at least trust that language can
express a gap between oneself and another. Unable to believe even in
that gap, the melancholic conveys mistrust both by muteness and by
charged forays into language.

Out of the melancholic's impulse to seal over a crucial break in his or
her personal history derive the intricate narratives which nonetheless
figure that rupture. Entrenched in baroque but repetitive psychic
configurations, these narratives do not evolve in a progressive way.
They are wayward, both in their movement and in their resistance to
interpretation. Rapt at their inaccessibility, the melancholic takes care
that they remain so: not solely to fend off the pain of loss and the
threat to one's sense of self that would presumably accompany any
efforts to recognize the sources of one's melancholy, but because, given
the indissoluble complexities of identifying with the lost object, the
melancholic is in some sense never recognizably at the heart of his or
her own fantasies. Were those fantasies to be distinguishable as such,
they would yield a shameful confusion at the point of revelation; or,
more neutrally and perhaps distressingly, they would be beside the
point, anachronistic.

Literary representations of melancholy – and for Kristeva all literary
representations have a melancholy aspect – are thus multiply vexed.
A fantasy based on fantasies defined by their unrepresentability, their
narrative entrenchment, their suspicion of signifying, literary melancholy
strains the limits of narrative credibility, emerging not simply in a
character's depressive affect, but also in more fleeting and stylized forms
of narrative disaffection. Jane Austen's *Persuasion* is a compelling instance
of the ways in which these issues configure when a novel undertakes to
treat *of* melancholy so as to treat melancholy: both its heroine's dolor and
that of the reader who turns to Austen for the consolations of gratified
fantasy in the name of rational persuasion. If the novel seems to be
invested in the meliatory effects of persuasion, even while recognizing
its potential dangers, this investment conflicts with the intransigence of
a structure of melancholy that remains devoted to an unacknowledged
narrative rupture. In undertaking to treat melancholy, the novel comes
to grips with certain narrative dilemmas which turn on the attempt
to regulate fantasy, to limit the effects of shame arising out of the
emergence of fantasies, and to make of reading a therapeutic act. In
what follows I will sketch out some of the narrative consequences that
emerge from these disruptive relations in the course of the novel.

*   *   *

For a writer disposed to indulge the gratification of fantasy, Jane
Austen systematically deprives a reader of such gratification throughout

the first half of *Persuasion*. The novel substitutes instead a series
of exquisite mortifications for its heroine, Anne Elliot, as if bent on
unleashing the vindictiveness of the critical faculty toward its previous
submission to its own prior fantasies. The persistent devaluation of
Anne Elliot by family, friends, and former lover appears otherwise as a
gratuitous narrative cruelty toward a character who ought, by virtue of
her status, gifts, and sensibility, to have everything. Fated repeatedly
to endure the insufferable, the morally circumspect Anne makes this
her metier, if by the insufferable we understand that indignity in
relation to which one moralizes one's suffering.

The first part of *Persuasion* mortifies not only its heroine, but
the reader's appetite for upscale identification. Anne Elliot is the
second daughter of a vain and foolish baronet. Her mother, a
woman of superior precepts whose only lapse of insight was to
have been briefly smitten with her husband, died when Anne was
fourteen. Sandwiched between a haughty elder sister, Elizabeth,
and a querulous younger sister, Mary, Anne has no confidante
but her mother's oldest friend, Lady Russell. At nineteen Anne
falls in love with a Captain Frederick Wentworth, whose ardent
confidence in his maritime future is not shared by Anne's father nor
by Lady Russell. Anne submits to Lady Russell's persuasions and
breaks the engagement. For the next eight years she goes into a
melancholy decline. In 1814, at the apparent end of the Napoleonic
Wars, Captain Wentworth returns to the area, having earned a fortune.
He is looking for a wife, and flirts with a Miss Louisa Musgrove,
whose determined temper he praises. His manner towards Anne
is distant; she endures exquisite torments in his company. Her
situation only begins to improve after a visit to the seaside town of
Lyme, where for the first time she is distinguished by the admiring
glances of an unknown gentleman. The visit ends in turmoil when
Louisa demands to be jumped down a flight of stone steps by
Captain Wentworth and, leaping a half-second too soon, falls nerveless
on the stone.

Faced with a rupture to her personal narrative, a rupture signified
by her mother's premature death and restaged in her lover's loss,
Anne refuses to accept its consequences while seeming to have
done so. Prematurely withered in her expectations as in her person,
Anne will not make claims for herself, will not market her griefs.
But this deprecatory stance arises from a sense of exclusivity that
makes her own social exclusion a point of pride. The melancholy that
distinguishes Anne in the first part of the novel derives partly from
the isolation of being a rare bit of psychic goods. Her refinement of
sensibility, her capacity for exquisite sensation, the tenacity of her
attachments, all price her out of the emotional market. No one can

value her properly. Her susceptibility to mortification testifies to
the lack of recognition from which her delicate constitution is also
mortified; she is fading and faded from too little regard. Even the
loving appraisal of her mother, now withdrawn, derives a melancholy
tinge from having been always marked by withdrawal; Anne's
tendency to melancholy emerges in reaction to the death of a mother
whose attachment to her home and daughters had, terribly, made
it 'no small matter of indifference to her to leave this life.'[4] To have
been raised by a mother, however attentive, whose attachments
have the character of compensations and whose domestic life has
at its basis the suppression of acute mortification at the buffoonish
self-aggrandizement of a vain and incompetent husband, so that her
suppressed contempt becomes the sign of that mortification – that is
surely grounds for the daughter's melancholy predilection. Lady Elliot's
premature death suggests, for Anne, that mortification can be deadly.
Yet Anne's early renunciation of Frederick Wentworth testifies to
mortification's allure, the allure of a loyal and hopeless affection that
equates attention humiliating both in itself and in its preciousness with
a reassuringly familiar and humiliating failure to be perceived. If it is
Anne's exquisite sensibility that makes her susceptible to mortification –
the refined palate has a morbid taste even for this, if the thrill be acute
enough – the sense of shame to which such mortifications expose her is
of a kind to shore up the system of outrages to which she is subjected.
Anne moralizes her submission to the insufferable as a means to
preserve a structure of melancholy in whose name she is willing
to accommodate, even perhaps to provoke, the sorts of outrage to
sensibility at whose portrayal Austen excels. Mortification thus becomes
a privileged effect of melancholy.

Yet, despite Anne's seemingly intransigent attachment to the
melancholy economy, the novel as a whole seems to be invested in a
system of melioration whose name is persuasion. While Anne's delicate
and highly trained sensibility predisposes her towards melancholy,
her educable nature also prompts her to overcome it. Even when her
condition seems most abject – when, exiled to Uppercross, she must
endure her peripherality amongst her sister Mary's relations and, most
especially, to her former lover – still, she cannot help trying to make
something of her worsening circumstances, in a compulsive interpretive
effort more desperate than her dutiful 'struggles with lowness.'
Only after she has been stripped of the illusions that sustained her
melancholy torpor – that she might live out her life at its familiar
source, without having to face the pain of anything new, or that she
might imagine Frederick to have esteemed her motives for rejecting
him – is she finally forced to an unextenuated vision of her object
losses. She ruefully recognizes that she has compulsively hoarded her

meager comforts so as to snatch solace even from her abandonment; but, while striving to transcend melancholy, she has managed only to prop it.

As if to dispel an intuition of this dilemma, Anne takes increasing risks to put melancholy behind her. Roused by the astringent claims of Lyme, she relinquishes the comforts of spinsterish obscurity for the hazards of a partially restored visibility, both when she eases Captain Benwick's grief over the lost Fanny Harville by taking on the role of substitute object, and when she submits to the passing admiration of the as-yet-unknown William Elliot, heir to Sir Walter's baronetcy. In a world where even the slightest change in decorum can be seen as a means of going for broke, her scarcely perceptible attempts to elude abandonment both to and within melancholy themselves seem almost abandoned. Louisa's fall providentially justifies Anne's gamble, prompting her to take the further risk of revealing her indispensability (previously hidden by her low-key usefulness – a spinster's trick), so that others will perceive and acknowledge their dependence on her. In living up to the crisis (and the melancholy temper, which battens on a crisis denied, is trained to live up to, and in a sense to live it up in, a crisis), Anne makes of Louisa's fall a crisis for her own melancholy situation. For not only might Anne recoup her losses should her oppressively high-spirited rival be removed, but she also seizes on the catastrophe as a means to escape her melancholy fatalism. By interpreting Louisa's fall to be a consequence of her obstinate temperament, not merely an accident of split-second timing, Anne shifts from a fatalistic sense that circumstances are working to thwart her to a more enterprising notion that one makes one's fate.

Thus, by the time Anne accompanies Lady Russell, albeit reluctantly, to Bath, the long-suffering heroine's fortunes have begun to reverse, as if by virtue of her readiness for them to do so. Her qualities, so neglected and abused in the first half of the novel, grant her a modest celebrity in the second. This is not to say that her mortifications have stopped, but they have changed in character; for the most part, they have become a form of charm, a means to forestall potentially harsh judgement by allowing her to recognize and blush for her flaws in advance. Her consciously correct manners, while still the mark of a shame-ridden vigilance, no longer have the effect of making Anne invisible, as the melancholy economy necessitated; instead, they mark the significant rarity of disposition and sensibility that everyone in Bath seems to take pleasure in having discovered. Mortification was for her initially a device by which one's own obscurity became a displaced mark of the melancholic's disavowal of an introjected loss; she deftly turns it into a device whereby one charmingly flaunts and mocks one's own and others' complicity in that melancholy deception. Anne proceeds in her own peculiar fashion to take her fate into her own hands by making melancholy a source of charismatic intrigue even while she moralizes its disinterestedness. *A propos* of the inconsolable Benwick's rash engagement to Louisa, Anne declares to the bemused Captain Harville, brother of the late Fanny, that 'All the privilege I claim for my sex (it is not a very enviable one, you need not covet it) is that of loving longest, when existence or when hope is gone' (p. 222) – a declaration made within earshot of the twice-shy Frederick as a strange, if unwitting, goad to his scribbled outburst of passion ('I can listen no longer in silence' [p. 223]). By identifying her own melancholy predilections with the 'privilege' of her sex – a privilege which makes her both more exalted and more accessible to the eavesdropping Frederick ('Too good, too excellent creature!' he exclaims in his hasty missive [p. 224]) – Anne puts melancholy to work as a form of persuasion and even of seduction wielded against itself.

By the end of the novel Anne appears to have shed melancholy; her lover has gently induced her to renounce the unenviable privilege of her sex. The confluence of ardor, judgement, sensibility, and the binding gratitude of both parties at having been granted a second chance promises a marriage rarer and more structurally enduring than any of Austen's previous happy endings. Not only Anne's own happiness, but the little lingering grin a reader – at least this sort of reader – finds on her face as she reads the ending, the grin of one abashed because fantasy has been so liberally gratified in a way rarely indulged except in one's most exalted reveries, testify to the success of the novel's meliatory powers. And yet that grin is the sort one doesn't want anyone to see; it reveals a shame-inducing shamelessness, a furtive consciousness of the performative quality of one's fantasy identification, that ropes one back into the queasy and coercive dynamic by which such narrative gratification requires the reader to conspire to dissimulate its melancholy sources. That uneasy consciousness registers a sense that the melancholy that Anne seemed to have vanquished nonetheless persists in displaced textual effects. Whether or not Frederick Wentworth is in fact a sufficient replacement for the loss he fills, the narrative as a whole seems tenaciously to sustain its own unenviable privilege of clinging faithfully to loss.

It does so by generating, as it were on Anne's behalf, what would look like a series of melancholy intrapsychic maneuvers, were they not situated outside her: as if, mimicking a psyche and adopting a narrative role at times almost indistinguishable from Anne's, the text accomplished her compensatory fantasies for her, through certain narrative effects. One such effect emerges in the very scene that seemed to offer a break in the heroine's own melancholy: the fall of Louisa Musgrove, the most sensational moment of physical violence in

Austen's work and *Persuasion*'s turning point, and one that precipitates
a disruption in the melancholy economy which, while looking like
its doom, presses it instead into a new and more ungovernable
mode. With Dantean precision the headstrong young woman's head
is permanently weakened; once fearless and determined, on her
recovery Louisa is timid and easily alarmed, possessed of a newfound
tenderness. The moment of narrative violence coincides with a carefully
dissimulated vindictiveness on the part of its heroine – a vindictiveness
that would seem out of character for her, were it not a familiar
feature of the unconscious recriminations chronically levelled by the
melancholic against herself. Soon after the catastrophe, as she rides
along in a coach next to the apparently bereft Captain Wentworth,
Anne reflects that he will perhaps realize from this contretemps the
folly of encouraging an obstinate, unpersuadable temper. Lest we
may have missed this message, Austen with uncharacteristic callous
appropriateness delivers it on the spot.

> 'Don't talk of it, don't talk of it,' he cried. 'Oh God! that I had not
> given way to her at the fatal moment! Had I done as I ought! But so
> eager and so resolute! Dear, sweet Louisa!'
>
> Anne wondered whether it ever occurred to him now, to question
> the justness of his own previous opinion as to the universal felicity
> and advantage of firmness of character; and whether it might not
> strike him, that, like all other qualities of the mind, it should have
> its proportions and limits. She thought it could scarcely escape him
> to feel, that a persuadable temper might sometimes be as much in
> favour of happiness, as a very resolute character. (p. 113)

This moralizing reflection has a drop of acid, a hint of triumph over
a fallen rival unlike the circumspect Anne, yet to be indulged, we
are led to feel, because, having endured insufferable comparison
to the lively Louisa, Anne by her hardheaded reflection shifts that
mortification onto Louisa's senseless body, which may be dying of
a lesson in humiliation. The presumption that the consequences of
Louisa's shameless, ingenuous pleasure in asserting her will should be
near-death and indeterminate injury is precisely *not* shocking because
the price of disavowal within a melancholy economy is high: in order
for the incident to be divested of a trace of fantasy gratification, for
the retributory passing on of mortification to be justified, for the
melancholic to begin to savor revenge as if it were some sort of cure,
there must be a lofty inattention to, or redirection of attention from,
these proceedings.

The narrative's dissimulation of the heightened activity at work in
the melancholy economy, an activity marked by characters' shifting

allegiances – the sort of mutual recriminations, endorsements, punishments and protectiveness that mark the melancholic's transactions with the introjected object – further emerges in the range of indulgent to savage irony directed at those who are incapable of change, of being anything but – and therefore caricatures of – themselves. The measure of the narrative need to display a careful negligence to this procedure is the uncanny reverberation of Anne's reflections when they are slightly 'off' with those of the narrative itself. Anne's father and sisters are identifiable by humors, their desires as limited as their tempers. The rigid alignments within the Elliot family, according to which each daughter is seemingly susceptible to only one parent's influence – Anne to her mother's, Elizabeth and, in a more tempered form, Mary, to their father's – diverts attention from the more fluid dynamics by which Mary's peevishness and hypochondria, Elizabeth's imperiousness and disdain, may be seen as melancholic reactions to their mother's withdrawals, of which her death is presumably the most final. Mary's peevishness might act out her mother's determinedly suppressed sense of ill-use; Elizabeth's hauteur might as easily mimic her mother's withheld contempt for her husband's unworthiness as her father's vanity. The splitting and hypostatization of qualities may be understood as forms of melancholy identification by which the narrative, in a preemptively melancholic gesture of its own, supplants Sir Walter's obsession with aristocratic heritage by an aristocracy of sensibility that carries its own code of valuable non-recognition as to the clamorous and unglamorous claims of those aspirants whom one does not even deign to vie with. Anne is barred by a highminded sense of the noblesse her melancholic isolation imposes from seizing on this spiritual aristocracy to explain her triumph in effectively routing her relations, particularly her father and Elizabeth. Hence she must fall back on gratitude and tenderness toward her beloved to express her unbudgeable sense of non-reliance on them: after her engagement, she 'had no other alloy to the happiness of her prospects than what arose from the consciousness of having no relations to bestow on him which a man of sense could value' (p. 236). She thus perpetuates the melancholy disavowal of mutual implication that sustains the silent and shifting struggle with apparently entrenched positions, and that makes the entry of any seemingly neutral figure into that struggle, a Louisa Musgrove or a William Wentworth or a Mrs. Clay, for example, so dangerous for them and for the narrative.

It is, ironically, the embattled Sir Walter, clinging to a belated aristocracy at a moment when it is threatened both personally and historically, who most clearly gives melancholy an historical resonance in the novel.[5] From the outset, Sir Walter's obsessive rereading of the

Baronetage, and particularly of the paragraph detailing the essentials of his family history, is subjected to barbed appraisal. His mindless admiration for aristocracy; his excessive sense of self-consequence; the near-idiocy of such fantastic resourcelessness, signified by his having inserted 'most accurately' the date of his wife's death into the family paragraph, as if it strained all his faculties to remember and transcribe that event (or as if such scrupulosity marked its negligibility) – all reveal Sir Walter's unworthiness to aspire to the rigors of melancholy. His incuriosity has preserved him from noticing any but the grossest effects or implications of the French Revolution; fourteen years of nearly continuous war, and he grouses at the need to nod and chat to those prematurely aged, ill-complected social inferiors who have been promoted for years of naval service. But if Sir Walter seems incapable of mourning, let alone recognizing, his own anachronistic status, he may be understood to be a melancholic precisely by virtue of his strenuous denial that anything has happened to shake his sense of history: a denial made more impressive by the fact that his still-born son – who presumably could not face the Oedipal stupidity of being his father's heir – died on November 5, 1789, a doubly revolutionary anniversary, memorializing Sir Walter's loss of the entail simultaneous with Guy Fawkes day in the opening year of the French Revolution. Reverting with undiminished ardor to the austere pleasures of the Baronetage, Sir Walter shows himself to be on the order of a conqueror or an historian, who needs no more than the barest marks to trace the lineaments of the past. Like Walter Benjamin's melancholy historian, Sir Walter obliterates any sense of an unbridgeable gap between the present and a prior historical moment, only he does not need to reanimate that past, merely to refer to it. It takes, in other words, a brooding or stuporous stupidity, an *interesting* stupidity, to ignore so utterly the theoretical chasm which separates one from a past that would rock one's otherwise insignificant present. Sir Walter's unswerving and unregenerate anachronism takes on a preemptive authority. If his excessive sense of self-consequence keeps him from seeing the consequences of his extravagances, it also operates as a melancholy shield. We can discern a corresponding, though more subtly suggested, internalization of a melancholy dynamic even in the career of Frederick Wentworth, which focuses the novel's dramatic and historical strategy of attempting to constrain the effects of melancholy, in the interests of articulating the passing of an aristocratic order and the triumph of a meritocratic mercantile power. His ardent prosecution of a career in service of a fervent nationalism is perhaps the novel's central antidote to melancholy quiescence. But the means by which he forges his career oddly mimics the dynamics of melancholy. He earns his way by capturing not only enemy ships but privateers, neutrals willing to trade with the enemy. The liberality with which the British defined privateering and the aggression with which they enforced its suppression tacitly recognized that such trading erodes distinctions between the enemy and one's own side. Melancholy shares some of these characteristics of privateering: the lost figure who commands one's loyalty is at the same time the object of hostility for having abandoned one; the melancholic profits emotionally by trading with this enemy. Frederick is at war both with privateering and with the melancholy that has been his rival for Anne. And yet, in trying to suppress privateering, he in fact perpetuates and even profits by its logic: making his fortune by capturing privateers, who frequently were sanctioned by their own governments, he profits by trade with these enemies. The dangers of making capital out of trade with entrenched positions, the volatilizing of any apparently neutral figure who enters the embattled scenario, the treacherous distinctions that discompose the identification of charged figures – all these features of the melancholy economy play themselves out in the historical register as well.

II

The novel's unease about the struggle between its meliorist and melancholic tendencies culminates in its violent condemnation of William Elliot, the only *outré* factor in the novel's late felicities. Having previously slighted the family and married a wealthy woman of inferior birth instead of his cousin Elizabeth, William Elliot has come a widower to repair the acquaintance. A sensible and refined man, he wins immediate favor. But while Anne respects him, she remains loyal to Frederick despite the temptation Lady Russell raises that Anne might take her mother's place by marrying William, heir to the baronetcy. Through an ailing and impoverished friend, a Mrs. Smith, Anne learns that William had initially despised the current baronet and the baronetcy, and had helped to ruin his friend Smith and refused to aid Smith's wife. William's attentiveness to Sir Walter comes of newly coveting the baronetcy; his courtship of Anne partly cloaks his desire to insinuate himself into the family circle so as to make sure no supervenient heirs are produced.

The plot does not need the revelation of his duplicity – Anne is already determined to marry or be forsaken by Frederick – so something else must need it. William Elliot's most heinous crime is to have reinstigated the very melancholy dynamic he had seemed to help dispel by his admiration of Anne. But this time melancholy emerges as a form of intervention on an historically quiescent narrative. He is unmasked as a Napoleonic figure, who had moved from a decrier to a coveter of aristocracy. Acute at deceit, ambitious and strategic, he denies the historical rupture he represents by validating structures of privilege while delegitimating their capacity to ennoble. He corrodes from within the system of values he embraces. He professionalizes anachronism. His complex system of allegiances and his perilously accurate representation of the refined sensibility embodied by his cousin Anne unleash the treacherous distinctions which expose both such refinement and susceptibility to mortification as symptoms of melancholy quiescence. In effect, he exposes the novel's dissimulation of the intransigence and anachronism of its melancholy structure. Melancholy appears as an absolute resistance to melioration, to the revisability of a symbolic system whose terms it has blasted and simultaneously kept intact.

William Elliot's initial admiring gaze at Anne, which apparently activated her to escape melancholy, accrues retroactively a brazenness that causes her shame at having been seen and measured too acutely. In retrospect that glance sees too much, sees in Anne the potential for a melancholy persistence that her happy fate seems now a means of denying. Thus Anne's acute mortification at William Elliot's contempt for her relatives – a contempt she has long been privy to and shared, so that his articulation of it should come only as the shock of seeing one's secret feelings publicized by someone not apparently privy to them – becomes a means of restoring the quiescence of the melancholy economy, rather than a form of dormant violence. The apparent indolence of a melancholy vision of history, as Walter Benjamin might describe it, becomes instead a volatile intervention on the limits and terms of the historical narrative. Anne Elliot's sense of shame becomes a means to reinvoke and restabilize an account of melancholy that denies historical rupture. But if the novel castigates and suppresses the danger represented by William Elliot, it does so by a narrative gesture as brazen and rhetorically treacherous as his own. For the two crucially dramatic moments of the novel, the fall of Louisa Musgrove and the revelation of William Elliot's treachery, both emerge, not as moments of rhetorical persuasion, but as acts of narrative violence. They violate the gentle exertions of persuasion and retaliate against those who have unwittingly interfered between Anne Elliot and her object with a ruthlessness that exceeds any belief in the meliatory possibilities of persuasion.

The punitive aspect of these apparently regulative dramatic moments – rebuking William's amorous pretensions by unmasking his cultivated viciousness, and chastening Louisa's obduracy by breaking her head – shows how the narrative impulse to gratify a fantasy of unprovoked retaliation mortifies itself in the guise of a disciplinary measure. The narrative is strangely ungracious to its most highly fraught fantasy scenarios; despite the apparently crucial dramatic function they serve, they are presented as if they were in fact unnecessary. Frederick claims that he never loved Louisa, Anne had decided not marry William before she knew of his treacheries or of Frederick's reawakened interest. Yet no villain throughout Austen's work is so contemptible as William, no physical act so violent as Louisa's fall, no proposal so furtive and breathless as Frederick's and no urge to accept so fraught as Anne's. Frederick's snatched proposal, in which the gradual escalation of fantasy gratification in the second half of the novel culminates, by its nerviness seems to convey the danger that the lovers might not claim one another so as to banish the final traces of melancholy; the fact that their mutual trepidation intensifies at a point when every significant obstruction has been swept away represents the narrative's staged but nonetheless potent sense that, while the proposal has taken place successfully in preceding Austen novels, *this time it just might not come off*: the effort in *Persuasion* to subdue the competing claims of the urge to gratify fantasy and the recognition that to do so is to unleash the melancholy dynamic appears too costly. At the same time that these highly-fraught moments discipline the characters who might interfere with the gratification of the heroine's desires, the narrative's denial of their necessity and significance disciplines the luxury of these fantasies, lest their vengeful character emerge too clearly. The stakes are curiously heightened and deflated: deflated from the impulse to suppress the exposed nature of such fantasy, and from a sense that the novel is impatient to divest itself of the need for fantasy regulation altogether. By meticulously marring the ground of its sensational structure, by its very insistence on the plausibility of its machinations, the novel shows the fantasy of discipline to be necessary to the disciplining of fantasy. But the fact that these moments regulate through a luxurious vindictiveness shows not only how difficult it is to distinguish the educative narrative from fantasy, but also how the slipperiness of identifications in these moments – exactly who is punishing and protecting whom, and to what end – reinforces the melancholy dynamic just at the point that it seems to be abolished.

While *Persuasion* sets itself up as a cure for melancholy by engendering a tutelary identification with its heroine and by educating the reader in the vicissitudes of melancholy narrative, the novel mortifies the reader's appetite for such identification by forcing it with a self-effacing heroine whose refusal to set forth her own claims makes her an increasingly elusive source of performative identification. Like the introjected lost object, Anne Elliot tantalizes the reader by her withheld and absorbing refusal to perform. A reproof to the encroaching tendencies of the reader's fantasies, her retiring disposition emphasizes a sense of competing and out-of-synch claims. The increasing rectitude and passivity of Austen's heroines in the course of her career seems to signify their heightened moral sensitivity and complexity, but in fact is the sign of their increasing reluctance to perform the role of fantasy displacement, for other characters but also in effect *as* characters, as if their exasperating willingness to shoulder unenviable tasks were a measure of their recognition of the costs of provoking envy. Thus, it is precisely when Anne appears to take on the role of fantasy displacement, to let her happiness become apparent, in the last stages of the novel, that she appears most attenuated and elusive as a character. Her newfound 'tenderness,' the mark of her delight and the relaxation of her melancholy watchfulness, emerges at the expense of the wry and often acerbic spinsterish vigilance she shared with the narrative voice. Like Louisa's tenderness after her fall, Anne's suggests that she too has been bruised into an even greater delicacy by relinquishing her sardonic acuity as she pitched toward happiness. Prone to 'quick alarm' by any political shift that might signify war and remobilize her husband, easily overcome by newly refined agitations, Anne appears to have been granted a precarious extension so as to be whittled away by apprehensions as to the fragility of her happiness. If her delicacy and tendency toward alarm are the signs of her insufficient inscription in the scene of her pleasure, her 'tenderness' indicates that the effort to revivify a fragile heroine – fragile *as* a heroine – to extricate her from the toils of melancholy by an access of grateful indebtedness, may serve only to strip her of the shield which melancholy provided. It is Anne's exquisite sensibility which makes her, finally, melancholy at the loss of melancholy.

Notes

1. SIGMUND FREUD, 'Mourning and Melancholia' (1917), in *The Standard Edition of the Complete Psychological Works of Sigmund Freud*, vol. 14, ed. James Strachey (London: Hogarth, 1957), pp. 243–58.

2. MELANIE KLEIN, 'The Psychogenesis of Manic-Depressive States' (1935), in *The Selected Melanie Klein*, ed. Juliet Mitchell (New York: Macmillan, 1987).

3. JULIA KRISTEVA, *Black Sun: Depression and Melancholia*, trans. Leon S. Roudiez (New York: Columbia University Press, 1989).

4. JANE AUSTEN, *Persuasion* (Oxford: Oxford University Press, 1990), p. 222. All further references to this edition will be given in the text.

5. This essay is part of a longer study of the role of history and melancholy in *Persuasion*, which examines the novel's relation to the French Revolution and the Napoleonic Wars in greater detail.

6 To the Lighthouse*

Daniel Ferrer

Virginia Woolf first met Freud in London in 1939, after his escape
from Nazi-occupied Vienna, and she remembered in her diary
that he presented her with a narcissus.† However, apart from
this resonant encounter, Woolf was curiously reticent about her
attitudes to psychoanalysis; even though the Hogarth Press, which
she founded with her husband Leonard Woolf, published the
Strachey translations of Freud's work; and even though she
suffered from recurrent bouts of mental illness, which were
treated by the most benighted methods. Perhaps she felt she
had discovered the unconscious on her own, and wanted no
companions in the netherworld. Of her novel *To the Lighthouse*,
she wrote, 'I suppose that I did for myself what psycho-analysts
do for their patients'; specifically, she exorcised her parents' ghosts,
who had haunted her throughout her life.‡ 'I used to think of
[father] & mother daily; but writing The Lighthouse, laid them
in my mind' (*Diary*, vol. 3, p. 208). This novel, with its cameos of
ardent mother and castrating father, has proved all too susceptible
to Freudian interpretation. But Daniel Ferrer argues that the novel's
attack against the father masks a more insidious attack against the
mother, Mrs Ramsay, who in spite of all attempts to murder her,
refuses to be laid to rest. In Lily Briscoe's painting, which epitomises
the ambivalence of mourning, the lost maternal body is resurrected
only to be mutilated: we learn almost nothing of the contents of the
painting, yet we are treated to a lurid recitation of the violence of its
creation. In the following essay, Ferrer argues that for Woolf, 'art is
not only a discharge of aggressivity, but simultaneously an attempt

---

*Daniel Ferrer, '*To the Lighthouse*', in *Virginia Woolf and the Madness of
Language*, trans. Geoffrey Bennington and Rachel Bowlby (London: Routledge,
1990) pp. 40–64; 157–63. © 1990 Daniel Ferrer, Geoffrey Bennington and
Rachel Bowlby.
†*The Diary of Virginia Woolf*, ed. Anne Olivier Bell with Andrew McNeillie
(Harmondsworth: Penguin, 1985), vol. 5, p. 202 (29 January 1939).
‡Woolf, *Moments of Being*, ed. Jeanne Schulkind (New York: Harcourt
Brace Jovanovich, 1985), p. 81.

at reparation, a will to fill in an empty space, to close the wounds opened in the maternal body' (below, p. 156).

The multitudinous mother

[The residual hallucination of *To the Lighthouse*. The subject: from madman to artist. The object: Mrs Ramsay, the Mother. Ambivalences. Biographical excursus. Death underlying. The Mother behind the Father. Painting and the return to archaic depths. Submersion, absorption, and anorexia. Art as combat. Art as compromise?]

Compared with the initial project formulated in the diary, the place occupied by Septimus in *Mrs Dalloway* was significantly reduced, even if his role remains crucial. Virginia Woolf even wondered whether the book would not have benefited from his absence: 'I am driving my way through the mad chapters of *Mrs Dalloway*. My wonder is whether the book would have been better without them. But this is an afterthought, consequent upon learning how to deal with her' (D. II: 321). Clarissa, instead of doubling him, threatens to absorb the character of Septimus. The apparent revelation of the preface is indeed an 'afterthought' projected on to the origin.

To the Lighthouse does without a 'mad' character of this kind, always threatening to particularize the problem by localizing madness, even if, as we have seen, this localization is constantly overrun. And yet hallucination is present in *To the Lighthouse*, if only on a single and unobtrusive occasion. It may be noted immediately that Lily Briscoe, who takes Septimus's place as subject of the hallucination, is an artist,[1] and that the hallucination happens during the composition of a work. Lily Briscoe, deep in reflection on the problems of her art (painting),[2] is contemplating, brush in hand, the subject she is trying to represent – a piece of wall, a window, a hedge, a tree – when something happens:

> Some wave of white went over the window pane. The air must have stirred some flounce in the room. Her heart leapt at her and seized her and tortured her.
> 'Mrs Ramsay! Mrs Ramsay!' she cried, feeling the old horror come back – to want and want and not to have. Could she inflict that still? And then, quietly, as if she refrained, that too became part of ordinary experience, was on a level with the chair, with the table. Mrs. Ramsay – it was part of her perfect goodness – sat there quite simply, in the chair, flicked her needles to and fro and knitted

her reddish-brown stocking, cast her shadow on the step. There
she sat.

(TL: 300)

Mrs Ramsay, dead for several years, has returned to the very place
where she was sitting ten years before, when Lily had made a first
attempt at painting the same subject. It is immediately apparent that
hallucination takes place within reality, on the same footing ('on a level
with the chair, with the table'); that it does not come to satisfy a desire
('to want and want and not to have'); that it is not accompanied by
pleasure – on the contrary, there is torture and 'horror'. This horror
is not provoked by the strangeness of the hallucinatory phenomenon,
since it has to do with an '*old* horror come *back*'. Who is the character
whose return is capable of producing so powerful an impression? Who
is Mrs Ramsay?

This time there is no possible ambiguity: Mrs Ramsay is defined
above all as a mother. She has eight children and enjoys playing a
maternal role for all those around her (including those of her guests
who do not like her, and whom she obstinately tries to mother whether
they like it or not), to the extent that another mother accuses her of
wanting to steal her daughter's affection (TL: 88). Lily Briscoe, who
lives alone with her father, is especially the object of this solicitude.
On a symbolic level, it is very clear that Mrs Ramsay embodies the
mythical universal mother, the fertile feeding element (whence her
caricatural obsession with the delivery of milk, her recriminations
against what she calls 'the iniquity of the English dairy system'
(TL: 155)).

It is generally agreed that this extremely appealing character is the
most seductive of all those created by Virginia Woolf. For a long time
after the appearance of *To the Lighthouse*, all those who studied the
novel sang the praises of Mrs Ramsay. The most recent criticism, on
the other hand, takes pleasure in emphasizing her faults. For the novel
clearly expresses a certain number of reproaches (for example: 'wishing
to dominate, wishing to interfere, making people do what she wished
– that was the charge against her' (TL: 88)). Her very seductiveness has
something sinister about it: 'There was something frightening about
her. She was irresistible. Always she got her own way at the end, Lily
thought' (TL: 152).

Now Virginia Woolf never hid the fact that she had conceived the
character of Mrs Ramsay in the image of her own mother – and indeed
it is for this reason that it was long considered that this character could
only be entirely positive. If we are to believe Vanessa, the depiction
is extremely lifelike: 'She says it is an amazing portrait of mother; a
supreme portrait painter; has lived in it; found the raising of the dead

almost painful' (WD: 107).[3] It seems difficult, then, to avoid another detour through biography, to present what is known of the relations between Virginia Woolf and her own mother.

It is generally thought that for her daughter Julia Stephen was, in Jean Guignet's words, 'a being loved without reservations or division'.[4] Yet if we look closely at the autobiographical writings, we realize that her attitude is, on the contrary, extremely divided: to put it mildly, she expresses some reservations (for example, MB: 42).

Woolf's first crisis of madness and first suicide attempt followed closely on the death of her mother, and it is generally considered that they were provoked by the shock of losing an object too much loved.[5] A passage from the diary shows that things were not so simple: 'Remember turning aside at mother's bed, when she had died, and Stella took us in, to laugh, secretly at the nurse crying. She's pretending, I said, aged thirteen, and was afraid I was not feeling enough' (MB: 42). This recalls Septimus ('the panic was on him – that he could not feel' (MD, 96)) and his indifference in the face of Evans's death. In both cases, it is clear that the surface indifference masks a considerable quantity of investments and is the result of a conflict of opposing feelings (well represented in *The Years* by the contradictory reactions of Milly and Delia at the time of their mother's death).

This mourning, relived through the deaths that followed it (Leslie Stephen, the father; Stella, the sister; Thoby, the brother), but itself referring to an earlier loss, profoundly marks Woolf's universe.[6] In all the novels, the invasive presence of the dead weighs on the living. In *The Voyage Out*, Rachel Vinrace's mother seems to look out from the frame of her photograph with a fairly friendly eye, but it is *in her name* that a particularly suffocating educational system is inflicted on Rachel (VO: 87–8). The ancestors of the Hilbery family (in *Night and Day*) are omnipresent and completely squash their descendants. In *Jacob's Room*, Mrs Flanders refers to her late husband thus:

> At first, part of herself; now one of a company, he had merged in the grass, the sloping hillside, the thousand white stones, some slanting, others upright, the decayed wreaths, the crosses of green tin, the narrow yellow paths, and the lilac that drooped in April, with a scent like that of an invalid's bedroom, over the churchyard wall. Seabrook . . . – the voice of the dead.
>
> (JR: 14)

Sometimes we have the impression that the entire landscape of this novel, strewn with skulls and bones (JR: 8, 128), peopled with 'death's head moths' (JR: 21), is a great corpse in the process of decomposing ('the blues settled on little bones and the painted ladies feasted upon bloody entrails' (JR: 22)). Everything suggests that death and its remains are integral parts of humanity and of its deepest reality, as opposed to the surface world of social conventions, 'thrown up in such black outline upon what we are; upon the reality; the moors and Byron; the sea and the lighthouse; the sheep's jaw with the yellow teeth in it' (JR: 33). We shall see in the next chapter the (in every sense) *fundamental* role of death in *The Waves*, but it is worth pointing out now that the memory of Percival, killed in an accident with a horse, haunts the whole of the second half of the book. *The Years* opens with the interminable agony of Mrs Pargiter, doubled by that of another mother, Mrs Levy. The improperly buried corpse for which funeral rites have not been decently carried out (Y: 66–9) will contaminate life ('life mixing with death, death becoming life' (Y: 68)) and run from that time forth over the sunny surface of things, 'cadaverous but brilliant' (Y: 329), surging up again at each interruption to the continuity of a text which is in every aspect the novel of fragmentation. All this appears particularly clearly at the start of the section '1907', at the point where Sally is daydreaming around the theme of Antigone. First a mouldering corpse appears, huge, across the broken words and the discontinuous reading, invading the familiar universe:

> From the litter of broken words, scenes rose, quickly, inaccurately, as she skipped. The unburied body of a murdered man lay like a fallen tree trunk, like a statue, with one foot stark in the air. Vultures gathered. Down they flopped on the silver sand. With a lurch, with a reel, the top-heavy birds came waddling; with a flap of the grey throat swinging, they hopped – she beat her hand on the counterpane as she read – to that lump there. Quick, quick, quick, with repeated jerks they struck the mouldy flesh. Yes. She glanced at the tree outside in the garden. The unburied body of the murdered man lay on the sand.
>
> (Y: 105)

Then there is Antigone and her attempt, ineffective from the outset, to accomplish the burial: 'Antigone? She came whirling out of the dust-cloud to where the vultures were reeling and flung white sand over the blackened foot. She stood there letting fall white dust over the blackened foot' (Y: 105). But, as we know, alongside the law which demands burial, requiring that the corpse of the relative be withdrawn from the actions of 'any low, irrational individuality' (the vultures) and from the 'forces of abstract matter' (rotting), there is another law opposed to it. This is what Hegel calls Human Law,[7] but for Virginia Woolf it is only the law of men, imposed by the fraternal

147

community of males, the law which leads inexorably – Woolf and
Hegel agree – to violence, war, and the destruction of the whole
community. But the cause of the failure of the burial and the imminent
catastrophe, individual and collective, is not only external, it is also
to be sought in the ambivalence, in regard to the dead body, of the
officiating woman herself (cf. 'There lay her mother; in that coffin –
the woman she had loved and hated so' (Y: 68)), in her own aggressive
tendencies projected across the blackening of the corpse and its
devouring by the vultures. Antigone–Sally finds herself buried alive,
in the place of the dead man who revenges himself by seizing hold of
the living:

> The man's name was Creon. He buried her. It was a moonlit
> night. The blades of the cactuses were sharp silver. The man in the
> loincloth gave three sharp taps with his mallet on the brick. She was
> buried alive. The tomb was a brick mound. There was just room for
> her to lie straight out. Straight out in a brick tomb, she said. And
> that's the end, she yawned, shutting the book.
> She laid herself out, under the cold smooth sheets, and pulled the
> pillow over her ears. The one sheet and the one blanket fitted softly
> around her. At the bottom of the bed was a long stretch of cool
> mattress. The sound of the dance music became dulled. Her body
> dropped suddenly, then reached ground. A dark wing brushed her
> mind . . .
>
> (Y: 105–6)

We shall see in Chapter six that death is not only represented
throughout the work, it is the very base on which Virginia Woolf
writes, a base which shows through at each failing in the continuity
of the writing, as the following words indicate, commenting on a
provisional interruption of her diary: 'That . . . seems to show the
signs of death already spreading in this book' (D, I: 58).

It is thus clear that when Virginia Woolf writes: 'I have never seen
anyone who reminded me of . . . my mother. [She does] not blend
in the world of the living at all' (MB: 97), this sentence (contradicted,
moreover, by another remark: 'Mrs Carlyle reminds me oddly of [my
mother], with her "coterie" speech' (MB: 36)) is to be read as denial or
exorcism. Death, and in particular the dead mother, is omnipresent,
it invades the universe of the living, and if this universal presence
always maintained the protective character with which it is sometimes
endowed (for example, MB: 40), it would not be necessary to exorcize
it. It is thus not entirely surprising to find, at the start of at least
one of Virginia Woolf's episodes of madness, a threatening maternal
apparition: 'One morning she was having breakfast in bed and I was

talking to her when without warning she became violently excited and distressed. She thought her mother was in the room and began to talk to her.'[8]

The writing of *To the Lighthouse* (and before, of *Mrs Dalloway*) seems to have coincided with Virginia Woolf's becoming conscious of certain things which she previously refused (of *To the Lighthouse*, she wrote: 'I suppose I did for myself what psychoanalysts do for their patients' (MB: 81)). This becomes clear, for example, in the diary entry for 17 March 1923. After remarking, about something completely different, 'exposed to electric light eggs show dark patches', Virginia Woolf recounts the following scene: 'We had the photographs out. Lytton said "I don't like your mother's character. Her mouth seems complaining" & a shaft of light fell across my dusky rich red past' (D, II: 239). Or again, 18 July 1925, in this very odd juxtaposition (and even superimposition) of the complacently drawn portrait of a bad mother and the conception of *To the Lighthouse*, with its very idiosyncratic form of (elegiac?) relationship to the lost being and the sea:

> [Jack Hill] became very intent & almost emotional. '. . . My mother now – she was a very able woman – we all owe her an awful lot – but hard.' She said an odd thing to Nessa once – that she hated motherless girls. 'There you go very deep – it was the terror of her life – that she was losing her charm. She would never have a girl in the house. It was a tragedy. She was a very selfish woman.' (But *while I try to write*, I am making up 'To the Lighthouse' – the sea is to be heard all through it. I have an idea that I will invent a new name for my books to supplant 'novel'. A new —— by Virginia Woolf. But what? Elegy?)
>
> (D, III: 34)

The evil side of maternal protection appears fairly clearly within *To the Lighthouse*. Lily Briscoe feels it: 'Mrs Ramsay, Lily felt, as she talked about the skins of vegetables, exalted that, worshipped that, held her hands over it to warm them, to protect it, and yet, having brought it all about, somehow laughed, led her victims, Lily felt, to the altar' (TL: 153). We cannot refrain from juxtaposing the following two passages: '[Mrs Ramsay] said, speaking to Prue in her own mind, You will be as happy as she is one of these days. You will be much happier, she added, because you are my daughter, she meant: her own daughter must be happier than other people's daughters' (TL: 165); and 'Prue Ramsay died that summer in some illness connected with childbirth, which was indeed a tragedy, people said, everything, they said, had promised so well' (TL: 199).

It is true that the revolt against the Father, quite classically Oedipal (even including the image of an injured foot (TL: 275)), is present in the foreground of the novel. But a closer look reveals that it is often the Mother who is the target, by way of the father. It turns out that the most virulent attacks against Mr Ramsay are diverted, without apparent justification, on to Mrs Ramsay.

In this sentence, Lily Briscoe's canvas appears first as a barrier against Mr Ramsay and his inhibiting influence: 'She set her clean canvas firmly upon the easel, as a barrier, frail, but she hoped sufficiently substantial to ward off Mr Ramsay and his exactingness' (TL: 223). But after a long diatribe against the tyranny of Mr Ramsay, we end up suddenly with this:

> *Really she was angry with Mrs Ramsay*. With the brush slightly trembling in her fingers she looked at the hedge, the step, the wall. *It was all Mrs Ramsay's doing*. She was dead. Here was Lily, at forty-four, wasting her time, unable to do a thing, standing there, playing at painting, playing at the one thing one did not play at, and *it was all Mrs Ramsay's fault*. She was dead. The step where she used to sit was empty. She was dead.
>
> (TL: 223–4)

Elsewhere, it is William Bankes who criticizes Mr Ramsay: 'he rather wished Lily to agree that Ramsay was, as he said, "a bit of a hypocrite"'. Then Lily falters once again: 'Mr Bankes expected her to answer. And she was about to say something *criticising Mrs Ramsay*, how she was alarming, too, in her way, high-handed, or words to that effect . . .' (TL: 72–3). James himself becomes aware that his aggressiveness is not directed against his father, but against a 'thing' which possesses him and which he compares to a female monster (the harpy, with the bust of a woman and the body of a bird, with steely beak and claws, perfect image of the phallic mother):

> He had always kept this old symbol of taking a knife and striking his father to the heart. Only now, as he grew older, and sat staring at his father in an impotent rage, it was not him, that old man reading, whom he wanted to kill, but it was the thing that descended on him – without his knowing it perhaps: that fierce sudden black-winged harpy, with its talons and its beak all cold and hard . . .
>
> (TL: 273)

It could even be said that the whole book manifests a similar sliding over, if we compare it to the original project as formulated in the diary:

'The centre is father's character, sitting in a boat, reciting We perished, each alone, while he crushes a dying mackerel' (WD: 77). In the work that we can read, this centre is obviously displaced: everyone agrees that at the centre of the book it is no longer the father, but the mother – and though the panting fish is still there (TL: 268), it is no longer the father who squeezes it, but the maternal abyss which engulfs it (more on this below).

How might all this enlighten us as to the function of Lily Briscoe's hallucination? We have noted that this hallucination occurs at the moment of completing a painting. Now the image of Mrs Ramsay seems to be closely bound up with the act of painting. After her death, Lily can only clearly call up the memory of her when she is in the middle of a painting (TL: 270). For painting, like the image of Mrs Ramsay, is drawn from a very distant past ('as she dipped into the blue paint, she dipped too into the past there. Now Mrs Ramsay . . .' (TL: 256)). The act of painting allows her to go back further and further, or more precisely to dig down ever deeper ('She went on tunnelling her way into her picture, into the past' (TL: 258)) and to recover images associating Mrs Ramsay with a world that resembles a vast matrix:

> she began to lay on a red, a grey, and she began to model her way
> *into the hollow there.* At the same time, she seemed to be sitting *beside
> Mrs Ramsay* on the beach.
>   'Is it a boat? Is it a cask?' Mrs Ramsay said. And she began
> hunting round for her spectacles. And she sat, having found them,
> silent, *looking out to sea.* And Lily, painting steadily, felt *as if a door
> had opened, and one went in and stood gazing silently about in a high
> cathedral-like place, very dark, very solemn.*
>
>   (TL: 255).[9]

Within the frame of her picture, Lily contemplates the depths of the maternal body and, by the mediation of Mrs Ramsay's gaze materialized by the frame of her spectacles, the sea. Indeed painting enables the closest approach to the sea ('It was an odd road to be walking, this of painting. Out and out one went, further and further, until at last one seemed to be on a narrow plank, perfectly alone, over the sea' (TL: 256)), and even to dive down ('she dipped into the blue paint' (TL: 256)) into this universal amniotic fluid, ready to submerge the whole world:

> Empty it was not, but full to the brim. She seemed to be standing up
> to the lips in some substance, to move and float and sink in it, yes,
> for these waters were unfathomably deep. Into them had spilled so

many lives. The Ramsays'; the children's; and all sorts of waifs and strays of things besides.

(TL: 285–6)

This engulfing is both desired[10] and feared, for this maternal sea is capable of astonishing cruelty:

'Mrs Ramsay!' she said aloud, 'Mrs Ramsay!' The tears ran down her face.

VI

[Macallister's boy took one fish and cut a square out of its side to bait his hook with. The mutilated body (it was alive still) was thrown back into the sea.]

VII

'Mrs Ramsay!' Lily cried, 'Mrs Ramsay!' But nothing happened. The pain increased. That anguish should reduce one to such a pitch of imbecility, she thought! . . . No one had seen her step off her strip of board into the waters of annihilation.

(TL: 268–9)

The insertion of this sixth chapter, eloquent in its brevity, a marine jump-cut in the midst of Lily Briscoe's maternal invocation, draws out the affinity between the ocean opening up to overwhelm the mutilated body and Mrs Ramsay dragging Lily off into the 'waters of annihilation'. At the same time, it marks the intensity of the vital lack (a square cut out of living flesh) for which her absence is responsible.

There is total ambiguity with regard to the maternal fluid. It cradles and overwhelms, nourishes and poisons. In spite of her crusade against 'the iniquity of the English dairy system', Mrs Ramsay is a bad nurse, incapable of assuring that the milk served at her table is not contaminated by insects (TL: 298). Lily plunged 'up to the lips' (TL: 298) in this invading liquid which wells up everywhere, including from herself, is forced to close her mouth, stiffen her lips ('Her eyes were full of hot liquid (she did not think of tears at first) which, *without disturbing the firmness of her lips,* made the air thick, rolled down her cheeks' (TL: 267)). She is like the damned of the eighth circle of Dante's Inferno, plunged into a river of excrement or into the burning pitch from which they try to get their faces to emerge (*Inferno*, XXII: 25–6), or even more, like those of the fifth circle, plunged into the muddy waters of the Styx which stifle their cries: 'Quest'inno si gorgolian ne la strozza, ché dir nol posson conparola integra'.[11] For it is clearly the possibility of an autonomous articulate expression, whether in language or painting, which is the first thing to be threatened by this process of dissolution into non-differentiation, by this eminently regressive resurgence of a universe of touch, from which all distance is abolished between the eye or the mouth and an object conceived as an invasive, even corrosive fluid, as agent of a disintegration of identity.

This should be related to Virginia Woolf'a anorexia – Leonard Woolf tells us that it manifested itself chiefly in relation to the *milk* allegedly necessary for her mental and physical health[12] – or even to her general attitude to the world as betrayed, for example, by her pursed lips in the face, say, of Joyce's stream of scatology in *Ulysses*.[13] It was not really a question of closing herself off to this ambivalent maternal substance, of refusing to let it into her,[14] but of trying to filter it off as much as possible, to make it as fluid as she could in order to get rid of the bad things in it, at the risk of depriving herself at the same time of its nutritive treasures.[15]

All this of course is not unconnected to the great fluidity of writing which is generally attributed to Virginia Woolf's texts. Hugh Kenner spoke of 'undifferentiated verbal soup',[16] but this type of comparison had been around for quite some time: 'One reviewer says that I have come to a crisis in the matter of writing style: it is now so fluent and fluid that it runs through the mind like water. That disease began in The Lighthouse. The first part came fluid – how I wrote and wrote' (D, III: 118). In fact the 'disease' goes back much further. Take for instance a letter from Lytton Strachey to Leonard Woolf concerning 'The Mark on the Wall': 'Virginia's [story] is, I consider, a work of genius. The liquidity of the style fills me with envy: really some of the sentences! – How on earth does she make the English language float and float?'[17] How on earth indeed . . .? Strachey adds a technical remark: 'My only criticism is that there doesn't seem to be quite enough ink.' A writing so fluid, then, that it verges on transparency and effacement . . . To pick up Kenner's image again, it is a constantly clarifying broth: the anorexia comes out in an ascesis in the writing, with the extreme stylization of *The Waves*, or the placing of multiple frames in *Between the Acts* around what proves to be almost nothing, or perhaps a complete absence.[18]

In the merciless struggle that must be waged so as not to be absorbed by this cruel sea, by this dead mother, there are moments of triumph:

But the dead, thought Lily . . . oh, the dead! she murmured, one pitied them, one brushed them aside, one had even a little contempt for them. They are at our mercy. Mrs Ramsay had faded and gone, she thought. We can over-ride her wishes, improve away her limited, old-fashioned ideas. She recedes further and further from us. Mockingly she seemed to see her there at the end of the corridor of years saying, of all incongruous things, 'Marry, marry!' (sitting very upright early in the morning with the birds beginning to cheep in the garden outside). And one would have to say to her, It has all gone against your wishes. They're happy like that; I'm happy like this. Life has changed completely. At that all her being, even her beauty, became for a moment, dusty and out of date. For a moment Lily, standing there, with the sun hot on her back, summing up the Rayleys, triumphed over Mrs Ramsay.

(TL: 260)

But these moments are followed by terrible defeats:

How that wrung the heart, and wrung it again and again! Oh Mrs Ramsay! she called out silently, to that essence which sat by the boat, that abstract one made of her, that woman in grey, as if to abuse her for having gone, and then having gone come back again. It had seemed so safe, thinking of her. Ghost, air, nothingness, a thing you could play with easily and safely at any time of day and night, she had been that, and suddenly she put her hand out and wrung the heart thus.

(TL: 266)

Art (painting in *To the Lighthouse*) is both an issue and a weapon. It is through her painting that Lily can resist the power of Mrs Ramsay's authority and, on aesthetic pretexts, annihilate the maternal image in a gesture that is deeply aggressive, despite her denials:

She had only escaped by the skin of her teeth though, she thought. She had been looking at the table-cloth, and it had flashed upon her that she would move the tree to the middle, and need never marry anybody, and she had felt an enormous exultation. She had felt, *now she could stand up to Mrs Ramsay – a tribute to the astonishing power that Mrs Ramsay had over one. Do this, she said, and one did it.* Even her shadow at the window with James was full of authority. She remembered how *William Bankes had been shocked by her neglect of the significance of mother and son. Did she not admire her beauty?* he said. But William, she remembered, had listened to her with his wise child's eyes when she explained how *it was not irreverence*: how a light there needed a shadow there and so on. *She did not intend to disparage a subject which, they agreed, Raphael had treated divinely. She was not cynical. Quite the contrary.*

(TL: 262)

In the first part, where the will to challenge in regard to Mrs Ramsay is less explicit, the consequences that Lily believes she can derive from a mere idea for the composition of her painting appear first of all quite out of proportion ('she need not marry, thank Heaven: she need not undergo that degradation. She was saved from that dilution. She would move the tree rather more to the middle' (TL: 154)). But the meaning of the word *dilution* becomes clear retrospectively. . . .

The implicit destination of the picture as a finished object takes us in the same direction. Lily wonders why she persists in painting this picture, while knowing perfectly well how her canvas will end up: 'it would be hung in the attics, she thought; it would be rolled up and flung under a sofa' (TL: 267). We can see that what motivates her is precisely here: to paint Mrs Ramsay is an indirect means of getting rid of her, of putting her away.[19]

But the effectiveness of this weapon turns out to be inadequate compared with its dangers. Artistic practice, by dint of prospecting an ever more distant past, brings out a world of very early representations grouped around the archaic figure of the mother. These representations bring back, tightly bound up with them, violent aggressive and libidinal drives (genital, but also, more deeply buried, anal, and urethral). What was inscription on a surface becomes spasm, coitus, excretion, a struggle, doomed to failure, against a jealous and implacable divinity. This appears in the long description of Lily painting, where the proliferation of words marking the dynamic, corporeal dimension of this true *action painting* suggests the quantity of drive energies discharged here: 'physical sensation', 'urged forward', 'quick decisive stroke', 'running mark', 'dancing rhythmical movement', 'striking, she scored her canvas', 'running nervous lines', 'it was an exacting form of intercourse', 'roused one to perpetual combat, challenged one to a fight in which one was bound to be worsted', 'as if some juice for the lubrication of her faculties were spontaneously squirted', and more (TL: 235–8).

This second state ('a trance' (TL: 238), 'an ecstasy' (TL: 300)) leads to a loss of consciousness of self and of external objects as distinct from self to plunge into a *current*; but it makes it possible to seize and be seized by the essence of reality ('this other thing, this truth, this reality, which suddenly laid hands on her (TL: 236)). It is not to be confused with a mere daydream cut off from the world, which misses what is essential ('It invaded her now when she thought of her picture. Phrases came. Visions came. Beautiful pictures. Beautiful phrases. But what she wished to get hold of was that very jar on the nerves, the thing itself' (TL: 287)). *Thinking about* Mrs Ramsay, dreaming about her in lovely, reassuring and deceptive images, is not really getting to grips with her. Coming into contact with her via artistic creation is infinitely more dangerous, it means engaging her in battle and running the risk of being conquered and even submerged by one's own aggressivity.

It seems that this is what is happening here. The usual defence mechanisms are momentarily overrun, and archaic mechanisms are reactivated. Expulsion into the real is what takes the place of impossible repression: with hallucination the limit separating creation from madness is momentarily crossed. The question for us is that of knowing whether this crossing is merely represented and whether, beyond the character, the limit is not reconstituted: but we shall only be in a position to begin to reply to this when we have defined more clearly the relationship between Lily Briscoe's painting and Virginia Woolf's novel.

We can see that here the hallucination does not go along with a generalized decomposition. The world of *To the Lighthouse* is much less broken up, much more serene than that of *Mrs Dalloway*. For within painting two aspects oppose and complement each other. Art is not only a discharge of aggressivity, but simultaneously an attempt at reparation, a will to fill in an empty space, to close the wounds opened in the maternal body.

The anal dimension of painting, 'a succession of small dirty deposits juxtaposed',[20] very clear in the description of Lily painting we have just quoted, is not just sadistic aggressivity; it is also a reparatory offering, a propitiatory oblativity. The same ambiguity is to be found in the writing of the novel itself. Virginia Woolf writes in her diary, 'I used to think of [father] and mother daily; but writing the *Lighthouse* has laid them to rest in my mind' (WD: 138). This can be taken as a murder – Virginia has buried once and for all these parents who came back so persistently – but also as a mark of piety, an expiatory rite which enables her to be reconciled to them.

Artistic practice attempts to operate an ordering and reintegration of the destructive drives. Already, in Lily Briscoe's action painting, the spasm was organized into a rhythm, a dance: 'she attained a dancing rhythmical movement, as if the pauses were one part of the rhythm and the strokes another . . . as if it had fallen in with some rhythm which was dictated to her . . . this rhythm was strong enough to bear her along with it' (TL: 236).

With enough distance (in other words by pulling away from contact, from the symbiotic plunge into the maternal universe), the succession of terrifying experiences could lead to a serene order: 'the waves shape themselves symmetrically from the cliff top, but to the swimmer among them are divided by steep gulfs and foaming crests' (TL: 235). In order to lead to a work of art, ecstasy must mix with ordinary experience: 'One wanted, she thought, dipping her brush deliberately, to be on a level with ordinary experience, to feel simply that's a chair, that's a table, and yet at the same time, it's a miracle, it's an ecstasy' (TL: 299–300). Ecstasy is forced to integrate with reality ('that too became part of ordinary experience, was on a level with the chair, with the table' (TL: 300)), but with a reality articulated by the Symbolic, under paternal authority. And indeed the table is not an innocent object here, chosen at random among others. For Lily Briscoe, it is closely associated with Mr Ramsay.[21] Its existence is thought, studied philosophically, guaranteed, by the father, the master of the symbolic.[22] Lily can repose on this paternal grid which attempts to divide the world into squares and tame the Real ('she let it uphold her and sustain her, this admirable fabric of the masculine intelligence, which ran up and down, crossed this way and that, like iron girders spanning the swaying fabric, upholding the world, so that she could trust herself to it utterly' (TL: 159)). But this encaging ('iron girders') also has its dangers.

The whole problem of artistic creation, an extraordinarily difficult one, is to find a compromise between stability and break-up; to arrive at a balance between antagonistic forces: those which are represented by Mr Ramsay and the more properly pictural forces attached to the image of the mother ('For whatever reason she could not achieve that razor edge balance between two opposite forces; Mrs Ramsay and the picture; which was necessary' (TL: 287)).

Looming white space versus unbroken black

[Between absence and re-covering: the space of creation. The pictorial detour. The picture and the act of painting. Textual modalities of the irruption of the lack.]

At the beginning of creation, there is a polarity of forces diversely specified as a polarity of white and black, void and excess, light and dark.[23] But we need to step back for a moment here, and tell a little story. Take an infinite expanse where white reigns supreme, a *blank*, a frozen immensity. At a spot which seems indistinguishable from all the rest, a sign arises: a great cross on which the following line can be read: 'To strive, to seek, to find, and not to yield.' This frozen vacuity is that of the great Antarctic desert. The signal is the monument set up at the South Pole to the memory of Scott. We can see how this excessively white page represented a challenge to the Victorian and Edwardian empire builders, was perhaps even more intolerable than the 'heart of darkness', the humid seethings of the 'dark continent'.[24] It was vital that the Empire make its mark, plant its footprint in this at once abstract and concrete place, this invisible point on the snowy mantle designated by cosmology as the navel of the globe. For these men died; but not in vain, since the cenotaph erected in their memory, adorned, inevitably, with a line from Tennyson,[25] extends the hold of the symbolic, of paternal speech, to the outposts of the universe. All this is not directly at issue in *To the Lighthouse*, but it crops up as a submerged image – one of the keys to the book – at numerous points.[26] At the opposite, and complementary, pole, is a sentence from 'A Sketch of the Past' describing the Stephens' mourning after the death of the mother: the total blackness ('unbroken black') of clothes, of the whole of existence, and even of the writing paper with its funereal border so wide that there was barely any space left for writing.[27]

It is between this white expanse of the father's mark and the invasive black of maternal mourning that art has to clear itself a space, writing inscribe itself – or painting, which has the advantage of putting the problem overtly in terms of the organization and occupation of surfaces, and the mastery of space.[28]

Painting also has the advantage of being ostensibly situated outside the field of language, outside the system of words alphabetically ordered by the father. This is an idea which recurs in Virginia Woolf's writings on the subject: painting leads us to the heart of a country where silence reigns. At first sight, this is only stating the obvious: of course painting is less noisy than music . . . But it is not so simple. For Virginia Woolf, there is a kind of bad painting which is noisy and garrulous: she speaks of the din at the Royal Academy ('The Fleeting Portrait' (CE, 4: 211)). In *Between the Acts*, as we shall see, two pictures face each other of which one, the portrait of a male ancestor, is just a 'talk producer', while the other, supposed to represent a *female* ancestor, is a 'true painting', inspiring only silence and emptiness (BA: 29–30). Above all, Virginia Woolf shows that this silence can also be recovered at the heart of literature; her example is 'Kubla Khan', a sonorous poem if ever there was one ('Walter Sickert', CE, 2: 236). Art of whatever kind must reach a point where the paternal language fails[29] – but in painting, things are more clear, more simple, for this silence is not covered by the rustling of words.[30]

This simplicity has as its counterpart a limitation. The painting is circumscribed by a frame. The impalpable space which the artist must open up for herself or himself, here materialized by the bounded area of the canvas, is naturally articulated with the space organized by the symbolic system, in which it will eventually find its place, its point of attachment (even if this place is that of rubbish, as with Lily's painting). There is a division of territory, not a struggle at the heart of language. This is no doubt what explains the relative serenity of this novel, organized around a painting. But at the same time, all these limitations inherent to painting are deflected by various means.

First of all, we may note that the painting itself is never described. We only get a very vague idea of what it might look like; on the other hand, we know everything about the different stages of its execution. It is the act of painting which is represented, while the object of the painting is bracketed off (or perhaps we ought to say *square* bracketed off – we shall see why in a moment). This execution of the painting is stretched out, beyond all probability, over a period of more than ten years. To be more precise, there is a *break* in the execution, and into the void there sneak loss, absence, death, which all come to break the canvas's desperately compact surface, causing the painting to explode outside its frame and the representation outside its limits.

It is the role of the section entitled 'Time Passes' to introduce this interval, this *spacing*. It has frequently been remarked that the interval resembles the brief moment of darkness separating the two flashes constituting the signal of the lighthouse of the title. Between two sections devoted to the stream of consciousness, 'Time Passes' has the task, obviously doomed to failure, of describing the world as it is outside any consciousness, any human gaze, and even in a way outside the grasp of the symbolic.

We shall return to the modalities of this attempt in relation to the 'interludes' of *The Waves*. These take up this project again, but avoid some of the faults to be found in 'Time Passes', which does sometimes end up in mere stylistic display, the over-written purple patch. For given that it is not possible to open up the hole of the real within discourse, it is a matter of *standing out*, of interrupting, even if this means adding on a layer of discourse to reveal what is interrupted as a *border* marking the contours of a gap, in the same way that the two luminous flashes of the lighthouse can function as simple limits to the interval of shadow.

Peter Greenaway's film *Z00* (*Z and Two Noughts*) may help us to see what is going on here. The film tells the story of two widowed biologists (Siamese twins, separated surgically) who cannot succeed in integrating into their mental universe that ultimate form of separation which is death. So they set about tracking it down in its real form, organic decomposition, which they try to grasp by observing the process of rotting in a series of plants and in the bodies of animals and finally humans. They do this by chrono-photography, a technique which involves speeding up time (*'time passes . . .'*), but also pinning it down, by taking a series of photos of the subject of the experiment at regular intervals and with a fixed angle and fixed lighting. The continuity of the lighting is obtained by placing the automatic experimental apparatus in the dark and accompanying each photo with a flash of intense light. It should be specified that this apparatus, which thus includes a double and regular cutting up of time by light (the flashes and the photographic displays), and which places space under the gaze of that child of geometric optics which is the camera, is established in the laboratory of a museum or a zoo (an operator of taxinomy) – at least until it is thrown out by the authorities, but at that point, as if in compensation, it is completed by a grid (a sort of Cartesian reference) on which will be placed the object of the ultimate experiment (the experiments follow the *historical order* of the evolution of the species). But it is all very well to multiply the surveys, to transform the decomposition into a sort of ballet or pantomime with the aid of the film obtained by the juxtaposition of the instants photographed.[31] The real does not let itself be symbolized; like the lighthouse beams, the flashes which relentlessly track the dead bodies watching over them night and day, do no more than track the borders of the intervals of darkness when, in a sense, it is the carcasses who are staring at the scientists.[32] It is thus logical that for their final experiment, the twin biologists take their objects' place and install themselves, reunited in death, under the eye of their own apparatus programmed to register their own decomposition. But the mechanism will get submerged by a flood of snails,[33] interrupting the programming and restoring the apparatus, after the final flash of a short-circuit, to the dark of nothingness.

In 'Time Passes', the socialization apparatus represented by the family household does not fall into a state of undifferentiation: it is rescued at the last minute, as if by a miracle; but of course it is only a patching up. Yet what is important is not the outcome of the story, which in spite of everything does get told in this central section, but rather its structural function. This corresponds to the hole of darkness between two luminous displays, the interruption necessary to mobilize the fixity of the image (the photo becoming a film) and engender the story which will be constructed as a denial of this nothingness. But this suture is here in a sense inverted, since the superimposition of story upon story, words upon words, tends to make the gap loom up again.

This process is doubled within 'Time Passes' itself by the incursion of passages *between square brackets*. These reintroduce human affairs, as if incidentally, into the course of this description of an inhuman, or rather non-human, universe. But the only human thing to be reintroduced is death, the massacres of the war: '[A shell exploded. Twenty or thirty young men were blown up in France, among them Andrew Ramsay, whose death, mercifully, was instantaneous.]' (TL: 201); a wedding that foreshadows death ('[Prue Ramsay, leaning on her father's arm, was given in marriage. What, people said, could have been more fitting? And, they added, how beautiful she looked.]'

(TL: 198); '[Prue Ramsay died that summer in some illness connected with childbirth, which was indeed a tragedy, people said, everything, they said, had promised so well.]' (TL: 199)); and a poetry which stands out against a background of death ('[Mr Carmichael brought out a volume of poems that spring, which had an unexpected success. The war, people said, had revived their interest in poetry.]' (TL: 202)). The same gesture, delineating the edge of the fundamental gap designated by the death of Mrs Ramsay, is repeated again inside the first of these passages, with the movement of Mr Ramsay's arm and the tottering of the syntax around this absence: '[Mr Ramsay, stumbling along a passage one dark morning, stretched his arms out, but Mrs Ramsay having died rather suddenly the night before, his arms, though stretched out, remained empty.]' (TL: 194).

But the parenthetical passage (square brackets, which generally point to a change of the enunciative level are sufficiently rare in fiction to attract our attention) cannot but recall that odd sixth chapter of the third section, also contained within square brackets, which was quoted earlier on p. 152.[34] It too is organized around a lack – and, as we saw, extends the lack outwards into the surrounding text which it brutally breaks up. In this way it can be seen that the process established in the central section is also diffused into the other ones, beginning from the image of the mother and her equivalents. They are there again, symmetrically arranged, in the middle of the famous Chapter five of the first section, a classical example of stream of consciousness fiction.[35] Indeed, while this text plunges into the intimacy of the thoughts of Mrs Ramsay, whom we have the impression of knowing better than any other character in the novel, more intimately perhaps than we have ever known anyone other than ourselves, this communion is suddenly shattered, rendered illusory by the appearance of a zone of impenetrable darkness:

> Never did anybody look so sad. Bitter and *black*, half-way down, in the *darkness*, in the shaft which ran from the sunlight into the *depths*, perhaps a tear formed; a tear fell; the *waters* swayed this way and that, received it, and were at rest. Never did anybody look so sad.
>
> But was it nothing but looks people said? *What was there behind it –* her beauty and splendour? Had he blown his brains out, they asked, had he died the week before they were married – some other, earlier lover, of whom rumours reached one? *Or was there nothing?* nothing but an incomparable beauty which she lived behind, and could do nothing to disturb? For easily though she might have said at some moment of intimacy when stories of great passion, of love foiled, of ambition thwarted came her way how she too had known, or felt or been through it herself, she never spoke. *She was silent always.*

(TL: 46)

161

The abrupt change in the point of view, the transition at the crucial moment from an internal to an external focus, works as an intense frustration. The full light which had been thrown on to Mrs Ramsay's consciousness appears as a strategy destined to intensify the zone of shadow.

But the most important of these resurgences of the lack coincides with Lily Briscoe's hallucination, and it is to this that we must now return after the long digression. Mrs Ramsay's appearance cannot but throw into doubt the set of conventions on which the reading was based. *To the Lighthouse* presents itself, both internally and externally, as a narrative. All the formal characteristics of this regime of enunciation can be found in it, and Virginia Woolf, against her express plan (D, III: 34), gave up the idea of placing her book in a category other than that of novel. The text refers to a series of events which are external to it (even though, since this is fiction, they do not precede it), and organized into a 'story', relatively autonomous in relation to the narrative from which it is deduced (it is possible to tell it in other terms, to make another narrative of it). This story has its own logic, which enables us to fill any silences in the narrative. For each event of the narrative can be recounted once (the most usual case), several times, or not at all (these are the narrative's ellipses). And to each segment of the narrative there correspond *always*, in normal cases, one or a number of elements of the story. This remains true for the stream of consciousness narrative, which simply doubles this correspondence. Here each segment of the narrative corresponds to two distinct events in the story, for the narrating of each perception refers both to the psychic event (the perception itself) and to an external event (what is perceived). In the same way the narrating of each memory refers to a psychic event (remembering) and to an external event that took place in the time of the story. A dream or fantasy is always a psychic event and opens up a story within the story, endowed in its turn with its own logic. The narrative of this dream will thus refer both to the psychic event of the dream within the main story and to the events of the interpolated story.

But here is a piece of narrative where the reference is not so clear:

> Mrs Ramsay – it was part of her perfect goodness – sat there quite simply, in the chair, flicked her needles to and fro, knitted her reddish-brown stocking, cast her shadow on the step. There she sat.
>
> (TL: 300)

Verisimilitude requires that this be Lily's hallucination (the dead never return). And yet nothing in the form of the utterance distinguishes this passage from the rest of the text. It is perfectly well linked to the following sentence: 'And as if she had something she must share, yet could hardly leave her easel, so full her mind was of what she was thinking, of what she was seeing, Lily went past Mr Carmichael holding her brush to the end of the lawn', objectively describing Lily's movements and analysing her thoughts from the outside. This continuity is even reinforced by the conjunction 'and', and by a chiasmus which brings together the two anaphoric *shes*, one referring to 'Mrs Ramsay' and the other to 'Lily'. Nothing allows us to decide that these words, syntactically equivalent, do not refer to the same level of reality (or irreality). And the suspicion gradually increases.

Unlike memory, whose effect is to anchor the narrative to two points of the unfolding of the story, the hallucination refers only to a double void. It does not correspond to any event that can be located in the present, and is only attached to an indefinitely receding past, thus inscribing itself in a temporality which is no longer that of the story but that of the unconscious.

In the face of this narrative which suddenly stops referring to a story without ceasing to be a narrative, the status of representation shifts, for the narrative takes on a value which is no longer representative but what we could call performative. The narrative starts functioning as discourse – in other words, it takes its value by reference to the subject of enunciation. But this subject can no longer be reduced to a grammatical construction, nor to a particular correlate of the representational apparatus. Instead, it is diffracted when it comes up against this gap; or rather, the gap suddenly reveals its irremediable fragmentation into numerous drives. For the underlying drives push their way across representational language and tend to emerge in the foreground through the sudden absence of the referent. This process is akin to the pictorial mechanism, founded on regression to the extent that the brush-stroke, the trace of the artist's hand, places us 'before the motor element in the sense of response, inasmuch as it engenders, backwards, its stimulus [in opposition to] that which, in the identificatory dialectic of the signifier and of the spoken, will project itself forwards as haste'.[36]

Take the sentence which marks the beginning of the hallucination: 'Some wave of white went over the window pane' (TL: 300). This refers to the window – the window which gave its name to the first section of the novel where it framed the figure of Mrs Ramsay, but also the window which has served as a model for western painting since the Renaissance. But what is going on here is neither what can be perceived through the window, nor what is framed by it, but an event which takes place in the thickness of the glass itself. Beyond the contradictory signals ('wave of white' evokes the sea and the milky fluid, both associated with the maternal figure of Mrs Ramsay, but also

163

the clarity opposed to the maternal shadows), which translate all the complexity of what is going on here and all the contradiction inherent in the advent within discourse of that beyond of discourse which is the hallucination, these words make playful use of the phonetic and accentual values, which are not exhausted by their distinctive value of second-degree articulation. We are poorly equipped to analyse these phenomena, which in fact exceed the limits of the logical organization of language on which analysis has to depend.[37] But we can note, for example, that the alliterative repetition of the semi-vowel *w*, perhaps the bearer of an oral sucking instinct, issues in the final explosion of *p*, a mark of anal rejection;[38] that the return of the letters *v* and *w*[39] traces an alternating graphic rhythm of rises and falls independent of their sounds. We can also note how, in the best tradition of English poetry, alliteration seems to emphasize the stressed syllables, and that these seem to be organized in an iambic rhythm – but this regularity, itself hyper-coded, is upset in the middle by a supplementary syllable and a displacement of stress, introducing into the fixed formula a lilt which gets it moving again. In the same way, a few lines below the phrase 'to want and want and not to have', which makes clear that the hallucination is *not* a substitute for the lack, does not operate as a perfect iambic tetrameter, but as a pentameter with one of its feet cut off, if we hear in it an ironic echo introducing the lack at the heart of the canonical line[40] 'To strive, to seek, to find, and not to yield', which, as we have seen, was inscribed on the Antarctic cenotaph: substitute for the lost body of Scott (sign of the father *in absentia*), intended to complete the universal hold of the Symbolic, and absolute antithesis of the maternal hallucination which is repetition of the lack, emergence of the a-symbolizable.

The transparent glass of representational language is momentarily darkened, or at least coloured by the passing through of a wave of instinct. Articulate, paternal language, which, by its very nature, represses an essential part of reality ('little words that broke up the thought and dismember it said nothing. "About life, about death; about Mrs Ramsay" – no, she thought, one could say nothing to nobody' (TL: 265)) is subtly contested, diverted from its usage, forced to let glimmer through what it normally keeps quiet, what by its nature it can only cover over.

We have seen how hallucination can be analysed as the invasion of an unreal inside reality. But the representation of the hallucination inside Virginia Woolf's fiction does not have the effect of inserting one unreal into another (this would be the case with a dream narrative or with what Gérard Genette calls the *metadiegetic*[41]). Instead, however fleetingly, it brings to the surface, within the space of representation, the real.

Notes

1. Artistic creation appears as a sort of double of madness, very close and yet distinct. It offers an alternative. Already in *Mrs Dalloway*, Septimus seemed to be momentarily cured through his participation in the artistic elaboration (choosing colours and materials) of Mrs Filmer's hat.

2. It is obvious that painting functions here as a metaphor of writing. We shall come back later to the significance of this detour via a 'sister' art, which was in fact the art form of Vanessa, the elder sister in regard to whom Virginia Woolf maintained a strange relationship of artistic rivalry and emulation (significantly, she had made a sort of high desk to enable her, she said, to write standing up, as if at an easel), not being in a position to compete with her as a mother.

3. Virginia Woolf simply repeats, word for word, her sister's terms: 'As far as portrait painting goes you seem to me to be a supreme artist'; 'It is almost painful to have *her* so raised from the dead' (quoted in the appendix to Virginia Woolf's *Letters*, vol. III). There is one slight difference: Vanessa specifies that what is difficult to tolerate is the return of the *mother*, thus confirming that for her this 'portrait painting' does not have the function of substitution.

4. Jean Guiguet, *Virginia Woolf and her Works* (1962) (New York: Harcourt, Brace and World, 1965), p. 257.

5. For example, Guiguet, *Virginia Woolf*, p. 257.

6. As Melanie Klein shows, 'the child goes through states of mind comparable to the mourning of the adult, or rather . . . this early mourning is revived whenever grief is experienced in later life'. As a result, mourning entails the reactivation of the defence processes previously used ('Mourning and its Relation to Manic-Depressive States' (1940), in Juliet Mitchell (ed.), *The Selected Melanie Klein* (Harmondsworth: Penguin, 1986), p. 147).

7. See Hegel's analysis of the Antigone myth in *The Phenomenology of Spirit*, trans. A.V. Miller (Oxford: Oxford University Press, 1977).

8. Leonard Woolf, *Beginning Again: An Autobiography of the Years 1919–1939* (New York: Harcourt, Brace, 1964), p. 172.

9. Cf. 'A Sketch of the Past': 'Certainly there she [my mother] was, in the very centre of that great cathedral space which was childhood; there she was from the very first' (MB: 81).

10. 'What device for becoming, like waters poured into one jar, inextricably the same, one with the subject one adored? Could the body achieve, or the mind, subtly mingling in the intricate passages of the brain? or the heart? Could loving, as people called it, make her and Mrs Ramsay one? for it was not knowledge but unity that she desired' (TL: 79); 'Against her will she had come to the surface, and found herself half out of the picture' (TL: 265).

11. 'They gurgle these phrases in their throats, for they cannot speak in complete words' (*Inferno*, VII, ll. 125f.).

12. 'Drink milk in bed' is given a prominent place in the list of trials imposed on Sir William Bradshaw's patients. There is also this: 'Sir William [made

England] prosper, secluded her lunatics, *forbade childbirth*, penalised despair'
(MD: 110). This 'obscurely evil' doctor has extremely close affinities with
the bad mother in Melanie Klein's description of archaic fantasies. The bad
mother dispenses a poisoned milk which is only the return against the
child of the surges of aggression which emanate from himself or herself
(as expressed in another mode by AGRIPPA D'AUBIGNÉ: 'Felons, you have
bloodied/the breast which nourishes you and which bore you;/therefore,
live off poison, bloody offspring,/I have no longer anything but blood to
feed you!' (*Les Tragiques*, I, ll. 127ff.)), and, especially, takes revenge on her
daughters' fantasmatic attacks by preventing them from having children
in their turn. It is interesting that Leonard Woolf, who was placed in a
maternal position in relation to his wife, was lèd to take his collection of
prescriptions and prohibitions upon himself (see, for example, *Beginning
Again*, p. 82). And so it is not surprising to find the main elements of the
maternal imagery coming up again in relation to him in the diary, with all
the ambivalence that underlies them.

13. 'First there is a dog that p's – then a man that farts, and one can be
    monotonous even on that subject', in VIRGINIA WOOLF and LYTTON
    STRACHEY, *Letters* (London: Hogarth Press, 1956), p. 73.

14. Cf. this image from 'A Sketch of the Past': 'This confirms me in my
    instinctive notion: (it will not bear arguing about; it is irrational) the
    sensation that we are sealed vessels afloat on what it is convenient to call
    reality; and at the same moment the sealing water cracks, in floods reality'
    (MB: 122).

15. The sea is a source of danger – there are many references to murderous
    shipwrecks and Mr Ramsay as well as his children compulsively recite lines
    from COWPER's 'Castaway': 'But I beneath a rougher sea / Was whelmed
    in deeper gulfs than he' – but also a source of inexhaustible richness ('a
    trophy fetched from the bottom of the sea, of Neptune's banquet' (TL: 146);
    'that underworld of water where the pearls stuck in clusters to white
    sprays' (TL: 272)). There is also the story Mrs Ramsay reads to her son,
    in which the poor fisherman finds riches and power, but also ruin, in the
    threatening deeps of the sea (TL: 86ff.). Augustus Carmichael, the poet,
    is presented as a marine deity, 'looking like an old pagan god, shaggy,
    with weeds in his hair and the trident (it was only a French novel) in
    his hand' (TL: 309), off to seek his artistic fortune from the heart of the
    ocean ('Augustus too feasted his eyes on the same plate of fruit [Neptune's
    Banquet], *plunged* in, broke off a bloom there, a tassel here, and returned
    after feasting, to his hive' (TL: 146), whence his artistic 'success' (TL: 202);
    'People said that his poetry was "so beautiful"' (TL: 288). Unlike Lily, he
    can make this dive at no risk, for he is utterly *impermeable* to Mrs Ramsay's
    seductiveness.
    For a rich and much fuller interpretation of the role of the liquid element
    in Virginia Woolf, see MARIE-PAULE VIGNE, *Le thème de l'eau dans l'oeuvre
    de Virginia Woolf* (Talence: Presses Universitaires de Bordeaux, 1984). Her
    psychoanalytic interpretation is rather different from this one.

16. HUGH KENNER, *Joyce's Voices* (Berkeley: University of California Press, 1962),
    p. 23.

17. Quoted by QUENTIN BELL, *Virginia Woolf*, vol. II (London: Hogarth Press,
    1972), p. 43.

18. This is why it is not good enough to make a simple opposition between Virginia Woolf's *dryness* and the *plethora* that characterizes the writing of her two great male contemporaries, Joyce and Faulkner. We should not forget that we are dealing with three variants of *stream* of consciousness. Moreover, if fasting or drinking, on the one hand refusing the nourishment of milk or gorging oneself on *white* wine and *moonshine* whisky on the other, are translated into contrasting modes of writing, it is still a matter of problems to do with incorporation, with the exchange between the inside and the outside. Alcoholism does not represent any more satisfying a relation to the maternal breast than anorexia. In both JOYCE and FAULKNER (on numerous occasions), we come across the image of the woman as receptacle filled with a monstrous liquid. The episode of Burrus and Caseus in *Finnegans Wake* (160.37–168.17) enacts, even in its phonic substance, an attempt at dissociating the milky material into cheese that stinks and creamy butter, at distinguishing the good from the bad object inside the maternal substance. The distinction does not manage to sustain itself or escape a homogenization which re-establishes ambivalence (see DANIEL FERRER, 'Hissheory ou le plaisir en trop', *Poétique*, **26** (1976)). At the end of the line, the outcome, whether dreamt or actually accomplished, is the same: drowning in the River Ouse or in a glass of liquor . . . .

19. This should be linked to Virginia Woolf's remark that she and her sister, on the pretext of aesthetic considerations, had relegated G.W. Watts's portraits of their parents to the basement (MB: 173).

20. J. LACAN, *The Four Fundamental Concepts of Psychoanalysis*, trans. Alan Sheridan (London: Hogarth Press, 1977), p. 117.

21. 'Whenever she "thought of [Mr Ramsay's] work" she always saw clearly before her a large kitchen table' (TL: 38); 'the scrubbed kitchen table, symbol of her profound respect for Mr Ramsay's mind' (TL: 41).

22. If the symbolic is represented in *To the Lighthouse* by the succession of the letters of the alphabet ('if thought is like the keyboard of a piano, divided into so many notes, or like the alphabet is ranged in twenty-six letters all in order, then his splendid mind had no sort of difficulty in running over those letters one by one, firmly and accurately, until it had reached, say, the letter Q. . . . But after Q? What comes next? After Q there are a number of letters the last of which is scarcely visible to mortal eyes, but glimmers red in the distance. Z is only reached once by one man in a generation. Still, if he could reach R it would be something. Here at least was Q. He dug his heels in at Q. Q he was sure of. Q he could demonstrate. If Q then is Q–R . . . R is then – what is R?' (TL: 53–4)), then Mr Ramsay is master up to the excluded letter R. This seems to suggest that Leslie Stephen, of whom he is only the effigy, went as far as the letter S, not included. And indeed the man who spent a large part of his life editing the (alphabetical) *Dictionary of National Biography* was never able to edit the necessarily posthumous article about himself (and which he could not stop himself from imagining while he lived: see *Sir Leslie Stephen's Mausoleum Book* (Oxford: Clarendon Press, 1977), p. 4n). It seems that Virginia Woolf (the author of several biographical essays on her father) implicitly places herself three or four laps ahead of him. . . . But at the most, it is a matter of being out of step, not enough to escape the grasp of the paternal signifier. Virginia Woolf is perfectly aware of this when she pretends to attribute her

own and her brother Adrian's lack of balance to the prenatal influence on them of the *DNB*, like the clock in *Tristram Shandy*: 'The D.N.B. crushed his life out before he was born. It gave me a twist of the head too. I shouldn't have been so clever, but I should have been more stable, without that contribution to the history of England' (D, 2: 277).

23. For example: 'For what reason had she introduced [Mrs Ramsay reading to James] then? he asked. Why indeed? – except that if there, in that corner, it was bright, here, in this, she felt the need of darkness' (TL: 81); 'William Bankes had been shocked by her neglect of the significance of mother and son. . . . She explained it was not irreverence: how a light here needed a shadow there and so on' (TL: 262). But we are going to find this polarity again soon, at a quite different level.'

24. See the Victorian vignette in *Between the Acts* and the analysis in Chapter five.

25. 'Ulysses', 1. 70. Tennyson is singled out as a target among the Victorians Virginia Woolf makes fun of in *Freshwater*.

26. Especially, of course, in the daydreams of Mr Ramsay, who likes picturing himself as a polar explorer, dying heroically before he attains his goal. (Leslie Stephen was in fact a well-known mountaineer). It should be recalled that Mr Ramsay is very keen on Tennyson, and that he goes back over the lines that celebrate the no less heroic end of the Light Brigade. Compare too this passage (pointed out to me by M. Durand), in which James Ramsay alludes to both his father and male solidarity in the form of a double imprint on a desert of snow: 'There was a waste of snow and rock very lonely and austere; and there he had come to feel, quite often lately, when his father said something or did something which surprised the others, there were two pairs of footprints only; his own and his father's' (TL: 275–6).

27. 'Even the notepaper was so black bordered that only a little space for writing remained' (MB: 93–4). It would be equally possible to take as a starting point the two scenes Virginia Woolf recounts as her very first memories, and which offer two images of the mother, one white, one black, linked by a whole network to the two complementary aspects of Mrs Ramsay (MB: 64–5). The oldness of these images (to which we shall return in relation to *The Waves*), certainly proves that the *accident* of the mother's death is only the replaying of a previous loss, the bringing to light again of a mourning that can never be completed.

28. Painters seem, in Virginia Woolf's eyes, to have a natural affinity with space. With admiration and envy, she writes of her sister and Duncan Grant that 'these painters . . . have smooth broad spaces in their minds' (D, I: 69).

29. Lily feels she must fight so as not to give up her gaze in favour of Mr Paunceforte's – at the risk of finding herself once more naked, defenceless, before the eyes of the world.

30. There is also the fact that Leslie Stephen was not a painter and knew nothing about painting. Virginia Woolf notes that her father did all he could to assist Vanessa in her vocation, although painting was something strange for him ('Leslie Stephen', CE: 4: 79). Does she not imply that in

reality, this was precisely why he helped her? She admits in her diary that she herself could never have written if her father, crushing emblem of the Victorian man of letters, had not died: 'His life would have entirely ended mine. What would have happened? No writing, no books; inconceivable' (WD: 138).

31. As much a conjuring away of evil as Lily's 'dance'.

32. Beneath the more smiling exteriors of the flowers of spring, it is the same terrible gaze of the world when it is not held in respect by the human gaze which 'Time Passes' describes: 'the flowers standing there, looking before them, looking up, yet beholding nothing, eyeless and terrible' (TL: 203).

33. Woolfian creatures *par excellence*. See 'Kew Garden', 'The Mark on the Wall', *The Waves* . . . but in 'Time Passes', they are replaced as the incarnation of what HEGEL calls the 'low individualities and the forces of abstract matter' (see p. 44) or, to put it differently, of time outside thought and human division, by rats, birds, and in particular draughts of sea air.

34. The playing with chapter length (varying from three lines to twenty or so pages) and the typographical fantasy obviously recall STERNE who, in a much more ostentatious way, pursues the same end as Virginia Woolf, shows up the gaps in discourse and enunciation by systematic recourse of interruption: '*Tristram!* child . . . of interruption!' (*The Life and Opinions of Tristram Shandy, Gentleman* (1759–67; Oxford: Oxford University Press, 1983), p. 236).

    It may be thought that the play with the square brackets is a pretty discreet form of daring compared with Sterne's extravagances, but Virginia Woolf was prepared to go as far as is possible in this direction. She had taken to Vita Sackville-West a copy of *To the Lighthouse* in which the pages had been replaced by white paper; the dedication read: 'Vita from Virginia (In my opinion the best novel I have ever written)' (L, 3: 372–3). In a number of letters she ponderously insists on how these words are to be interpreted: 'When I wrote it was my best book I merely meant because all the pages were empty'; "my best book" referred to the blank pages of her dummy copy'. It is clearly a private joke, but one addressed to the privileged reader who is the woman she loves.

35. Famous in particular because of ERICH AUERBACH's reading of it in *Mimesis* (1946), trans. Willard R. Trask (Princeton: Princeton University Press, 1953), pp. 525ff.

36. JACQUES LACAN, *The Four Fundamental Concepts*, 114; tr. mod.

37. Probably they are derived from what Virginia Woolf called 'rhythm', of which she speaks in these terms in a letter to V. Sackville-West at the very time when she was in the process of writing *To the Lighthouse*: 'Once you get that, you can't use wrong words. But on the other hand here am I sitting after half the morning, crammed with ideas, and visions, and so on, and can't dislodge them, for lack of the right rhythm. Now this is very profound, what rhythm is, and goes far deeper than words. A sight, an emotion creates this *wave* in the mind, long before it makes words to fit it; . . . and then, as it breaks and tumbles in the mind, it makes words to fit it' (L, 3: 247). Similarly, she will write of *The Waves*: 'I am writing *The Waves* to a rhythm not to a plot' (D, 3: 316). See also the letter to Ethel Smyth of 28 August 1930 (L, 4: 204).

38. See I. FONAGY, 'Les bases pulsionnelles de la phonation', *Revue française de la psychanalyse* (January 1970 and July 1971), and JULIA KRISTEVA, *Revolution in Poetic Language* (1974), trans. Margaret Waller (New York: Columbia University Press, 1984).

39. Should we read the writer's initials here, ironically (see note 22) disseminated by a process resembling the one Ferdinand de Saussure thought he had spotted in classical poetry? See FERDINAND DE SAUSSURE, 'Anagrammes', *Mercure de France* (February 1964), and JULIA KRISTEVA, 'Pour une sémiologie des paragrammes', *Séméiotike* (Paris: Seuil, 1969).

40. No doubt because of its rigidity, it is often chosen as a didactic illustration of iambic rhythm. See for example WEBSTER's *College Dictionary*.

41. 'D'un récit baroque', *Figures* II (Paris: Editions du Seuil, 1969), p. 202.

Abbreviations of Virginia Woolf's Works

References to texts by Virginia Woolf are included within the main text, using abbreviations and editions as in the following list. The date given is that of the first publication.

VO   *The Voyage Out*. New York: Harcourt Brace & World, 1915.

ND   *Night and Day*. London: Duckworth, 1919.

JR   *Jacob's Room*. St Albans: Panther, 1922.

MD   *Mrs Dalloway*. Harmondsworth: Penguin, 1925.

TL   *To the Lighthouse*. New York: Modern Library, 1927.

W   *The Waves*. Harmondsworth: Penguin, 1931.

Y   *The Years*. London: Granada, 1937.

BA   *Between the Acts*. Harmondsworth: Penguin, 1941.

WD   *A Writer's Diary*. London: Hogarth Press, 1947.

CE   *Collected Essays*. Vols 1–4. London: Chatto and Windus, 1967.

MB   *Moments of Being: Unpublished Autobiographical Writings*. London: Hogarth Press, 1976.

L   *Letters*. Vols 1–6. London: Chatto and Windus, 1980.

D   *The Diary of Virginia Woolf*. Vols 1–5. London: Hogarth Press, 1984.

Part Three

Poetry

7 Freud and the Sublime: A Catastrophe Theory of Creativity*

HAROLD BLOOM

Harold Bloom is best known for his work on the 'anxiety of influence', in which he argues that 'strong poets' must struggle for priority against the overwhelming influence of their precursors; in the same way that the sons, in Freud's conception of the 'primal horde', must overthrow the father. 'To live, the poet must *misinterpret* the father, by the crucial act of misprision, which is the re-writing of the father', Bloom declares.† The newcomer or 'ephebe' turns against the works of his precursor by means of tropes, which correspond to the ego's 'mechanisms of defence', mapped out by Anna Freud.‡ An inventory of the tropes of 'misprision' [literally mis-taking], together with their corresponding psychic defences, may be found in Bloom's manifesto, *A Map of Misreading* (1975). Here he writes:

Influence, as I conceive it, means that there are *no* texts, but only relationships *between* texts. These relationships depend upon a critical act, a misreading or misprision, that one poet performs upon another, and that does not differ in kind from the necessary critical acts performed by every strong reader upon every text he encounters. The influence-relation governs reading as it governs writing, and reading is therefore a miswriting just as writing is a misreading. As literary history lengthens, all poetry necessarily

---

*HAROLD BLOOM, 'Freud and the Sublime: A Catastrophe Theory of Creativity', in *Agon: Towards a Theory of Revisionism* (New York: Oxford University Press, 1982), pp. 91–118. © 1982, Oxford University Press, Inc.
†HAROLD BLOOM, *A Map of Misreading* (Oxford: Oxford University Press, 1975), p. 19.
‡ANNA FREUD, *The Ego and the Mechanisms of Defense* (1937; rev. edn, New York: International Universities Press, 1966). I would suggest that Bloom's true precursor, whom he disavows, is Melanie Klein, since it is she who anticipates his notion that tropes arise out of anxiety; unlike Lacan, who regards desire as the wellspring of figurative language. It is typical of Bloom to disavow the foremother; in his conception of literary history, sires beget sons in an unending chain without the interference of a feminine progenitor.

becomes verse-criticism, just as all criticism becomes prose-poetry. (p. 3)

In the following article, Bloom interprets Freud as a great 'prose-poet of the Sublime', and traces his descent from Goethe, Schiller, and Schopenhauer, rather than from the nineteenth-century psychologists. The Sublime is rather a confusing term: in eighteenth-century aesthetics, it referred to the quality of awesome grandeur, as distinguished from the merely beautiful. According to Kant, the sense of the Sublime may be aroused by nature's incalculable power, manifest in whirlwinds, waterfalls, and earthquakes; but also by numerical proliferation, when the mind undergoes a 'momentary checking of the vital powers' in the face of overwhelming multiplicity. This moment of 'blockage', however, is quickly overcome by the mind's 'exultation in its own rational faculties, in its ability to think a totality that cannot be taken in through the senses'.* Thus the Sublime involves two contradictory emotions, one of awe, the other of omnipotence: the mind, appalled by the experience of vastness, triumphs nonetheless in its ability to contemplate the magnitude of its beyond.

According to Bloom, Freud's work *Beyond the Pleasure Principle* may best be understood as a late Romantic meditation on the principle of the Sublime. In this work Freud argues that the psyche strives to master trauma *after* the event by generating the anxiety that should have been aroused *before* the unforeseen catastrophe. Anxiety, as a mode of expectation, overrides the pastness of the past, taking possession of the lost unliveable event by transforming 'it was' into 'I am'. Through this ruse, anxiety converts itself into omnipotence, in the same way that terror in the face of the Sublime (according to the aestheticians of the eighteenth century) coverts itself into the triumph of the ego. The anxiety of influence, Bloom argues, also represents the struggle to pre-empt the past: the latecomer strives to anticipate his forerunner so as to invent himself anew, self-born and self-begotten. In Freud's vision of the primal horde, the sons consume the father after they have murdered him, and every totem feast commemorates this act of cannibalism; in Bloom, however, poetry itself becomes the totem feast in which the power of the father is 'introjected' or 'transumed' into the son.

---

*See IMMANUEL KANT, *Critique of Judgment*, trans. J.H. Bernard (New York: Hafner, 1966), esp. pp. 83, 91. See also NEIL HERTZ, 'The Notion of Blockage in the Literature of the Sublime', in *The End of the Line: Essays on Psychoanalysis and the Sublime* (New York: Columbia University Press, 1985), pp. 40–60.

Jacques Lacan argues that Freud 'derived his inspiration, his ways of thinking and his technical weapons' from imaginative literature rather than from the sciences. On such a view, the precursors of Freud are not so much Charcot and Janet, Brücke and Helmholtz, Breuer and Fliess, but the rather more exalted company of Empedocles and Heraclitus, Plato and Goethe, Shakespeare and Schoepenhauer. Lacan is the foremost advocate of a dialectical reading of Freud's text, a reading that takes into account those problematics of textual interpretation that stem from the philosophies of Hegel, Nietzsche and Heidegger, and from developments in differential linguistics. Such a reading, though it has attracted many intellectuals in English-speaking countries, is likely to remain rather alien to us, because of the strong empirical tradition in Anglo-American thought. Rather like Freud himself, whose distaste for and ignorance of the United States were quite invincible, Lacan and his followers distrust American pragmatism, which to them is merely irritability with theory. Attacks by French Freudians upon American psychoanalysis tend to stress issues of societal adjustment or else of a supposed American optimism concerning human nature. But I think that Lacan is wiser in his cultural vision of Freud than he is in his polemic against ego psychology, interpersonal psychoanalysis or any other American school. Freud's power *as a writer* made him the contemporary not so much of his rivals and disciples as of the strongest literary minds of our century. We read Freud not as we read Jung or Rank, Abraham or Ferenczi, but as we read Proust or Joyce, Valéry or Rilke or Stevens. A writer who achieves what once was called the Sublime will be susceptible to explication either upon an empirical *or* upon a dialectical basis.

The best brief account of Freud that I have read is by Richard Wollheim (1971), and Wollheim is an analytical philosopher, working in the tradition of Hume and Wittgenstein. The Freud who emerges in Wollheim's pages bears very little resemblance to Lacan's Freud, yet I would hesitate to prefer either Wollheim's or Lacan's Freud, one to the other. There is no 'true' or 'correct' reading of Freud because Freud is so strong a writer that he *contains* every available mode of interpretation. In tribute to Lacan, I add that Lacan in particular has uncovered Freud as the greatest theorist we have of what I would call the necessity of misreading. Freud's text both exemplifies and explores certain limits of language, and therefore of literature, insofar as literature is a linguistic as well as a discursive mode. Freud is therefore as much the concern of literary criticism as he is of psychoanalysis. His intention was to found a science; instead he left as legacy a literary canon and a discipline of healing.

It remains one of the sorrows, both of psychoanalysis and of literary criticism, that as modes of interpretation they continue to be antithetical to one another. The classical essay on this antithesis is still Lionel Trilling's *Freud and Literature*, first published back in 1940, and subsequently revised in *The Liberal Imagination* (1950). Trilling demonstrated that neither Freud's notion of art's status nor Freud's use of analysis on works of art was acceptable to a literary critic, but nevertheless praised the Freudian psychology as being truly parallel to the workings of poetry. The sentence of Trilling's eloquent essay that always has lingered in my own memory is the one that presents Freud as a second Vico, as another great rhetorician of the psyche's twistings and turnings:

> In the eighteenth century Vico spoke of the metaphorical, imagistic language of the early stages of culture; it was left to Freud to discover how, in a scientific age, we still feel and think in figurative formations, and to create, what psychoanalysis is, a science of tropes, of metaphor and its variants, synecdoche and metonymy.

That psychoanalysis is a science of tropes is now an accepted commonplace in France, and even in America, but we do well to remember how prophetic Trilling was, since the *Discours de Rome* of Jacques Lacan dates from 1953. Current American thinkers in psychoanalysis like Marshall Edelson and Roy Schafer describe psychic defenses as fantasies, not mechanisms, and fantasies are always tropes, in which so-called 'deep structures,' like desires, become transformed into 'surface structures,' like symptoms. A fantasy of defense is thus, in language, the recursive process that traditional rhetoric named a trope or 'turning,' or even a 'color,' to use another old name for it. A psychoanalyst interpreting a symptom, dream or verbal slip and a literary critic interpreting a poem thus share the burden of having to become conceptual rhetoricians. But a common burden is proving to be no more of an authentic unifying link between psychoanalysts and critics than common burdens prove to be among common people, and the languages of psychoanalysis and of criticism continue to diverge and clash.

Partly this is due to a certain over-confidence on the part of writing psychoanalysts when they confront a literary text, as well as to a certain over-deference to psychoanalysis on the part of various critics. Psychoanalytic over-confidence, or courageous lack of wariness, is hardly untypical of the profession, as any critic can learn by conducting a seminar for any group of psychoanalysts. Since we can all agree that the interpretation of schizophrenia is a rather more desperately urgent matter than the interpretation of poetry, I am in no way inclined to sneer at psychoanalysts for their instinctive privileging of their own kinds of interpretation. A critical self-confidence, or what Nietzsche might have called a will-to-power over the text-of-life, is a working necessity for a psychoanalyst, who otherwise would cease to function. Like the shaman, the psychoanalyst cannot heal unless he himself is persuaded by his own rhetoric. But the writing psychoanalyst adopts, whether he knows it or not, a very different stance. As a writer he is neither more nor less privileged than any other writer. He cannot invoke the trope of the Unconscious as though he were doing more (or less) than the poet or critic does by invoking the trope of the Imagination, or than the theologian does by invoking the trope of the Divine. Most writing psychoanalysts privilege the realm of what Freud named as 'the primary process.' Since this privileging, or valorization, is at the center of any psychoanalytic account of creativity, I turn now to examine 'primary process,' which is Freud's most vital trope or fiction in his theory of the mind.

Freud formulated his distinction between the primary and secondary processes of the psyche in 1895, in his *Project for a Scientific Psychology*, best available in English since 1954 in *The Origins of Psychoanalysis* (ed. Bonaparte, A. Freud and Kris). In Freud's mapping of the mind, the primary process goes on in the system of the unconscious, while the secondary process characterizes the preconscious-conscious system. In the unconscious, energy is conceived as moving easily and without check from one idea to another, sometimes by displacement (dislocating) and sometimes by condensation (compression). This hypothesized energy of the psyche is supposed continually to reinvest all ideas associated with the fulfilment of unconscious desire, which is defined as a kind of primitive hallucination that totally satisfies, that gives a complete pleasure. Freud speaks of the primary process as being marked by a wandering-of-meaning with meaning sometimes dislocated onto what ought to be an insignificant idea or image, and sometimes compressed upon a single idea or image at a crossing point between a number of ideas or images. In this constant condition of wandering, meaning becomes multiformly determined, or even over-determined, interestingly explained by Lacan as being like a palimpsest, with one meaning always written over another one. Dreaming is of course the principal Freudian evidence for the primary process, but wishing construed as a primitive phase of desiring may be closer to the link between the primary process and what could be called poetic thinking.

Wollheim calls the primary process 'a primitive but perfectly coherent form of mental functioning.' Freud expounded a version of the primary process in Chapter VII of his masterwork, *The Interpretation of Dreams* (1900), but his classic account of it is in the essay of 1911, *Formulations on the Two Principles of Mental Functioning*. There the primary process is spoken of as yielding to the secondary process when the person abandons the pleasure principle and yields to the reality principle, a surrender that postpones pleasure only in order to render its eventuality more certain.

The secondary process thus begins with a binding of psychic energy, which subsequently moves in a more systematic fashion. Investments in ideas and images are stabilized, with pleasure deferred, in order to make possible trial runs of thought as so many path-breakings towards a more constant pleasure. So described, the secondary process also has its links to the cognitive workings of poetry, as to all other cognitions whatsoever. The French Freudians, followers of Lacan, speak of the primary and secondary process as each having different laws of syntax, which is another way of describing these processes as two kinds of poetry or figuration, or two ways of 'creativity,' if one would have it so.

Anthony Wilden observes in his *System and Structure* (1972): 'The concept of a primary process or system applies in both a synchronic and a diachronic sense to all systemic or structural theories.' In Freudian theory, the necessity of postulating a primary process precludes any possibility of regarding the forms of that process as being other than abnormal or unconscious phenomena. The Lacanian psychoanalyst O. Mannoni concludes his study *Freud* (English translation 1971) by emphasizing the ultimate gap between primary process and secondary process as being the tragic, unalterable truth of the Freudian vision, since 'what it reveals profoundly is a kind of original fracture in the way man is constituted, a split that opposes him to himself (and not to reality or society) and exposes him to the attacks of his unconscious.'

In his book *On Art and the Mind* (1973), Wollheim usefully reminds us that the higher reaches of art 'did not for Freud connect up with that other and far broader route by which wish and impulse assert themselves in our lives: Neurosis.' Wollheim goes on to say that, in Freudian terms, we thus have no reason to think of art as showing any single or unitary motivation. Freud first had developed the trope or conceptual image of the unconscious in order to explain repression, but then had equated the unconscious with the primary process. In his final phase, Freud came to believe that the primary process played a positive role in the strengthening of the ego, by way of the fantasies or defenses of introjection and projection. Wollheim hints that Freud, if he had lived, might have investigated the role of art through such figures of identification, so as to equate art 'with recovery or reparation on the path back to reality.' Whether or not this surmise is correct, it is certainly very suggestive. We can join Wollheim's surmise to Jack Spector's careful conclusion in his *The Aesthetics of Freud* (1972) that Freud's contribution to the study of art is principally 'his dramatic view of the mind in which a war, not of good and evil, but of ego, super-ego, and id forces occurs as a secular *psychomachia.*' Identification, through art, is clearly a crucial weapon in such a civil war of the psyche.

Yet it remains true, as Philip Rieff once noted, that Freud suggests very little that is positive about creativity as an intellectual process, and therefore explicit Freudian thought is necessarily antithetical to nearly any theory of the imagination. To quarry Freud for theories of creativity, we need to study Freud where he himself is most imaginative, as in his great phase that begins with *Beyond the Pleasure Principle* (1920), continues with the essay *Negation* (1925) and then with *Inhibitions, Symptoms, and Anxiety* (1926, but called *The Problem of Anxiety* in its American edition), and that can be said to attain a climax in the essay *Analysis Terminable and Interminable* (1937). This is the Freud who establishes the priority of anxiety over its stimuli, and who both imagines the origins of consciousness as a catastrophe and then relates that catastrophe to repetition-compulsion, to the drive-towards-death, and to the defense of life as a drive towards agonistic achievement, an agon directed not only against death but against the achievements of anteriority, of others, and even of one's own earlier self.

Freud, as Rieff also has observed, held a catastrophe theory of the genealogy of drives, but *not* of the drive-towards-creativity. Nevertheless, the Freudian conceptual image of a catastrophe-creation of our instincts is perfectly applicable to our will-to-creativity, and both Otto Rank and more indirectly Sandor Ferenczi made many suggestions (largely unacceptable to Freud himself) that can help us to see what might serve as a Freudian theory of the imagination-as-catastrophe, and of art as an achieved anxiety in the agonistic struggle both to repeat and to defer the repetition of the catastrophe of creative origins.

Prior to any pleasure, including that of creativity, Freud posits the 'narcissistic scar,' accurately described by a British Freudian critic, Ann Wordsworth, as 'the infant's tragic and inevitable first failure in sexual love.' Parallel to this notion of the narcissistic scar is Freud's speculative discovery that there are early dreams whose purpose is not hallucinatory wish-fulfillment. Rather they are attempts to master a stimulus retroactively by first developing the anxiety. This is certainly a creation, though it is the *creation of an anxiety*, and so cannot be considered a sublimation of any kind. Freud's own circuitous path-breaking of thought connects this creation-of-an-anxiety to the function of a repetition-compulsion, which turns out, in the boldest of all Freud's tropes, to be a regressive return to a death-instinct.

Freud would have rejected, I think, an attempt to relate this strain in his most speculative thinking to any theory of creativity, because for Freud a successful repression is a contradiction in terms. What I am suggesting is that any theory of artistic creation that wishes to use Freud must depart from the Freudian letter in order to develop the Freudian spirit, which in some sense is already the achievement of Lacan and his school, though they have had no conspicuous success in speculating upon art. What the Lacanians *have* seen is that Freud's system, like Heidegger's, is a science of anxiety, which is what I suspect the art of belatedness, of the last several centuries, mostly is also. Freud, unlike Nietzsche, shared in the Romantics' legacy of over-idealizing art, of accepting an ill-defined trope of 'the Imagination' as a kind of mythology of creation. But Freud, as much as Neitzsche (or Vico, before them both), provides the rational materials for demythologizing our pieties about artistic creation. Reading the later Freud teaches us that our instinctual life is agonistic and ultimately self-destructive and that our most authentic moments tend to be those of negation, contraction and repression. Is it so unlikely that our creative drives are deeply contaminated by our instinctual origins?

Psychoanalytic explanations of 'creativity' tend to discount or repress two particular aspects of the genealogy of aesthetics: first, that the creative or Sublime 'moment' is a negative moment; second, that this moment tends to rise out of an encounter with someone else's prior moment of negation, which in turn goes back to an anterior moment, and so on. 'Creativity' is thus always a mode of repetition *and* of memory and also of what Nietzsche called the will's revenge against time and against time's statement of: 'It was.' What links repetition and revenge is the psychic operation that Freud named 'defense,' and that he identified first with repression but later with a whole range of figurations, including identification. Freud's rhetoric of the psyche, as codified by Anna Freud in *The Ego and the Mechanisms of Defense* (1946), is as comprehensive a system of tropes as Western theory has devised. We can see now, because of Freud, that rhetoric always was more the art of defense than it was the art of persuasion, or rather that defense is always *prior* to persuasion. Trilling's pioneering observation that Freud's science shared with literature a reliance upon trope has proved to be wholly accurate. To clarify my argument, I need to return to Freud's trope of the unconscious and then to proceed from it to his concern with catastrophe as the origin of drive in his later works.

'Consciousness,' as a word, goes back to a root meaning 'to cut or split,' and so to know something by separating out one thing from another. The unconscious (Freud's *das Unbewusste*) is a purely inferred division of the psyche, an inference necessarily based only upon the supposed effects that the unconscious has upon ways we think and act that can be *known*, that are available to consciousness. Because there are gaps or disjunctions to be accounted for in our thoughts and acts, various explanatory concepts of an unconscious have been available since ancient times, but the actual term first appears as the German *Unbewusste* in the later eighteenth century, to be popularized by Goethe and by Schelling. The English 'unconscious' was popularized by Coleridge, whose theory of a poem as reconciling a natural outside with a human inside relied upon a formula that 'the consciousness is so impressed on the unconscious as to appear in it.' Freud acknowledged often that the poets had been there before him, as discoverers of the unconscious, but asserted his own discovery as being the scientific *use* of a concept of the unconscious. What he did not assert was his intense narrowing down of the traditional concept, for he separated out and away from it the attributes of creativity that poets and other speculators always had ascribed to it. Originality or invention are not mentioned by Freud as rising out of the unconscious.

There is no single concept of the unconscious in Freud, as any responsible reading of his work shows. This is because there are two Freudian topographies or maps of the mind, earlier and later (after 1920), and also because the unconscious is a dynamic concept. Freud distinguished his concept of the unconscious from that of his closest psychological precursor, Pierre Janet, by emphasizing his own vision of a civil war in the psyche, a dynamic conflict of opposing mental forces, conscious against unconscious. Not only the conflict was seen thus as being dynamic, but the unconscious peculiarly was characterized as dynamic in itself, requiring always a contending force to keep it from breaking through into consciousness.

In the first Freudian topography, the psyche is divided into Unconscious, Preconscious, and Conscious, while in the second the divisions are the rather different triad of id, ego, and super-ego. The Preconscious, descriptively considered, is unconscious, but can be made conscious, and so is severely divided from the Unconscious proper, in the perspective given either by a topographical or a dynamic view. But this earlier system proved simplistic to Freud himself, mostly because he came to believe that our lives began with all of the mind's contents in the unconscious. This finally eliminated Janet's conception that the unconscious was a wholly separate mode of consciousness, which was a survival of the ancient belief in a creative or inaugurating unconscious. Freud's new topology insisted upon the dynamics of relationship between an unknowable unconscious and consciousness by predicating three agencies or instances of personality: id, ego, super-ego. The effect of this new system was to devalue the unconscious, or at least to demystify it still further.

In the second Freudian topography, 'unconscious' tends to become merely a modifier, since all of the id and very significant parts of the ego and super-ego are viewed as being unconscious. Indeed, the second Freudian concept of the ego gives us an ego which is *mostly* unconscious, and so 'behaves exactly like the repressed – that is, which produces powerful effects without itself being conscious and which requires special work before it can be made conscious,' as Freud remarks in *The Ego and the Id*. Lacan has emphasized the unconscious element in the ego to such a degree that the Lacanian ego must be considered, despite its creator's protests, much more a revision of Freud than what ordinarily would be accounted an interpretation. With mordant eloquence, Lacan keeps assuring us that the ego, every ego, is essentially paranoid, which as Lacan knows *sounds* rather more like Pascal than it does like Freud. I think that this insistence is at once Lacan's strength and his weakness, for my knowledge of imaginative literature tells me that Lacan's conviction is certainly true if by the ego we mean the literary 'I' as it appears in much of the most vital lyric poetry of the last three hundred years, and indeed in all literature that achieves the Sublime. But with the literary idea of 'the Sublime' I come at last to the sequence of Freud's texts that I wish to examine, since the first of them is Freud's theory of the Sublime, his essay *The 'Uncanny'* of 1919.

The text of *The 'Uncanny'* is the threshold to the major phase of Freud's canon, which begins the next year with *Beyond the Pleasure Principle*. But quite aside from its crucial place in Freud's writings, the essay is of enormous importance to literary criticism because it is the only major contribution that the twentieth century has made to the aesthetics of the Sublime. It may seem curious to regard Freud as the culmination of a literary and philosophical tradition that held no particular interest for him, but I would correct my own statement by the modification, no *conscious* interest for him. The Sublime, as I read Freud, is one of his major *repressed* concerns, and this literary repression on his part is a clue to what I take to be a gap in his theory of repression.

I come now, belatedly, to the definition of 'the Sublime,' before considering Freud as the last great theorist of that mode. As a literary idea, the Sublime originally meant a style of 'loftiness,' that is of verbal power, of greatness or strength conceived agonistically, which is to say against all possible competition. But in the European Enlightenment, this literary idea was strangely transformed into a vision of the terror that could be perceived both in nature and in art, a terror uneasily allied with pleasurable sensations of augmented power, and even of narcissistic freedom, freedom in the shape of that wildness that Freud dubbed 'the omnipotence of thought,' the greatest of all narcissistic illusions.

Freud's essay begins with a curiously weak defensive attempt to separate his subject from the aesthetics of the Sublime, which he insists deals only 'with feelings of a positive nature.' This is so flatly untrue, and so blandly ignores the long philosophical tradition of the negative Sublime, that an alert reader ought to become very wary. A year later, in the opening paragraphs of *Beyond the Pleasure Principle*, Freud slyly assures his readers that 'priority and originality are not among the aims that psycho-analytic work sets itself.' One sentence later, he charmingly adds that he would be glad to accept any philosophical help he can get, but that none is available for a consideration of the meaning of pleasure and unpleasure. With evident generosity, he then acknowledges G.T. Fechner, and later makes a bow to the safely distant Plato as author of *The Symposium*. Very close to the end of *Beyond the Pleasure Principle*, there is a rather displaced reference to Schopenhauer, when Freud remarks that 'we have unwittingly steered our course into the harbor of Schopenhauer's philosophy.' The apogee of this evasiveness in regard to precursors comes where it should, in the marvelous essay of 1937, *Analysis Terminable and Interminable*, which we may learn to read as being Freud's elegiac *apologia* for his life's work. There the true precursor is unveiled as Empedocles, very safely remote at two and a half millennia. Perhaps psychoanalysis does not set priority and originality as aims in its *praxis*, but the first and most original of psychoanalysts certainly shared the influence-anxieties and defensive misprisions of all strong writers throughout history, and particularly in the last three centuries.

Anxieties when confronted with anterior powers are overtly the concerns of the essay on the 'uncanny.' E.T.A. Hoffmann's *The Sand-Man* provides Freud with his text, and for once Freud allows himself to be a very useful practical critic of an imaginative story. The repetition-compulsion, possibly imported backwards from *Beyond the Pleasure Principle* as work-in-progress, brilliantly is invoked to open up what is hidden in the story. Uncanniness is traced back to the narcissistic belief in 'omnipotence of thought,' which in aesthetic terms is necessarily the High Romantic faith in the power of the mind over the universe of the senses and of death. *Das Heimliche*, the homely or canny, is thus extended to its only apparent opposite, *das Unheimliche*, 'for this uncanny is in reality nothing new or foreign, but something familiar and old-established in the mind that has been estranged only by the process of repression.'

Freud weakens his extraordinary literary insight by the latter part of his essay, where he seeks to reduce the 'uncanny' to either an infantile or a primitive survival in our psyche. His essay knows better, in its wonderful dialectical play on the *Unheimlich* as being subsumed by the larger or parental category of the *Heimlich*. Philip Rieff finely catches this interplay in his comment that the effect of Freud's writing is itself rather uncanny, and surely never more so than in this essay. Rieff sounds like Emerson or even like Longinus on the Sublime when he considers the condition of Freud's reader:

> The reader comes to a work with ambivalent motives, learning what he does not wish to know, or, what amounts to the same thing, believing he already knows and can accept as his own intellectual property what the author merely 'articulates' or 'expresses' for him. Of course, in this sense, everybody knows everything—or nobody could learn anything. . . .

Longinus had said that reading a sublime poet '. . . we come to believe we have created what we have only heard.' Milton, strongest poet of the modern Sublime, stated this version of the reader's Sublime with an ultimate power, thus setting forth the principle upon which he himself read, in Book IV of his *Paradise Regained*, where his Christ tells Satan:

> . . . who reads
> Incessantly, and to his reading brings not
> A spirit and judgment equal or superior
> (And what he brings, what needs he elsewhere seek?),
> Uncertain and unsettled still remains. . . .

Pope followed Boileau in saying that Longinus 'is himself the great Sublime he draws.' Emerson, in his seminal essay *Self-Reliance*, culminated this theme of the reader's Sublime when he asserted that 'in every work of genius we recognize our own rejected thoughts; they come back to us with a certain alienated majesty.' The 'majesty' is the true, high, breaking light, aura or lustre, of the Sublime, and this realization is at the repressed center of Freud's essay on the 'uncanny.' What Freud declined to see, at that moment, was the mode of conversion that alienated the 'canny' into the 'uncanny.' His next major text, *Beyond the Pleasure Principle*, clearly exposes that mode as being catastrophe.

Lacan and his followers have centered upon *Beyond the Pleasure Principle* because the book has not lost the force of its shock value, even to Freudian analysts. My contention would be that this shock is itself the stigma of the Sublime, stemming from Freud's literary achievement here. The text's origin is itself shock or aura, the trauma that a neurotic's dreams attempt to master, *after the event*. 'Drive' or 'instinct' is suddenly seen by Freud as being catastrophic in its origins, and as being aimed, not at satisfaction, but at death. For the first time in his writing, Freud overtly assigns priority to the psyche's fantasizings over mere biology, though this valorization makes Freud

uneasy. The pleasure principle produces the biological principle of
constancy, and then is converted, through this principle, into a drive
back to the constancy of death. Drive or instinct thus becomes a
kind of defense, all but identified with repression. This troping of
biology is so extreme, really so literary, that I find it more instructive
to seek the aid of commentary here from a Humean empiricist like
Wollheim than from Continental dialecticians like Lacan and Laplanche.
Wollheim imperturbably finds no violation of empiricism or biology
in the death-drive. He even reads 'beyond,' *jenseits,* as meaning
only 'inconsistent with' the pleasure principle, which is to remove
from the word the transcendental or Sublime emphasis that Freud's
usage gave to it. For Wollheim, the book is nothing more than the
working through of the full implication of the major essay of 1914,
On Narcissism: An Introduction. If we follow Wollheim's lead quite
thoroughly here, we will emerge with conclusions that differ from his
rather guarded remarks about the book in which Freud seems to have
shocked himself rather more than he shocks Wollheim.

The greatest shock of *Beyond the Pleasure Principle* is that it ascribes
the origin of all human drives to a catastrophe theory of creation
(to which I would add: 'of creativity'). This catastrophe theory is
developed in *The Ego and the Id,* where the two major catastrophes, the
drying up of ocean that cast life onto land and the Ice Age, are said to
be repeated psychosomatically in the way the latency period (roughly
from the age of five until twelve) cuts a gap into sexual development.
Rieff again is very useful when he says that the basis of catastrophe
theory, whether in Freud or in Ferenczi's more drastic and even
apocalyptic *Thalassa* (1921), 'remains Freud's *Todestrieb,* the tendency
of all organisms to strive toward a state of absence of irritability
and finally "the death-like repose of the inorganic world"'. I find it
fascinating from a literary critical standpoint to note what I think has
not been noted, that the essay on narcissism turns upon catastrophe
theory also. Freud turns to poetry, here to Heine, in order to illustrate
the psychogenesis of Eros, but the lines he quotes actually state a
psychogenesis of creativity rather than of love:

> . . . whence does that necessity arise that urges our mental life to
> pass on beyond the limits of narcissism and to attach the libido to
> objects? The answer which would follow from our line of thought
> would once more be that we are so impelled when the cathexis of
> the ego with libido exceeds a certain degree. A strong egoism is
> a protection against disease, but in the last resort we must begin
> to love in order that we may not fall ill, and must fall ill if, in
> consequence of frustration, we cannot love. Somewhat after this
> fashion does Heine conceive of the psychogenesis of the creation:

Krankheit ist wohl der letzte Grund
Des ganzen Schöpferdrangs gewesen;
Erschaffend konnte ich genesen,
Erschaffend wurde ich gesund.

To paraphrase Heine loosely, illness is the ultimate ground of the drive to create, and so while creating the poet sustains relief, and by creating the poet becomes healthy. Freud transposes from the catastrophe of creativity to the catastrophe of falling in love, a transposition to which I will return in the final pages of this chapter.

Beyond the Pleasure Principle, like the essay on narcissism, is a discourse haunted by images (some of them repressed) of catastrophe. Indeed, what Freud verges upon showing is that to be human is a catastrophic condition. The coloring of this catastrophe, in Freud, is precisely Schopenhauerian rather than, say, Augustinian or Pascalian. It is as though, for Freud, the Creation and the Fall had been one and the same event. Freud holds back from this abyss of Gnosticism by reducing mythology to psychology, but since psychology and cosmology have been intimately related throughout human history, this reduction is not altogether persuasive. Though he wants to show us that the daemonic is 'really' the compulsion to repeat, Freud tends rather to the 'uncanny' demonstration that repetition-compulsion reveals many of us to be daemonic or else makes us daemonic. Again, Freud resorts to the poets for illustration, and again the example goes beyond the Freudian interpretation. Towards the close of section III of *Beyond the Pleasure Principle*, Freud looks for a supreme instance of 'people all of whose human relationships have the same outcome' and he finds it in Tasso:

. . . The most moving poetic picture of a fate such as this is given by Tasso in his romantic epic *Gerusalemme Liberata*. Its hero, Tancred, unwittingly kills his beloved Clorinda in a duel while she is disguised in the armor of an enemy knight. After her burial he makes his way into a strange magic forest which strikes the Crusaders' army with terror. He slashes with his sword at a tall tree; but blood streams from the cut and the voice of Clorinda, whose soul is imprisoned in the tree, is heard complaining that he has wounded his beloved once again.

Freud cites this episode as evidence to support his assumption 'that there really does exist in the mind a compulsion to repeat which overrides the pleasure principle.' The repetition in Tasso is not just incremental, but rather is qualitative, in that the second wounding is 'uncanny' or Sublime, and the first is merely accidental. Freud's citation is an allegory of Freud's own passage into the Sublime. When Freud writes (and the italics are his): *'It seems, then, that a drive is an urge inherent in organic life to restore an earlier state of things,'* then he slays his beloved trope of 'drive' by disguising it in the armor of his enemy, mythology. But when he writes (and again the italics are his): *'the aim of all life is death,'* then he wounds his figuration of 'drive' in a truly Sublime or 'uncanny' fashion. In the qualitative leap from the drive to restore pure anteriority to the apothegm that life's purpose is death, Freud himself has abandoned the empirical for the daemonic. It is the literary authority of the daemonic rather than the analytical which makes plausible the further suggestion that

. . . sadism is in fact a death instinct which, under the influence of the narcissistic libido, had been forced away from the ego. . . .

This language is impressive, and it seems to me equally against literary tact to accept it or reject it on any supposed biological basis. Its true basis is that of an implicit catastrophe theory of meaning or interpretation, which is in no way weakened by being circular and therefore mythological. The repressed rhetorical formula of Freud's discourse in *Beyond the Pleasure Principle* can be stated thus: *literal meaning equals anteriority equals an earlier state of meaning equals an earlier state of things equals death equals literal meaning.* Only one escape is possible from such a formula, and it is a simpler formula: *Eros equals figurative meaning.* This is the dialectic that informs the proudest and most moving passage in *Beyond the Pleasure Principle,* which comprises two triumphant sentences *contra* Jung that were added to the text in 1921, in a Sublime afterthought:

Our views have from the very first been *dualistic,* and today they are even more definitely dualistic than before – now that we describe the opposition as being, not between ego-instincts and sexual instincts, but between life instincts and death instincts. Jung's libido theory is on the contrary *monistic*; the fact that he has called his one instinctual force 'libido' is bound to cause confusion, but need not affect us otherwise.

I would suggest that we read *dualistic* here as a trope for 'figurative' and *monistic* as a trope for 'literal.' The opposition between life drives and death drives is not just a dialectic (though it *is* that) but is a great writer's Sublime interplay between figurative and literal meanings, whereas Jung is exposed as being what he truly was, a mere literalizer of anterior mythologies. What Freud proclaims here, in the accents of sublimity, is the power of his own mind over language, which in this context *is* the power that Hegelians or Lacanians legitimately could term 'negative thinking.'

I am pursuing Freud as prose-poet of the Sublime, but I would not concede that I am losing sight of Freud as analytical theorist. Certainly the next strong Freudian text is the incomparable *Inhibitions, Symptoms, and Anxiety* of 1926. But before considering that elegant and somber meditation, certainly the most illuminating analysis of anxiety our civilization has been offered, I turn briefly to Freud's essay on his dialectic, *Negation* (1925).

Freud's audacity here has been little noted, perhaps because he packs into fewer than five pages an idea that cuts a considerable gap into his theory of repression. The gap is wide enough so that such oxymorons as 'a successful repression' and 'an achieved anxiety,' which are not possible in psychoanalysis, are made available to us as literary terms. Repressed images or thoughts, by Freudian definition, *cannot* make their way into consciousness, yet their content can, on condition that it is *denied*. Freud cheerfully splits head from heart in the apprehension of images:

> Negation is a way of taking account of what is repressed; indeed, it is actually a removal of the repression, though not, of course, an acceptance of what is repressed. It is to be seen how the intellectual function is here distinct from the affective process. Negation only assists in undoing *one* of the consequences of repression – namely, the fact that the subject-matter of the image in question is unable to enter consciousness. The result is a kind of intellectual acceptance of what is repressed, though in all essentials the repression persists. . . .

I would venture one definition of the literary Sublime (which to me seems always a negative Sublime) as being that mode in which the poet, while expressing previously repressed thought, desire, or emotion, is able to continue to defend himself against his own created image by disowning it, a defense of *un-naming* it rather than *naming* it. Freud's word *Verneinung* means both a grammatical negation and a psychic disavowal or denial, and so the linguistic and the psychoanalytical have a common origin here, as Lacan and his school have insisted. The ego and the poet-in-his-poem both proceed by a kind of 'misconstruction,' a defensive process that Lacan calls *méconnaissance* in psychoanalysis, and that I have called 'misprision' in the study of poetic influence (a notion formulated before I had read Lacan, but which I was delighted to find supported in him). In his essay *Aggressivity in Psychoanalysis* Lacan usefully connects Freud's notion of a 'negative' libido to the idea of Discord in Heraclitus.

Freud himself brings his essay on *Verneinung* to a fascinating double conclusion. First, the issue of truth or falsehood in language is directly related to the defenses of introjection and projection; a true image thus would be introjected and a false one projected. Second, the defense of introjection is aligned to the Eros-drive of affirmation, 'while negation, the derivative of expulsion, belongs to the instinct of destruction,' the drive to death beyond the pleasure principle. I submit that what Freud has done here should have freed literary discussion from its persistent over-literalization of his idea of repression. Freud joins himself to the tradition of the Sublime, that is, of the strongest Western poetry, by showing us that negation allows poetry to free itself from the aphasias and hysterias of repression, *without* however freeing the poets themselves from the unhappier human consequences of repression. Negation is of *no* therapeutic value for the individual, but it *can* liberate him into the linguistic freedoms of poetry and thought.

I think that of all Freud's books, none matches the work on inhibitions, symptoms and anxiety in its potential importance for students of literature, for this is where the concept of defense is ultimately clarified. Wollheim says that Freud confused the issue of defense by the 'overschematic' restriction of repression to a single species of defense, but this is one of the very rare instances where Wollheim seems to me misled or mistaken. Freud's revised account of anxiety *had* to distinguish between *relatively* non-repressive and the more severely repressive defenses, and I only wish that both Freud and his daughter after him had been even more schematic in mapping out the defenses. We need a rhetoric of the psyche, and here the Lacanians have been a kind of disaster, with their simplistic over-reliance upon the metaphor/metonymy distinction. Freud's revised account of anxiety is precisely at one with the poetic Sublime, for anxiety is finally seen as a technique for mastering anteriority by *remembering* rather than *repeating* the past. By showing us that anxiety is a mode of expectation, closely resembling desire, Freud allows us to understand why poetry, which loves love, also seems to love anxiety. Literary and human romance both are exposed as being anxious quests that could not bear to be cured of their anxieties, even if such cures were possible. 'An increase of excitation underlies anxiety,' Freud tells us, and then he goes on to relate this increase to a repetition of the catastrophe of human birth, with its attendant trauma. Arguing against Otto Rank, who like Ferenczi had gone too far into the abysses of catastrophe-theory, Freud enunciated a principle that can help explain why the terror of the literary Sublime must and can give pleasure:

Anxiety is an affective state which can of course be experienced only by the ego. The id cannot be afraid, as the ego can; it is not an organization, and cannot estimate situations of danger. On the contrary, it is of extremely frequent occurrence that processes are initiated or executed in the id which give the ego occasion to develop anxiety; as a matter of fact, the repressions which are probably the earliest are motivated, like the majority of all later ones, by such fear on the part of the ego of this or that process in the id. . . .

Freud's writing career was to conclude with the polemical assertion that 'mysticism is the obscure self-perception of the realm outside the ego, of the id,' which is a splendid farewell thrust at Jung, as we can see by substituting 'Jung' for 'the id' at the close of the sentence. The id perceiving the id is a parody of the Sublime, whereas the ego's earliest defense, its primal repression, is the true origin of the Sublime. Freud knew that 'primal repression' was a necessary fiction, because without some initial fixation his story of the psyche could not begin. Laplanche and Pontalis, writing under Lacan's influence in their *The Language of Psychoanalysis*, find the basis of fixation

in primal moments at which certain privileged ideas are indelibly inscribed in the unconscious, and at which the instinct itself becomes fixated to its psychical representative – perhaps by this very process constituting itself *qua* instinct.

If we withdrew that 'perhaps,' then we would return to the Freudian catastrophe-theory of the genesis of all drives, with fixation now being regarded as another originating catastrophe. How much clearer these hypotheses become if we transpose them into the realm of poetry! If fixation becomes the inscription in the unconscious of the privileged idea of a Sublime poet, or strong precursor, then the drive towards poetic expression originates in an agonistic repression, where the agon or contest is set against the pattern of the precursor's initial fixation upon an anterior figure. Freud's mature account of anxiety thus concludes itself upon an allegory of origins, in which the creation of an unconscious implicitly models itself upon poetic origins. There was repression, Freud insists, before there was anything to be repressed. This insistence is neither rational nor irrational; it is a figuration that knows its own status as figuration, without embarrassment.

My final text in Freud is *Analysis Terminable and Interminable*. The German title, *Die Endliche und die Unendliche Analyse*, might better be translated as 'finite or indefinite analysis,' which is Lacan's suggestion. Lacan amusingly violates the taboo of discussing how long the analytic session is to be when he asks:

. . . how is this time to be measured? Is its measure to be that of what Alexander Koyré calls 'the universe of precision'? Obviously we live in this universe, but its advent for man is relatively recent, since it goes back precisely to Huyghens' clock – in other words, to 1659 – and the *malaise* of modern man does not exactly indicate that this precision is in itself a liberating factor for him. Are we to say that this time, the time of the fall of heavy bodies, is in some way sacred in the sense that it corresponds to the time of the stars as they were fixed in eternity by God who, as Lichtenberg put it, winds up our sundials?

I reflect, as I read Lacan's remarks, that it was just after Huyghens's clock that Milton began to compose *Paradise Lost*, in the early 1660's, and that Milton's poem is *the* instance of the modern Sublime. It is in *Paradise Lost* that temporality fully becomes identified with anxiety, which makes Milton's epic the most Freudian text ever written, far closer to the universe of psychoanalysis than such more frequently cited works, in Freudian contexts, as *Oedipus Tyrannus* and *Hamlet*. We should remember that before Freud used a Virgilian tag as epigraph for *The Interpretation of Dreams* (1908), he had selected a great Satanic utterance for his motto:

Seest thou yon dreary plain, forlorn and wild,
The seat of desolation, void of light,
Save what the glimmering of these livid flames
Casts pale and dreadful? Thither let us tend
From off the tossing of these fiery waves,
There rest, if any rest can harbour there,
And reassembling our afflicted powers,
Consult how we may henceforth most offend
Our enemy, our own loss how repair,
How overcome this dire calamity,
What reinforcement we may gain from hope;
If not, what resolution from despair.

This Sublime passage provides a true motto for all psychoanalysis, since 'afflicted powers' meant 'cast-down powers,' or as Freud would have said, 'repressed drives.' But it would be an even apter epigraph for the essay on finite and indefinite analysis than it could have been for the much more hopeful *Interpretation of Dreams*, thirty years before. Freud begins his somber and beautiful late essay by brooding sardonically on the heretic Otto Rank's scheme for speeding up analysis in America. But this high humor gives way to the melancholy of considering every patient's deepest resistance to the analyst's influence, that 'negative transference' in which the subject's anxiety-of-influence seeks a bulwark. As he reviews the main outlines of his theory, Freud emphasizes its *economic* aspects rather

191

than the dynamic and topographical points of view. The *economic* modifies any notion that drives have an energy that can be measured. To estimate the magnitude of such excitation is to ask the classical, agonistic question that *is* the Sublime, because the Sublime is always a comparison of two forces or beings, in which the agon turns on the answer to three queries: more? equal to? or less than? Satan confronting hell, the abyss, the new world, is still seeking to answer the questions that he sets for himself in heaven, all of which turn upon comparing God's force and his own. Oedipus confronting the Sphinx, Hamlet facing the mystery of the dead father, and Freud meditating upon repression are all in the same economic stance. I would use this shared stance to re-define a question that psychoanalysis by its nature cannot answer. Since there is *no* biological warrant for the Freudian concept of libido, what is the energy that Freud invokes when he speaks from the economic point of view? Wollheim, always faithful to empiricism, has only one comment upon the economic theory of mind, and it is a very damaging observation:

> . . . though an economic theory allows one to relate the damming up of energy or frustration at one place in the psychic apparatus with discharge at another, it does not commit one to the view that, given frustration, energy will seek discharge along all possible channels indifferently. Indeed, if the system is of any complexity, an economic theory would be virtually uninformative unless some measure of selectivity in discharge was postulated. . . .

But since Freud applied the economic stance to sexual drives almost entirely, no measure of selectivity *could* be postulated. This still leaves us with Freud's economic obsessions, and I suggest now that their true model was literary, and not sexual. This would mean that the 'mechanisms of defense' are dependent for their formulaic coherence upon the traditions of rhetoric, and not upon biology, which is almost too easily demonstrable. It is hardly accidental that Freud, in this late essay which is so much his *summa*, resorts to the textual analogue when he seeks to distinguish repression from the other defenses:

> Without pressing the analogy too closely we may say that repression is to the other methods of defense what the omission of words or passages is to the corruption of a text. . . . For quite a long time flight and an avoidance of a dangerous situation serve as expedients. . . . But one cannot flee from oneself and no flight avails against danger from within; hence the ego's defensive mechanisms are condemned to falsify the inner perception, so that it transmits to us only an imperfect and travestied picture of our id. In its relations

with the id the ego is paralysed by its restrictions or blinded by its errors. . . .

What is Freud's motive for this remarkably clear and eloquent recapitulation of his theory of repression and defense (which I take to be the center of his greatness)? The hidden figuration in his discourse here is his economics of the psyche, a trope which is allowed an overt exposure when he sadly observes that the energy necessary to keep such defenses going 'proves a heavy burden on the psychical economy.' If I were reading this essay on finite and indefinite analysis as I have learned to read Romantic poems, I would be on the watch for a blocking-agent in the poetic ego, a shadow that Blake called the Spectre and Shelley a daemon or *Alastor*. This shadow would be an anxiety narcissistically intoxicated with itself, an anxiety determined to go on being anxious, a drive towards destruction in love with the image of self-destruction. Freud, like the great poets of quest, has given all the premonitory signs of this Sublime terror determined to maintain itself, and again like the poets he suddenly makes the pattern quite explicit:

> The crux of the matter is that the mechanisms of defense against former dangers recur in analysis in the shape of *resistances* to cure. It follows that the ego treats recovery itself as a new danger.

Faced by the patient's breaking of the psychoanalytic compact, Freud broods darkly on the war between his true Sublime and the patient's false Sublime:

> Once more we realize the importance of the quantitative factor and once more we are reminded that analysis has only certain limited quantities of energy which it can employ to match against the hostile forces. And it does seem as if victory were really for the most part with the big battalions.

It is a true challenge to the interpreter of Freud's text to identify the economic stance here, for what is the source of *the energy of analysis*, however limited in quantity it may be? Empiricism, whether in Hume or in Wittgenstein, does not discourse on the measurement of its own libido. But if we take Freud as Sublime poet rather than empirical reasoner, if we see him as the peer of Milton rather than of Hume, of Proust rather than of the biologists, then we can speculate rather precisely about the origins of the psychoanalytical drive, about the nature of the powers made available by the discipline that one man was able to establish in so sublimely solitary a fashion. Vico teaches us that the Sublime or severe poet discovers the origin of his rhetorical drive, the catastrophe of his creative vocation, in *divination*, by which Vico meant both the process of foretelling dangers to the self's survival and the apotheosis of becoming a daemon or sort of god. What Vico calls 'divination' is what Freud calls the primal instinct of Eros, or that 'which strives to combine existing phenomena into ever greater unities.' With moving simplicity, Freud then reduces this to the covenant between patient and analyst which he calls 'a love of truth.' But, like all critical idealisms about poetry, this idealization of psychoanalysis is an error. No psychic economy (or indeed *any* economy) can be based upon 'a love of truth.' Drives depend upon fictions, because drives *are* fictions, and we want to know more about Freud's enabling fictions, which grant to him his Sublime 'energy of analysis.'

We can acquire this knowledge by a very close analysis of the final section of Freud's essay, a section not the less instructive for being so unacceptable to our particular moment in social and cultural history. The resistance to analytical cure, in both men and women, is identified by Freud with what he calls the 'repudiation of femininity' *by both sexes*, the castration complex that informs the fantasy-life of everyone whatsoever: '. . . in both cases it is the attitude belonging to the sex opposite to the subject's own which succumbs to repression.' This is followed by Freud's prophetic lament, with its allusion to the burden of Hebraic prophecy. Freud too sees himself as the *nabi* who speaks to the winds, to the winds only, for only the winds will listen:

> . . . At no point in one's analytic work does one suffer more from the oppressive feeling that all one's efforts have been in vain and from the suspicion that one is 'talking to the winds' than when one is trying to persuade a female patient to abandon her wish for a penis on the ground of its being unrealizable, or to convince a male patient that a passive attitude towards another man does not always signify castration and that in many relations in life it is indispensable. The rebellious over-compensation of the male produces one of the strongest transference-resistances. A man will not be subject to a father-substitute or owe him anything and he therefore refuses to accept his cure from the physician. . . .

It is again one of Lacan's services to have shown us that this is figurative discourse, even if Lacan's own figurative discourse becomes too baroque a commentary upon Freud's wisdom here. Freud prophesies to the winds because men and women cannot surrender their primal fantasies, which are their poor but desperately prideful myths of their own origins. We cannot let go of our three fundamental fantasies: the primal scene, which accounts for our existence; the seduction fantasy, which justifies our narcissism; and the castration complex, which explains to us the mystery of sexual differentiation. What the three fantasy-scenes share is the fiction of an originating catastrophe, and so a very close relation to the necessity for defense. The final barrier to Freud's heroic labor of healing, in Freud's own judgment, is the human imagination. The original wound in man cannot be healed, as it is in Hegel, by the same force that makes the wound.

Freud became a strong poet of the Sublime because he made the solitary crossing from a realm where effect is always traced to a cause, to a mode of discourse which asked instead the economic and agonistic questions of comparison. The question of how an emptiness came about was replaced by the question that asks: more, less, or equal to? which is the agonistic self-questioning of the Sublime. The attempt to give truer names to the rhetoric of human defense was replaced by the increasing refusal to name the vicissitudes of drive except by un-namings as old as those of Empedocles and Heraclitus. The ambition to make of psychoanalysis a wholly positive *praxis* yielded to a skeptical and ancient awareness of a rugged negativity that informed every individual fantasy.

Lacan and his school justly insist that psychoanalysis has contributed nothing to biology, despite Freud's wistful hopes that it could, and also that the life sciences inform psychoanalysis hardly at all, again in despite of Freud's eager scientism. Psychoanalysis is a varied therapeutic *praxis*, but it is a 'science' only in the peculiar sense that literature, philosophy and religion are also *sciences of anxiety*. But this means that no single rhetoric or poetic will suffice for the study of psychoanalysis, any more than a particular critical method will unveil all that needs to be seen in literature. The 'French way' of reading Freud, in Lacan, Derrida, Laplanche, and others, is no more a 'right' reading than the way of the ego-psychologists Hartmann, Kris, Erikson, and others, which Lacan and his followers wrongly keep insisting is the only 'American reading.' In this conflict of strong misreadings, partisans of both ways evidently need to keep forgetting what the French at least ought to remember: strong texts become strong by mis-taking all texts anterior to them. Freud has more in common with Proust and Montaigne than with biological scientists, because his interpretations of life and death are mediated always by texts, first by the literary texts of others, and then by his own earlier texts, until at last the Sublime mediation of otherness begins to be performed by his text-in-process. In the *Essays* of Montaigne or Proust's vast novel, this ongoing mediation is clearer than it is in Freud's almost perpetual self-revision, because Freud wrote no definitive, single text; but the canon of Freud's writings shows an increasingly uneasy sense that he had become his own precursor, and that he had begun to defend himself against himself by deliberately audacious arrivals at final positions.

8 Gérard de Nerval, The Disinherited Poet*

JULIA KRISTEVA

Gérard de Nerval was born Gérard Labrunie in Paris on 22 May 1808. His mother died when he was two. In 1828 he published his first important literary work, a translation of Goethe's *Faust* (Part I), after which he worked as a literary journalist and freelance writer. Collaborating on plays with Dumas and others, he fell in love with the actress Jenny Colon, and spent most of an inheritance on a short-lived theatre magazine which he founded in 1835. An eccentric figure, famous for walking a lobster on a lead in the gardens of the Palais Royal, he suffered his first mental breakdown in 1841. Dr Emile Blanche, who treated him at Montmartre, later offered him an attic room in his clinic at Passy, where Nerval wrote the sonnet sequence *Les chimères*, of which 'El Desdichado' is the leading poem. After its publication in 1854, Nerval quickly degenerated: for the last few weeks of his life he was homeless, having discharged himself against his doctor's wishes from Passy. On 25 January 1855 he wrote a letter to his aunt which ended, 'Don't expect me this evening, for the night will be black and white.' At dawn the next day he was found hanged from a grating at the foot of the stone steps in the snow-covered rue de la Vieille Lanterne.†

Nerval's sonnet 'El Desdichado' [The Disinherited] is probably more familiar to English readers through T.S. Eliot, who quoted its second line directly in *The Waste Land* (*'Le prince d'Aquitaine à la tour abolie'*), and alluded to it many times throughout his early work. Julia Kristeva's book *Black Sun* (named after the 'soleil noir' of 'El Desdichado') argues that Nerval's melancholia represents the 'impossible mourning for the maternal object': impossible

*JULIA KRISTEVA, 'Gérard de Nerval, The Disinherited Poet', in *Black Sun: Depression and Melancholia*, trans. Leon S. Roudiez (New York: Columbia University Press, 1989), pp. 139–72; 272–5. © 1989, English translation, Columbia University Press.
†See the biographical note on Gérard de Nerval in *Les chimères*, trans. Peter Jay (London: Anvil Press, 1984), pp. 41–2. 'El Desdichado' is usually printed as the first poem in *Les chimères*, which was first published with *Les filles du feu* in 1854.

because this primordial bereavement occurs before the advent of signification, whereby objects might be named or exorcised or laid to rest. What the melancholic mourns, Kristeva argues, is not an object but 'the Thing', which is prior to the object and resembles the archaic 'breast' in Klein's fantasia: 'an unnameable, supreme good . . . something unrepresentable, that perhaps only devouring might represent, or an *invocation* might point out, but no word could signify' (*Black Sun*, p. 13). This Thing is 'abject' rather than 'object', in Kristeva's terms, because it cannot be distinguished from the self, but undermines the boundaries of subjectivity: 'it is a waste into which, in my sadness, I merge. It is Job's ashpit in the Bible' (for 'abjection', see Introduction above, p. 26). There is something luxurious, as well as sickening, in this collapse of boundaries, as the cliché 'wallowing in grief' implies: for 'sadness is really the sole object' of the melancholic, cherished in defence against the absence of an object and the failure of the whole objectifying faculty. According to Kristeva, melancholia eludes the 'symbolic' side of language in which objects are identified and named; it is only through the 'semiotic' that the melancholy Thing can be articulated: 'through melody, rhythm, semantic polyvalency' (*Black Sun*, p. 14). 'El Desdichado', for example, uses rhyme, rhythm, and alliteration to emphasise the 'network of intensities, sounds, significances rather than communicating univocal information'. In this way Nerval brings meaning closer to the body, which 'asserts itself through a glottic and oral presence'. Like Melanie Klein, Kristeva believes that art performs a reparative function: by transposing melancholy into rhythms, signs, forms, poetry at once communicates its sorrow to the reader yet also brings that sorrow under domination by the sign (below, pp. 212, 217).

El Desdichado *(The Disinherited)*
(As published in *Le Mousquetaire* on December 10, 1853)

1   Je suis le ténébreux, le veuf, l'inconsolé,
2   Le prince d'Aquitaine à la tour abolie;
3   Ma seule étoile est morte, et mon luth constellé
4   Porte le soleil noir de la mélancolie.

5   Dans la nuit du tombeau, toi qui m'a consolé,
6   Rends-moi le Pausilippe et la mer d'Italie,
7   La fleur qui plaisait tant à mon coeur désolé,
8   Et la treille où le pampre à la vigne s'allie.

9   Suis-je Amour ou Phoebus, Lusignan ou Byron?
10   Mon front est rouge encor du baisers de la reine;
11   J'ai dormi dans la grotte où verdit la sirène.

12   Et j'ai deux fois vivant traversé l'Achéron,
13   Modulant et chantant sur la lyre d'Orphée
14   Les soupirs de la sainte et les cris de la fée.

1   *I am saturnine, bereft, disconsolate,*
2   *The Prince of Aquitaine whose tower has crumbled;*
3   *My lone star is dead, and my bespangled lute*
4   *Bears the black sun of melancholia.*

5   *In the night of the grave, you who brought me solace,*
6   *Give me back Posilipo and the sea of Italy,*
7   *The flower that so pleased my distressed heart,*
8   *And the arbor where vine and grape combine.*

9   *Am I Cupid or Phoebus, Lusignan or Byron?*
10   *My brow is still red from the kisses of the queen;*
11   *I have slept in the cave where the siren turns green,*

12   *I've twice, yet alive, been across the Acheron,*
13   *Modulating and singing on Orpheus' lyre*
14   *The sighs of the saint and the screams of the fay.*

El Desdichado *(The Disinherited)*
(As published in *Les Filles du feu* 1854)

1 Je suis le ténébreux, – le veuf, – l'inconsolé,
2 Le prince d'Aquitaine à la tour abolie;
3 Ma seule *étoile* est morte, – et mon luth constellé
4 Porte le *Soleil noir* de la *Mélancolie.*

5 Dans la nuit du tombeau, toi qui m'a consolé,
6 Rends-moi le Pausilippe et la mer d'Italie,
7 La *fleur* qui plaisait tant à mon coeur désolé,
8 Et la treille où le pampre à la rose s'allie.

9 Suis-je Amour ou Phébus? . . . Lusignan ou Byron?
10 Mon front est rouge encor du baiser de la reine;
11 J'ai rêvé dans la grotte où nage la sirène . . .

12 Et j'ai deux fois vainqueur traversé l'Achéron,
13 Modulant tour à tour sur la lyre d'Orphée
14 Les soupirs de la sainte et les cris de la fée.

1 *I am saturnine – bereft – disconsolate,*
2 *The Prince of Aquitaine whose tower has crumbled;*
3 *My lone star is dead – and my bespangled lute*
4 *Bears the* Black Sun *of* Melancholia.

5 *In the night of the grave, you who brought me solace,*
6 *Give me back Posilipo and the sea of Italy,*
7 *The* flower *that so pleased my distressed heart,*
8 *And the arbor where grapevine and rose combine.*

9 *Am I Cupid or Phebus? . . . Lusignan or Byron?*
10 *My brow is still red from the kiss of the queen;*
11 *I have dreamt in the cave where the siren swims . . .*

12 *I've twice, as a conqueror, been across the Acheron;*
13 *Modulating by turns on Orpheus' lyre*
14 *The sighs of the saint and the screams of the fay.*

I am alone, I am bereft, and the night falls upon me

            –Victor Hugo, Booz

. . . it is melancholia that becomes his Muse
       – Gérard de Nerval, To Alexandre Dumas

'El Desdichado' and 'Artémis,' written in red ink, were sent to Alexandre Dumas by Nerval in a letter dated November 14, 1853. 'El Desdichado' was first published in *Le Mousquetaire* on December 10, 1853, with an essay by Dumas serving as introduction. A second version appeared in *Les Filles du feu* in 1854. The manuscript of that poem, which belonged to Paul Eluard, bears the title *Le Destin* and is essentially the same as the *Les Filles du feu* version.

After his fit of madness of May 1853, Gérard de Nerval (1808–1855) set out for his native Valois (Chaalis Abbey, Senlis, Loisy, Mortefontaine) in order to seek nostalgic refuge and relief.[1] The tireless wanderer who never grew weary of crisscrossing Southern France, Germany, Austria, and the East, withdrew for a while into the crypt of a past that haunted him. In August the symptoms showed up again: there he was, like a threatened archeologist, visiting the osteology wing at the Jardin des Plantes, convinced, in the rain, that he was witnessing the Flood. Graves, skeletons, the irruption of death indeed continually haunted him. Within such a context, 'El Desdichado' was his Noah's Ark. Albeit a temporary one, it nevertheless secured him a fluid, enigmatic, spellbinding identity. Orpheus, once again, retained victory over the Black Prince.

The title, 'El Desdichado,' at once points to the strangeness of the text that follows; its Spanish resonance, however, shrill and trumpeting beyond the word's woeful meaning, contrasts sharply with the shaded, discreet vowel pattern of the French language and appears to herald some triumph or other in the very heart of darkness.

Who is 'El Desdichado'? On the one hand, Nerval might have borrowed the name from Walter Scott's *Ivanhoe* (chapter 8); it refers to one of King John's knights whom the king dispossessed of the castle that Richard Lion-Heart had bequeathed to him. The unfortunate, disinherited knight then decided to embellish his shield with the picture of an uprooted oak and the words 'El Desdichado.' On the other hand, a 'French source for El Desdichado' has been suggested; this would be Don Blaz Desdichado, a character in Alain René Lesage's *Le Diable boiteux* [The Lame Devil] who goes mad because, lacking heirs, he is forced to return his wealth to his in-laws after his wife's death.[2] If it be true that for many French readers the Spanish 'el desdichado' translates as 'disinherited,' an accurate, literal rendition of the word would be 'wretched,' 'unfortunate,' 'pitiful.' Nerval, however, appears to have been attached to 'disinherited' – which was, moreover, Alexandre Dumas' choice in his translation of *Ivanhoe*. It is also the term Nerval used to refer to himself in another context ('Thus, myself, once a brilliant actor, an unknown prince, a mysterious lover, disinherited, excluded from happiness, handsome and saturnine. . . .').[3]

Lost 'thing' or 'object'

Disinherited of what? An initial deprivation is thus indicated at once; it is not, however, the deprivation of a 'property' or 'object' constituting a material, transferable heritage, but the loss of an unnameable domain, which one might, strangely enough, evoke or invoke, from a foreign land, from a constitutional exile. This 'something' would be previous to the detectable 'object': the secret and unreachable horizon of our loves and desires, it assumes, for the imagination, the consistency of an archaic mother, which, however, no precise image manages to encompass. The untiring quest for mistresses or, on the religious level, the accumulation of feminine divinities or mother goddesses that Eastern and particularly Egyptian religions lavish on the 'subject,' points to the elusive nature of that *Thing* – necessarily lost so that this 'subject,' separated from the 'object,' might become a speaking being.

If the melancholy person ceaselessly exerts an ascendency, as loving as it is hateful, over that Thing, the poet finds an enigmatic way of being both subordinate to it and . . . elsewhere. Disinherited, deprived of that lost paradise, he is wretched; writing, however, is the strange way that allows him to overcome such wretchedness by setting up an 'I' that controls both aspects of deprivation – the darkness of disconsolation and the 'kiss of the queen.'

The 'I' then asserts itself on the field of artifice: there is a place for the 'I' only in play, in theater, behind the masks of possible identities, which are as extravagant, prestigious, mythical, epic, historical, and esoteric as they are incredible. Triumphant, but also uncertain.

This 'I' that pins down and secures the first line, 'I am saturnine – bereft – disconsolate,' points, with a knowledge as certain as it is illuminated with a hallucinatory nescience, to the necessary condition for the poetic act. To speak, to venture, to settle within the legal fiction known as symbolic activity, that is indeed to lose the Thing.

Henceforth the dilemma can be stated as follows: will the traces of that lost Thing sweep the speaker along, or will he succeed in carrying them away – integrating them, incorporating them in his discourse, which has become a song by dint of seizing the Thing. In other words: is it the bacchantes who tear Orpheus to pieces, or is it Orpheus who carries the bacchantes away through his incantation, as in a symbolic anthropophagy?

I am that which is not

The fluctuation will be permanent. After an unbelievable assertion of presence and certainty, recalling Victor Hugo's self-confidence as a patriarch whom solitude does not disturb but brings peace to ('I am alone, I am bereft, and the night falls upon me'), we are once more amid misfortune. The qualities of that triumphant 'I' are negative ones; deprived of light, deprived of wife, deprived of solace, he is that which *is not*. He is 'saturnine,' 'bereft,' 'disconsolate.'

Nerval's interest in alchemy and esoterica render perfectly plausible Georges Le Breton's interpretation, according to which the first lines of *El Desdichado* follow the tarot cards' order (cards 15, 16, 17). 'Saturnine' would refer to hell's great demon (the fifteenth card of the tarot is the devil's card); he also might well be Pluto the alchemist, who died celibate, whose deformity caused the goddesses to flee (hence he is bereft), and who figured the earth at the bottom of a caldron where all alchemical processes have their source.[4]

Nonetheless, those references that make up Nerval's ideology are inserted into a poetic web – uprooted, transposed, they achieve a multivalency and a set of connotations, all of which are often undecidable. The polyvalency of symbolism within the new symbolic order structured by the poem, combined with the rigidity of symbols within esoteric doctrines, endow Nerval's language with a twofold advantage: on the one hand, insuring a stable meaning as well as a secret community where the disconsolate poet is heard, accepted, and, in short, solaced; on the other, slipping away from monovalent meaning and that same community in order to reach as closely as possible the specifically Nervalian object, sorrow – and this through the uncertainty of naming. Before attaining the level of erased meaning where poetic language accompanies the disappearance of the melancholy subject foundering in the lost object, let us follow those processes of Nerval's text that are logically easy to pin down.

Inversions and a double

The qualifier 'saturnine' [Nerval's word: *ténébreux*] is consonant with the Prince of Darkness already suggested by the tarot pack as well as with night deprived of light. It conjures up the melancholy person's complicity with the world of darkness and despair.

The 'black sun' (line 4) again takes up the semantic field of 'saturnine,' but pulls it inside out, like a glove: darkness flashes as a solar light, which nevertheless remains dazzling with black invisibility.

'Bereft' [Nerval's word: *veuf* = widower] is the first sign pointing to mourning. Would the saturnine mood then be the consequence of his having lost a wife? At this spot the Eluard manuscript adds a note, 'in the past: Mausolus?' which replaces words that have been crossed out, 'the Prince/dead/' or 'the poem.' Mausolus was the fourth-century B.C. king of Caria who married his sister Artemisia and died before she did. If the widower were Mausolus, he would have been incestuous – married to his sister, his mother, . . . to an erotic, familiar, and domestic Thing. That figure's ambivalence is yet further muddled by what Nerval does with him; having died first he cannot be a widower but leaves *a widow*, his sister Artemisia. Nerval makes her name masculine in the sonnet 'Artémis' and perhaps plays with the two members of the couple as if each were the *double* of the other – interchangeable but also, consequently, imprecise in their sexuality, nearly androgynous. We are here at an extremely compact stage of Nerval's poetic process: the widow Artemisia identifies with her dead double (brother + husband), *she* is *he*, hence a widower, and this identification, the encrypting of the other, installing the other's vault in oneself, would be the equivalent of the poem. (There are indeed commentators who believe they can read the word 'poem' under the obliteration.) The text as mausoleum?

Using the word 'disconsolate' [*inconsolé*] as opposed to 'inconsolable' suggests a paradoxical temporality: the one who speaks has not been solaced in the past, and the effect of that frustration lasts up to the present. While 'inconsolable' would anchor us in the present, 'disconsolate' turns the present into the past when the trauma was experienced. The present is beyond repair, without the slightest hope of solace.

Imaginary memory

The 'Prince of Aquitaine' is doubtless Waifer (or Guaifer) of Aquitaine who, pursued by Pepin III, the Short, hid in the forests of Périgord. In his mythical genealogy, partially published by Aristide Marie and then fully by Jean Richer,[5] Nerval assumed a prestigious lineage and had his own Labrunie family descend from the knights of Odo [also called Eudon or Eudes]; one of its branches supposedly came from Périgord, just like the Prince of Aquitaine. He also specified that Broun or Brunn means tower and grain-drying structure. The coat of arms of the Labrunies, who were said to have owned three châteaux on the banks of the Dordogne, would bear three silver towers, and also stars and crescents evoking the East, somewhat like the 'star' and 'bespangled lute' that appear in the next line of the text.

To the polyvalency of Aquitaine as a symbol – the land of waters [according to folk etymology, though the word actually derives from Auscetani] – one can add the note sent by Nerval to George Sand (quoted by Richer) in which one reads, 'GASTON PHOEBUS D'AQUITAINE,' whose esoteric meaning would be that of solar initiate. It will be noted more simply, following Jacques Dhaenens,[6] that Aquitaine is the land of troubadours, and thus, by evoking the Black Prince, the widower begins, through courtly song, his transformation into Orpheus . . . We are still, nevertheless, in the domain of despondent statement: 'crumbled' [*abolie* = abolished] confirms the meaning of destruction, deprivation, and lack that has been woven since the beginning of the text. As Emilie Noulet has noted,[7] the phrase 'whose tower has crumbled' [*à la tour abolie*] functions as 'a single mental grouping' and endows the Prince of Aquitaine with a complex qualifier where words merge and syllables stand out, sounding a litany: 'à-la-tour-a-bo-lie,' which might also be seen as a loose anagram of Labrunie. There are three instances of the word 'abolie' in Nerval's work, and Emilie Noulet has noted that this uncommon word seemed essential to Mallarmé, who used it at least six times in his poems.

A dispossessed prince, the glorious subject of a destroyed past, El Desdichado belongs to a history, but to a depreciated history. His past without future is not a historical past – it is merely a *memory* all the more present as it has no future.

The next line again takes up the personal trauma; the tower that has crumbled, the height that is henceforth lacking, was a 'star' that is now dead. The star is the image of the muse, also that of a lofty universe, of the cosmos, which is higher still than the medieval tower or the presently wrecked destiny. We shall keep in mind, following Jacques Geninasca,[8] the proud, exalted, stellar scope of this first quatrain where the poet stands with his equally star-spangled lute, as if he were the negative version of the celestial, artistic Apollo. Probably, too, the 'star' is also a theater star – the actress Jenny Colon, who died in 1842, catalyzed several of Nerval's crises. The star-spangled lute was elaborated through the identification with the 'dead star,' through scattering her in his song, as in a resonant replica of Orpheus' being torn to pieces by the bacchantes. The art of poetry asserts itself as the memory of a posthumous harmony, but also, through a Pythagorean resonance, as the metaphor of universal harmony.

On the threshold of the invisible and the visible

As a result of the absorption of the 'dead star' into the 'lute,' the 'Black Sun' of 'Melancholia' emerges. Beyond its alchemical scope, the 'Black Sun' metaphor fully sums up the blinding force of the despondent mood – an excruciating, lucid affect asserts the inevitability of death, which is the death of the loved one and of the self that identifies with the former (the poet is 'bereft' of the 'star').

This intrusive affect, however, which irrigates the celestial realm with a hidden Apollo, or one who is not conscious of being such, attempts to find its expression. The verb 'bears' points to that bursting out, that reaching the signs of darkness, while the learned word *melancholia* serves to bespeak the struggle for conscious mastery and precise meaning. Heralded in Nerval's letter to Alexandre Dumas, evoked in *Aurélia* ('A creature of enormous proportions – man or woman I do not know – was fluttering painfully through the air. . . . It was colored with ruddy hues and its wings glittered with a myriad changing reflections. Clad in a long gown of antique folds, it looked like Albrecht Dürer's *Angel of Melancholia*'),[9] *Melancholia* belongs in the celestial realm. It changes darkness into redness or into a sun that remains black, to be sure, but is nevertheless the sun, source of dazzling light. Nerval's introspection seems to indicate that *naming the sun* locates him on the threshold of a crucial experience, on the divide between appearance and disappearance, abolishment and song, nonmeaning and signs. Nerval's reference to the alchemical metamorphosis may be read as a metaphor more in keeping with the borderline experience of the psyche struggling against dark asymbolism than with a para-scientific description of physical or chemical reality.

Who are you?

The second stanza takes the reader down from celestial, star-spangled heights to the 'night of the grave.' The underground, nightly realm assumes the somber mood of the saturnine poet but changes gradually throughout the quatrain into a realm of consolation, of luminous and vital bond. The haughty, princely 'I' of passive cosmic space (the 'star' and 'sun' of the first stanza) meets with a partner in the second stanza: a 'you' appears for the first time, initiating solace, light, and the arrival of plant life. The star [*étoile*] of the celestial vault [*toit*] is henceforth someone the poet can speak to – a 'you' [*toi*] who lies within.

The constant ambiguity, the continuous inversions of Nerval's world deserve emphasis; they increase the instability of its symbolism and reveal the object's ambiguity – and also that of the melancholy stance.

Who is this 'you'? Scholars have asked the question and provided many answers – it is Aurélia, the saint, Artemisia/Artémis, Jenny Colon, the dead mother . . . The undecidable concatenation of these real and imaginary figures recedes once more toward the position of the archaic 'Thing' – the elusive preobject of a mourning that is endemic with all speaking beings and a suicidal attraction for the depressive person.

Nevertheless – and this is not the least of its ambiguities – the 'you' that the poet meets with only in 'the night of the grave' can console only and precisely in that place. Joining her in the tomb, identifying with her dead body, but perhaps also joining her truly by means of a suicide, the 'I' finds solace. The paradox in this action (suicide alone allows me to unite with the lost being, suicide alone brings me peace) can be grasped through the placidness, serenity, and that kind of happiness that veils a number of suicidal people, once they have made the fatal decision. A narcissistic fullness seems to build up in imaginary fashion; it is one that removes the disastrous anguish over loss and finally gratifies the dismayed subject: there is no need to be distressed any more, solace comes through joining the beloved being in death. Death then becomes the phantasmal experience of returning to the lost paradise. The past tense of 'you who brought me solace' will be noted.

Henceforth the grave brightens; the poet finds in it the luminous bay of Naples and the Posilipo promontory (in Greek, *pausilypon* means the 'cessation of sadness'), and a watery billowing, maternal expanse ('the sea of Italy'). One should add to the polyvalency of this liquid, luminous, Italian universe – as opposed to the Apollonian or medieval, interstellar, and mineral universe of the first stanza – first the fact that Nerval tried to commit suicide on Posilipo out of love for Jenny Colon.[10] Second, there is the connection made by Hoffman between 'Aurélia and the picture of Santa Rosalia,' which was confirmed by Nerval who, during this stay in Naples (October 1834), gazed upon the 'likeness of Santa Rosalia' that embellished the abode of an anonymous mistress.[11]

A flower, a saint: the mother?

The virgin Rosalia links the symbolism of feminine Christian purity with the esoteric connotations of the text that have already been mentioned. This way of thinking seems justified by the note, 'Vatican Gardens,' which Nerval inserted in the Eluard manuscript on line 8: 'where grapevine and rose combine' [in French, *à la rose s'al-lie* = Rosalie].

The flowery connotation of the saint's name becomes explicit on line 7, 'the *flower* that so pleased my distressed heart.' The dead *star* of the previous stanza (line 3) resurrects as a *flower* within the identification of the poet with the dead woman. The identification is evoked in the metaphor of the 'arbor,' climbing network, interpenetration of twigs and leaves, which 'combines' the grapevine and the rose and moreover evokes Bacchus or Dionysus, the god of a plant-loving intoxication, as opposed to the black, astral Apollo of the first stanza. Let us note that, for some contemporary commentators, Dionysus is less a phallic deity than the one who, in his body and dancing intoxication, conveys an intimate complicity, even an identification, with femininity.[12]

The Bacchic 'grapevine' and the mystical 'rose,' Dionysus and Venus, Bacchus and Ariadne . . . one can imagine a series of mystical couples implicitly evoked in this funeral *and* resurrectional grouping. Let us recall Nerval's naming of the Virgin Mary as 'white Rose' and, among others, 'Les Cydalises': 'Where are our lovers? / They are in the grave / They are far happier / In a more beautiful region! . . . Oh white betrothed! / Oh blossoming young virgin!'[13]

The 'flower' can be interpreted as being the flower into which the melancholy Narcissus was changed – finally solaced by his drowning in the reflection-spring. It is also the 'myosotis'[14]: this foreign-sounding word evokes the artifice of the poem ('An answer is heard in a soft foreign tongue') at the same time as it invokes the memory of those who will love the writer ('Forget me not!'). Let me finally suggest a semantic possibility for this flowery universe appended to the evocation of the other: Nerval's mother, who died when he was two years old, was named Marie-Antoinette-*Marguerite-Laurent* and usually called Laurence – a saint and a flower (marguerite [daisy], laurel), while Jenny Colon's real first name was . . . Marguerite. Enough to nourish a 'mystical rose.'

Ancholia and hesitation: who am I?

There is a merging that is consoling but also lethal – the luminous fulfilment arrived at by uniting with the rose, but also the darkness of the grave; temptation to commit suicide, but also flowery resurrection . . . Did such a mingling of opposites appear to Nerval, as he reread his text, as 'madness'?

On line 7 (referring to 'flower') he noted in the Eluard manuscript:

'ancholia' – symbol of sadness for some, emblem of madness for others.* *Melancholia/ancholia*. The rhyme leads me once again to read both similitude and opposition between the first two stanzas. Mineral sadness (first stanza) is superimposed on a death-bearing merger that is also madly attractive, like the promise of an other life, beyond the grave (second stanza).

The first tercet clarifies the uncertainty of the 'I.' Triumphant at first, then linked with 'you,' he now ponders the question, 'Am I?' It is the turning point of the sonnet, a moment of doubt and lucidity. The poet searches, precariously, for his specific identity, on a level one can assume to be neutral, neither Apollonian nor Dionysian, neither dismayed nor exhilarated. The interrogative removes us, for a while, from the almost hallucinatory world of the two quatrains, their changeable, undecidable connotations and symbolisms. It is the time for choice: are we dealing with Cupid, in other words Eros, psyche's lover (reminder of the second quatrain), or with Phoebus/Apollo (reminder of the first quatrain) who, according to Ovid's *Metamorphoses*, pursued the nymph Daphne? She escapes by being changed into a laurel tree – and one will recall the flowery transformation suggested in the second quatrain. Is this the case of a gratified lover or a frustrated one?

As to Lusignan d'Agenais, he would be one of the Labrunie's forebears, according to Nerval's imaginary filiation, who was crushed by the desertion of his serpent-wife Melusina. Biron takes us back to an ancestor of the Dukes of Biron, the crusader Elie de Gontaut in the Third Crusade; or perhaps to Lord Byron, for Nerval confused the spellings Biron/Byron.[15]

What is the precise logical relation within those two pairs (Cupid and Phebus, Lusignan and Biron) and between them as well? Are we dealing with a listing of more or less unhappy lovers in quest of an always elusive mistress? Or with two kinds of lovers, gratified and disheartened? Exegeses pile up and diverge, some favoring the idea of a listing, others the chiasmus.

Nonetheless, the basic polyvalency of Nerval's semantics (thus, among others, 'Fair-haired or dark / Must we choose? / The Lord of the World / Is called Pleasure')[16] leads one to believe that here, too, logical relationships are doubtful. Perhaps in the image of that butterfly whose fascinating uncertainty the writer describes in this fashion: 'The butterfly, stemless flower, / That flutters about, / That one harvests in

---

Ancolie is the common French name for a flower of the Aquilegia genus – the columbine, which does not convey the symbolic connotation and rhyme of the French word. The neologism 'ancholia', which preserves the link with 'melancholia', may be thought of as referring to an imaginary flower – L.S.R.

a net; / Within infinite nature, / It provides harmony / Between plants and birds! . . .'[17]

Ultimately, the proper names gathered in this tercet perhaps work more as signs of various identities (see 'Names as Clues' below). If the 'persons' that have been named belong to the same world of love and loss, they suggest – through the poet's identification with them – a dispersal of the 'I,' loving as well as poetic, among a constellation of elusive identities. It is not certain that those figures had for Nerval the semantic fullness of their mythological or medieval source. The litaneutical, hallucinatory gathering of their names allows one to suppose that they might merely have the value of signs, broken up and impossible to unify, of the lost Thing.

An underlying violence

The question as to the speaker's own identity has barely been suggested when line 10 recalls his dependency on the queen; the questioning 'I' is not supreme, he has a sovereign ('My brow is still red from the kiss of the queen'). With the alchemical evocation of the king and queen and their union and redness as sign of infamy and murder ('I sometimes bear Cain's inexorable redness!'), we are once more steeped in an ambiguous world. The brow bears the memory of the loved one's kiss and thus signifies loving joy at the same time as redness recalls the blood of a murder and, beyond Cain and Abel, signifies the destructive violence of archaic love, the hatred underlying lovers' passion, the revenge and the persecution that underlie their romance. The powerful Anteros of the melancholy person seethes behind a dashing Eros: 'You ask me why my heart is raging so / . . . Yes, I am one of those whom the Avenger drives, / He has scarred my forehead with his angry lip, / And sometimes, alas, Abel's pallor is covered with blood, / For I carry from Cain that inexorable red.'[18]

Does the despairer's paleness hide the avenging and to himself unavowed anger of the murderous violence directed at his loved one? While such aggressiveness is heralded on line 10, the speaker does not assume it. It is projected: not I but the kiss of the queen wounds, cuts, bloodies. Then, immediately, the outburst of violence is suspended, and the dreamer appears in a protected haven – uterine refuge or swinging cradle. The red queen is changed into a siren who swims or 'turns green' (*Le Mousquetaire* version). The floral, vital, resurrectional value of the second quatrain has been pointed out, as well as the frequent oppositions of red and green with Nerval. Red asserts itself as metaphor of revolt, of insurrectional fire. It is Cainish, diabolical, infernal, while green is saintly, and Gothic stained glass assigned it to John [the Divine].[19] Need I emphasize once more the mistress' royal function, the more dominating as she is undominated, filling the entire space of authority and fatherhood and for that very reason enjoying an insuperable ascendency over the saturnine poet? – she is the queen of Sheba, Isis, Mary, queen of the Church . . . Facing her, the act of writing alone is implicitly master and avenger: let us remember that the sonnet was written in *red ink*.

We thus find only a simple, slight allusion to sexual desire and its ambivalence. The erotic connection does, in fact, bring to their climax the conflicts of a subject who experiences both sexuality and the discourse that refers to it as destructive. One understands why the melancholy withdrawal is a fugue in the face of the dangers of eroticism.

Such an avoidance of sexuality and its naming confirms the hypothesis according to which the 'star' of *El Desdichado* is closer to the archaic Thing than to an object of desire. Nevertheless, and although such an avoidance seems necessary for the psychic balance of some, one could wonder if, by thus blocking the way toward the *other* (threatening, to be sure, but also insuring the conditions for setting up the boundaries of the self), the subject does not sentence itself to lie in the Thing's grave. Sublimation alone, without elaborating the erotic and thanatoid contents, seems a weak recourse against the regressive tendencies that break up bonds and lead to death.

The Freudian way, on the contrary, aims at planning (in all circumstances and no matter what difficulties there might be with so-called narcissistic personalities) for the advent and formulation of sexual desire. Such a design, often disparaged as reductionist by detractors of psychoanalysis, is imperative – in the perspective of considerations on melancholy imagination – as an ethical option, for *named* sexual desire insures securing the subject to the other and, consequently, to meaning – to the meaning of life.

I narrate

The poet, however, returns from his descent into hell. He goes 'twice' across the Acheron, remaining 'alive' (*Le Mousquetaire* version) or being a 'conqueror' (*Les Filles du feu* version), and the two crossings recall the two previous major attacks of madness suffered by Nerval.

Having assimilated an unnamed Eurydice into his song and the chords of his lyre, he adopts the pronoun 'I' as his own. Not as strict as in the first line and beyond the uncertainties of the ninth, this 'I' is, at the conclusion of the sonnet, an 'I' who narrates a story. The untouchable, violent past, black and red, and also the verdant dream of a lethal resurrection have been modulated into an artifice that includes temporal distance ('I've . . . been across') and belongs to another reality, that of the lyre. The beyond of melancholy hell would thus be a modulated, sung narrative, an integration of prosody into a narration that has only been started here.

Nerval does not specify the cause, the motive, or the reason that lead him to this miraculous modification ('I've twice, as a conqueror, been across the Acheron'), but he unveils the economy of his metamorphosis, which consists in transposing into his melody and song 'the sighs of the saint and the screams of the fay.' The figure of the loved one is divided at first: ideal *and* sexual, white and red, Rosalia and Melusina, the virgin and the queen, spiritual and carnal, Adrienne and Jenny, and so forth. Besides and even more so, these women are henceforth *sounds* borne by characters in a *story* that narrates a past. Neither unnameable beings resting in the depths of polyvalent symbolism nor mythical objects of destructive passion, they attempt to turn into the imaginary protagonists of a cathartic narrative that endeavors to name, by differentiating them, ambiguities and pleasures. The 'sighs' and the 'screams' connote jouissance, and one distinguishes idealizing love (the 'saint') from erotic passion (the 'fay').

By means of a leap into the orphic world of artifice (of sublimation), the saturnine poet, out of the traumatic experience and object of mourning, remembers only a gloomy or passional tone. He thus comes close, through the very components of language, to the lost Thing. His discourse identifies with it, absorbs it, modifies it, transforms it: he takes Eurydice out of the melancholy hell and gives her back a new existence in his text/song.

The rebirth of the two, the 'bereft' and the 'star' – 'flower,' is nothing but the poem strengthened by the start of a narrative stance. That particular imagination is granted with the economy of a resurrection.

Nevertheless, Nerval's narrative is simply suggested in 'El Desdichado.' In the other poems it remains scattered and always incomplete. In the prose texts, in order to maintain their difficult linear motion toward a limited goal and message, he resorts to the subterfuge of the voyage or the biographic reality of a literary character whose adventures he takes up. *Aurelia* is the very instance of a narrative dispersal, replete with dreams, splittings, musings, incompletions . . .

One should not speak of a 'failure' faced with that dazzling narrative kaleidoscope foreshadowing contemporary experiments in novelistic fragmentation. Just the same, narrative continuity, which, beyond the certainty of syntax, builds space and time and reveals the mastery of an existential judgment over hazards and conflicts, is far from being Nerval's favorite realm. Any narrative already assumes that there is an identity stabilized by a completed Oedipus and that, having accepted the loss of the Thing, it can concatenate its adventures through failures and conquests of the 'objects' of desire. If such be the narrative's internal logic, one can understand why the telling of a story seems too 'secondary,' too schematic, too unessential to capture the 'black sun's' incandescence with Nerval.

Prosody will then be the basic, fundamental sieve that will sift the 'black prince's' sorrow and joy into language. A fragile filter but often the only one. Does one not, when all is said and done, and beyond the multifarious and contradictory meanings of words and syntactic structures, hear the vocal gesture? With the very first alliterations, rhythms, melodies, and transposition of the speaking body asserts itself through a glottic and oral presence. T: *t*énébreux (saturnine), Aqui*t*aine, *t*our (tower), é*t*oile (star), mor*t*e (dead), lu*t*h (lute), cons*t*ellé (bespangled), por*t*e (bears); BR-PT-TR: Téné*br*eux (saturnine, *pr*ince, *t*our (tower), *m*or*t*e (dead), *port*e (bears); S: *s*uis (am), incon*s*olé (disconsolate), prin*c*e, *s*eule (lone), con*s*tellé (bespangled), *s*oleil (sun); ON: inc*on*solé (disconsolate), m*on* (my), c*on*stellé (bespangled) . . .

Repetitive, often monotonous, such a prosody[20] forces on the affective flow a grid that is as rigorous to decipher (it presupposes precise knowledge of mythology or esoterics) as it is flexible and unsettled on account of its very allusiveness. Who are the Prince of Aquitaine, the 'lone dead star,' Phebus, Lusignan, Biron . . . ? We can find out, we do find out, interpretations pile up or differ . . . But the sonnet can also be read by ordinary readers who know nothing about such referents, if they will simply allow themselves to be caught up in the sole phonic and rhythmic coherence, which at the same time limits and permits the free associations inspired by each word or name.

It can thus be understood that the triumph over melancholia resides as much in founding a symbolic family (ancestor, mythical figure, esoteric community) as in constructing an independent symbolic object – a sonnet. Attributable to the author, the construction becomes a substitute for the lost ideal in the same way as it transforms the woeful darkness into a lyrical song that assimilates 'the sighs of the saint and the screams of the fay.' The nostalgic focus – 'my lone star is dead' – turns into feminine voices incorporated into the symbolic cannibalism constituted by the poem's composition, into the prosody created by the artist. One is to interpret in analogous fashion the massive presence of proper nouns in Nerval's texts, particularly in his poetry.

Names as clues: it is

The series of names attempts to fill the space left empty by the lack of
a sole name. Paternal name, or Name of God. 'Oh father! Is it you that
I sense within myself? / Do you have the power to live and to conquer
death? / Might you have succumbed after a final effort / From that
angel of darkness who was anathematized . . . / For I feel completely
alone, crying and suffering, / Alas! And if I die, it is because everything
is going to die!'[21]

This first person Christly lament is very much like the biographical
complaint of an orphan or one lacking paternal support (Mme Labrunie
died in 1810, Nerval's father, Etienne Labrunie, was wounded at Vilna
in 1812). Christ forsaken by his father, Christ's passion as he descends
into hell alone, attract Nerval who interprets this as a signal, at the
very heart of Christian religion, of the 'death of God' proclaimed by
Jean Paul [Richter], whom Nerval quotes in the epigraph. Abandoned
by his father who thus renounces his almightiness, Christ dies and
drags every creature down into the abyss.

The melancholy Nerval identifies with Christ forsaken by the Father;
he is an atheist who seems no longer to believe in the myth of 'this
madman, this sublime demented person . . . This forgotten Icarus who
ascended back into heaven.'[22] Is Nerval afflicted with the same nihilism
that shook Europe from Jean Paul to Dostoyevsky and Nietzsche and
echoes Jean Paul's well-known utterance all the way to the epigraph
of *Christ at the Mount of Olives:* 'God is dead! The sky is empty . . . /
Weep! Children, you no longer have a father!'? Identifying with Christ,
the poet appears to suggest it: '"No, God does not exist!" / They were
asleep. "Friends, have you heard *the news?* / With my brow I touched
the eternal vault; / I am covered in blood, exhausted, I shall suffer for
many days! / Brethren, I misled you. Abyss! Abyss! Abyss! / God is
missing from the altar where I am the victim . . . / God is no more!
God is no more!" / But they were still asleep!'[23]

His philosophy, however, is perhaps more of an immanent
Christianity coated with esoterica. For the dead God he substitutes the
hidden God – the God not of Jansenism but of a diffuse spirituality,
the ultimate refuge of a psychic identity in catastrophic anguish:
'Often, in an obscure being, lives a hidden God; / And, like a new-born
eye covered by its lids, / A pure spirit grows under the covering of
stones.'[24]

The amassing of names (which refer to historical, mythical, and
above all esoteric figures) achieves first this impossible naming of the
One, then its pulverizing, finally its reversal towards the dark region of
the unnameable Thing. This means that we are not engaged here in a
debate internal to Jewish or Christian monotheism, about the possibility

or impossibility of naming God, about the oneness or multiplicity of his names. Within Nerval's subjectivity the crisis of naming and that of the authority answerable for subjective oneness went deeper.

Since the One or His Name is deemed dead or negated, there looms the possibility of replacement through a series of imaginary filiations. Such mythical, esoteric, or historical families or brotherhoods or doubles that Nerval feverishly imposes in place of the One, however, seem finally to be endowed with incantatory, conspiratorial, ritual value. Instead of pointing to their concrete referent, those names indicate, rather than mean, a massive, uncircumventable, unnameable presence, as if they were the anaphora of the unique object; not the mother's 'symbolic equivalence,' but the shifter 'this,' empty of meaning. Names are the gestures that point to the lost being out of which the 'black sun of melancholia' first breaks out, before the erotic *object* separated from the mournful subject settles in, along with the linguistic *artifice of signs* that transposes that object to the symbolic level. In the final analysis, and beyond the anaphoras' ideological value, the poem integrates them as signs without signifieds, as *infra* or *supra*-signs, which, beyond communication, attempt to reach the dead or untouchable object, to take over the unnameable being. Thus the sophistication of polytheist knowledge has the ultimate aim of taking us to the threshold of naming, to the edge of the unsymbolized.

By representing that unsymbolized as a maternal object, a source of sorrow and nostalgia, but of ritual veneration as well, the melancholy imagination sublimates it and gives itself a protection against collapsing into asymbolism. Nerval formulates the temporary triumph of that genuine arbor of names hauled up from the abyss of the lost 'Thing' in the following fashion: 'I cried out at length, invoking my mother under the names given to ancient divinities.'[25]

Commemorating mourning

Thus the melancholy past does not pass. Neither does the poet's past. He is the continuous historian less of his real history than of the symbolic events that have led his body towards significance or threatened his consciousness with foundering.

A poem by Nerval thus has a highly mnemonic function ('a prayer to the goddess Mnemosyne,' he writes in *Aurélia*),[26] in the sense of a commemoration of the genesis of symbols and phantasmal life into texts that become the artist's only 'true' life: 'Here began what I shall call the overflowing of the dream into real life. From that moment on, everything took on at times a double aspect' (p. 120). One can follow, for instance, in a section of *Aurélia*, the concatenation of the following sequences: death of the loved woman (mother), identifying with her and with death, setting up a space of psychic solitude buttressed by the perception of a bisexual or asexual form, and finally bursting forth of the sadness that is summed up by the mention of Dürer's *Melancholia*. The following excerpt can be interpreted as a commemoration of the 'depressive position' dear to the disciples of Melanie Klein [see above, p. 129]: 'I saw in front of me a woman with deathly pale complexion, hollow eyes, whose features seemed to me like Aurélia's. I said to myself: "I am being warned of either her *death* or mine." . . . I was wandering about a vast building composed of several rooms. . . . A creature of enormous proportions – man or woman I do not know – was fluttering painfully through the air . . . it looked like Dürer's *Angel of Melancholia*. I could not keep myself from crying out in terror and this woke me up with a start' (p. 118). The symbolics of language and, more markedly, of the text takes over from terror and triumphs, for a while, through the death of the other or of the self.

Variations of the 'double'

Widower or poet, stellar or funereal being, identifying with death or Orphic conqueror – such are merely a few of the ambiguities that a reading of 'El Desdichado' reveals, and they require us to view *doubling* as the central image of Nerval's imagination.

Far from repressing the trouble that the loss of the object entails (whether archaic or present loss), melancholy persons settle the lost Thing or object within themselves, identifying with the loss's beneficial features on the one hand, with its maleficent ones on the other. This presents us with the first state of the self's doubling, which initiates a series of contradictory identifications that the work of the imagination will attempt to reconcile – tyrannical judge and victim, unreachable ideal or sick person beyond recovery, and so forth. Figures follow one upon another, meet, pursue or love one another, love, look after, reject one another. Brothers, friends, or enemies, doubles might be involved in a true dramatic staging of homosexuality.

Nevertheless, when one of the figures becomes identified with the female sex of the lost object, the attempt at reconciliation beyond the splitting leads up to a feminization of the speaker or to androgyny. 'From that moment on, everything took on at times a double aspect' (p. 120). Aurélia, 'a woman whom I had loved for a long while,' is dead. But 'I said to myself: "I am being warned of either her *death* or mine"!' (pp. 115, 118). Having found Aurélia's funereal bust, the

215

narrator recounts the melancholy state caused by the knowledge of his illness: 'I believed that I myself had only a short while longer to live. . . . Besides, she belonged to me much more in her death than in her life' (p. 132). She and he, life and death, here are entities that reflect each other in mirrorlike fashion, interchangeable.

After evoking the process of creation, prehistoric animals, and various cataclysms ('Everywhere the suffering image of the eternal Mother was dying, weeping, or languishing' (p. 136)), he sees another double. It is an oriental prince whose face is that of the narrator: 'It was my own face, my whole form magnified and idealized' (p. 138).

Having been unable to unite with Aurélia, the narrator changes her into an idealized and, this time, masculine double: '"Every man has a double," I said to myself. "I feel two men in myself"' (p. 139). Spectator and actor, speaker and respondent, all nevertheless rediscover the projective dialectic of good and evil: 'In any case, my *other* is hostile to me.' Idealization turns into persecution and entails a 'double meaning' in everything the narrator hears. Because he is being visited by this bad double, by 'an evil genius [who] had my place in the soul world,' Aurélia's lover gives in to a greater despair. To crown it all, he imagines that his double 'was going to marry Aurélia' – 'Immediately a mad rage seized me,' while all around him they laughed at his impotence. As a result of this dramatic doubling, women's screams and foreign words – other signs of doubling, this time sexual and verbal – pierce Nerval's dream (p. 142). Meeting, under an arbor, a woman who is Aurélia's physic double, he is again thrust into the idea that he must die in order to be with her, as if he were the dead woman's alter ego (p. 157).

The episodes of doubling follow one upon the other and vary, but they all lead up to a celebration of two fundamental figures: the universal Mother, Isis or Mary, and Christ, who is praised and of whom the narrator wishes to be the ultimate double. 'A kind of mysterious choir chanted in my ears. Children's voices were repeating in chorus: *Christe! Christe! Christe!* . . . "But Christ is no more," I said to myself' (p. 157). The narrator descends to hell as Christ did and the text comes to a stop with that image, as if it were not sure of forgiveness and resurrection.

The theme of forgiveness asserts itself indeed in the last pages of Aurélia: guilty because he did not mourn for his old parents as strongly as he mourned for 'that woman,' the poet cannot hope for forgiveness. And yet, 'Christ's pardon was pronounced for you also!' (p. 175). Thus the longing for forgiveness, an attempt to belong to the religion that promises an afterlife, haunts the struggle against melancholia and doubling. Confronting the 'black sun of melancholia' the narrator asserts, 'God is the Sun' (p. 156). Is this a resurrectional metaphor or a reverse with respect to a solidary obverse seen as the 'black sun'?

Speaking the breakup

At times, the doubling becomes a 'molecular' breakup that is metaphorized by currents crisscrossing a 'sunless day.'

> I felt myself carried painlessly along on a current of molten metal, and a thousand similar streams, the colors of which indicated different chemicals, criss-crossed the breast of the world like those blood-vessels and veins that writhe in the lobes of the brain. They all flowed, circulated and throbbed just like that, and I had a feeling that their currents were composed of living souls in a molecular condition, and that the speed of my own movement alone prevented me from distinguishing them. (p. 124)

Strange insight, admirable knowledge of the accelerated dislocation subtending the process of melancholia and its underlying psychosis. The language of that breathtaking acceleration assumes a combinatory, polyvalent, and totalizing aspect, dominated by primary processes. Such a symbolic activity, often not lending itself to representation, 'nonfigurative,' 'abstract,' is brilliantly perceived by Nerval.

> The speech of my companions took *mysterious turns* whose sense I alone could understand, and *formless*, inanimate objects lent themselves to the *calculations* of my mind; from *combinations* of pebbles, from *shapes in corners, chinks* or openings, from the *outlines* of leaves, colors, smells, and sounds, emanated for me hitherto unknown harmonies. 'How have I been able to live so long,' I asked myself, 'outside nature and without identifying myself with it? Everything lives, moves, everything corresponds . . . it is a transparent *network* that covers the world.'
>
> (pp. 166–67; see also chapter 1)

Cabalism or esoteric theories involving 'correspondences' show up here. All the same, the quotation is also an extraordinary allegory of the prosodic polymorphism characteristic of a writing in which Nerval appears to favor the network of intensities, sounds, significances rather than communicating univocal information. Indeed, this 'transparent network' refers to Nerval's very text, and we can read it as a metaphor of sublimation – a transposition of drives and their objects into destabilized and recombined signs that make the writer capable of 'sharing my joys and sorrows' (p. 167).

Whatever allusions to freemasonry and initiation there may be, and perhaps at the same time, Nerval's writing conjures up (as in analysis) archaic psychic experiences that few people reach through their conscious speech. It appears obvious that Nerval's psychotic conflicts could favor such an access to the limits of the speaking being and of humanity. With Nerval, melancholia represented only one aspect of such conflicts, which could reach the point of schizophrenic fragmentation. Nevertheless, because of its key position in the organization and disorganization of psychic space, at the limits of affect and meaning, of biology and language, of asymbolia and breathtakingly rapid or eclipsed significance, it is indeed melancholia that governed Nerval's representations. Creating prosody and an undecidable polyphony with symbols centered in the 'black spot' or the 'black sun' of melancholia thus provided an antidote to depression, a temporary salvation.

Melancholia subtends the 'crisis of values' that shook up the nineteenth century and was expressed in esoteric proliferation. The legacy of Catholicism became involved, but the elements pertaining to states of psychic crisis were recovered and inserted in a polymorphic and polyvalent spiritualistic syncretism. The Word was experienced less as incarnation and euphoria than as a *quest for a passion* remaining unnameable or secret, and as *presence of an absolute meaning* that seems as omnivalent as it is elusive and prone to abandon. A true melancholy experience of man's symbolic resources was then undergone on the occasion of the religious and political crisis caused by the French Revolution. Walter Benjamin has stressed the melancholy substratum of the imagination that has been deprived of both classical and religious stability but is still anxious to give itself a new meaning (as long as we speak, as long as artists create), which nevertheless remains basically disappointed, racked by the evil or the irony of the Prince of Darkness (so long as we live as orphans but creating, creators but forsaken . . .).

'El Desdichado,' however, like all Nerval's poetry and poetic prose, attempted a tremendous *incarnation* of the unbridled significance that leaps and totters within the polyvalence of esoterisms. By accepting the dispersal of meaning – the text's replica of a fragmented identity – the themes of the sonnet relate a true archeology of affective mourning and erotic ordeal, overcome by assimilating the archaic state into the language of poetry. At the same time, the assimilation is also accomplished through oralization and musicalization of the signs themselves, thus bringing meaning closer to the lost body. At the very heart of the value crisis, poetic writing mimics a resurrection. 'I've twice, as a conqueror, been across the Acheron . . .' There would be no third time.

Sublimation is a powerful ally of the Disinherited, provided, however, that he can receive and accept another one's speech. As it happened, the other did not show up at the appointment of him who went to join – without a lyre this time, but alone in the night, under a street lamp – 'the sighs of the saint and the screams of the fay.'

Notes

1. See JEANINE MOULIN, *Les Chimères, Exégèses* (Lille: Giard, 1949). During the summer of 1954, a few months before his suicide, it seems that Nerval went on a pilgrimage to his mother's tomb in Glogau, Germany [now Glogów, Poland]; this was followed by a relapse.

2. See JACQUES DHAENENS, *Le Destin d'Orphée, 'El Desdichado' de Gérard de Nerval* (Paris: Minard, 1972).

3. 'A Alexandre Dumas', in *Oeuvres complètes* (hereafter *OC*), Bibliothèque de la Pléiade (Paris: Gallimard, 1952), 1: 175–6.

4. A rather precise and striking similarity has been noted between the first three lines of 'El Desdichado' and the seventh volume of COURT DE GEBELIN's *Monde primitif, analysé et comparé avec le monde moderne* (1781). Likewise, sources have been found for the five sonnets of *Chimères* ('El Desdichado', 'Myrtho', 'Horus', 'Antéros', and 'Artémis') in *Les Fables égyptiennes et grecques* (1758) by DOM ANTOINE-JOSEPH PERNETY, a Benedictine monk of the Saint Maur congregation. Nerval must also have read PERNETY's *Dictionnaire mytho-hermétique*. The following excerpts from PERNETY can be related to Nerval's work:

   > The real key for the work is this blackness at the start of its process. . . . Blackness is the true sign of a perfect solution. Matter is then dissolved into a powder more minute. . . . than the atoms that flit about in the rays of the sun, and its atoms are changed into permanent water.
   >   Philosophers have given that disintegration such names as death, . . . hell, Tartarus, *the shades, night . . . the grave . . . melancholia . . . overshadowed sun* or *eclipse of the sun* and moon. . . . They have finally named it by using all the words that might express or designate corruption, disintegration, and blackness. It is what furnished Philosophers the stuff for so many allegories about deaths and tombs . . .
   >   (*Fables égyptiennes et grecques*, 1: 154–5; emphasis mine)

   Pernety quotes RAYMOND LULLE on the topic of blackness: 'Let the body of the sun be putrefied for thirteen days, at the end of which the dissolution becomes black as ink; but its inside will be red like a ruby, or like a carbuncle. Now take this tenebrous sun, darkened by its sister's or mother's embrace, and place it in an alembic . . .' (ibid., 2: 136). His definition of melancholia is as follows: 'Melancholia signifies the putrefaction of matter. . . . This name has been given to matter turned black, doubtless because there is something sad about the color black, and because the human body's humor called melancholia is considered to be a black, twice-cooked bile that produces sad, lugubrious vapors' (*Dictionnaire mytho-hermétique*, p. 289). 'Sadness and melancholia . . . are also names that Adepts give to their matter when it has turned black' (*Les Fables égyptiennes et grecques*, **2**: 300).

Those connections between Nerval's text and the alchemical corpus have been established by GEORGES LE BRETON, 'La Clé des *Chimères*: l'alchimie', *Fontaine* (1945), **44**: 441–60; see also 'L'Alchimie dans *Aurélia*: "Les Mémorables"', *Fontaine* (1945), **45**: 687–706. Many works have dealt with Nerval and esoterism, among which JEAN RICHER, *Expérience et création* (Paris: Hachette, 1963); FRANÇOIS CONSTANT, "Le Soleil noir et l'étoile ressuscitée," *La Tour Saint Jacques* (January–April 1958), nos. 13–14, and so forth.

5. RICHER, *Expérience et création*, pp. 33–8.

6. See DHAENENS, *Le Destin d'Orphée*.

7. See EMILIE NOULET, *Etudes littéraires, l'hermétisme de la poésie française moderne* (Mexico: Talleres Gráficos de la Editorial Cultura, 1944).

8. JACQUES GENINASCA, 'El Desdichado', *Archives Nervaliennes*, no. 59, pp. 9–53.

9. NERVAL, *Selected Writings*, trans. Geoffrey Wagner (Ann Arbor: University of Michigan Press, 1957), pp. 118–19.

10. See 'Lettres à Jenny Colon', in *OC* **1**: 726ff.

11. See JEAN GUILLAUME, *Aurélia: prolégomène à une édition critique* (Namur: Presses Universitaires de Namur, 1972).

12. See MARCEL DÉTIENNE, *Dionysos à ciel ouvert* (Paris: Hachette, 1986).

13. NERVAL, *Selected Writings*, p. 209. [Trans. slightly modified by LSR.]

14. *Aurelia*, in *Selected Writings*, p. 173.

15. See DHAENENS, *Le Destin d'Orphée*, p. 49.

16. NERVAL, 'Chanson gothique', in *OC* **1**: 59.

17. 'Les Papillons', in *OC* **1**: 53.

18. 'Anteros', in *Selected Writings*, p. 219.

19. See DHAENENS, *Le Destin d'Orphée*, p. 59.

20. See M. JEANNERET, *La Lettre perdue: écriture et folie dans l'oeuvre de Nerval* (Paris: Flammarion, 1978).

21. NERVAL, 'Le Christ des Oliviers', in *OC* **1**: 37.

22. *Ibid.*, p. 38.

23. *Ibid.*, p. 36.

24. 'Gilded Verses', in *Selected Writings*, p. 225.

25. 'Fragments du manuscrit d'Aurélia', in *OC* **1**: 423.

26. *Aurelia*, in *Selected Writings*, p. 118. Further page references are given in the text.

9 'Daddy'*

JACQUELINE ROSE

'Plath is a fantasy', writes Jacqueline Rose (*The Haunting of Sylvia Plath* [London: Virago, 1991], p. 5.) This is because Plath's works have been conflated with her personality, and their violence construed as the unmediated expression of her own. In particular, Plath's use of the Holocaust as metaphor has earned her much opprobrium for cashing in on the afflictions of the Jews. Her critics argue that she had no right to identify herself with a catastrophe so far exceeding any tribulations of her own. Rose, however, insists that images of fascism and the Holocaust in Plath's writing represent the points at which the psychic and the social interpenetrate. Fascism, Rose argues,

is one of the few historical moments which historians have generally recognised as needing psychoanalytic concepts of desire and identification in order . . . to be fully understood. At this level fascism could be described as the historical annexing, or collective seizure, of unconscious drives . . . In fascism, the realm of politics reveals itself as massively invested with the most private and intimate images of our fantasy life. Plath's writing presents us with those images at work . . .

(*The Haunting of Sylvia Plath*, p. 7)

In her notorious poem 'Daddy', for example, Plath explores the fantasy of persecution by a feared and desired father: the Daddy of the poem, while standing for her own dead father, Otto Plath, also stands for the paternal figure of the Führer, as well as for the fathers of the literary tradition in which Plath must struggle for a voice: 'Barely daring to breathe or Achoo.'† 'Daddy' thus provides 'an extraordinary instance of the inseparability of history

---

*SYLVIA PLATH, 'Daddy' (1962), in *Collected Poems*, ed. Ted Hughes (London: Faber, 1981), p. 222.
†JACQUELINE ROSE, 'Daddy', in *The Haunting of Sylvia Plath* (London: Virago, 1991), pp. 205–38; 267–72. © 1991, Jacqueline Rose.

and subjectivity', Rose argues (*The Haunting of Sylvia Plath*, p. 7). By forcing us to recognise our own investments in the fantasies of fascism, such poetry may help us to internalise those fantasies and prevent them from erupting in the Real; for as Freud warns us, 'that which [is] abolished internally returns from without' (SE XII 71).

Who will forgive me for the things I do . . .
I think it would be better to be a Jew.
(Anne Sexton, 'My Friend, My Friend', 1959)

I am lame in the memory.
(Sylvia Plath, 'Little Fugue', 1962)

For a writer who has so consistently produced outrage in her critics, nothing has produced the outrage generated by Sylvia Plath's allusions to the Holocaust in her poetry, and nothing the outrage occasioned by 'Daddy', which is just one of the poems in which those allusions appear. Here is one such critic, important only for the clarity with which he lays out the terms of such a critique. Leon Wieseltier is reviewing Dorothy Rabinowicz's *New Lives: Survivors of the Holocaust* in an article entitled 'In a Universe of Ghosts', published in *The New York Review of Books*:

Auschwitz bequeathed to all subsequent art perhaps the most arresting of all possible metaphors for extremity, but its availability has been abused. For many it was Sylvia Plath who broke the ice . . . In perhaps her most famous poem, 'Daddy,' she was explicit . . . There can be no disputing the genuineness of the pain here. But the Jews with whom she identifies were victims of something worse than 'weird luck'. Whatever her father did to her, it could not have been what the Germans did to the Jews. The metaphor is inappropriate . . . I do not mean to lift the Holocaust out of the reach of art. Adorno was wrong – poetry *can* be made after Auschwitz and out of it . . . But it cannot be done without hard work and rare resources of the spirit. Familiarity with the hellish subject must be earned, not presupposed. My own feeling is that Sylvia Plath did not earn it, that she did not respect the real incommensurability to her own experience of what took place.[1]

It is worth looking at the central terms on which this passage turns – the objection to Plath's identification with the Jew: 'the Jews with whom she identifies'; to the terms of that identification for introducing chance into Jewish history (into history): 'victims of something worse than "weird luck"'; above all, to Plath's failure to recognise the 'incommensurability to her experience of what took place'. Wieseltier is not alone in this criticism. Similarly, Joyce Carol Oates objects to Plath 'snatching [her word] metaphors for her predicament from newspaper headlines'; Seamus Heaney argues that in poems like 'Lady Lazarus', Plath harnesses the wider cultural reference to a 'vehemently self-justifying purpose'; Irving Howe describes the link as 'monstrous, utterly disproportionate'; and Marjorie Perloff describes Plath's references to the Nazis as 'empty' and 'histrionic', 'cheap shots', 'topical trappings', 'devices' which 'camouflage' the true personal meaning of the poems in which they appear.[2] On a separate occasion, Perloff compares Plath unfavourably to Lowell for the absence of any sense of personal or social history in her work.[3] The two objections seem to cancel and mirror each other – history is either dearth or surplus, either something missing from Plath's writing or something which shouldn't be there.

In all these criticisms, the key concept appears to be metaphor – either Plath trivialises the Holocaust through that essentially personal (it is argued) reference, or she aggrandises her experience by stealing the historical event. The Wieseltier passage makes it clear, however, that if the issue is that of metaphor ('Auschwitz bequeathed to all subsequent art perhaps the most arresting of all possible metaphors for extremity'), what is at stake finally is a repudiation of metaphor itself – that is, of the necessary difference or distance between its two terms: 'Whatever her father did to her it cannot be what the Germans did to the Jews.' Plath's abuse (his word) of the Holocaust as metaphor (allowing for a moment that this is what it is) rests on the demand for commensurability, not to say identity, between image and experience, between language and event. In aesthetic terms, what Plath is being criticised for is a lack of 'objective correlative' (Perloff specifically uses the term[4]). But behind Wieseltier's objection, there is another demand – that only those who directly experienced the Holocaust have the right to speak of it – speak of it in what must be, by implication, non-metaphorical speech. The allusion to Plath in his article is there finally only to make this distinction – between the testimony of the survivors represented in Rabinowicz's book and the poetic metaphorisation (unearned, indirect, incommensurate) of Plath.

Turn the opening proposition of this quotation around, therefore, and we can read in it, not that 'Auschwitz bequeathed the most *arresting* of all possible metaphors for extremity', but that in relation to literary representation – or at least this conception of it – Auschwitz is the place where metaphor is *arrested*, where metaphor is brought to a halt. In this context, the critique of Plath merely underlines the fact that

223

the Holocaust is the historical event which puts under greatest pressure – or is most readily available to put under such pressure – the concept of linguistic figuration. For it can be argued (it has recently been argued in relation to the critic Paul de Man) that, faced with the reality of the Holocaust, the idea that there is an irreducibly figurative dimension to all language is an evasion, or denial, of the reality of history itself.[5] But we should immediately add here that in the case of Plath, the question of metaphor brings with it – is inextricable from – that of fantasy and identification in so far as the image most fiercely objected to is the one which projects the speaker of the poem into the place of a Jew. The problem would seem to be, therefore, not the *slippage* of meaning, but its *fixing* – not just the idea of an inherent instability, or metaphoricity, of language, but the very specific fantasy positions which language can be used to move into place. Criticism of 'Daddy' shows the question of fantasy, which has appeared repeatedly as a difficulty in the responses to Plath's writing, in its fullest historical and political dimension.

In this final chapter, I want to address these objections by asking what the representation of the Holocaust might tell us about this relationship between metaphor, fantasy and identification, and then ask whether Sylvia Plath's 'Daddy' might not mobilise something about that relationship itself. The issue then becomes not whether Plath has the right to represent the Holocaust, but what the presence of the Holocaust in her poetry unleashes, or obliges us to focus, about representation as such.

To pursue this question, I want first to take a detour through psychoanalysis, as the discourse which makes language and fantasy the direct object of its concern – specifically through the 1985 Hamburg Congress of the International Association of Psycho-Analysis, as the psychoanalytic event which illustrated most acutely the shared difficulty of language and fantasy in relation to the Holocaust itself.[6] To say that the Congress was 'about' Nazism and the Holocaust would, however, be a simplification given the conditions and difficulties in which it took place. It was the first Congress of the Association to be held in Germany since the Congress of Wiesbaden in 1932, and it was held in Hamburg only because an original invitation to Berlin had caused such an outcry that it had had to be withdrawn. Hamburg, then, was the result of a compromise, the first of a series of compromises which continued with the organisational committee's decision that Nazism would not be referred to directly – not as history – but only in terms of clinical practice; that is, in terms of what patients who were survivors, the children of survivors or the children of Nazis brought to the psychoanalytic couch.[7] From the very beginning, therefore, and at every level of organisation, it was the problem of direct address, of direct representation, in relation to this historical moment, that was at stake.

Despite that decision to avoid direct historical reference, history and politics erupted on the fringes of the Congress in the inaugural meeting of 'International Psychoanalysts against Nuclear Weapons'. There is of course a direct connection to the Holocaust in the shared terminology: the term 'holocaust' was used to refer to the nuclear threat in 1949 before being projected back on to the camps. There is also a connection at the level of fantasy, made clearest by Hanna Segal's opening address on nuclear rhetoric, which she analysed in terms of the psychotic mechanisms of splitting and denial – the same mechanisms which were being negotiated and renegotiated in the cases described in the papers of the main event.[8] If all this was a sign of compromise, therefore, like all compromise-formations, it spoke as much as it concealed. Specifically, it spoke the fact that experience is no guarantee of memory since the Congress itself, like the cases it transcribed and in transcribing repeated, was so clearly operating under the dual imperative to remember and to forget. The very title of Hanna Segal's paper, 'Silence is the Real Crime', with all that it implied by way of an injunction, a historical urgency, to speak, was matched by the recognition, endlessly rehearsed in the main Congress, that speech itself is the problem, caught up as it is in the very fantasies she was describing, and nowhere more so than in relation to the Holocaust itself.

To say that the Congress was not addressing Nazism directly is, therefore, misleading inasmuch as the Congress found itself acting out, or repeating, the problem – or impossibility – of direct address in relation to Nazism and the Holocaust as such. At the opening session, Janine Chasseguet-Smirgel quoted these famous words from Freud: 'what has been abolished internally returns from the outside in the form of a delusion'.[9] In the memories of the patients, the Holocaust endlessly recurred in the form of such a delusion, demonstrating with painful clarity the detours which lie, of necessity, between memory and this (any) historical event.

No simple memory, therefore, especially for a second generation shown by analysis as in need of remembering to the precise extent that they did not participate concretely in the event. And no simple identification – not for this second generation but, equally and more crucially perhaps, not for the first generation. For if the experience of this generation was, historically, so unequivocal, their identifications at the level of fantasy constantly dislocated that certainty of historical place. I am referring here not only to what one writer described as the 'sacrilege' or 'disjunct parallelism' involved in juxtaposing the cases of the children of survivors to the children of Nazis (and the reverse)[10] but also, and even more, to the internal vicissitudes of identification revealed in the individual case-histories (two papers had the title 'Identification and its Vicissitudes in the Context of the Nazi Phenomenon').[11] Over and over again these patients found themselves in fantasy occupying either side of the victim/aggressor divide. Like the daughter of a German military family caught in a double role as victor and vanquished, and who thus mirrored, her analyst commented, the children of Jewish survivors who identify with the aggressor and victim alike[12]; or the two sons of the Third Reich fathers oscillating between the 'polar extremes of submission and exertion of power' as the 'defence of experiencing oneself as a victim' gradually met up with the 'repressed experience of harbouring the intentions of the perpetrator'[13]; or the daughter of a member of the SS whose analyst comments – and not only in relation to her – on the conflict between the 'partial identities of the shame of the victim and the guilt of the culprit'.[14]

Suspended between these partial identities, these patients lived in a world of fantasy where actuality and memory both did and did not correspond (it would be ridiculous to suggest – even in cases of quasi-psychotic denial – that there was no connection between these fantasies and what they had concretely and historically experienced in the past). But what did emerge from these case-histories was that the question of historical participation in no sense exhausted that of identification and of fantasy – it did not settle the question of from where, and in what form, memory takes place. For being a victim does not stop you from identifying with the aggressor; being an aggressor does not stop you from identifying with the victim. To which we can add a formula only deceptively tautological – that being a victim (or aggressor) does not stop you from identifying with the victim (or aggressor). Identification is something that always has to be constructed. Wherever it is that subjects find themselves historically, this will not produce any one, unequivocal, identification as its logical effect.[15]

Look again at the term 'holocaust' and the ambivalence of identification can be seen to reside inside the very term. What special relationship – Zev Garber and Bruce Zuckerman have asked – does the concept of 'holocaust' set up between Nazi and Jew, what idea of supreme or chosen purpose, carrying as it does the biblical meaning of a sacrifice that is divinely inspired?[16] Track the term through Plath's poetry and the word appears first in this earlier biblical sense: 'Then hurl the bare world like a bluegreen ball/back into the holocaust' ('Song For a Revolutionary Love'), 'till the Announcer's voice is lost/in heresies of holocaust' ('Insolent Storm Strikes at the Skull').[17] This meaning persists throughout Plath's writing – it could be said to be the meaning of *Ariel* itself: 'The meaning of Isaiah 29:1–2 seems to be that Jerusalem, here (prophetically?) called Ariel, is to become like an altar, i.e., a scene of holocaust' . . . 'The altar of holocausts is called the "ariel of God".'[18] This also suggests another interpretation of the passage: 'hoping for houses in a holocaust . . . .'

This is not to deny that the oscillations revealed by these patients can be analysed partly in terms of a logic of the event – the perpetrators experience themselves as victims in order both to deny and to legitimate their role (to be a perpetrator you *have* first to 'be' a victim); the victim identifies with the aggressor out of retaliation in a situation where not only psychic but concrete survival is at stake. Primo Levi made this logic central to what he describes as 'ambiguity fatally provoked by oppression' in his last book, *The Drowned and the Saved*, in which he insists that there must be no historical confusion between the two roles ('precious service rendered (intentionally or not) to the negators of truth').[19]

There is no disagreement with this analysis, therefore, even if one suggests that it leaves a residue unexplained. And that is the very process of alternation – what it is that these partial and transferable identities reveal about the workings of fantasy itself. They show subjects taking up positions in the unconscious which are the opposite of the ones they occupy at the level of their conscious life. The one-sidedness of that conscious identity, even where it corresponds to the concretely lived experience (especially where it does so), is what causes the difficulty. The problem for Mrs B, for example, was not just the violence to which she had been subjected in the camps, but the fact that the extremity of it had made it impossible for her to accept those violent and extreme elements in herself.[20] Her need then was to recognise her own participation in the psychic positions she most desired to exclude. For it is the psychic exclusion or repudiation of those positions which, for psychoanalysis, is most likely to precipitate their projection or acting out. Exclusion turns into unconscious repetition.

For Hanna Segal at least, it is this mechanism which constitutes the political as much as the psychic threat. Thus nuclear rhetoric endlessly reproduces and legitimates a violence which it always locates outside itself, whose cause always, and by definition, belongs somewhere else – a rhetoric of violence which mobilises, not aggression (it denies, projects, splits off aggression) but defence. It is these mechanisms which, it can be argued, were at work in Nazism itself, and were rediscovered here in the fantasies of Nazis and their children, and then (risking that 'sacrilege' of 'disjunct parallelism') in those of the survivors and their children in turn. In *Night and Hope*, one of his collections of short stories about the camps, the Czech author Arnost Lustig writes: 'fear was merely the transformation of one's own thoughts into those of the enemy'.[21]

Projection is not, therefore, something that we can safely locate in the world of the psychotic alone. In his discussion of Schreber, Freud wrote:

> . . . [projection] has a regular share assigned to it in our attitude towards the external world. For when we refer the causes of certain sensations to the external world, instead of looking for them (as we do in the case of others) inside ourselves, this normal proceeding, too, deserves to be called projection.[22]

As if he was suggesting that the way we distribute causality – the way we distinguish – between ourselves and others is something of a paranoid mechanism in itself. Think back to that analysis of Plath as answerable for everything in her life, to the battle that has constantly taken place around her over the location (inner or outer) of the cause, and her story can then be read as a saga of projection, whose fullest historical ramifications can be traced out beneath the surface of responses to, as well as inside, her late texts. Against the entire logic that has so often been brought to bear on Plath as woman and as writer, these cases suggest that psychological innocence is not guaranteed by the historical attribution of guilt (nor the reverse).

Is it going too far to suggest that what is being asked for in the cases described at the Hamburg Congress is a further act of identification, or rather a recognition on the part of these subjects that such an identification has *already* taken place? In the field of sexuality, such a demand has become fairly well known. As Freud puts it with reference to homosexual object-choice: 'By studying sexual excitations other than those that are manifestly displayed, [psychoanalytic research] has found that all human beings are capable of making a homosexual object-choice and *have in fact made one* in their unconscious' (my emphasis).[23] 'Recognise that unconscious desire' has become a commonplace of a recent sexual political version of Freud, meaning: 'Beyond that apparently assumed heterosexual identity in which you think you know yourself so well, know your unconscious participation in its other side.' For it is the homophobic who is most deeply and compulsively involved in the repudiation of homosexuality in him/herself (the social implications of such a general recognition would clearly be vast).

But what happens if we extend that demand beyond the world of neurosis and repression to that of psychosis and projection, where it is not a socially outlawed object of desire but a physically and ethically unmanageable identification which is at stake? Could it be that the very different encounter between psychoanalysis and politics precipitated here (partially and tardily of necessity) by the Holocaust cannot help but produce this demand as its effect? Note just how far this takes us from those who criticise Plath for putting herself in the wrong place in 'Daddy', for putting herself – the two are, as we will see, inseparable in her poem – in the place of the Nazi as well as in the place of the Jew.

Go back once again to that criticism of Plath, specifically on the issue of metaphor, and it then appears that such a demand, such an identification, relies on the possibility of metaphor: the problem is not the presence of metaphor, but the risk that metaphor, along with the possibility of language itself, may be lost. Loss of metaphor is in itself a form of defence which threatens memory and identification alike. This is the central point of a paper by Ilse Grubrich-Simitis, 'From Concretism to Metaphor: Thoughts on Some Theoretical and Technical Aspects of the Psychoanalytic Work with Children of Holocaust Survivors', a paper not given at the Congress but one to which several of the other papers referred.[24] According to Grubrich-Simitis, the problem for these children of survivors is that the metaphoric function is *impaired*. They reify language into an object world whose blunt and repetitious literality, whose loss of figurality, signals the impossibility for these patients of grasping the nature of the event. They regard what they say as 'thinglike', unable to see it as 'something imagined or remembered', as something having the character of a sign.[25] As one analyst at the Congress put it, with direct reference to the paper: losing metaphor, they have lost that function 'without which the origins of language are unthinkable'.[26] Take metaphor out of language and there is no memory, no history, left.

In the analytic setting, this requires a return to the event, to what Grubrich-Simitis calls a 'non-metaphorical' recognition that it took place (a reversal, as she acknowledges, of that famous and infamous move from actuality to fantasy made by Freud).[27] But this return is made in order to *restore* the function of metaphor, to release the essentially metaphorical work of analysis itself: 'alongside poetry perhaps the metaphorical enterprise *par excellence*'.[28] Only in this way will these patients be freed from the literalness of a language which makes memory impossible – which, paradoxically, is the sign that they have no real knowledge that the Holocaust even took place. Only in this way, too, will they be able to acknowledge the aggressive side of fantasy which the loss of metaphor allows them simultaneously to erase. For metaphor is the recognition and suspension of aggression (the second as the condition of the first), allowing the subject to take up any one of these propositions in turn:

I want X but I do not intend to do it
I want X but I am not doing it
I do X (in fantasy) but I do not (actually) do it
I want X but I do not want to want it

– all mutations of an unspeakable desire, or rather one that can be spoken only to the extent that, as in analysis, as in poetry (the poetry of Plath, for example), it remains within the bounds of speech.

There is a sense here, therefore, in which we can truly say that metaphor was arrested in Auschwitz, in so far as the figural possibilities of language, without which 'the origins of language are unthinkable', are one of the things that the Holocaust put at risk. We can turn that criticism of Plath around again and ask: not whether the Holocaust is 'abused' by metaphor, but rather under what conditions of representation can the fantasies underpinning metaphor itself be spoken?

There is of course an inverse position on the representation of the Holocaust which situates it on the other side of representation itself, and can sometimes take the form of a *privileging* of poetry. According to Hannah Arendt, the judges at the trial of Eichmann rested their right to judge him on the distinction between 'deeds and motives' that belonged in the courtroom, and 'sufferings on so gigantic a scale' as to be '"beyond human understanding"', a matter for the '"great authors and poets"' of the world.[29] When George Steiner praises 'Daddy' as the 'Guernica of modern poetry', he makes the same point: 'perhaps it is only those who had no part in the events who *can* focus on them rationally and imaginatively' (Wieseltier takes issue with Steiner specifically on this).[30] Steiner underlines the metaphoric status of Plath's writing in the poem: 'committing the whole of her poetic and formal authority to metaphor, to the mask of language'; but in doing so he seems to attribute the fact of metaphor to poetic language alone. For the Holocaust theologian Emil Fackenheim, the Holocaust is a 'more than poetic truth', a truth that can be measured only by its failure to represent itself: 'each and every explanation is false, if not downright obscene, unless it is accompanied by a sense of utter inadequacy'.[31]

In this case, literature has become the repository for the non-representability of the event. For both positions, however – the rejection of metaphor, the demand for poetic representation alone – the Holocaust seems to be placed outside the domain of language proper, either in the before or beyond of language itself. The question of uniqueness and particularity is latent to the debate about language. The Holocaust can only represent itself, the Holocaust can only fail to be represented. The singularity of the Holocaust is that it is proper only to itself. Without taking sides in the dispute over the uniqueness of the

Holocaust, we can notice its implications for – or rather, the extent of its implication *in* – the problem of what can and cannot, what should and should not, be represented in speech. Compare these lines from Karl Kraus, cited in one of the papers at the Hamburg Congress:

> Don't ask me why all this time I never spoke.
> Worldless am I,
> and won't say why . . .
> The word expired when that world awoke.[32]

with these lines from the epigraph to Primo Levi's *If This Is A Man*:

> I commend these words to you . . .
> Repeat them to your children,
>   Or may your house fall apart,
>   May illness impede you,
>   May your children turn their faces from you.[33]

An end to language that can be figured only in words, and an injunction to speech, to bear a witness whose impossibility Levi himself has described: 'I must repeat – we, the survivors, are not the true witnesses.'[34] Compare Paul Celan: 'Niemand/zeugt für den/Zeugen' ('Aschenglorie': 'No one/bears witness/for the witness').[35] How can one argue that certain writers do, or do not, have the right to represent the Holocaust, unless one has settled in advance, or suspended, these most fundamental paradoxes that the Holocaust opens up at the heart of language?

One more term, finally, from the criticism of Plath with which this chapter began – the concept of luck ('The Jews with whom she identifies were victims of something worse than "weird luck"'). It can be set against a moment from another representation of the Holocaust by the Ukrainian writer Piotr Rawicz, a survivor of the camps. At the end of his 1961 novel *Le sang du ciel* (translated in 1964 as *Blood From the Sky*), he adds this postscript:

> This book is not a historical record. If the notion of chance (like most other notions) did not strike the author as absurd, he would gladly say that any reference to a particular period, territory or race is purely coincidental. The events that he describes could crop up in any place, at any time, in the minds of any man, planet, mineral . . .[36]

By introducing the element of chance back into the story, Rawicz opens up the issue of who should be able – who should be required

– to recognise themselves in what took place. As he himself has argued in debate with Fackenheim, the experience of the Holocaust exceeds concrete participation in the event: 'those who physically lived through the Holocaust are not the only ones who experienced it'.[37] This observation is merely the other side of the recognition that experience and memory do not simply coincide. Note too the date of Rawicz's novel (1961), the historical gap which it signals between event and memory, between memory and writing. Add to this book a list of the other novels of the Holocaust that appeared in the early 1960s – Josef Bor's *Terezin Requiem* (1963), Elie Wiesel's *Night* (1960), Ilse Aichinger's *Herod's Children* (1963) – and we start to get a sense of the general, collective nature of that delay.[38] All these books are discussed in Alvarez's article 'Literature of the Holocaust', first published in *Commentary* in 1964, and reprinted in *Beyond All This Fiddle*, the collection which also includes the article he wrote on Plath at the time of her death.[39] If, therefore, the Holocaust appears as historical reference only in the last years of Plath's writing, the delay is coincident with the memory of the survivors themselves. Her tardiness mimics, or chimes in with, their own.

Forget in order to remember. Somewhere in the trials of this process, Plath's writing – at the most basic level – finds its place. Remember Hughes's statement on his destruction of Plath's last journals: that forgetting, the destruction of memory, was essential in order to survive: 'Two more notebooks *survived* for a while' . . . 'in those days I regarded forgetfulness as essential to *survival*' (my emphasis).[40] The repetition is eloquent of the internal contradiction of this statement (its self-abolition?), which Hughes partly seems to recognise himself: 'in those days'. Annotating T.S. Eliot's *Four Quartets*, Plath writes: 'We live by memory of the past (the dead).'[41]

To all of this must be added another point of instability, and that is the instability of Jewishness itself. In his essay on Paul Celan, Jacques Derrida links this hesitancy of identity, of self-situating in relation to the Jew, to the question of holding, naming, remembering a moment by dating it in time. On 'Conversation in the Mountains' – the line 'July is not July' – he comments:

> This is in the course of a meditation on the Jew, son of a Jew, whose name is 'unpronounceable,' and who has nothing of his own, nothing that is not borrowed, so that, like a date, what is proper to the Jew is to have no property or essence. Jewish is not Jewish.[42]

But that very instability – of Jewishness and of the date – establishes the conditions of a general recognition: 'The Jew is also the other,

myself and the other; I am Jewish in saying: the Jew is the other who
has no essence, who has nothing of his own or whose essence is not to
have one.'[43] Hence both the 'alleged universality of Jewish witness
("All the poets are Jews," says Marina Tsvetayeva, cited in epigraph
to "Und mit dem Buch aus Tarussa") and the incommunicable secret
of the Judaic idiom, the singularity of its "unpronounceable name"'.[44]
What I am focusing on here, however, what I read in Plath, is a
related but distinct form of uncertainty – the point at which the abyss
at the centre of Jewish identity, for the one who is Jewish and not
Jewish, appears in the form of a drama about psychic aggression
and guilt.

Most obviously, this is the subject of Anne Sexton's poem 'My Friend,
My Friend', on which, it has been argued, Plath's 'Daddy' was
based.[45] The poem was written in the year Sexton and Plath attended
Lowell's poetry class in Boston together. In this poem, Jewish is an
enviable state. It confers origin and divine paternity – the conditions of
forgiveness for a crime that is never named:

> Who will forgive me for the things I do?
> With no special legend or God to refer to,
> With my calm white pedigree, my yankee kin.
> I think it would be better to be a Jew.

Victim, without agency, the Jew escapes the burden of historic (of
any) guilt:

> I forgive you for what you did not do.
> I am impossibly guilty. Unlike you,
> My friend, I cannot blame my origin
> With no special legend or God to refer to.

For the speaker of this poem, Jewishness offers the possibility of a
symbolic deferral of guilt. Blaming one's origin – the poem makes its
own diagnosis – is nothing less than the ultimate, divinely sanctioned,
attribution, or projection, of the cause. Victimisation becomes an
advantage of which its bearer can then be *accused*: 'I forgive you for
what you did not do.' The total innocence of the Jew, for the one who
is not Jewish, turns into a form of guilt. According to the strictest logic
of projection, the Jew becomes culpable for the fact that she cannot be
blamed.

As the poem progresses, the guilt comes to centre on the death of
the mother, a death experienced as the 'first release' of the speaker of
the poem:

> Watching my mother slowly die I knew
> My first release. I wish some ancient bugaboo
> Followed me. But my sin is always my sin.

This is the only content attributed, albeit indirectly, to that impossible
burden of guilt, other than the guilt, collective, of simply not being
a Jew: 'my calm white pedigree, my yankee kin'. At another level,
guilt can remain without content, precisely in so far as it takes the
form of a relentless self-accusation, one that the speaker of the poem
makes over and again of herself: the repeated refrain 'Who will forgive
me for the things I do?', to which the line 'I think it would be better
to be a Jew' comes as the repeated reply. In this little-known poem
by Anne Sexton, only recently unearthed from the *Antioch Review* of
1959 and published in a selection of her work, Jewishness is offered
unequivocally, if not unapologetically, as an object of desire. It is as
if Sexton is answering in advance those who criticise Plath on the
grounds that her identification with the Jew serves some personal
purpose. For what could be an identification *without* purpose? In
Sexton's poem, the desire to be Jewish reveals the tendentiousness
(and guilt) of identification as such.

  In Sexton's poem, the guilt centres on the mother. By transposing
the dilemma on to the father, Plath shifts this drama into the realm
of symbolic as well as personal law. The father carries the weight,
not only of guilt, but of historic memory. In 'Little Fugue', one of the
less well known poems from *Ariel* and forerunner of 'Daddy', Plath
presents the relation to the father most directly in terms of a language
or communication that fails:

> The yew's black fingers wag;
> Cold clouds go over.
> So the deaf and dumb
> Signal the blind, and are ignored.[46]

In fact the poem does not start with failed communication, but with
the complete loss of the physical conditions that make communication
possible. Deaf and dumb signalling to blind – there are no words here,
and what there is in the place of words still goes astray. Likewise, the
memory of the speaker's father takes the form of a confusion in the
register of signs:

> Deafness is something else.
> Such a dark funnel, my father!
> I see your voice
> Black and leafy, as in my childhood.

A yew hedge of orders,
Gothic and barbarous, pure German.
Dead men cry from it.
I am guilty of nothing.

What does it mean here to 'see a voice'? To be deaf to it? – not in the
sense of hearing nothing, but of hearing, of seeing too much. That
voice is pure German, a surfeit of orders that is full of the cries of
dead men. The poem proposes an impossible alternative at the level of
language: signs that are empty because they cannot be heard, either by
those who utter or by those who fail to see them, and a language pure
only in its powers of destruction, which can speak finally only from
the place of the dead. Before the first of these two stanzas, the original
draft has: 'The yew is many-footed./Each foot stops a mouth./ So the
yew is a go-between: talks for the dead.' According to Robert Graves,
there is a belief in Brittany that churchyard yews spread a root to the
mouth of each corpse.[47]

In all this, guilt is not located. Isolated at the end of the verse, the
line 'I am guilty of nothing' can be read back retroactively into the
cries of the dead men heard in the voice of the father, into – as a
consequence – the father's own voice, or into the voice of the speaker
herself. The line works at once as denial and as plaint. Doubling over
or disappearing into itself as utterance – dead men inside the voice of
the father inside the voice of the poet who speaks – it stages a crisis
in the historical location of guilt. Plath removes from the first draft at
the start of the stanza: 'This dominates me', which offers a more exact,
more precisely and directly oppressive, distribution of roles.

In fact, 'Little Fugue' repeatedly unsettles the subjective positions
on which such a distribution depends. In the second stanza of the
poem, the yew's 'black fingers' meet the 'featurelessness' of a cloud
that is 'white as an eye all over!/ The eye of the blind pianist'. Black
and white, yew and eye, you and I – in the finger alphabet described
by Graves, the letter of the yew tree is the 'I' which is also the death
vowel. Death belongs on either side of the binaries – yew/eye: you/I –
on which the poem repeatedly puns. It slides from the yew tree to the
father, but then, since 'yew' equals 'I', on to the speaker herself. The
slippage of the pronouns produces an identity between the speaker
and the father she accuses. In 'Little Fugue', therefore, the relationship
to the father belongs on the axis of identification, as much as – in this
poem to the exclusion of – that of desire (this point will be crucial for
'Daddy').

But if the poem produces such a radical destabilisation, such an
unsettling of its enunciative place, it equally offers a more direct
sequence, something in the order of a transmission or inheritance

passed from the father to the child. The speaker takes on, finds herself
forced to utter, words silenced by her father's refusal to speak:

> And you, during the Great War
> In the California delicatessen
>
> Lopping the sausages!
> They color my sleep,
> Red, mottled like cut necks.
> There was a silence!
>
> Great silence of another order.
> I was seven, I knew nothing.
> The world occurred.
> You had one leg, and a Prussian mind.
>
> Now similar clouds
> Are spreading their vacuous sheets.
> Do you say nothing?
> I am lame in the memory.

The sequence seems to offer a narrative of silence. This silence ensures
that the war can be known only in the sleep of the child who did
not live through it, the same child for whom it also represents the
coming into being of the world: 'I was seven, I knew nothing./ The
world occurred.' It cripples the speaker's memory, maims her like her
one-legged father. The identification between them is only one part of
a repetition already guaranteed by the fact that what happened has still
not been spoken in words. As the poem shifts from the general 'There
was a silence!' to the particular 'Do you say nothing?', the father's
silence becomes accountable for the speaker's inability to write her own
history – 'I am lame in the memory' – as well as for the destiny of the
world: 'Now similar clouds/ Are spreading their vacuous sheets'. In an
article published in *Encounter* in September 1963, 'In Search of a Lost
Language', Hans Magnus Enzensberger describes Germany as 'mute',
a 'speechless country' – hence the linguistic paralysis which afflicted
German poets after the war.[48] The silence figured in this poem thus
mimics, as Judith Kroll has pointed out, a more general postwar silence
that was laid on the German tongue. This silence can therefore be
called historical in two senses – accountable for the future, a product
of the trauma of the past. The tense of 'Little Fugue' then becomes the
psychoanalytic tense of the future perfect: 'What I shall have been for
what I am in the process of becoming'.[49] Remembering for the future
– the very formula that has been chosen for returning to the Holocaust
today.[50]

To argue that the personal accusation against the father is part of a
more collective dilemma about memory is not, however, to substitute
a historical for the more common, personal and psychological reading
of Plath's work (the alternative that Perloff seems to propose) but to
suggest that Plath is writing from a place where they are precisely
inseparable. As a title, 'Little Fugue' condenses these different levels
in itself – fugue as (historic) flight, fugue as a technical term for
psychological amnesia, a temporary flight from reality, according to
Webster (cause and/or effect of the first), as well as the music of the
blind pianist (a little, not gross, fugue). The last lines of the poem are
particularly apposite here:

> I survive the while
> Arranging my morning.
> These are my fingers, this my baby.
> The clouds are a marriage dress, of that pallor.

They move the poem into the speaker's personal present – temporary
survivor: 'I survive the while'. So easily reduced, after the fact, to the
level of personal, biographical premonition (only a while to survive),
the line can equally be read as 'this transitional time is the medium in
which – or what – I have to survive'. Note too the allusion to the line
'I sing the while' from Blake's 'Infant Joy', an allusion which evokes
a poetic and linguistic tradition in which the speaker cannot take
her place: she does not sing to her child, she *only* survives (like the
Holocaust survivor who, until approximately this moment, survives
but does not speak). The dilemma is thus both more and less than
the dilemma of the woman writer oppressed by a male tradition in
which she cannot find her voice. Likewise, 'Arranging my morning'
– the speaker prepares her death (arranging her own mourning), or
the speaker completes a mourning that has been historically denied:
'The second generation mourns the denied mourning of their parents'
(Hillel Klein and Ilany Kogan, 'Identification Processes and Denial in
the Shadow of Nazism').[51]

In 'Little Fugue', the personal present is engendered in its possibility
– provisional, precarious – by the drama of a fully historical past. To
say, in this context, that Plath uses history as metaphor is to establish
a hierarchy of levels – the historic simply signifies the personal drama
– and by implication a hierarchy of values between the two levels,
which overlooks something presented here more as a sequence, more
in the nature of a logic of the event. Inside that sequence, the form
of determination between the historic and the psychic instance is
impossible to pin down in any easy way. What the poem seems to

narrate is at once the historical engendering of personal time and the psychic engendering of history.

'Daddy' is a much more difficult poem to write about.[52] It is of course the poem of the murder of the father which at the very least raises the psychic stakes. It is, quite simply, the more aggressive poem. Hence, no doubt, its founding status in the mythology of Sylvia Plath. Reviewing the American publication of *Ariel* in 1966, *Time* magazine wrote:

> Within a week of her death, intellectual London was hunched over copies of a strange and terrible poem she had written during her last sick slide toward suicide. 'Daddy' was its title; its subject was her morbid love-hatred of her father; its style was as brutal as a truncheon. What is more, 'Daddy' was merely the first jet of flame from a literary dragon who in the last months of her life breathed a burning river of bale across the literary landscape.[53]

Writing on the Holocaust, Jean-François Lyotard suggests that two motifs tend to operate in tension, or to the mutual exclusion of each other – the preservation of memory against forgetfulness and the accomplishment of vengeance.[54] Do 'Little Fugue' and 'Daddy' take up the two motifs one after the other, or do they present something of their mutual relation, the psychic economy that ties them even as it forces them apart? There is a much clearer narrative in 'Daddy' – from victimisation to revenge. In this case it is the form of that sequence which has allowed the poem to be read purely personally as Plath's vindictive assault on Otto Plath and Ted Hughes (the transition from the first to the second mirroring the biographical pattern of her life). Once again, however, it is only that preliminary privileging of the personal which allows the reproach for her evocation of history – more strongly this time, because this is the poem in which Plath identifies with the Jew.

The first thing to notice is the trouble in the time sequence of this poem in relation to the father, the technically impossible temporality which lies at the centre of the story it tells, which echoes that earlier impossibility of language in 'Little Fugue':

DADDY

You do not do, you do not do
Any more, black shoe
In which I have lived like a foot

For thirty years, poor and white,
Barely daring to breathe, or Achoo.

Daddy, I have had to kill you.
You died before I had time –
Marble-heavy, a bag full of God,
Ghastly statue, with one gray toe
Big as a Frisco seal

And a head in the freakish Atlantic
Where it pours bean green over blue
In the waters off beautiful Nauset.
I used to pray to recover you.
Ach, du.

What is the time sequence of these verses? On the one hand, a time
of unequivocal resolution, the end of the line, a story that once and
for all will be brought to a close: 'You do not do, you do not do/ Any
more'. This story is legendary. It is the great emancipatory narrative
of liberation which brings, some would argue, all history to an end.
In this case, it assimilates, combines into one entity, more than one
form of oppression – daughter and father, poor and rich – licensing
a reading which makes of the first the meta-narrative of all forms of
inequality (patriarchy the cause of all other types of oppression, which
it then subordinates to itself). The poem thus presents itself as protest
and emancipation from a condition which reduces the one oppressed
to the barest minimum of human, but inarticulate, life: 'Barely daring
to breathe or Achoo' (it is hard not to read here a reference to Plath's
sinusitis). Blocked, hardly daring to breathe or to sneeze, this body
suffers because the father has for too long oppressed.

If the poem stopped here then it could fairly be read, as it has often
been read, in triumphalist terms – instead of which it suggests that
such an ending is only a beginning, or repetition, which immediately
finds itself up against a wholly other order of time: 'Daddy, I have had
to kill you./ You died before I had time.' In Freudian terms, this is the
time of '*Nachträglichkeit*' or after-effect: a murder which has taken place,
but after the fact, because the father who is killed is already dead; a
father who was once mourned ('I used to pray to recover you') but
whose recovery has already been signalled, by what precedes it in the
poem, as the precondition for his death to be repeated. Narrative as
repetition – it is a familiar drama in which the father must be killed in
so far as he is already dead. This at the very least suggests that, if this
is the personal father, it is also what psychoanalysis terms the father
of individual prehistory, the father who establishes the very possibility
(or impossibility) of history as such.[55] It is through this father that the

subject discovers – or fails to discover – her own history, as at once personal and part of a wider symbolic place. The time of historical emancipation immediately finds itself up against the problem of a no less historical, but less certain, psychic time.

This is the father as godhead, as origin of the nation and the word – graphically figured in the image of the paternal body in bits and pieces spreading across the American nation state: bag full of God, head in the Atlantic, big as a Frisco seal. Julia Kristeva terms this father '*Père imaginaire*', which she then abbreviates 'PI'.[56] Say those initials out loud in French and what you get is 'pays' (country or nation) – the concept of the exile. Much has been made of Plath as an exile, as she goes back and forth between England and the United States. But there is another history of migration, another prehistory, which this one overlays – of her father, born in Grabow, the Polish Corridor, and her mother's Austrian descent: 'you are talking to me as a general American. In particular, my background is, may I say, German and Austrian.'[57]

If this poem is in some sense about the death of the father, a death both willed and premature, it is no less about the death of language. Returning to the roots of language, it discovers a personal and political history (the one as indistinguishable from the other) which once again fails to enter into words:

> In the German tongue, in the Polish town
> Scraped flat by the roller
> Of wars, wars, wars.
> But the name of the town is common.
> My Polack friend
>
> Says there are a dozen or two.
> So I never could tell where you
> Put your foot, your root,
> I never could talk to you.
> The tongue stuck in my jaw.
>
> It stuck in a barb wire snare.
> Ich, ich, ich, ich,
> I could hardly speak.
> I thought every German was you.
> And the language obscene

Twice over, the origins of the father, physically and in language, are lost – through the wars which scrape flat German tongue and Polish town, and then through the name of the town itself, which is so common that it fails in its function to identify, fails in fact to name. Compare Claude Lanzmann, the film-maker of *Shoah*, on the

Holocaust as 'a crime to forget the name', or Lyotard: 'the destruction of whole worlds of names'.[58] Wars wipe out names, the father cannot be spoken to, and the child cannot talk, except to repeat endlessly, in a destroyed obscene language, the most basic or minimal unit of self-identity in speech: 'ich, ich, ich, ich' (the first draft has 'incestuous' for 'obscene'). The notorious difficulty of the first-person pronoun in relation to identity – its status as shifter, the division or splitting of the subject which it both carries and denies – is merely compounded by its repetition here. In a passage taken out of her journals, Plath comments on this 'I':

> I wouldn't be I. But I am I now; and so many other millions are so irretrievably their own special variety of 'I' that I can hardly bear to think of it. I: how firm a letter; how reassuring the three strokes: one vertical, proud and assertive, and then the two short horizontal lines in quick, smug, succession. The pen scratches on the paper I . . . I . . . I . . . I . . . I . . . I.[59]

The effect, of course, if you read it aloud, is not one of assertion but, as with 'ich, ich, ich, ich', of the word sticking in the throat. Pass from that trauma of the 'I' back to the father as a 'bag full of God', and 'Daddy' becomes strikingly resonant of the case of a woman patient described at Hamburg, suspended between two utterances: 'I am God's daughter' and 'I do not know what I am' (she was the daughter of a member of Himmler's SS).[60]

In the poem, the 'I' moves backwards and forwards between German and English, as does the 'you' ('Ach, du'). The dispersal of identity in language follows the lines of a division or confusion between nations and tongues. In fact language in this part of the poem moves in two directions at once. It appears in the form of translation, and as a series of repetitions and overlappings – 'ich', 'Ach', 'Achoo' – which dissolve the pronoun back into infantile patterns of sound. Note too how the rhyming pattern of the poem sends us back to the first line, 'You do not do, you do not do', and allows us to read it as both English and German: 'You du not du', 'You you not you' – 'you' as 'not you' because 'you' do not exist inside a space where linguistic address would be possible.

I am not suggesting, however, that we apply to Plath's poem the idea of poetry as *écriture* (women's writing as essentially multiple, the other side of normal discourse, fragmented by the passage of the unconscious and the body into words). Instead the poem seems to be outlining the conditions under which that celebrated loss of the symbolic function takes place. Identity and language lose themselves in the place of the father whose absence gives him unlimited powers. Far from presenting this as a form of liberation – language into pure body and play – Plath's poem lays out the high price, at the level of fantasy, that such a psychic process entails. Irruption of the semiotic (Kristeva's term for that other side of normal language), which immediately transposes itself into an alien, paternal tongue.

Plath's passionate desire to learn German and her constant failure to do so, is one of the refrains of both her journals and her letters home: 'Wickedly didn't do German for the last two days, in a spell of perversity and paralysis' . . . 'do German (that I *can* do)' . . . 'German and French would give me self-respect, why don't I act on this?' . . . 'Am very painstakingly studying German two hours a day' . . . 'At least I have begun my German. Painful, as if "part were cut out of my brain"' . . . 'Worked on German for two days, then let up' . . . 'Take hold. Study German today.'[61] In *The Bell Jar*, Esther Greenwood says: 'every time I picked up a German dictionary or a German book, the very sight of those dense, black, barbed wire letters made my mind shut like a clam'.[62]

If we go back to the poem, then I think it becomes clear that it is this crisis of representation in the place of the father which is presented by Plath as engendering – forcing, even – her identification with the Jew. Looking for the father, failing to find him anywhere, the speaker finds him everywhere instead. Above all, she finds him everywhere in the language which she can neither address to him nor barely speak. It is this hallucinatory transference which turns every German into the image of the father, makes for the obscenity of the German tongue, and leads directly to the first reference to the Holocaust:

And the language obscene

An engine, an engine
Chuffing me off like a Jew.
A Jew to Dachau, Auschwitz, Belsen.
I began to talk like a Jew.
I think I may well be a Jew.

The snows of the Tyrol, the clear beer of Vienna
Are not very pure or true.
With my gypsy ancestress and my weird luck
And my Taroc pack and my Taroc pack
I may be a bit of a Jew.

The only metaphor here is that first one that cuts across the stanza break – 'the language obscene//An engine, an engine' – one of whose halves is language. The metaphor therefore turns on itself, becomes a comment on the (obscene) language which generates the metaphor as such. More important still, metaphor is by no means the dominant trope when the speaker starts to allude to herself as a Jew:

> Chuffing me off *like* a Jew.
> I began to talk *like* a Jew.
> I *think* I may well be a Jew.
> I may be a *bit* of a Jew.

Plath's use of simile and metonymy keeps her at a distance, opening up the space of what is clearly presented as a partial, hesitant, and speculative identification between herself and the Jew. The trope of identification is not substitution but displacement, with all that it implies by way of instability in any identity thereby produced. Only in metaphor proper does the second, substituting term wholly oust the first; in simile, the two terms are co-present, with something more like a slide from one to the next; while metonymy is, in its very definition, only ever partial (the part stands in for the whole).

If the speaker claims to be a Jew, then, this is clearly not a simple claim ('claim' is probably wrong here). For this speaker, Jewishness is the position of the one without history or roots: 'So I never could tell where you/Put your foot, your root'. Above all, it is for her a question, each time suspended or tentatively put, of her participation and implication in the event. What the poem presents us with, therefore, is precisely the problem of trying to claim a relationship to an event in which – the poem makes it quite clear – the speaker did not participate. Given the way Plath stages this as a problem in the poem, presenting it as part of a crisis of language and identity, the argument that she simply uses the Holocaust to aggrandise her personal difficulties seems completely beside the point. Who can say that these were not difficulties which she experienced in her very person?[63]

If this claim is not metaphorical, then, we should perhaps also add that neither is it literal. The point is surely not to try and establish whether Plath was part Jewish or not. The fact of her being Jewish could not *legitimate* the identification – it is, after all, precisely offered as an identification – any more than the image of her father as a Nazi which now follows can be *invalidated* by reference to Otto Plath. One old friend wrote to Plath's mother on publication of the poem in the review of *Ariel* in *Time* in 1966 to insist that Plath's father had been nothing like the image in the poem (the famous accusation of distortion constantly brought to bear on Plath).[64]

Once again these forms of identification are not exclusive to Plath. Something of the same structure appears at the heart of Jean Stafford's most famous novel, *A Boston Adventure*, published in 1946.[65] The novel's heroine, Sonie Marburg, is the daughter of immigrants, a

Russian mother and a German father who eventually abandons his wife and child. As a young woman, Sonie finds herself adopted by Boston society in the 1930s. Standing in a drawing-room, listening to the expressions of anti-Semitism, she speculates:

> I did not share Miss Pride's prejudice and while neither did I feel strongly partisan towards Jews, the subject always embarrassed me because, not being able to detect Hebraic blood at once except in a most obvious face, I was afraid that someone's toes were being trod on.[66]

It is only one step from this uncertainty, this ubiquity and invisibility of the Jew, to the idea that she too might be Jewish: 'And even here in Miss Pride's sitting-room where there was no one to be offended (unless I myself were partly Jewish, a not unlikely possibility) . . . .'[67] Parenthetically and partially, therefore, Sonie Marburg sees herself as a Jew. Like Plath, the obverse of this is to see the lost father as a Nazi: 'what occurred to me as [Mrs. Hornblower] was swallowed up by a crowd of people in the doorway was that perhaps my father, if he had gone back to Würzburg, had become a Nazi'[68] – a more concrete possibility in Stafford's novel, but one which turns on the same binary, father/daughter, Nazi/Jew, that we see in Plath.

In Plath's poem, it is clear that these identities are fantasies, not for the banal and obvious reason that they occur inside a text, but because the poem addresses the production of fantasy as such. In this sense, I read 'Daddy' as a poem about its own conditions of linguistic and phantasmic production. Rather than casually produce an identification, it asks a question about identification, laying out one set of intolerable psychic conditions under which such an identification with the Jew might take place.

Furthermore – and this is crucial to the next stage of the poem – these intolerable psychic conditions are also somewhere the condition, or grounding, of paternal law. For there is a trauma or paradox internal to identification in relation to the father, one which is particularly focused by the Holocaust itself. At the Congress, David Rosenfeld described the 'logical-pragmatic paradox' facing the children of survivors: 'to be like me you must go away and not be like me; to be like your father, you must not be like your father'.[69] Lyotard puts the dilemma of the witness in very similar terms: 'if death is there [at Auschwitz], you are not there; if you are there, death is not there. Either way it is impossible to prove that death is there'[70] (compare Levi on the failure of witness). For Freud, such a paradox is structural, Oedipal, an inseparable part of that identification with the father of individual prehistory which is required of the child: '[The relation of the superego] to the ego is not exhausted by the precept: "You *ought to be* like this (like your father)." It also comprises the prohibition: "You *may not be* like this (like your father)".'[71] Paternal law is therefore grounded on an injunction which it is impossible to obey. Its cruelty, and its force, reside in the form of the enunciation itself.

'You stand at the blackboard, Daddy/In the picture I have of you' – it is not the character of Otto Plath, but his symbolic position which is at stake. In her story 'Among the Bumblebees', Plath writes of the father: 'Alice's father feared nothing. Power was good because it was power.'[72] Commenting on what he calls the '*père*-version' of the father, the French psychoanalyst Jacques Lacan writes: 'nothing worse than a father who proffers the law on everything. Above all, spare us any father educators, rather let them be in retreat on any position as master.'[73] The reference is to the father of Schreber, eminent educationalist in pre-Nazi Germany, whose gymnasia have been seen as part of the institutional and ideological prehistory of what was to come.[74] It might then be worth quoting the following lines from Otto Plath's 'Insect Societies' (he was a professor of entomology, famous for his work *Bumblebees and their Ways*).[75] Whether or not they tell us anything about what he was like as a person, they can be cited as one version of such paternal 'perversion', of such an impossible paternal ideal: 'When we see these intelligent insects dwelling together in orderly communities of many thousands of individuals, their social instincts developed to a high degree of perfection, making their marches with the regularity of disciplined troops . . .', or this citation from another professor, with which he concludes:

> Social instincts need no machinery of control over antisocial instincts. They simply have no antisocial tendencies. These were thoroughly eliminated many millions of years ago and the insects have progressed along a path of perfect social coordination. They have no need for policemen, lawyers, government officials, preachers or teachers because they are innately social. They have no need of learning the correct social responses. These are predetermined by their social constitution at the time of birth.[76]

Loss or absence of the father, but equally symbolic overpresence of the father (only the first is normally emphasised in relation to Plath) – it is the father as master who encapsulates the paradox at the heart of the paternal function, who most forcefully demands an identification which he also has to withhold or refuse. On more than one occasion, Plath relates the celebrated violence of her writing to the violence of that function. In 'Among the Bumblebees', the father sits marking scripts: 'the vicious little red marks he made on the papers were the color of the blood that oozed out in a thin line the day she cut her finger with the bread knife'.[77] And if we go back for a moment to 'Little Fugue', the same image can be traced out underneath the repeated 'blackness' of that text. On the back of the first draft is the passage from *The Bell Jar* in which Esther Greenwood is almost raped. The typescript has this line – 'In that light, the blood looked black' – crossed out and replaced with this one written by hand: 'Blackness, like ink, spread over the handkerchief.'[78] Underneath the poem to the father, a violence of writing – the poem's writing (the ink on the page), but equally his own. For those who would insist that what mattered most for Plath was the loss of her father, we might add that the only other father who can stand in for this overmastery of the paternal function is the father who is dead.

One could then argue that it is this paradox of paternal identification that Nazism most visibly inflates and exploits. For doesn't Nazism itself also turn on the image of the father, a father enshrined in the place of the symbolic, all-powerful to the extent that he is so utterly out of reach? (and not only Nazism – Ceauşescu preferred orphans to make up his secret police). By rooting the speaker's identification with the Jew in the issue of paternity, Plath's poem enters into one of the key phantasmic scenarios of Nazism itself. As the poem progresses, the father becomes more and more of a Nazi (note precisely that this identity is not given, but is something which emerges). Instead of being found in every German, what is most frighteningly German is discovered retrospectively in him:

> I have always been scared of *you*
> With your Luftwaffe, your gobbledygoo.
> And your neat moustache,
> And your Aryan eye, bright blue.
> Panzer-man, panzer-man, O You –
>
> Not God but a swastika
> So black no sky could squeak through.

The father turns into the image of the Nazi, a string of clichés and childish nonsense ('your gobbledygoo'), of attributes and symbols (again the dominant trope is metonymy) which accumulate and cover the sky. This is of course a parody – the Nazi as a set of empty signs. The image could be compared with Virginia Woolf's account of the trappings of fascism in *Three Guineas*.[79]

Not that this makes him any the less effective, any the less frightening, any the less desired. In its most notorious statement, the poem suggests that victimisation by this feared and desired father

is one of the fantasies at the heart of fascism, one of the universal
attractions for women of fascism itself. As much as predicament,
victimisation is also *pull*:

> Every woman adores a fascist,
> The boot in the face, the brute
> Brute heart of a brute like you.

For feminism, these are the most problematic lines of the poem –
the mark of a desire that should not speak its name, or the shameful
insignia of a new licence for women in the field of sexuality which has
precisely gone too far: 'In acknowledging that the politically correct
positions of the Seventies were oversimplified, we are in danger of
simply saying once more that sex is a dark mystery, over which we
have no control. "Take me – I'm yours", or "Every woman adores
a fascist".'[80] The problem is only compounded by the ambiguity of
the lines which follow that general declaration. Who is putting the
boot in the face? The fascist certainly (woman as the recipient of a
sexual violence she desires). But, since the agency of these lines is
not specified, don't they also allow that it might be the woman herself
(identification *with* the fascist being what every woman desires)?

There is no question, therefore, of denying the problem of these
lines. Indeed, if you allow that second reading, they pose the question
of women's implication in the ideology of Nazism more fundamentally
than has normally been supposed.[81] But notice how easy it is to start
dividing up and sharing out the psychic space of the text. Either
Plath's identification with the Jew is the problem, or her desire
for/identification with the fascist. Either her total innocence or her total
guilt. But if we put these two objections or difficulties together? Then
what we can read in the poem is a set of reversals which have meaning
only in relation to each other: reversals not unlike those discovered in
the fantasies of the patients described at Hamburg, survivors, children
of survivors, children of Nazis – disjunct and sacrilegious parallelism
which Plath's poem anticipates and repeats.

If the rest of the poem then appears to give a narrative of resolution
to this drama, it does so in terms which are no less ambiguous than
what has gone before. The more obviously personal narrative of
the next stanzas – death of the father, attempted suicide at twenty,
recovery of the father in the image of the husband – is represented as
return or repetition: 'At twenty I tried to die/And get back, back, back
to you' . . . 'I made a model of you', followed by emancipation: 'So
Daddy I'm finally through', and finally 'Daddy, daddy, you bastard,
I'm through'. They thus seem to turn into a final, triumphant sequence
the two forms of temporality which were offered at the beginning of

the poem. Plath only added the last stanza – 'There's a stake in your fat black heart', etc. – in the second draft to drive the point home, as it were (although even 'stake' can be read as signalling a continuing investment).

But for all that triumphalism, the end of the poem is ambiguous. For that 'through' on which the poem ends is given only two stanzas previously as meaning both ending: 'So daddy, I'm finally through' and the condition, even if failed in this instance, for communication to be possible: 'The voices just can't worm through.' How then should we read that last line – 'Daddy, daddy, you bastard, I'm through'? Communication *as* ending, or dialogue *without end*? Note too how the final vengeance in itself turns on an identification – 'you bastard' – that is, 'you father without father', 'you, whose father, like my own, is in the wrong place'.[82]

A point about the more personal narrative offered in these last stanzas, for it is the reference to the death of the father, the attempted suicide, and the marriage which calls up the more straightforward biographical reading of this text. Note, however, that the general does not conceal – 'camouflage' – the particular or personal meaning. It is, again, the relationship of the two levels which is important (it is that relationship, part sequence, part overdetermination, which the poem transcribes). But even at the most personal level of this poem, there is something more general at stake. For the link that 'Daddy' represents between suicide and a paternity, at once personal and symbolic, is again not exclusive to Plath.

At the end of William Styron's *Lie Down in Darkness*, Peyton, with whose suicide the book opened, is allowed to tell her story; the book has worked backwards from her death to its repetition through her eyes. In one of her last moments, she thinks – encapsulating in her thoughts the title of the book – 'I've sinned only in order to lie down in darkness and find, somewhere in the net of dreams, a new father, a new home.'[83] And then, as if in response to that impossible dream – impossible amongst other things because of the collapse of the myth of America on Nagasaki day, the day Peyton dies – the book ends with a 'Negro' revival baptism, as the servants of the family converge on the mass congregation of 'Daddy Faith'. As if the book was suggesting that the only way forward after the death of Peyton was into a grossly inflated symbolic paternity definitively lost to middle America, available only to those whom that same America exploits.[84] 'Daddy' is not far from this – if it is a suicide poem, it is so only to the extent that it locates a historically actualised vacancy, and excess, at the heart of symbolic, paternal law.

*   *   *

I have said relatively little about the sexual politics of the poem. Although there is nothing to mark its gender identity until fairly late, the poem can none the less be read as offering – after Sherry Ortner – the equation 'as father to daughter' so 'Nazi to Jew' (Ortner's formula was 'as nature to culture' so 'woman to man').[85] According to this interpretation, the representation of the father as Nazi would reveal something about the violence of patriarchy (patriarchy as violence). The speaker's own violence would then be a legitimate and triumphant retaliation – one feminist reading of the text. Clearly this is one way in which the poem can be read, but, taken on its own, the celebration of this narrative seems as problematic as that other feminist celebration of the breakdown or fragmentation of language to which I have already referred.

Assertion of the ego versus a body and language without identity or form – these are two positions on the poetic language of women which correspond respectively to the political demand for equality and to the demand for difference in the most fundamental psychic sense of the term. But perhaps more than any other poem by Plath, 'Daddy' seems to offer a type of corrective in advance to them both. It demonstrates the psychic and political cost of that desire for fragmentation (both in terms of origin and effects); but it also insists on the speaker's (and reader's) full participation in the most awkward of fantasies, fantasies which the feminist assertion of selfhood can read only as a type of psychic false consciousness, as the internalisation of patriarchy and mimicry of the eternal behaviour of men. It is particularly awkward for this second reading that the father oppresses to the precise extent that he is not there. Once again it is the category of fantasy that these readings have to play down – which also means, perhaps paradoxically, that they have to play down the concrete history in which the poem is set. For fascism must surely be distinguished from patriarchy, even if in some sense it can be seen as its effect. Fantasy and history are both lost in these two readings – in the eternal sameness of patriarchy and of women's singular relationship to it, in the eternal sameness of the femininity which erupts against its law.

Writing on Nazism in their famous book *The Inability to Mourn*, Alexander and Margarete Mitscherlich describe how vengeance as an alternative to failed mourning constitutes one of the unconscious sub-texts of what they call 'a particular German way of loving'.[86] If we add the mourning to the vengeance, then we cannot read 'Daddy' simply in terms of revenge against the oppressor. If we take the revenge and the mourning together, as the poem seems to do, we can reintroduce the concept of fantasy as that which links the motifs of memory and revenge, whose separation in responses to the Holocaust is discussed by Lyotard. More important, if we take their co-presence as a counter-narrative or caution against any straightforward narrative reading of the poem as a whole, then 'Daddy' appears as a poem that represents a set of fantasies which, at a precise historical moment and with devastating consequences, found themselves at the heart of our collective political life. In this context, there seems no point in trying to establish a one-way relation between the personal and the wider political history the poem evokes. The poem offers the implication of the one in the other – implication, rather than determination, precisely because one cannot establish a single, one-track relation between the two.

Whether the poem reproduces these fantasies or exposes them, whether it offers them to the reader for a further identification or critique, is not a question which I think can be answered. Saul Friedlander makes the difficulty of this distinction central to his book *Reflections of Nazism*, which describes the preoccupation with Nazi fantasies in our contemporary cultural life.[87] But the question is not yet historically settled as to whether knowledge of our implication in these fantasies, or the idea that we can and should separate ourselves from them completely, is most likely to prevent their repetition in the world today. Somewhere in the space between the inside and outside of the Hamburg Congress, between the Holocaust and nuclear rhetoric, it was this question that was being posed. In this context, what is most striking about 'Daddy' is its mobility of fantasy, the extent to which it takes up psychic positions which, it is often argued, if they cannot be clearly distinguished, lead to the collapse of morality itself. Plath, on the other hand, moves from one position to the other, implicating them in each other, forcing the reader to enter into something which she or he is often willing to consider only on condition of seeing it as something in which, psychically no less than historically, she or he plays absolutely no part.

Plath was a pacifist. The question then arises of the relation between her politics and these fantasies – between her pacifism and the psychic violence she represents in this poem, and of course not only here. In a much earlier psychoanalytic conference on the psychology of peace and war, held in London in 1934, two years after Wiesbaden, Edward Glover discusses the different relationships between violence in the inner and outer worlds.[88] Pacifism, he suggests, can be as much a repetition of, as a solution to, the problem of inner war. The militarist, on the other hand, is too desperately in search of inner peace to forgo war. But normality, or equilibrium, far from being the ideal scenario, is in many ways the most risky state of all:

The drawbacks to this state of equilibrium are threefold. First, having no urgent inner problem to solve, the man in the street is likely to ignore the real external urgency of war problems; secondly, the equilibrium will not withstand the panic and excitement of a war crisis; thirdly, it prevents the man in the street ever realising that the problem of war is his own unconscious problem.[89]

I offer Glover's remarks not as an analysis of Plath, nor indeed of pacifism, but in order to suggest something of the reversibility that might hold between pacifism and the commitment to (inner) war. (As Plath puts it in the *Journals*: 'I know it is too simple to wish for war, for open battle.'[90]) In order to suggest too – although Glover does not say it – something of the possible link between knowing the war is in fact one's own unconscious war, and working for peace. More simply, to note how little concepts such as antagonism, illegitimate appropriation, or theft (the terms of that critique of Plath with which this chapter began) can help us to understand the relation of these two concerns, the coexistence of external and inner urgency, in Plath's work.

Finally, I would suggest that 'Daddy' does allow us to ask whether the woman might not have a special relationship to fantasy – the only generalisation in the poem regarding women is, after all, that most awkward of lines: 'Every woman adores a fascist.' It is invariably taken out of context, taken out of the ghastly drama which shows where such a proposition might come from – what, for the woman who makes it, and in the worse sense, it might *mean*. Turning the criticism of Plath around once more, could we not read in that line a suggestion, or even a demonstration, that it is a woman who is most likely to articulate the power – perverse, recalcitrant, persistent – of fantasy as such? Nor would such an insight be in any way incompatible with women's legitimate protest against a patriarchal world. This is for me, finally, the wager of Plath's work.

Marguerite Duras's *La douleur* is her wartime diary. It describes the time when she was waiting for her husband to return from the camps, and her resistance during the war. At the end of this narrative, she introduces two stories:

> Thérèse is me. The person who tortures the informer is me. So also is the one who feels like making love to Ter, the member of the Militia. Me. I give you the torturer along with the rest of the texts. Learn to read them properly: they are sacred.[91]

The psychic terrain that Duras is covering here seems to be not unconnected to that represented in 'Daddy' by Plath – as if the story

of the victim (concretely and historically in this instance) had to be
followed by the story of herself as torturer, as well as by the story
of desire. The last word, however, goes to Sylvia Plath. It is her
first outline for the story 'The Shadow', a passage from the unedited
journals at Smith, not included in the published text:

> My present theme seems to be the awareness of a complicated guilt
> system whereby Germans in a Jewish and Catholic community are
> made to feel, in scapegoat fashion, the pain, psychically, the Jews
> are made to feel in Germany by the Germans without religion. The
> child can't understand the wider framework. How does her father
> come into this? How is she guilty for her father's deportation to
> a detention camp? [As (*sic*)] this is how I think the story will end.
> Joanna will come in on her own with the trapeze, Uncle Frank and
> the fiction of perfect goodness.[92]

Notes

1. LEON WIESELTIER, 'In a Universe of Ghosts', *New York Review of Books*,
   25 November 1976, pp. 20–23 (p. 20).

2. JOYCE CAROL OATES, 'The Death Throes of Romanticism', in PAUL
   ALEXANDER, (ed.) *Ariel Ascending* (New York: Harper and Row, 1973), p. 39;
   SEAMUS HEANEY, 'The indefatigable hoof-taps', *Times Literary Supplement*,
   (5–11 February 1988), 134–44 (p. 144); IRVING HOWE, 'The Plath Celebration:
   A Partial Dissent', in Edward Butscher (ed.), *Sylvia Plath: The Woman
   and the Work*, (New York: Dodd Mead and Company, 1977), pp. 224–35
   (p. 233); MARJORIE PERLOFF, 'The Two Ariels', *The American Poetry Review*,
   (November-December 1984), 14–15.

3. 'The sense of history, both personal and social, found in a poem like "For
   the Union Dead" is conspicuously absent from the *Ariel* poems. This is not
   mere coincidence: for the oracular poet, past and future are meaningless
   abstractions . . . For Sylvia Plath, there is only the given moment, only
   now.' MARJORIE PERLOFF, '*Angst* and Animism in the Poetry of Sylvia Plath',
   in LINDA W. WAGNER, (ed., *Critical Essays on Sylvia Plath* (Boston: Hall
   and Company, 1984), p. 121. For a much more positive assessment of
   Plath's relationship to history, see STAN SMITH, *Inviolable Voice: History and
   Twentieth-Century Poetry* (Dublin: Gill & Macmillan, 1982), ch. 9, 'Waist-Deep
   in History: Sylvia Plath', pp. 200–25.

4. PERLOFF, 'The Two Ariels', op. cit., p. 15.

5. The criticism was first directed at FERDINAND DE SAUSSURE's *Course in General
   Linguistics* (1915) (London: Fontana, 1974), for what has been seen as an
   emphasis on the synchronic, at the expense of the diachronic, dimension
   of language, and on the arbitrary nature of the linguistic sign which,
   it was argued, made it impossible to theorise the relationship between

language and reference. It has become a commonplace to reproach post-Saussurian literary theory with ahistoricism. For discussion of some of these debates, see DEREK ATTRIDGE, GEOFF BENNINGTON and ROBERT YOUNG (eds), *Post-Structuralism and the Question of History* (Cambridge: Cambridge University Press, 1987), especially Geoff Bennington and Robert Young, 'Introduction: posing the question', pp. 1–11. More specifically, I am referring here to the controversy which has followed the discovery of Paul de Man's wartime writings for the Belgian collaborationist newspaper *Le Soir*. See WERNER HAMACHER, NEIL HERTZ and THOMAS KEENAN (eds), *Responses* (Lincoln, NB/London: University of Nebraska Press, 1989).

6. The conference took place in Hamburg in 1985. The papers were published in a special issue of the *International Journal of Psycho-Analysis*, **67**, 1986.

7. I take this account from JANINE CHASSEGUET-SMIRGEL, '"Time's White Hair We Ruffle", Reflections on the Hamburg Conference', *International Review of Psycho-Analysis*, **14** (1987): 433–44.

8. HANNA SEGAL, 'Silence is the Real Crime', *International Review of Psycho-Analysis*, **14** (1987): 3–12. For the main Congress, see F.-W. EICKHOFF, 'Identification and its Vicissitudes in the Context of the Nazi Phenomenon', *International Journal of Psycho-Analysis*, **67** (1986): 33–44; HILLEL KLEIN and ILANY KOGAN, 'Identification Processes and Denial in the Shadow of Nazism', pp. 45–52; DAVID ROSENFELD, 'Identification and its Vicissitudes in Relation to the Nazi Phenomenon', pp. 53–64; MORTIMER OSTOW, 'The Psychodynamics of Apocalyptic: Discussion of Papers on Identification and the Nazi Phenomenon', pp. 277–85; DINORA PINES, 'Working with Women Survivors of the Holocaust: Affective Experiences in Transference and Counter-Transference', pp. 295–307; IRA BRENNER and JUDITH S. KESTENBERG, 'Children who Survived the Holocaust: The Role of Rules and Routines in the Development of the Superego', pp. 309–16; ANITA ECKSTAEDT, 'Two Complementary Cases of Identification Involving Third Reich Fathers', pp. 317–27. See also STEVEN A. LUEL and PAUL MARCUS, *Psychoanalytic Reflections on the Holocaust: Selected Essays*, Denver: Holocaust Awareness Institute and Center for Judaic Studies/New York: Ktav Publishing, 1984. I am grateful to Nina Farhi and Rachel Sievers for bringing my attention to this book, and to the article by Chasseguet-Smirgel cited above.

9. FREUD, 'Psycho-Analytic Notes on an Autobiographical Account of a Case of Paranoia (Schreber)', 1911, *Standard Edition*, vol. XII p. 71; Pelican Freud, **9**, p. 210, cited by Janine Chasseguet-Smirgel, opening comments, *International Journal of Psycho-Analysis*, **67** (1986): 7. Compare also the opening address of Adam Limentani, President of the International Association of Psycho-Analysis: '. . . we also hope that it will facilitate the mending of old wounds in typically psychoanalytic fashion – through remembering and understanding, rather than denial, rationalisation and forgetting' (p. 5); and of Deiter Olmeier, President of the German Psycho-Analytic Association: 'It is only possible to work through things which are accessible to the conscious, which can again and again and ever more clearly become conscious, which can and must be remembered' (p. 6).

10. EICKHOFF, 'Identification and its Vicissitudes in the Context of the Nazi Phenomenon', op. cit., p. 34.

11. Ibid., and ROSENFELD, op. cit.

12. The reference here is to an earlier paper by ANITA ECKSTAEDT, one of the contributors to the Hamburg Conference, cited by Henry Krystal in a review of Martin S. Bergmann and Milton E. Jucovy, *Generations of the Holocaust*, (New York: Basic Books, 1982), in the *Psycho-Analytic Quarterly*, **53**: 466–73 (p. 469).

13. ECKSTAEDT, op. cit., p. 326.

14. EICKHOFF (citing L. Wurmser), op. cit., p. 37.

15. I am aware of the danger of reducing the complexities of these individual case-histories to a formula. Each of them showed a particular set of vicissitudes, not only in relation to the historical position of the patient's parents and their own history in relation to Nazism, but also as regards other details of the patient's personal history (whether or not the parents chose to speak, the death of one or other parent, exile, reinstatement, etc.). Readers are encouraged to refer to the papers, which make an extraordinary historical document in themselves.

16. ZEV GARBER and BRUCE ZUCKERMAN, 'Why Do We Call the Holocaust "The Holocaust"? An Inquiry into the Psychology of Labels', in *Remembering For the Future* (Oxford: Oxford University Press, 1988), vol. 2, *The Impact of the Holocaust on the Contemporary World*, pp. 189–92.

17. Both poems are included in the 'Juvenilia' section of the *Collected Poems*, pp. 320, 325.

18. *Encyclopedia Judaica and Catholic Encylopedia*, both cited by JUDITH KROLL, *Chapters in a Mythology: The Poetry of Sylvia Plath* (New York: Harper & Row, 1976) p. 181.

19. PRIMO LEVI, *The Drowned and the Saved* (London: Michael Joseph, 1988), pp. 43, 33. See this whole chapter, Chapter 2, 'The Grey Zone', pp. 22–51.

20. PINES, 'Working with Women Survivors of the Holocaust', op. cit., p. 300.

21. ARNOST LUSTIG, 'Rose Street', in *Night and Hope* (New York: Dutton, 1962), p. 78.

22. FREUD, 'Psycho-Analytic Notes on an Autobiographical Account of a Case of Paranoia (Schreber)', op. cit., *Standard Edition*, p. 66; Pelican Freud, p. 204.

23. FREUD, *Three Essays on the Theory of Sexuality*, 1905, *Standard Edition*, vol. VII, pp. 123–245 (p. 145n); Pelican Freud, 7, pp. 31–169 (p. 56n).

24. ILSE GRUBRICH-SIMITIS, 'From Concretism to Metaphor: Thoughts on Some Theoretical and Technical Aspects of the Psychoanalytic Work with Children of Holocaust Survivors', *Psychoanalytic Study of the Child*, **39** (1984): 301–29.

25. Ibid., p. 302.

26. EICKHOFF, op. cit., p. 34.

27. GRUBRICH-SIMITIS, op. cit., pp. 313, 309n.

28. Ibid., p. 316.

29. HANNAH ARENDT, *Eichmann in Jerusalem: A Report on the Banality of Evil* (New York: Viking, 1963), revised and enlarged edition 1965; Harmondsworth: Penguin, 1977, p. 211.

30. GEORGE STEINER, 'Dying is an art', *The Reporter*, (7 October 1975), in Charles Newman (ed.), *The Art of Sylvia Plath* (Bloomington: Indiana University Press, 1970), p. 217.

31. EMIL L. FACKENHEIM, 'From Bergen-Belsen to Jerusalem: Contemporary Implications of the Holocaust' (The Cultural Department World Jewish Congress, Jerusalem, Institute of Contemporary Jewry, The Hebrew University of Jerusalem, 1975), pp. 17, 12.

32. KARL KRAUS, *Das Karl Kraus Lesebuch* (Zurich: Diogenes, 1980), cited Eickhoff, op. cit., p. 40; Eickhoff discusses these lines in relation to lines from a poem by Brecht – quoted as epigraph to his paper (p. 33) – who had attacked Kraus for raising his voice 'only in complaint that it was insufficient'.

33. LEVI, *If This Is A Man* (Oxford: The Bodley Head, 1960), first published in Italian in 1947; Harmondsworth: Penguin, 1979 (with *The Truce*), p. 17.

34. LEVI, *The Drowned and the Saved*, op. cit., p. 63.

35. PAUL CELAN, 'Aschenglorie', *Atemwende*, 1967; *Gedichte* (Frankfurt: Suhrkamp Verlag, 1975), p. 72. The line is discussed by JACQUES DERRIDA, 'Shibboleth' (for Paul Celan), in G.H. Hartman and S. Budick (eds) *Midrash and Literature* (New Haven: Yale University Press, 1986), pp. 307–47 (p. 326).

36. PIOTR RAWICZ, *Le sang du ciel* (Paris: Gallimard, 1961); *Blood From the Sky* (London: Secker & Warburg, 1964). These lines are quoted at the end of ALVAREZ, 'Literature of the Holocaust', op. cit., p. 33.

37. FACKENHEIM, op. cit. 'Discussion', p. 26.

38. JOSEF BOR, *Terezin Requiem* (New York: Knopf, 1963) (original date not given, in translation); ELIE WIESEL, *Night* (New York: Hill & Wang, 1960), first published in Yiddish in 1956; ILSE AICHINGER, *Herod's Children* (New York: Atheneum, 1963) (Alvarez refers to this work as a recent novel); ARNOST LUSTIG, *Night and Hope*, op. cit., was first published in Prague in 1962.

39. A. ALVAREZ, 'Literature of the Holocaust', in *Beyond all this Fiddle* (London: Allen Lane, 1968). Alvarez comments that the Polish writer Tadeusz Borowski is one of the few to have written about the camps close to the time. See 'This Way for the Gas – A Story', *Commentary*, 1: 34 (July 1962) 39–47. See also the Hungarian poet and camp survivor JANOS PILINSKY's *Selected Poems*, trans. Ted Hughes (Manchester: Carcanet Press, 1976) (his first collection of poems appeared in 1946); and LEVI, *If This Is A Man*, op. cit. The history of the publication of Levi's book is interesting in itself. Levi wrote it as soon as he returned from the camps. It was rejected by several large publishers and then published by a small publishing house run by Franco Antonicelli in 1947; 2500 copies were published. Antonicelli then collapsed and the book was not republished until 1958 by Enaudi. Levi comments: 'in that harsh post-war world, people didn't have much desire to go back in their memories to the painful years that had just finished.' LEVI, *Se questo è un uomo* (Turin: Enaudi, 1982), Author's Note, p. 231.

40. HUGHES, Foreword, *J*, p. xv.

41. KROLL, p. 243n.

42. DERRIDA, op. cit., p. 329.

43. Ibid., p. 338.

44. Ibid., and PAUL CELAN, op. cit., vol. 1, pp. 287–9.

45. DIANE WOOD MIDDLEBROOK and DIANA HUME GEORGE (eds), *Selected Poems of Anne Sexton* (Boston: Houghton Mifflin, 1988), p. 5; originally published in *The Antioch Review*, **19**, 1959; see HEATHER CAM, '"Daddy": Sylvia Plath's Debt to Anne Sexton', in Diana Hume George (ed.), *Sexton: Selected Criticism* (Urbana/Chicago: University of Illinois Press, 1988), pp. 223–6. I am grateful to Diane Middlebrook for drawing my attention to this poem.

46. *CP*, 2 April 1962, pp. 187–9, first published in *Encounter*, 21 October 1963, and in *Ariel*. The poem was not included in Plath's own list for *Ariel*.

47. ROBERT GRAVES, *The White Goddess*, (1946; London: Faber & Faber, 1961), p. 194.

48. HANS MAGNUS ENZENSBERGER, 'In Search of a Lost Language', *Encounter* (September 1963): 44–51. The article is discussed by Judith Kroll in relation to 'Little Fugue'. She compares Plath's poem to a poem by Gunter Eich cited by Enzensberger, but the historical allusion is finally synthesised into the overall mythological schema. KROLL, op. cit., pp. 114–15, 246–7n.

49. The concept comes from JACQUES LACAN, who formulates it thus: 'What is realised in my history is not the past definite of what was, since it is no more, or even the present perfect of what has been in what I am, but the future anterior of what I shall have been for what I am in the process of becoming', 'The function and field of speech and language in psychoanalysis', 1953, in *Ecrits: A Selection* (London: Tavistock, 1977), pp. 30–113 (p. 86). See also D.W. WINNICOTT: 'This search [for a past detail which is not yet experienced] takes the form of looking for this detail in the future', 'Fear of Breakdown', in Gregorio Kohon (ed.), *The British School of Psychoanalysis: The Independent Tradition* (London: Free Association Books, 1986), pp. 173–82 (p. 178).

50. *Remembering for the Future*, op. cit.

51. KLEIN and KOGAN, op. cit., p. 48.

52. *CP*, 12 October 1962, pp. 222–4 (strangely, the poem is omitted from the Index), first published in *Encounter*, 21 October 1963, and in *Ariel*.

53. 'The Blood Jet is Poetry', review of *Ariel*, *Time*, 10 June 1966, pp. 118–20 (p. 118). The review is copiously illustrated with photographs from Aurelia Plath's personal collection. A letter from her to Ted Hughes suggests that she felt she had been tricked by the reviewer and that this, plus the cover of the issue of *The Atlantic* which published 'Johnny Panic and the Bible of Dreams' ('Sylvia Plath on Going Mad'), had contributed to her reluctance to see *The Bell Jar* published in the United States. Letter from Aurelia Plath to Ted Hughes, 11 April 1970, Correspondence, Lilly, op. cit.

54. JEAN-FRANÇOIS LYOTARD, *The Differend: Phrases in Dispute* (Manchester: Manchester University Press, 1988) p. 27. Lyotard is discussing the issue of Holocaust denial or the Faurisson debate, see pp. 3ff. See also GILL SEIDAL, *The Holocaust Denial: Antisemitism, Racism and the New Right* (Brighton: Beyond the Pale Collective, 1986).

55. The concept comes from FREUD, *The Ego and the Id*, 1923, *Standard Edition*, vol. XIX pp. 31–2; Pelican Freud, 11, pp. 370–71, and *Group Psychology and the Analysis of the Ego*, 1921, *Standard Edition*, vol. XVIII, pp. 105–6; Pelican Freud, 12, pp. 134–5. It has been most fully theorised recently by JULIA KRISTEVA in *Tales of Love* (New York: Columbia University Press, 1987), pp. 24–9.

56. For Kristeva this father founds the possibility of identification for the subject and is critically linked to – enables the subject to symbolise – the orality, and hence the abjection, which was the focus of discussion of 'Poem for a Birthday', in Chapter 2 of Rose, *The Haunting of Sylvia Plath*, pp. 40–63.

57. 'Sylvia Plath', in PETER ORR (ed.), *The Poet Speaks* (London: Routledge & Kegan Paul, 1966), pp. 167–72 (p. 169).

58. Claude Lanzmann in discussion of the film *Shoah*, Channel 4 Television, 27 October 1987; see also LANZMANN, *Shoah, An Oral History of the Holocaust: The Complete Text of the Film* (New York: Pantheon, 1985); LYOTARD, 'Judiciousness in Dispute, or Kant after Marx', in Murray Krieger (ed.), *The Aims of Representation: Subject, Text, History* (New York: Columbia University Press, 1987), pp. 24–67 (p. 64).

59. *Journals*, Smith, July 1950–July 1953, September 1950, p. 60 (*J*, p. 20).

60. EICKHOFF, op. cit., p. 38.

61. 4 July 1958, 7 July 1958, 11 October 1959, *J*, pp. 244, 246, 319; 13 October 1959, *LH*, p. 356; 13 October 1959, 19 October 1959, *J*, pp. 319, p. 321; *Journals*, Smith, 12 December 1958–15 November 1959, 7 November 1959, p. 94 (*J*, p. 327).

62. *The Bell Jar*, p. 35.

63. 'On one side I am a first generation American, on one side I'm a second generation American, and so my concern with concentration camps and so on is uniquely intense', ORR, op. cit., p. 169.

64. Letter from Thomas J. Clohesy to Aurelia Plath, 4 September 1966, Smith, Section 5, Biography.

65. JEAN STAFFORD, *A Boston Adventure*, 1946 (London: Hogarth, 1986).

66. Ibid., p. 335.

67. Ibid.

68. Ibid., p. 482.

69. ROSENFELD, op. cit., p. 62.

70. LYOTARD, 'Judiciousness in Dispute', op. cit., p. 59. In a reply to Lyotard, Stephen Greenblatt takes issue with him on this specific question: GREENBLATT, 'Capitalist Culture and the Circulatory System', in KRIEGER, op. cit., pp. 257–73 (pp. 260–61).

71. FREUD, *The Ego and the Id*, op. cit., *Standard Edition*, p. 34; Pelican Freud, p. 374.

72. 'Among the Bumblebees' (early 1950s), *Johnny Panic*, pp. 259–66 (p. 263).

73. LACAN, 'Seminar of 21 January 1975', in Juliet Mitchell and Jacqueline Rose (eds), *Feminine Sexuality: Jacques Lacan and the École Freudienne* (London: Macmillan, 1982), pp. 162–71 (p. 167).

74. FREUD, 'Psycho-Analytic Notes on an Autobiographical Account of a Case of Paranoia (Schreber)', op. cit.; see also SAMUEL WEBER, Introduction to DANIEL PAUL SCHREBER, *Memoirs of My Nervous Illness*, ed. Ida Macalpine and Richard Hunter, 1955, new edition (Cambridge, MA/London: Harvard University Press, 1988), pp. vii–liv.

75. OTTO PLATH, *Bumblebees and their Ways* (New York: Macmillan, 1934).

76. OTTO E. PLATH, 'Insect Societies', in Carl Murchison (ed.), *A Handbook of Social Psychology* (Massachusetts: Clark University Press; London: Oxford University Press, 1935), pp. 83–141 (pp. 83, 136–7). The first quotation comes from the epigraph to the chapter and is part of a quotation from THOMAS BELT, *The Naturalist in Nicaragua*, 1874; its account of the perfect regiment belongs to a more generally utopian image of community which ends with a quotation from Thomas More.

77. 'Among the Bumblebees', op. cit., p. 262.

78. 'Little Fugue', Draft 1, page 2, verso, Smith, *Ariel Poems*.

79. VIRGINIA WOOLF, *Three Guineas* (London: Hogarth, 1938); (Harmondsworth: Penguin, 1977), p. 162.

80. ELIZABETH WILSON, 'Coming out for a brand new age', the *Guardian*, 14 March 1989. The same line has also been taken as a slogan to explain German women's involvement in Nazism; see MURRAY SAYLE, 'Adolf and the Women', *The Independent Magazine*, 9 November 1988: '"Every woman adores a Fascist," wrote Sylvia Plath. Is this why so many German women voted for Hitler, despite the male emphasis of the Nazi regime?' (caption under title).

81. For a study of this difficult question, see CLAUDIA KOONZ, *Mothers in the Fatherland: Women, the Family and Nazi Politics* (London; Jonathan Cape, 1987).

82. Thanks to Natasha Korda for pointing this out to me.

83. STYRON, *Lie Down in Darkness* (Indianapolis/New York: Bobbs-Merrill, 1951), p. 379.

84. On the question of racism, see JOHN HENRIK CLARKE (ed.), *William Styron's Nat Turner: Ten Black Writers Respond* (Boston: Beacon Press, 1968); and RICHARD OHMANN, *Politics of Letters*, ch. 5, 'The Shaping of a Canon: US Fiction, 1960–1975' (Middletown: Wesleyan University Press, 1987), p. 68.

85. SHERRY ORTNER, 'Is Female to Male as Nature Is to Culture?', in Michelle Zimbalist Rosaldo and Louise Lamphere (eds.), *Woman, Culture and Society* (California: Stanford University Press, 1974), pp. 67–87. For a critique of this article, see CAROL P. MACCORMACK, 'Nature, culture and gender: a critique', in CAROL P. MACCORMACK and MARILYN STRATHERN, *Nature, Culture and Gender* (Cambridge: Cambridge University Press, 1980), pp. 1–24.

86. ALEXANDER and MARGARETE MITSCHERLICH, *The Inability to Mourn* (London: Grove Press, 1975) ch. 1 'The Inability to Mourn – With Which Is Associated A German Way of Loving', pp. 3–68.

87. SAUL FRIEDLANDER, *Reflections of Nazism* (New York: Harper & Row, 1984).

88. EDWARD GLOVER and MORRIS GINSBERG, 'A Symposium on the Psychology of Peace and War', *British Journal of Medical Psychology*, **14** (1934): 274–93.

89. Ibid., p. 277.

90. Excerpt from a letter to Richard Sassoon, 15 January 1956, *J*, p. 97.

91. MARGUERITE DURAS, *La douleur* (Paris: POL, 1985); (London: Fontana, 1987), introductory statement to 'Albert of the Capitals' and 'Ter of the Militias', p. 115.

92. *Journals*, Smith, 12 December 1958–15 November, 1959, op. cit., 28 December 1958, p. 28 (*J*, p. 283).

Abbreviations of Sylvia Plath's Works

LH	*Letters Home: Correspondence 1950–1963*. Selected and edited with a commentary by Aurelia Schober Plath. London: Faber & Faber, 1975.
Johnny Panic	*Johnny Panic and the Bible of Dreams and Other Prose Writings*. Introduction by Ted Hughes. London: Faber & Faber, 1977. Revised edition, 1979.
CP	*Collected Poems*. Edited by Ted Hughes. London: Faber & Faber, 1981.
J	*The Journals of Sylvia Plath*. Edited by Frances McCullough with Ted Hughes. New York: Random House, 1982.
Smith	The Sylvia Plath Collection. Smith College Library, Rare Book Room, Smith College, Northampton, Massachusetts.
Lilly	The Sylvia Plath Collection. Lilly Library, University of Indiana, Bloomington, Indiana.

Note: Whenever reference is made to extracts from the Smith and Lilly collections which have been omitted from published texts, the page of the published version where the omission occurs is given in parentheses after the full reference.

Notes on Authors

In the case of translated works, only the date of the translation is given below.

HAROLD BLOOM is Sterling Professor of the Humanities at Yale University. His many books include *The Anxiety of Influence: A Theory of Poetry* (1973); *A Map of Misreading* (1975); *Figures of Capable Imagination* (1976); and *Agon: Towards a Theory of Revisionism* (1982).

CYNTHIA CHASE is Associate Professor of English at Cornell University. She is the author of *Decomposing Figures: Rhetorical Readings in the Romantic Tradition* (1986) and the editor of the Longman Critical Reader in *Romanticism* (1993).

SHOSHANA FELMAN is Professor of French at Yale University and an editor of *Yale French Studies*. She is the author of *The Literary Speech Act: Don Juan with J.L. Austin, or Seduction in Two Languages* (1983); *Madness and Literature: Literature / Philosophy / Psychoanalysis* (1985); and *Jacques Lacan and the Adventure of Insight: Psychoanalysis in Contemporary Culture* (1987).

DANIEL FERRER is a researcher at the Centre National de la Recherche Scientifique. He is the author of *Virginia Woolf and the Madness of Language* (1990); and the co-editor, with Derek Attridge, of *Post-Structuralist Joyce: Essays from the French* (1984). He is currently working on genetic criticism: he has edited, with Claude Jacquet, *Genèse de Babel: Joyce et la Création* (1985); and, with Jean-Louis Lebrave, *L'Écriture et ses doubles: genèse et variation textuelle* (1991).

ANDRÉ GREEN is a practising psychoanalyst: his essay in this volume is taken from his book *The Tragic Effect: The Oedipus Complex in Tragedy* (1979). His other works in English include *Psychoanalysis and Ordinary Modes of Thought* (1982) and *On Private Madness* (1986).

JULIA KRISTEVA, born in Bulgaria, is a practising psychoanalyst and holds the chair in Linguistics at the Université de Paris VII. An early member of the Tel Quel group, her books include *About Chinese Women* (1977); *Desire in Language: A Semiotic Approach to Literature and Art* (1980); *Powers of Horror: An Essay on Abjection* (1982); *Revolution in Poetic Language* (1984); *Black Sun: Depression and Melancholia* (1989); and a novel, *The Samurai* (1992).

JACQUELINE ROSE is Professor of English at Queen Mary and Westfield College, University of London. She is the editor, with Juliet Mitchell, of *Feminine Sexuality: Jacques Lacan and the Ecole Freudienne* (1982); and the author of *The Case of Peter Pan; or The Impossibility of Children's Fiction* (1984); *Sexuality in the Field of Vision* (1986); *The Haunting of Sylvia Plath* (1991); and *Why War?* (1993).

ANITA SOKOLSKY is Associate Professor of English at Williams College. She has written articles on modern literature, cinema, popular culture, and literary theory, and is currently writing a book on depression and melancholia in literature.

Slavoj Žižek is a researcher at the Institute for Sociology at Ljubljana, Slovenia. His many books include *The Sublime Object of Ideology* (1989); *For They Know Not What They Do: Enjoyment as a Political Factor* (1990); *Looking Awry: An Introduction to Jacques Lacan through Popular Culture* (1991); *Everything you always wanted to know about Lacan (but were afraid to ask Hitchcock)* (ed.) (1992); and *Enjoy your Symptom! Jacques Lacan in Hollywood and Out* (1992).

Further Reading

The following bibliography includes only works published in English. It is divided into three sections, corresponding roughly to the structure of the Introduction: the first section consists of works on psychoanalytic theory, including those of Freud and Lacan; the second covers psychoanalysis and literature, with a few works discussing the other arts; the third is devoted to psychoanalysis and feminism, including the works of Kristeva and Irigaray.

(1) Psychoanalytic Theory: Primary and Secondary Works

ABRAHAM, NICOLAS 'Notes on the Phantom: A Complement to Freud's Metapsychology', in Françoise Meltzer (ed.) *The Trial(s) of Psychoanalysis* (1988), pp. 75–80. Introduces Abraham's fascinating concept of intergenerational haunting.

ABRAHAM, NICOLAS and TOROK, MARIA 'The Shell and the Kernel', *Diacritics* 9:1 (1979), 16–31.

——'Psychoanalytic Esthetics: Time, Rhythm, and the Unconscious', *Diacritics* 16:3 (1986), 3–14.

——*The Wolf Man's Magic Word: A Cryptonomy.* Trans. Nicholas Rand. Foreword by Jacques Derrida. Minneapolis: University of Minnesota Press, 1986. With Derrida's famous introduction, 'Fors,' this strange and fascinating reinterpretation of the case history of the Wolf Man has become a key text in contemporary discussions of mourning.

BORCH-JACOBSEN, MIKKEL *The Freudian Subject.* Trans. Catherine Porter. Stanford: Stanford University Press, 1988.

——*Lacan: The Absolute Master.* Trans. Douglas Brink. Stanford: Stanford University Press, 1991.

BOWIE, MALCOLM *Lacan.* London: Fontana, 1991. The fullest, most impartial and eloquent introduction to Lacan.

CADAVA, EDUARDO, CONNOR, PETER and NANCY, JEAN-LUC (eds) *Who Comes after the Subject?* London: Routledge, 1991. Essays on the deconstruction of the subject in psychoanalysis and philosophy.

CHASSEGUET-SMIRGEL, JANINE *Creativity and Perversion.* London: Free Association, 1985.

CLÉMENT, CATHERINE *The Lives and Legends of Jacques Lacan.* Trans. Arthur Goldhammer. New York: Columbia University Press, 1983.

DERRIDA, JACQUES 'Freud and the Scene of Writing', in *Writing and Difference.* London: Routledge, 1978, pp. 196–230. On Freud's essay 'A Note upon the "Mystic Writing Pad"' (1925).

——*The Post Card: From Socrates to Freud and Beyond.* Trans. Alan Bass. Chicago: Chicago University Press, 1987. The second half of the book, 'To Speculate

– on Freud', contains Derrida's famous deconstructive reading of *Beyond the Pleasure Principle*.

EAGLETON, TERRY *Literary Theory: An Introduction.* Oxford: Blackwell, 1983. Includes a succinct and provocative introduction to psychoanalysis in Chapter 5.

FELDSTEIN, RICHARD and SUSSMAN, HENRY (eds) *Psychoanalysis and . . . .* London: Routledge, 1990. An excellent collection of essays examining the uneasy relationships between psychoanalysis and Marxism, femininism, semiotics, deconstruction, and literary criticism.

FELMAN, SHOSHANA *Jacques Lacan and the Adventure of Insight: Psychoanalysis in Contemporary Culture.* Cambridge, MA: Harvard University Press, 1987.

FORRESTER, JOHN *The Seductions of Psychoanalysis: Freud, Lacan, and Derrida.* Cambridge: Cambridge University Press, 1990. Mainly on the theory and transmission of psychoanalysis, and including a thought-provoking essay on psychoanalytic literary criticism and Dostoevsky's *The Gambler*.

FREUD, ANNA *The Ego and the Mechanisms of Defense.* New York: International Universities Press, 1966. A central text for Harold Bloom's poetics.

FREUD, SIGMUND *The Complete Psychological Works.* Standard Edition. Trans. James Strachey. London: Hogarth, 1953–1974. Works cited in the introduction to this volume, and those frequently cited by literary critics and feminist theorists, include:

——*The Interpretation of Dreams* (1900), IV and V.

——*The Psychopathology of Everyday Life* (1901), VI.

——'Screen Memories' (1903), III, p. 301–22.

——*Three Essays on the Theory of Sexuality* (1905), VII, pp. 125–246.

——'Psychopathic Characters on the Stage' (1905/6), VII, pp. 305-10. Interesting comments on *Hamlet*.

——*Fragment of an Analysis of a Case of Hysteria* ('Dora') (1905[1901]), XVII, pp. 3–122.

——*Jokes and their Relation to the Unconscious* (1905), VIII.

——*Delusions and Dreams in Jensen's 'Gradiva'* (1907), IX, pp. 3–97. Freud's fullest interpretation of a literary text.

——'Creative Writers and Day-Dreaming' (1908), IX, pp. 143–54.

——'On the Sexual Theories of Children' (1908), IX, pp. 207–26.

——'Family Romances' (1909), IX, pp. 237–41.

——'Leonardo da Vinci and a Memory of his Childhood' (1910), XI, pp. 59–138.

——'The Theme of the Three Caskets' (1913), XII, pp. 291–301. A fascinating exploration of the *King Lear* story.

——'Remembering, Repeating, and Working-Through' (1914), XII, pp. 147–56.

——*From the History of an Infantile Neurosis* ('Wolf Man') (1918[1914]), XVII, pp. 3–122.

——'The "Uncanny"' (1919), XVII, pp. 219–56. On E.T.A. Hoffman's 'The Sandman'.

——*Beyond the Pleasure Principle* (1920), XVIII, pp. 3–64.

——'The Dissolution of the Oedipus Complex' (1924), XIX, pp. 173–9.

——'Medusa's Head' (1940 [1922]), XVIII, pp. 273–4.

——'A Note on the "Mystic Writing-Pad"' (1925), XIX, pp. 227–32.

——'Negation' (1925), XIX, pp. 235–9.

——'Some Psychical Consequences of the Anatomical Distinction Between the Sexes' (1925), XIX, pp. 243–60.

——'Fetishism' (1927), XXI, pp. 149–57.

——'Dostoevsky and Parricide' (1928), XXI, pp. 175–96.

——*Moses and Monotheism: Three Essays* (1939), XXIII, pp. 3–238. A fascinating psychoanalytic reading of the Book of Exodus.

——'Female Sexuality' (1931), XXI, pp. 223–43.

GALLOP, JANE *Reading Lacan*. Ithaca: Cornell University Press, 1985. Vivid and irreverent essays on Lacanian theory.

GILMAN, SANDER L. (ed.) *Introducing Psychoanalytic Theory*. New York: Brunner/Mazel, 1982. Contains essays on psychoanalytic theory and two interesting essays on Freud's study of Hoffman's story 'The Sandman'.

GREEN, ANDRÉ *Psychoanalysis and Ordinary Modes of Thought*. London: University College London, 1982.

——*On Private Madness*. London: Hogarth, 1986.

KLEIN, MELANIE *Love, Guilt and Reparation and other Works, 1921–1945*. New York: Dell, 1977.

——*The Selected Melanie Klein*. Ed. Juliet Mitchell. Harmondsworth: Penguin, 1986. A useful collection of key works.

——*Envy and Gratitude and Other Works, 1946–1963*. London: Virago, 1988.

LACAN, JACQUES *The Language of the Self: The Function of Language in Psychoanalysis*. Ed. Anthony Wilden. New York: Dell, 1968. Extensive commentary by Wilden on a crucial essay of Lacan's.

——*Écrits: A Selection*. Trans. Alan Sheridan. London: Tavistock, 1977.

——*The Four Fundamental Concepts of Psycho-Analysis*. Trans. Alan Sheridan. London: Hogarth Press, 1977.

——'Desire and the Interpretation of Desire in *Hamlet*', in Shoshana Felman (ed.) *Literature and Psychoanalysis* (1982), pp. 11–52.

——*The Seminar of Jacques Lacan. Book I: Freud's Papers on Technique 1953–1954*. Ed. Jacques-Alain Miller. Trans. John Forrester. Cambridge: Cambridge University Press, 1988.

——*The Seminar of Jacques Lacan. Book II: The Ego in Freud's Theory and in the Technique of Psychoanalysis 1954–1955*. Ed. Jacques-Alain Miller. Trans. Sylvana Tomaselli. Cambridge: Cambridge University Press, 1988.

——*The Ethics of Psychoanalysis, 1959–1960: The Seminar of Jacques Lacan, Book VII*. Ed. Jacques-Alain Miller. Trans. Dennis Porter. London: Routledge, 1992.

LACOUE-LABARTHE, PHILLIPPE 'Theatrum Analyticum' *Glyph*, 2 (1977), 122–43. On the theatrical space of psychoanalysis.

LAPLANCHE, JEAN *Life and Death in Psychoanalysis*. Trans. Jeffrey Mehlman. Baltimore: Johns Hopkins University Press, 1976. An influential deconstruction of key Freudian terms.

LAPLANCHE, JEAN and PONTALIS, JEAN-BAPTISTE *The Language of Psycho-Analysis*. Trans. Donald Nicholson-Smith. London: Hogarth Press, 1973. An invaluable dictionary of psychoanalytic terms.

LEMAIRE, ANIKA *Jacques Lacan*. Trans. David Macey. London: Routledge, 1977. An early popularisation: useful but not as good as Malcolm Bowie's *Lacan*.

MACCABE, COLIN (ed.) *The Talking Cure: Essays in Psychoanalysis and Language*. London: Macmillan, 1981.

MEHLMAN, JEFFREY 'How to Read Freud on Jokes: The Critic as Schadchen', *New Literary History*, **6** (1975), 439–61. The Schadchen is the marriage-broker, a figure in many of the Jewish jokes discussed by Freud in *Jokes and their Relation to the Unconscious* (1905).

MEISEL, PERRY (ed.) *Freud: A Collection of Critical Essays*. Englewood Cliffs, NJ: Prentice-Hall, Inc., 1981. A judicious selection of essays by such eminent American critics as Lionel Trilling, Kenneth Burke, and Harold Bloom, together with famous essays on Freud by Thomas Mann and W.H. Auden. Meisel's elegant and knowledgeable introduction does much to discredit Lacan's prejudice against the American Freudians.

MULLER, JOHN P. and RICHARDSON, WILLIAM J. *Lacan and Language: A Reader's Guide to Écrits*. New York: International Universities Press, 1982. A closely annotated commentary on every part of the text of Lacan's *Écrits*, containing a useful index of terms.

RAGLAND-SULLIVAN, ELLIE *Jacques Lacan and the Philosophy of Psychoanalysis*. London: Croom Helm, 1986. An important analysis of Lacan's work.

RESNIK, SALOMON *The Theatre of the Dream*. Trans. Alan Sheridan. London: Tavistock, 1987.

RICOEUR, PAUL *Freud and Philosophy: An Essay in Interpretation*. Trans. Denis Savage. New Haven: Yale University Press, 1970.

ROUSTANG, FRANÇOIS *Dire Mastery: Discipleship from Freud to Lacan*. Trans. Ned Lukacher. Baltimore: Johns Hopkins University Press, 1982.

——*Psychoanalysis Never Lets Go*. Trans. Ned Lukacher. Baltimore: Johns Hopkins University Press, 1983. Useful books for understanding French psychoanalysis, with a pleasing lightness of touch.

SAFOUAN, MOUSTAFA *Pleasure and Being: Hedonism from a Psychoanalytic Point of View*. Trans. Martin Thom. London: Macmillan, 1983.

SCHNEIDERMAN, STUART (ed.) *Returning to Freud: Clinical Psychoanalysis in the School of Lacan*. New Haven: Yale University Press, 1980.

——*Jacques Lacan: The Death of an Intellectual Hero*. Cambridge, MA: Harvard University Press, 1983. An entertaining introduction.

SHARPE, ELLA FREEMAN *Collected Papers on Psycho-Analysis*. Ed. Marjorie Brierley. London: Hogarth, 1950. Scarcely known outside analytic circles, Sharpe's essay on 'Psycho-Physical Problems Revealed in Language: An Examination of Metaphor' is extremely suggestive for literary critics; see also her essay, 'The Impatience of *Hamlet*', for an interesting refutation of the long-standing view of Hamlet as a hesitator.

SILVERMAN, KAJA *The Subject of Semiotics*. Oxford: Oxford University Press, 1983. Chapter 4, on 'The Subject', is one of the most illuminating introductions to Freudian and Lacanian theory, making use of well-chosen examples from cinema.

TIMPANARO, SEBASTIANO *The Freudian Slip: Psychoanalysis and Textual Criticism*. Trans. Kate Soper. London: Verso, 1985. An interesting Marxist refutation of psychoanalysis.

TURKLE, SHERRY *Psychoanalytic Politics: Freud's French Revolution*. London: André Deutsch, 1979. An intelligent and entertaining account of the cultural events surrounding the French rediscovery of Freud.

WOLLHEIM, RICHARD *Freud*. London: Fontana, 1971. Particularly interesting on Freud's unfinished 'Project for a Scientific Psychology' (written 1887–1902).

(2) Works on Psychoanalysis and Literature

ABEL, ELIZABETH *Virginia Woolf and the Fictions of Psychoanalysis*. Chicago: Chicago University Press, 1989. An accomplished study with a Kleinian orientation.

APTER, EMILY *Feminizing the Fetish: Psychoanalysis and Narrative Obsession in Turn-of-the-Century France*. Ithaca: Cornell University Press, 1991. Discusses the theme of 'female fetishism' – mourning, collecting, and dressing – in fiction and psychoanalysis at the *fin de siècle*.

BALMARY, MARIE *Psychoanalyzing Psychoanalysis: Freud and the Hidden Fault of the Father*. Trans. Ned Lukacher. Baltimore: Johns Hopkins University Press, 1982. Contains a fascinating reinterpretation of Sophocles's Theban plays.

BERMAN, JEFFREY *The Talking Cure: Literary Representations of Psychoanalysis*. New York: New York University Press, 1987.

BERSANI, LEO *A Future for Astyanax: Character and Desire in Literature*. 1976; London: Marion Boyars, 1978.

——*Baudelaire and Freud*. Berkeley: University of California Press, 1977.

——*The Freudian Body: Psychoanalysis and Art*. New York: Columbia University Press, 1986. Placing masochism at the centre of the Freudian theory of sexuality, Bersani examines psychoanalysis, literature, and art as forms of self-undoing, thus challenging the Kleinian view of creativity as reparation. Contains, among other pleasures, a masterly reading of Henry James's *Portrait of a Lady*.

——*The Culture of Redemption*. Cambridge, MA: Harvard University Press, 1990. Bersani argues that the view that art can redeem life – make it whole, correct its errors, sublimate its passions – trivialises both life and, paradoxically, art. Ingenious and unsettling essays on psychoanalysis, philosophy, and literature, including Flaubert, Melville, Joyce, and Pynchon.

BLOOM, HAROLD *The Anxiety of Influence: A Theory of Poetry*. New York: Oxford University Press, 1973.

——*A Map of Misreading*. New York: Oxford University Press, 1975.

——*Agon: Towards a Theory of Revisionism*. New York: Oxford University Press, 1982.

BOHEEMEN, CHRISTINE VAN *The Novel as Family Romance: Language, Gender, and Authority from Fielding to Joyce*. Ithaca: Cornell University Press, 1987.

BOWIE, MALCOLM. *Freud, Proust and Lacan: Theory as Fiction*. Cambridge: Cambridge University Press, 1987. A superb study of the interpenetration of literature and psychoanalysis.

——*Psychoanalysis and the Future of Theory*. Oxford: Blackwell, 1993.

BROOKS, PETER *Reading for the Plot: Design and Intention in Narrative*. New York: Vintage, 1985. Masterly readings of literary and psychoanalytic texts.

——'The Idea of a Psychoanalytic Literary Criticism', in Françoise Meltzer (ed.) *The Trial(s) of Psychoanalysis* (1988), pp. 145–59; and in Shlomith Rimmon-Kenan (ed.) *Discourse in Psychoanalysis and Literature* (1987), pp. 1–18.

CARUTH, CATHY *Empirical Truths and Critical Fictions: Locke, Wordsworth, Kant, Freud*. Baltimore: Johns Hopkins University Press, 1991.

CHASE, CYNTHIA *Decomposing Figures: Rhetorical Readings in the Romantic Tradition*. Baltimore: Johns Hopkins University Press, 1986.

CREWS, FREDERICK *Out of My System: Psychology, Ideology, and Critical Method*. New York: Oxford University Press, 1976.

——'The American Critic Explains Why He Has Rejected Freud', *London Review of Books* (4 December 1980) 3–6.

DAVIS, ROBERT CON (ed.) *The Fictional Father: Lacanian Readings of the Text*. Amherst: University of Massachusetts Press, 1981. Contains a superb essay by Jean-Michel Rabaté on Joyce's *Ulysses* and *Finnegans Wake*.

——(ed.) *Lacan and Narration: The Psychoanalytic Difference in Narrative Theory*. Baltimore: Johns Hopkins University Press, 1983.

EAGLETON, TERRY *The Rape of Clarissa*. Oxford: Blackwell, 1982. Combines Marxist and psychoanalytic insight in a fascinating exploration of Richardson's *Clarissa*.

ELLMANN, MAUD 'The Ghosts of Ulysses', in Augustine Martin (ed.) *James Joyce: The Artist in the Labyrinth*. London: Ryan Publishing Co., 1990, pp. 193–227. On ghosts in Freud and Joyce.

FELMAN, SHOSHANA (ed.) *Literature and Psychoanalysis: The Question of Reading: Otherwise*. Baltimore: Johns Hopkins, 1982. Includes Felman's admirable reading of James, 'Turning the Screw of Interpretation', together with other influential essays by Jacques Lacan, Gayatri Chakravorty Spivak, Fredric Jameson, Barbara Johnson, and Peter Brooks.

——*Madness and Literature: Literature / Philosophy / Psychoanalysis*. Trans. Martha Noel Evans and Shoshana Felman. Ithaca: Cornell University Press, 1985.

FERRER, DANIEL *Virginia Woolf and the Madness of Language*. Trans. Geoffrey Bennington and Rachel Bowlby. London: Routledge, 1990.

GIRARD, RENÉ *Deceit, Desire and the Novel: Self and Other in Literary Structure*.
Trans. Yvonne Freccero. Baltimore: Johns Hopkins University Press, 1965.
GREEN, ANDRÉ 'The Double and the Absent', in Alan Roland (ed.)
Psychoanalysis, Creativity, and Literature: A French-American Inquiry, pp. 271–92.
——*The Tragic Effect: The Oedipus Complex in Tragedy*. Trans. Alan Sheridan.
Cambridge: Cambridge University Press, 1979.
GUNN, DANIEL *Psychoanalysis and Fiction: An Exploration of Literary and
Psychoanalytic Borders*. Cambridge: Cambridge University Press, 1988.
HARTMAN, GEOFFREY H. (ed.) *Psychoanalysis and the Question of the Text*.
Baltimore: Johns Hopkins University Press, 1978. A collection of influential
essays by Jacques Derrida, Barbara Johnson, Neil Hertz, and others.
HERTZ, NEIL *The End of the Line: Essays on Psychoanalysis and the Sublime*. New
York: Columbia University Press, 1985. Exemplary psychoanalytic readings of
Wordsworth, George Eliot, Henry James, and Freud himself.
JOHNSON, BARBARA *The Critical Difference: Essays in the Contemporary Rhetoric of
Reading*. Baltimore: Johns Hopkins University Press, 1980. Contains Johnson's
famous essay 'The Frame of Reference: Poe, Lacan, Derrida' (on Poe's
'Purloined Letter' and its repercussions in Lacan and Derrida), also published
in Muller and Richardson (eds) *The Purloined Poe* (1988), and elsewhere.
JONES, ERNEST *Hamlet and Oedipus*. 1949; New York: Norton, 1976.
KOFMAN, SARAH *The Childhood of Art: An Interpretation of Freud's Aesthetics*.
Trans. Winifred Woodhull. New York: Columbia University Press, 1988.
KURRIK, MAIRE JAANUS *Literature and Negation*. New York: Columbia University
Press, 1979. Makes use of Hegelian and Freudian concepts of negation in the
analysis of literary texts.
KURZWEIL, EDITH and PHILLIPS, WILLIAM (eds) *Literature and Psychoanalysis*. New
York: Columbia University Press, 1983.
LUKACHER, NED *Primal Scenes: Literature, Philosophy, Psychoanalysis*. Ithaca:
Cornell University Press, 1986.
MAHONY, PATRICK *Freud as a Writer*. New York: International Universities Press,
1982. A skilful study of Freudian rhetoric.
——*Psychoanalysis and Discourse*. London: Tavistock, 1987.
MARCUS, STEVEN *Freud and the Culture of Psychoanalysis: Studies in the Transition
from Victorian Humanism to Modernity*. Boston: Allen and Unwin, 1984.
MACCANNELL, JULIET FLOWER *Figuring Lacan: Criticism and the Cultural
Unconscious*. London: Croom Helm, 1986.
MEHLMAN, JEFFREY *Revolution and Repetition: Marx/Hugo/Balzac*. Berkeley:
California University Press, 1977.
MEISEL, PERRY *The Myth of the Modern: A Study in British Literature and Criticism
after 1850*. New Haven: Yale University Press, 1978. Uses the Freudian notion
of deferred action (*Nachträglichkeit*) to explore the anxiety of influence in
modern literature.
MELTZER, FRANÇOISE (ed.) *The Trial(s) of Psychoanalysis*. Chicago: University
of Chicago Press, 1988. Contains Nicolas Abraham's influential 'Notes on
the Phantom' and other interesting essays on psychoanalysis, feminism,
Marxism, and literature.
MOI, TORIL 'The Missing Mother: The Oedipal Rivalries of Reñe Girard',
Diacritics **12**:2 (1982) 21–31.
MULLER, JOHN P. and RICHARDSON, WILLIAM J. (eds) *The Purloined Poe: Lacan,
Derrida, and Psychoanalytic Reading*. Baltimore: Johns Hopkins University Press,
1988. A useful compilation of essays on Poe's much-psychoanalysed tale,
'The Purloined Letter'.
NORRIS, MARGOT *The Decentred Universe of Finnegans Wake: A Structuralist
Analysis*. Baltimore: Johns Hopkins University Press, 1976. Uses Lacanian
theory to make surprising sense of a notoriously impenetrable work.
OXFORD LITERARY REVIEW, Vol. 12, nos. 1–2 (1990). Special issue on

Psychoanalysis and Literature: New Work, edited by Nicholas Royle and Ann Wordsworth. Particularly useful for its introductions to the work of Nicolas Abraham and Maria Torok.

NEW LITERARY HISTORY, Vol. 12, no. 1 (1980). Special issue on *Psychology and Literature: Some Contemporary Directions*.

ORLANDO, FRANCESCO *Toward a Freudian Theory of Literature*. Baltimore: Johns Hopkins University Press, 1978.

RABATÉ, JEAN-MICHEL 'A Clown's Inquest into Paternity: Fathers, Dead or Alive, in *Ulysses and Finnegans Wake*', in Robert Con Davis (ed.) *The Fictional Father* (1981), pp. 73–114.

——*Language, Sexuality and Ideology in Ezra Pound's Cantos*. Albany: State University of New York Press, 1986.

——*James Joyce: Authorised Reader*. Baltimore: Johns Hopkins University Press, 1991.

——*Joyce Upon the Void: The Genesis of Doubt*. London: Macmillan, 1991. Rabaté is the foremost psychoanalytic critic of modernism.

RAGLAND-SULLIVAN, ELLIE and BRACHER, MARK (eds) *Lacan and the Subject of Language*. London: Routledge, 1991.

RIEFF, PHILIP *Freud: The Mind of the Moralist*. 1959; Chicago: Chicago University Press, 1979. A lucid and intelligent introduction to Freudian theory and its wider cultural implications.

RIMMON-KENAN, SHLOMITH *Discourse in Psychoanalysis and Literature*. London: Methuen, 1987. Peter Brooks's introductory essay on 'The Idea of a Psychoanalytic Literary Criticism' is particularly useful, and there are other interesting articles by Cynthia Chase, Mieke Bal, Elizabeth Wright, Susan Rubin Suleiman, Julia Kristeva, and others.

ROLAND, ALAN (ed.) *Psychoanalysis, Creativity, and Literature: A French-American Inquiry*. New York: Columbia University Press, 1978.

ROSE, JACQUELINE *The Case of Peter Pan; or The Impossibility of Children's Fiction*. London: Macmillan, 1984.

——*Sexuality in the Field of Vision*. London: Verso, 1986. Contains excellent psychoanalytic readings of *Hamlet* and *Daniel Deronda*.

——*The Haunting of Sylvia Plath*. London: Virago, 1991.

——*Why War? – Psychoanalysis, Politics, and the Return to Melanie Klein*. Oxford: Blackwell, 1993.

ROYLE, NICHOLAS 'The Distraction of 'Freud': Literature, Psychoanalysis, and the Bacon-Shakespeare Controversy', *Oxford Literary Review*, **12**: 1–2 (1990) 101–38. A fascinating reading of *Hamlet*.

——*Telepathy and Literature: Essays on the Reading Mind*. Oxford: Blackwell, 1991. Combines Freudian and Derridean theory in analyses of literary works ranging from Jane Austen to Raymond Chandler.

SACKS, PETER *The English Elegy*. Baltimore: Johns Hopkins University Press, 1985. Makes use of Freudian concepts of mourning and melancholia in an eloquent study of elegy.

SCHWARTZ, MURRAY M. and KAHN, COPPÉLIA *Representing Shakespeare: New Psychoanalytic Essays*. Baltimore: Johns Hopkins University Press, 1980.

SEDGWICK, EVE *Between Men: English Literature and Male Homosocial Desire*. New York: Columbia University Press, 1985. Sedgwick challenges Freudian theory, yet her ingenious analysis of the workings of desire in literary texts provides a model for an undogmatic psychoanalytic criticism.

——*Epistemology of the Closet*. Berkeley: University of California Press, 1990.

——*Tendencies*. Durham, North Carolina: Duke University Press, 1993.

SKURA, MEREDITH ANNE *The Literary Use of the Psychoanalytic Process*. New Haven: Yale University Press, 1981.

SMITH, JOSEPH H. (ed.) *The Literary Freud: Mechanisms of Defense and the Poetic Will*. New Haven: Yale University Press, 1980.

SMITH, JOSEPH H. and KERRIGAN, WILLIAM (eds) *Taking Chances: Derrida, Psychoanalysis, and Literature.* Baltimore: Johns Hopkins University Press, 1984.

SOKOLSKY, ANITA 'The Case of the Juridical Junkie: *Perry Mason* and the Dilemma of Confession', *Yale Journal of Law and Humanities* **2** (1990) 189–99.

STOKES, ADRIAN 'Form in Art', in Melanie Klein, Paula Heimann, and Roger Money-Kyrle (eds) *New Directions in Psycho-Analysis.* London: Maresfield Reprints, 1977.

——*Michelangelo* (1955), in Lawrence Gowing (ed.) *The Critical Writings of Adrian Stokes.* London: Thames and Hudson, 1978. A thrilling essay, which uses Melanie Klein's theories to reinterpret the art of Michelangelo.

SWANN, KAREN '"Christabel": The Wandering Mother and the Enigma of Form', *Studies in Romanticism* **23** (1984) 533–53.

——'Public Transport: Adventuring on Wordsworth's Salisbury Plain', *English Literary History,* **55** (1988) 811–34. Swann's ingenious readings of Romantic poetry are informed by psychoanalysis and deconstruction.

TANNER, TONY *Adultery in the Novel: Contract and Transgression.* Baltimore: Johns Hopkins University Press, 1979. A masterly analysis of works by Rousseau, Goethe, and Flaubert, subtly informed by psychoanalytic theory.

TENNENHOUSE, LEONARD (ed.) *The Practice of Psychoanalytic Criticism.* Detroit: Wayne State University Press, 1976.

TIFFT, STEPHEN 'The Parricidal Phantasm: Irish Nationalism and the *Playboy* Riots', in Andrew Parker, Mary Russo, Doris Sommer, and Patricia Yaeger (eds) *Nationalisms and Sexualities.* London: Routledge, 1992, pp. 313–32. Uses psychoanalysis to understand the convergence of the literary and the political.

WEBER, SAMUEL *The Legend of Freud.* Minneapolis: Minnesota University Press, 1982. A deconstructive reading of Freud's writings, particularly ingenious on the subjects of jokes and dreams.

WORDSWORTH, ANN 'An Art that will not Abandon the Self to Language: Bloom, Tennyson, and the Blind World of the Wish', in Robert Young (ed.) *Untying the Text* (1981), pp. 207–22.

WRIGHT, ELIZABETH *Psychoanalytic Criticism: Theory in Practice.* London: Methuen, 1984. Wide-ranging, concise, and judicious introduction to psychoanalytic concepts and their uses in literary criticism, with a full annotated bibliography.

YALE FRENCH STUDIES, **48** (1972). Special issue on *French Freud: Structural Studies in Psychoanalysis.* See especially Jean Laplanche and Serge Leclaire, 'The Unconscious: A Psychoanalytic Study', 118–78; and Derrida, 'Freud and the Scene of Writing', 73–117, rpt. in Derrida's *Writing and Difference* (1978).

YOUNG, ROBERT (ed.) *Untying the Text: A Post-Structuralist Reader* (London: Routledge, 1981). Section on psychoanalysis and literature, with an illuminating introduction and headnotes.

ŽIŽEK, SLAVOJ *Looking Awry: An Introduction to Jacques Lacan through Popular Culture.* Cambridge, MA: MIT Press, 1991.

——(ed.) *Everything you always wanted to know about Lacan (but were afraid to ask Hitchcock).* London: Verso, 1992.

——*Enjoy your Symptom! Jacques Lacan in Hollywood and Out.* New York: Routledge, 1992.

(3) Feminism and Psychoanalysis

ADAMS, PARVEEN and COWIE, ELIZABETH (ed.) *The Woman in Question: m/f.* London: Verso, 1990.

APPIGNANESI, LISA and FORRESTER, JOHN, *Freud's Women*. London: Weidenfield and Nicolson, 1992.

BOWLBY, RACHEL *Still Crazy after all these Years: Women, Writing, and Psychoanalysis*. London: Routledge, 1982. Witty and imaginative readings of literary and psychoanalytic texts.

BRENNAN, TERESA (ed.) *Between Feminism and Psychoanalysis*. London: Routledge, 1989. Contains excellent essays by Rachel Bowlby, Elizabeth Wright, Morag Shiach, Joan Copjec, Naomi Segal, Parveen Adams, and others, with an incisive introduction by Teresa Brennan.

——*The Interpretation of the Flesh: Freud and Femininity*. London: Routledge, 1992.

BUTLER, JUDITH *Gender Trouble: Feminism and the Subversion of Identity* . London: Routledge, 1990.

FELMAN, SHOSHANA 'Women and Madness: The Critical Phallacy', *Diacritics*, 7 (1975) 2–10. Rpt. in Catherine Belsey and Jane Moore (eds) *The Feminist Reader: Essays in Gender and the Politics of Literary Criticism*. London: Macmillan, 1989, pp. 133–53. Also rpt. in Robyn R. Warhol and Diane Price Herndl (eds) *Feminisms: An Anthology of Literature and Criticism*. New Brunswick, NJ: Rutgers University Press, 1991, pp. 6–19.

FLETCHER, JOHN and BENJAMIN, ANDREW *Abjection, Melancholia, and Love: The Work of Julia Kristeva*. London: Routledge, 1990. Contains Kristeva's important essay on 'The Adolescent Novel'; and a fine essay by Makiko Minow-Pinkney on Virginia Woolf.

GALLOP, JANE *The Daughter's Seduction: Feminism and Psychoanalysis*. Ithaca: Cornell University Press, 1982.

GARNER, SHIRLEY NELSON, KAHANE, CLAIRE and SPRENGNETHER, MADELON (eds) *The (M)other Tongue: Essays in Feminist Psychoanalytic Interpretation*. Ithaca: Cornell University Press, 1985.

GROSZ, ELIZABETH *Jacques Lacan: A Feminist Introduction*. London: Routledge, 1990.

HORNEY, KAREN *Feminine Psychology*. London: Routledge and Kegan Paul, 1967.

IRIGARAY, LUCE Interview in *Ideology and Consciousness*, 1 (1977) 64–65.

——*Speculum of the Other Woman*. Trans. Gillian C. Gill. Ithaca: Cornell University Press, 1985.

——*This Sex Which Is Not One*. Trans. Catherine Porter with Carolyn Burke. Ithaca: Cornell University Press, 1985.

——*The Irigaray Reader*. Ed. Margaret Whitford. Oxford: Blackwell, 1991.

——*Sexes and Genealogies*. Trans. Gillian C. Gill. New York: Columbia, 1993.

——*je, tu, nous: Toward a Culture of Difference*. Trans. Alison Martin. New York: Routledge, 1993.

JACOBUS, MARY *Reading Woman: Essays in Feminist Criticism*. London: Longman, 1983. Close analyses of literary texts informed by feminist and psychoanalytic theory.

——'"The Third Stroke": Reading Woolf with Freud', in Susan Sheridan (ed.) *Grafts: Feminist Cultural Criticism*. London: Verso, 1988, pp. 93–110. Rpt. in Rachel Bowlby (ed.) *Virginia Woolf*. London: Longman, 1992, pp. 102–20. An illuminating psychoanalytic reading of *To the Lighthouse*.

KRISTEVA, JULIA *About Chinese Women*. Trans. Anita Barrows. London: Boyar, 1977.

——*Desire in Language: A Semiotic Approach to Literature and Art*. Ed. Leon S. Roudiez. Trans. Thomas Gorz, Alice Jardine, and Leon S. Roudiez. Oxford: Blackwell, 1980.

——*Powers of Horror: An Essay on Abjection*. Trans. Leon S. Roudiez. New York: Columbia University Press, 1982.

——*Revolution in Poetic Language*. Trans. Margaret Waller. New York: Columbia University Press, 1984.

——*Tales of Love*. Trans. Leon S. Roudiez. New York: Columbia University Press, 1987.

——*In the Beginning was Love: Psychoanalysis and Faith*. Trans. Arthur Goldhammer. New York: Columbia University Press, 1987.

——*Black Sun: Depression and Melancholia*. Trans. Leon S. Roudiez. New York: Columbia University Press, 1989.

——*Strangers to Ourselves*. Trans. Leon S. Roudiez. London: Harvester, 1989.

MITCHELL, JULIET *Psychoanalysis and Feminism*. Harmondsworth: Penguin, 1974.

MITCHELL, JULIET and ROSE, JACQUELINE (eds) *Feminine Sexuality: Jacques Lacan and the École Freudienne*. London: Macmillan, 1982. Contains Lacan's writings on femininity and two excellent introductions by Mitchell and Rose.

MONTEFIORE, JAN *Feminism and Poetry: Language, Experience, Identity in Women's Writing*. London: Pandora, 1987.

ROWLEY, HAZEL and GROSZ, ELIZABETH 'Psychoanalysis and Feminism', in Sneja Gunew (ed.) *Feminist Knowledge: Critique and Construct*. London: Routledge, 1990, pp. 175–204. A lucid and concise survey.

SAYERS, JANET *Mothering Psychoanalysis: Helene Deutsch, Karen Horney, Anna Freud, Melanie Klein*. Harmondsworth: Penguin, 1992.

WHITFORD, MARGARET 'Irigaray', in Brennan (ed.) *Between Psychoanalysis and Feminism*, pp. 106–26. A concise and useful introduction to Irigaray, expanded in Whitford's *Luce Irigaray: Philosophy in the Feminine* (London: Routledge, 1991).

WRIGHT, ELIZABETH (ed.) *Feminism and Psychoanalysis: A Critical Dictionary*. Oxford: Blackwell, 1992. An indispensable guide to a prolific literature.

Index

Index

275